Divided Bodies

CRITICAL

GLOBAL

HEALTH:

EVIDENCE,

EFFICACY,

ETHNOGRAPHY

A series edited by

Vincanne Adams

and João Biehl

Divided Bodies

LYME DISEASE, CONTESTED ILLNESS, AND EVIDENCE-BASED MEDICINE

Abigail A. Dumes

DUKE UNIVERSITY PRESS

Durham and London   2020

Library of Congress Cataloging-in-
Publication Data
Names: Dumes, Abigail Anne,
    [date] author.
Title: Divided bodies : Lyme disease,
    contested illness, and evidence-
    based medicine / Abigail Dumes.
Other titles: Critical global health.
Description: Durham : Duke
    University Press, 2020. | Series:
    Critical global health: evidence,
    efficacy, ethnography | Includes
    bibliographical references and
    index.
Identifiers: LCCN 2020006168 (print)
LCCN 2020006169 (ebook)
ISBN 9781478005988 (hardcover)
ISBN 9781478006664 (paperback)
ISBN 9781478007395 (ebook)
Subjects: LCSH: Lyme disease—
    United States. | Lyme disease—
    Patients—United States. | Lyme
    disease—Psychological aspects.
Classification: LCC RA644.L94 D864
    2020 (print) | LCC RA644.L94
    (ebook) | DDC 616.9/24600973—
    dc23
LC record available at https://lccn.loc
    .gov/2020006168
LC ebook record available at https://
    lccn.loc.gov/2020006169

Cover art: Hannah Rose Dumes,
Nine Five, 2014. Collage, rice paper
on panel. 20 × 16 inches. Courtesy of
the artist.

FOR JOHN, ABE, AND ROSE,
MY HEART AND HOME

Contents

Acknowledgments

From inception to completion, this project was made possible by the support, participation, and collaboration of others. My gratitude is unending. Thank you—a thousand times over—to:

Each individual who participated in this project, from patients and physicians to scientists and politicians. This book is *your* book. Thank you for sharing your stories with me, for patiently answering my questions, and for trusting me with the responsibility of representing your ideas and experiences. I hope this book conveys how much each of you shaped this project.

My undergraduate mentors at Washington University in St. Louis, who paved the road to anthropology. Lois Beck introduced me to the wondrous world of fieldwork and ethnographic writing, Joseph Loewenstein taught me the importance of being an engaged reader and writer, and Shanti Parikh redirected my freshman focus from primatology to cultural anthropology. I never looked back.

The Yale Department of Anthropology, for providing an academic and intellectual home during my doctoral training and research. The staff at the Yale Human Research Protection Program, who helped to ensure that my project fully protected the privacy and well-being of those who participated in it. My incomparable cohort mates, Minhua Ling and Ryan Sayre, who provided critical conversation and social sustenance, inside and outside the seminar room. The brilliant bevy of other students and faculty at Yale—Omolade Adunbi, Jeffrey Alexander, Allison Alexy, Lucia Cantero, Annie Claus, Michael Degani, Susanna Fioratta, Ajay Gandhi, Radhika Govindrajan, David Graeber, Dana Graef, Thomas Blom Hansen, Joseph Hill, William Kelly, Molly Margaretten, Michael McGovern, Christopher Miller, Gabriela Morales, Jessica Newman, Tina Palivos, Dhooleka Raj, Joshua Rubin, David Scales, Harold Scheffler, Shaila Seshia-Galvin, Maria Sidorkina, Helen Siu, Nathaniel Smith, John Szwed, Angelica Torres, Laura Wexler, Gavin

Whitelaw, Eric Worby, and Amy Zhang—who provided community, guidance, and the comfort of shared experience. And the American Council of Learned Societies, the National Science Foundation, the Wenner-Gren Foundation, and Yale University, whose support made possible the research and writing of the dissertation on which this book is based.

My extraordinary graduate mentors, who are as generous as they are brilliant. Sean Brotherton helped shape my thoughts about evidence-based medicine in the earliest stages of this project and provided incisive feedback; Kamari Clarke fostered an insatiable hunger for the kind of thinking that makes anthropology so addictive and has been an unending source of support and counsel; and Didier Fassin, who first took a chance on me when he agreed to be my mentor during my Fulbright year in France in 2004, thoughtfully reviewed material, critically engaged with this book's evolving ideas, and provided trail markers to sharper critique. Last but not least, my advisor and academic compass, Marcia Inhorn, for whom there are not enough words to express my gratitude and appreciation. Marcia unfailingly guided me through each step of this project, read and offered insightful comments and suggestions on writing at all stages, masterfully refined and improved the arc of my arguments, and showered me with encouragement. Lucky am I to call Marcia my mentor and dear friend.

Colleagues and friends in the departments of Women's Studies, Anthropology, and Afroamerican and African Studies at the University of Michigan, whose support and guidance nurtured this book's writing: Omolade Adunbi, Donna Ainsworth, Allison Alexy, Kelly Askew, Abigail Bigham, Melissa Burch, Rosario Ceballo, Jason De Leon, Jatin Dua, Sarah Ellerholz, Matthew Hull, Anna Kirkland, Stuart Kirsch, Michael Lempert, Zhying Ma, Sara McClelland, Michael McGovern, John Mitani, Yasmin Moll, Damani Partridge, Christine Sargent, Andrew Shryock, Abigail Stewart, Scott Stonington, and Elizabeth Wingrove.

Fellow panelists, discussants, and audience members at American Anthropological Association meetings, American Ethnological Society meetings, and the Michigan University-Wide Sustainability Environment Conference, who engaged with and provided feedback on a range of ideas that animate this book. In addition, faculty and students in the Department of Sociology and Anthropology at Elon University, the Department of Anthropology at California State University, Sacramento, the Department of Humanities and Social Sciences at Clarkson University, the Department of Anthropology at Tulane University, the Department of Women's Studies at the University of Michigan, and the Department of Anthropology at William Paterson University of New Jersey, whose members invited me to present work in progress and, through their questions and comments, helped that work progress.

Two fabulous anonymous reviewers at Duke University Press, whose incredibly thoughtful and thorough feedback made this a better book. Editor extraordinaire Elizabeth Ault, for her patient guidance, anchoring encouragement, and remarkable gift for always being able to see to the heart of things. Kate Herman, whose editorial assistance, attention to detail, and anthropological eye made preproduction so much breezier. Ellen Goldlust, Lisa Lawley, and Melanie Mallon, for their project management and copyediting wizardry. And three wonderful research assistants—Zoe Boudart, Anna Deming, and Jeremy Ray—for their meticulous help with in-text citations and the bibliography. Portions of chapter 2 appeared in a chapter titled "Paradise Poisoned: Nature, Environmental Risk, and the Practice of Lyme Disease Prevention in the United States" in *A Companion to the Anthropology of Environmental Health* (2016), a volume edited by Merrill Singer and published by Wiley-Blackwell. Portions of chapter 2 also appeared in an essay titled "Ticks, Pesticides, and Biome-Subjectivity" on the Anthropology and Environment Society's blog, *Engagement* (2017). Portions of chapter 3 were previously published by Wiley-Blackwell in an article titled "Putting Ethnographic Flesh on New Materialist Bones: Lyme Disease and the Sex/Gender Binary" in *Feminist Anthropology* (2020), and portions of chapter 4 were previously published by Taylor and Francis in an article titled "Lyme Disease and the Epistemic Tensions of 'Medically Unexplained Illnesses'" in *Medical Anthropology* (2019). Heartfelt thanks to the reviewers and editors who reviewed and improved that work and to this book's series editors, Vincanne Adams and João Biehl, for supporting the project and for the honor of including me in such luminous company.

Amanda Henriques and Angela Sheppard, talented, creative, and loving caregivers who spent time with my children so that I could write. The gift of knowing that my children were happy and nurtured while I worked was priceless.

My web of dear friends between coasts and across seas, whose enduring friendship over the years has provided a much-needed antidote to the socially isolating forces of book writing: Katy and Robbie Botta, Hannah and Peter Christensen, and Daniel Leisawitz and Daniela Viale; Lauren Abele, Joshua Barocas, Rachel Brown, Christopher Davies, Karishma Desai, Mollie Jacobs, Melinda Kramer, Daniel Lightheart, Phil Valko, Joshua Vogelstein, and Aaron Weinblatt; Kate Bredeson and Lauren Tompkins; Naomi Dalglish, Mia Dalglish, and the entire Dalglish-Klein and Bass-Burger clans; Barbara

Wilde and Denis Gardeur; Elin Raun-Royer, Emilie Rex, and Roberto Vega-Morales; and Irene Soléa Antonellis, Emilie Engelhard, Nori Flautner, Molly Hudson, Kim Monroe, and Reiko Watanabe.

My loving extended family, whom I cherish and treasure: Grandma Phyl, Philip Crouse, Stanley Dumes Crouse, and Ashby Dumes Crouse; Carol Millet, Cathy Millet, Austin Luangasa, and John Luangasa; and Jyoti and Ashwin Shukla.

Hannah Rose Dumes, my beloved sister and steadfast other half, who, in her unmatched coolness, kindness, maturity, humor, artistry, and wisdom, has generously held my hand as we've walked life's path together. To top it off, she spent countless unglamorous but infinitely appreciated hours mending this book's bibliography. Thank you, Bo: life is better and so much more beautiful with you in it.

My father, Harold Dumes, who taught me how to write a thesis sentence in fourth grade and modeled a love for reading. And my mother, Marsha Bradford, whose editing, grammar, and critical thinking prowess knows no equal, and who has devotedly read and copyedited almost every paper I have ever written. This book is no exception. From the beginning, I have been buoyed by the unconditional love and encouragement of my parents. I am because they are.

My husband, John Millet, my true love, best friend, and other brain, whose technical, medical, and emotional expertise sustained eleven years of crafting and completing a project. From EndNote and Microsoft Word assistance to listening to late night and early morning digests of new ideas to the unwavering belief that I would not only finish this project but also be happy with it, John's support has known no bounds.

And, finally, my children, Abe and Rose Dumes Millet, who are my reasons for being and doing. Your presence in my world gives it meaning beyond measure.

Introduction

LYME DISEASE OUTSIDE IN

On October 5, 2013, Lyme disease advocates organized a protest against the Infectious Diseases Society of America (IDSA). The protest took place in San Francisco, in front of the convention center where the IDSA was holding its annual conference. Protesters wore lime green clothing and displayed signs that read, "IDSA: Revise Lyme Guidelines," "IDSA Ticks Me Off," and "Chronic Lyme Affects Me Every Day. Revise Your Guidelines." The protest also featured speeches by patients and advocates and an original song by a Lyme patient rapper. In the weeks leading up to the protest, a Lyme advocacy group circulated a petition urging the National Guidelines Clearinghouse (NGC), an organization that, at the time, housed all US clinical practice guidelines, to remove the IDSA's Lyme disease guidelines from its website. Although the IDSA maintained that its guidelines for diagnosing and treating Lyme disease were based on the "best available evidence," Lyme disease advocates argued that the guidelines were "outdated," did not recognize the biological basis of chronic Lyme disease, and denied access to the care that patients need.

Over the past four decades, patient advocacy events like the IDSA protest, increased media attention, and growing numbers of reported Lyme disease cases have brought the controversy over how to diagnose and treat Lyme disease into the national spotlight. Indeed, Lyme disease is one of the most controversial medical issues in the United States, and, like other illnesses whose biological reality is contested, including chronic fatigue syndrome, Gulf War syndrome, and multiple chemical sensitivity, it is replete with class action lawsuits, patient protests, polarizing documentaries, congressional hearings, and state and federal investigations. The crux of Lyme's controversy is whether the disease can persist beyond standard antibiotic treatment. While proponents of the "mainstream" standard of care claim that Lyme disease is easily diagnosed and treated, proponents of the "Lyme-literate" standard of care claim that diagnostic tests are unreliable and that Lyme disease can persist in the form of "chronic Lyme disease," a condition that mainstream proponents do not recognize but which Lyme-literate proponents argue should be treated with extended courses of antibiotics.[1] The response to this medical impasse has been twofold: individuals on both sides of the divide have taken legal and political action to try to regulate how Lyme patients are diagnosed and treated; many have also turned to environmental measures (e.g., deer hunting, pesticides, and landscaping) to protect those at risk and to prevent the further spread of Lyme disease.

This book sits at the heart of the disagreement over how to diagnose and treat Lyme disease, and it explores why, in an era of evidence-based medicine, the systematic production and standardization of evidence has *amplified* rather than *diminished* disagreement related to contested illnesses. Institutionalized in the United States in the late 1980s and early 1990s, evidence-based medicine is an approach to standardizing clinical care that promotes the use of clinical guidelines and the hierarchization of scientific evidence, at the top of which is the "objective" evidence of randomized controlled trials and at the bottom of which is the "subjective" evidence of expert opinion. As the introductory vignette reveals, Lyme disease draws attention to the emerging centrality of evidence-based medicine—particularly clinical guidelines—to the experiences and practices of American biomedicine. As the basis for treatment, insurance, and public health decisions, clinical guidelines are an increasingly salient dimension of patients' and physicians' everyday lives. Because Lyme's controversy hinges on differences over how to clinically manage Lyme disease and, more critically, whether chronic Lyme disease has an objective evidentiary basis, clinical guidelines are urgently relevant to Lyme patients and physicians. For all patients with contested illnesses, which evidence gets to count toward the substantiation and formal recognition of their suffering is paramount.

Over the course of my research for this book, as I spent time with Lyme patients at support group meetings or observed physicians who treat Lyme disease at their offices, I was often asked whether my research would "solve" the controversy. In response to this question, I was quick to manage expectations because, for many, this question ultimately meant, "Will your research determine whether chronic Lyme disease exists?," which is beyond the purview of an anthropological engagement. But for others, this question meant, "Why has the controversy lasted so long? And what is preventing its resolution?" At the time, I assumed this question was also tangential to my project, since anthropologists are often better equipped to answer questions that begin with *how* instead of *why*. In the end, however, the countless stories and observations I collected suggested otherwise. Drawing from eighteen months of research among Lyme patients, physicians, and scientists in the United States, this book attempts to answer *why* the rise of evidence-based medicine has made contested illnesses like Lyme disease even *more contested* despite the fact that the aim of evidence-based medicine is to resolve medical dispute.

To the anticipated disappointment of some, my answer to this question has less to do with a *cover-up* and more to do with an *uncovering*. As the stories of Lyme patients, physicians, and scientists show, the emergence of evidence-based medicine has contributed to the perceived delegitimation of contested illnesses through the formal categorization of "medically unexplainable illness." This term has often been used interchangeably in biomedical practice with somatoform disorder and is understood by many biomedical physicians to be "the repeated medical help-seeking for multiple medical symptoms without organic disease" and, in many cases, "the expression of psychological illness through physical symptoms" (Burton 2003, 231; see also Hatcher and Arroll 2008; Nimnuan, Hotopf, and Wessely 2001). Although the history of physical ailments perceived to lack a biological basis is long (S. Johnson 2008, 13), it was only with the rise of evidence-based medicine that these ailments became formally recognized as medically unexplainable and, as a result, were excluded from the trappings of medical legibility, including an insurance code, eligibility to be the object of clinical studies, and corresponding pharmaceutical treatments and clinical guidelines. Through formal categorization, patients with contested illnesses (chronic Lyme patients foremost among them) have become bound together in a more cohesive and more visible "biosociality" of "delegitimized" suffering that has allowed them to mobilize against their medical marginalization, mobilizations no more clearly demonstrated than in the Lyme patient community's protest against the IDSA.[2]

At the same time that evidence-based medicine has hardened the boundary between explainable and unexplainable illnesses, it has also unexpectedly offered patients a path to perceived biological legitimacy by providing a platform on which individuals inside and outside the medical arena can make claims to medical truth. In the case of Lyme disease, these truth claims are made in two ways. The first are the embodied and symptomatic expressions of unwellness that Lyme patient advocates and Lyme-literate physicians (as their patients' proxies) make heard through digital and social media, legislative lobbying, the design of clinical trials, and the writing of clinical guidelines. The second are scientific claims based on interpretations of a range of published evidence. As "citizen experts," Lyme patients' claims to the biological reality of their ill health are simultaneously grounded in embodied experience *and* scientific knowledge—a phenomenon nicely captured in the bannered backdrop to the Lyme patient community's 2014 protest against the IDSA in Philadelphia, which read, "IDSA Stop Rejecting Science! Lyme Patients are Suffering!" (Orsini 2008, 111).[3] Intended to streamline medical opinion, evidence-based medicine has instead produced a proliferation of opinions and, more critically, has created the opportunity for patients as well as practitioners to draw on the authority of evidence-based medicine to validate their experiences and make their opinions heard. In its exploration of Lyme's fractured reality, this book not only offers the first ethnographic analysis of the Lyme disease controversy but also brings into focus the social complexities of contested illness within the increasingly standardized bounds of US biomedicine.

Contextualizing Lyme

With more than three hundred thousand estimated new cases each year, Lyme disease is the most commonly reported vector-borne infectious disease in the United States.[4] Discovered in 1982, *Borrelia burgdorferi*, the bacterium that causes Lyme disease, is transmitted by the bite of *Ixodes scapularis*, the blacklegged tick, in the eastern United States and *Ixodes pacificus* in the western United States.[5] Although Lyme disease affects women and men of all ages, it disproportionately affects those who live in areas that deer, small rodents, and ticks prefer to inhabit: the suburbs or areas on the periphery of forested land (Stafford 2007). More critically, because of the geopolitics of suburban development, Lyme disease is understood to primarily affect those above and well above the national poverty level. For example, only 3 percent of Connecticut residents who are below the poverty line live in towns in the "highest quintile of Lyme disease rates" (Cromley and Cromley 2009, 10). For this reason and others, Lyme disease has become known by some as a "yuppie disease."[6] Like other illnesses perceived to be medically unexplainable, chronic Lyme disease is also perceived to be more common among women. In contrast to the perceived environmental and social specificity of its risk, Lyme disease's biophysical manifestations are understood by many to be characterized by marked generality. Aside from a diagnostic "bull's-eye" rash known as erythema migrans (EM), many across the standard-of-care divide argue that both early and late Lyme disease are characterized by nonspecific symptoms (i.e., symptoms associated with a spectrum of other disorders) and, because of their clinical ambiguity, are often misdiagnosed.

Differences in biomedical practice and opinion are the rule not the exception.[7] It is exceptional, however, that a disagreement over the diagnosis and treatment of one disease would be so pronounced that it would manifest in the institutionalization of two biomedical standards of care.[8] Proponents of the mainstream standard of care diagnose early Lyme by an EM rash or a positive antibody test, treat with two to four weeks of antibiotics, and in doing so, adhere to the clinical guidelines formulated by the IDSA and adopted by the Centers for Disease Control and Prevention (CDC). Mainstream proponents argue that the bacterium that causes Lyme disease, Borrelia burgdorferi, does not persist in the body at pathogenic levels after standard antibiotic therapy. As a result, these physicians perceive chronic Lyme disease (the attribution of symptoms that persist beyond antibiotic treatment to persistent Borrelia infection) to be one of a range of medically unexplained illnesses. That is, they classify chronic Lyme as an "illness" (a subjective experience of physical distress) rather than a "disease" (a condition substantiated by biophysical markers that warrants biophysical intervention). In this way, the mainstream standard of care can be more fully understood as a "dominant epidemiological paradigm," one that is "produced by a diverse set of social actors who draw on existing stocks of institutional knowledge to identify and define a disease and determine its etiology, proper treatment, and acceptable health outcomes" (P. Brown, Morello-Frosch, and Zavestoski 2012, 84). As a "belief system and a practice" that is "historically contingent," a dominant epidemiological paradigm becomes entrenched and endures, but it is also changeable, even if that change occurs over protracted periods of time (2012, 105).

On the other side of the debate, proponents of the Lyme-literate standard of care diagnose Lyme based on a complex manifestation of symptoms with or without a positive antibody test, treat patients with extended oral and intravenous antibiotics, and in doing so, adhere to the clinical guidelines published by the International Lyme and Associated Diseases Society (ILADS), the professional organization created in opposition to the IDSA in 1999.[9] Unlike the mainstream camp, the Lyme-literate camp is supported by a patient base of "activated health citizens" who are organized around their shared delegitimized suffering (G. Davis and Nichter 2015).[10] In this way, chronic Lyme patients take part in what sociologist Phil Brown and colleagues have described as "embodied health movements" and "boundary movements," movements that are centered around the "embodied experience of illness" and that actively challenge medical and scientific doxa (P. Brown, Morello-Frosch, and Zavestoski 2012, 16, 27–29).[11] That is, patients engage in "boundary work," attempting to reconfigure the boundaries between "science" and "nonscience" (2012, 27–28; see Gieryn 1983) while also engaging with "boundary objects," such as evidence-based medicine, that move across boundaries between scientists and "lay experts" and can be differentially deployed depending on whose hands they are in (Star and Greisemer 1989; Epstein 1995, 1996; see also Cordner 2016).[12]

Despite critical differences in how the mainstream and Lyme-literate communities interpret Lyme disease, both seek to establish credibility through the scientific authority of evidence-based medicine. To date, scientists have conducted five randomized controlled trials on the therapeutic effects of extended antibiotics for Lyme disease patients. Although intended to resolve dispute, randomized controlled trials have, in this case, provided a means by which each camp, through different "styles of scientific practice," has reinforced its respective standard of care (Fujimura and Chou 1994, 1017). Grounded in interdisciplinary explorations of medical epistemologies, biopower, and environmental health, this book intervenes to explore how the controversy over how to diagnose and treat Lyme disease sheds light on the tangled relationship between contested illness and evidence-based medicine in the United States.

The Divided Bodies of Contested Illness

To make sense of the Lyme disease controversy, I have described Lyme disease as a contested illness. But what do I mean by contested illness? This term is most often used by sociologists, and most notably by Phil Brown and those affiliated with the former Contested Illness Research Group at Brown University, to mean "diseases or conditions in which there is dispute over environmental causation."[13] For these sociologists, approaches to understanding contested illness are "situated at the intersection of environmental health and environmental justice."[14] More recently, anthropologist Joseph Dumit has described "emerging, contested illnesses," such as chronic fatigue syndrome, Gulf War syndrome, and multiple chemical sensitivity, as "illnesses you have to fight to get" (2006) or "new sociomedical disorders" (2000) and has suggested that they are characterized by five features: chronicity, biomentality, therapeutic diversity, cross-linkage, and legal explosivity (2006, 578).[15]

My use of contested illness is a departure from previous applications because in more broadly describing contested illness as any bodily condition whose biological basis is disputed, it insists that these illnesses are not limited to environmental causation and highlights the inextricability of their relationship with evidence-based medicine. This approach to contested illness has less to do with causation, the effects of contestation, and defining features than with the conditions of possibility that produce "medically unexplainable illness" as a diagnostic category.[16] For example, because evidence-based medicine has formalized the importance of objective over subjective evidence in the diagnosis of disease, illnesses that present with more symptoms (subjective markers of disease) than they do signs (objective markers of disease) bring out epistemic differences *within* biomedical practice over the extent to which symptoms can be used to substantiate and explain the biological reality of illness. And because of these epistemic differences, patients with contested illnesses straddle the divide between the experience of living a disease and the experience of being perceived to have a medically unexplainable illness.

The analysis in this book, then, draws on the concept of "divided bodies" to highlight the epistemic and embodied tensions that characterize the phenomenon of contested illnesses in an era of evidence-based medicine; that is, contested illnesses are disorders over which bodies of *thought* are divided, and they are also bodily conditions that are always *experienced* as diseases but are often *perceived* to be illnesses. As a result, those who live, diagnose, and treat contested illness often make corollary and competing claims to, on the one hand, biological legitimacy and, on the other, "epistemo-legitimacy" (the legitimacy of how contested illness should be known) (Fassin 2018a). For example, in the case of Lyme disease, and within an evidence-based framework that privileges the legitimacy of objective over subjective evidence, claims to biological legitimacy hinge on the biological reality of bacterial persistence in patients' bodies, while competing claims to epistemo-legitimacy hinge on divergent approaches to the relationship between symptoms and signs in how Lyme disease should be known.

Over the course of this book, I also suggest that evidence-based medicine's role in amplifying disagreement over the biological reality of contested illnesses is the product of a foundational feature of biomedicine: the relative importance of the *sign* versus the *symptom* in the diagnosis and treatment of ill health. While evidence-based medicine attempts to achieve a more scientific medicine by eliminating bias and, in particular, clinical reliance on the subjectivity of symptoms, the rub is that no matter how many randomized controlled trials are performed and no matter how sophisticated technology becomes, patients continue to experience ill health through their symptoms. As a result, symptomatic experience continues to remain the bedrock of clinical care. This is no truer than for contested illnesses, in which patients and practitioners must often navigate a range of perplexing symptoms in the absence of definitive signs.

And yet, just because patients experience their ill health symptomatically as an *illness* does not mean that they do not also experience their ill health as a *disease*, if by disease we mean an organic pathological process that affects organs and systems of the body. As anthropologist Stefan Ecks observes, the "illness/disease opposition" has been a hallmark feature of medical anthropology since the late 1970s, "when medical anthropologists insisted on recovering subjective 'illness' experiences from below medicine's overpowering definitions of objective 'disease'" (2008, s83). First outlined by psychiatrist Leon Eisenberg in 1977 and soon after elaborated on by medical anthropologist Arthur Kleinman, illness has been understood within anthropology as the "innately human experience of symptoms and suffering," while disease has been understood as "what the practitioner creates in the recasting of illness in terms of theories of disorder," that is, "an alteration in biological structure or functioning" (1988, 3–6). Although the distinction between illness and disease—and a subsequent shift in scholarly focus to the sociocultural dimensions of health and medicine—has been one of medical anthropology's most significant contributions, its equally significant flaw is that it reproduces and reifies biomedicine's binaries of experience/knowledge, subjectivity/objectivity, and patient/practitioner and, in doing so, does not take into account the possibility that patients actually live—or in Annemarie Mol's words "do"—disease (Mol 2002).[17] In the case of Lyme disease, *living* disease means that in addition to the symptomatic feeling of unwellness, Lyme patients also feel, imagine, internalize, enact, and act on ideas of the Lyme bacterium living inside them, morphing into different states, hiding in their tissues and other parts of their bodies, proliferating and dying, and interacting with their immune system, all of which are ideas drawn from a scientific understanding of Lyme disease as a biological entity. It is precisely this divided experience of living a disease while being perceived to have an illness within the context of divided bodies of thought that uniquely characterizes the phenomenon of contemporary contested illness.

While proponents of evidence-based medicine have assumed that a more scientific medicine would help to create an amoral and apolitical foundation for clinical care, in practice, as this book underscores, evidence-based medicine has reinforced biomedicine's moral and political dimensions. Indeed, within the now immanent institutional framework of evidence-based medicine, the distinction between medically explainable and medically unexplainable conditions can be more fully understood as a normative delineation between the "right" and "wrong" ways of being sick.[18] In the everyday lives of Lyme patients and other patients with contested illness, being sick in the wrong way means that they are at risk for being perceived by physicians and other patients as good or bad individuals who make good or bad choices about their health, a reality that, of course, has consequences for the delivery and distribution of their medical care. Much has been written about medicalization and biomedicalization and the process by which features of everyday life become the objects of biomedical attention and intervention; less has been written about bodily conditions that are actively excluded from biomedicine's embrace and the epistemic processes by which they are categorized as *unexplainable* and, as a result, *unmedicalizable*.[19] Approaching biomedicine as a "stratified process" that is "simultaneously expansionist and exclusionary," this book explores biomedicine's exclusionary features by attending to one condition perceived to be unexplainable—chronic Lyme disease—and the implications of its unexplainability (Klawiter 2008, 28).

The Biopower and Biolegitimacy of Evidence-Based Medicine

If evidence-based medicine has succeeded in adjudicating the right and wrong ways to be sick in the United States according to a rubric of medical explainability that privileges certain types of evidence over others, it is because it is a potent site of power. But what is the nature of this power? And what is the source of its potency? In this book, I suggest that evidence-based medicine can be more fully understood as both a technology of biopower *and* a form of "biolegitimacy," an argument that builds on Didier Fassin's critical interpretation of Michel Foucault's work on biopower.[20] Against the grain of much biopolitical scholarship, Fassin suggests that Foucauldian biopower—or power "situated and exercised at the level of life"—actually has little to do with "life as such" and is much more about how, through "biopolitics" (the regulation of populations) and "anatomo-politics" (the "set of disciplines practiced on the body"), populations and individuals are governed (Rabinow and Rose 2006, 196; Fassin 2011, 185). In this way, Fassin argues that biopower can be more accurately described as "power over life," and that an attendant and perhaps more salient feature of the contemporary world is biolegitimacy: a "legitimacy of life" that "affirms" "the value of life as supreme good" but is always in tension with a "politics of life" that simultaneously produces an "inequality of the worth of lives in the real world" (2018b, 66, 116).[21] As a technology whose object is the improvement of individual and collective health *and* a means through which bodies are legitimated at the same time that they are hierarchized, assigned "unequal worth," and "differentially treated," evidence-based medicine invites analytical attention to how biopower *and* biolegitimacy operate in everyday life (92).

For example, as a "form of truth discourse" and a "strategy for intervention upon collective existence in the name of life and health," evidence-based medicine is animated by the biopolitical idea that "making live" can be made more "effective and efficient" through the taxonomic organization of medical evidence (Rabinow and Rose 2006, 203–4; Foucault [1997] 2003, 247).[22] And because, as Foucault observes, "power is everywhere," the source of evidence-based medicine's power is not uniquely held by the state but flows through and is operationalized simultaneously by state, nonstate, and individual entities (Foucault [1976] 1990, 93).[23] Indeed, state institutions (e.g., departments of health, the CDC, the Food and Drug Administration, and the National Institutes of Health), nonstate institutions (e.g., medical boards and professional societies), *and* individual bodies police the boundaries between "normal" and "pathological," "risk" and "benefit," "good practice" and "bad practice," and "science" and "quackery." To do this, as Lyme disease and other contested illnesses reveal, these regulatory bodies have increasingly come to rely on medicine's "'soft' biomedical technology" of legibility and standardization: evidence-based medicine (and, in particular, the randomized controlled trial) (Lowy 2000, 49).[24] More critically, evidence-based medicine is intensely biopolitical because, in its uptake by patients as well as physicians and scientists, it is also produced and sustained through individual and everyday "practices of the self, in the name of individual or collective life or health" (Rabinow and Rose 2006, 204).[25]

As I explore in this book, however, evidence-based medicine is much more than a set of biopolitical practices, technologies, and institutions that regulate clinical care—it is also a form of biolegitimacy that produces epistemic truths about the biological body and legitimizes differences between the right (or medically explainable) and wrong (or medically unexplainable) ways to be sick. The case of Lyme disease suggests that evidence-based medicine's power over life can be more fully attributed to its democratic and ecumenical appeal and the attendant perception of its innocuous—if not benevolent—nature. That evidence is widely understood and promoted to be "a good thing" and that clinical guidelines are widely understood and promoted to be "voluntary" are key to evidence-based medicine's strength, for these features widen evidence-based medicine's reach and allow it to be used as a lingua franca that makes biological life "sacred" through coordinated efforts to improve it *and* reinforces the "differential evaluation of concrete lives" (Fassin 2018b, 126).[26] The ethnographic study of the relationship between evidence-based medicine and contested illness also highlights how, in the context of biomedicine, claims to biological legitimacy are inextricably linked to epistemo-legitimacy, since claims to the biological legitimacy of contested illnesses are validated and strengthened by knowledge about the body that is recognized as legitimate *at the same time* that knowledge about the body is validated and strengthened by the biological legitimacy of patients' embodied experiences. Here, I make a distinction between biolegitimacy and biological legitimacy. Where biolegitimacy is a pervasive "legitimacy of life," biological legitimacy is a desired state of biomedical inclusion to which individuals make claims—for themselves and on behalf of others—within a framework of biolegitimacy (66).

In its attention to "life as biology" and "life as biography," this book explores the experience and practice of evidence-based medicine as both a technology of biopower and a form of biolegitimacy, and it sheds light on the *lived* political implications of the institutionalization of medical standards in the United States (Fassin 2011, 190). In doing so, this book reveals the extent to which standardization has become a critical component of the management of individual and collective health and a means by which certain conditions of the body come to matter more than others.

Researching Lyme

Between 2010 and 2011, I spent eighteen months traveling by car, train, ferry, and plane throughout the northeastern, mid-Atlantic, and western United States to spend time with and observe Lyme patients, physicians, and scientists. The research methods I used were a familiar anthropological combination of participant observation, unstructured and semistructured interviews, and popular, academic, and social media analysis. As a participant observer, I shadowed physicians on either side of the standard-of-care divide, and I regularly attended critical sites of discourse and practice in the Lyme disease controversy, including patient support group meetings, scientific laboratory and public health meetings, fundraising events, and scientific conferences. In addition to conducting hundreds of informal interviews at these sites, I also conducted 145 semistructured interviews with patients, physicians, and scientists, in addition to health officials, politicians, and patient advocates.[27] Finally, because a significant portion of Lyme disease discourse takes place online, I tracked the publication and circulation of relevant articles, blog posts, and listserv emails. Together, the data derived from the range of methods I used allowed me to piece together analytical insights into the lived experience of Lyme's controversy.

My first points of contact were with support group leaders and patient advocates. Within a matter of months, I was attending and observing the weekly and monthly meetings of five patient support groups, all of which were located within the same state in the northeastern United States. Although they differed in size and the regularity of their meetings, all the support group meetings I attended followed a similar format. Members would begin by introducing themselves to others and would then describe their experiences with Lyme disease; many would provide updates about remedies they had tried since the last meeting or about changes in their health status. The task of describing their experiences often brought members to tears, the reason why many group leaders kept a box of tissues on hand. Relevant issues that surfaced when members shared their stories often led to lively discussions that would eventually be reined in by the group leader so that the next member could share their story.

All five of the support groups I observed had a core group of members that attended every meeting; other members attended when they could, and each meeting was often attended by one or two new members. Members' experiences with Lyme disease were wide ranging: many had been undergoing treatment for years, while others had just been diagnosed with Lyme disease and were hoping to learn more information, having heard from friends and family that Lyme disease could be a persistent problem. Some members were unaware of the Lyme disease controversy, while others were acutely aware, having participated in advocacy events and read a range of advocacy-related materials. Attending patient support group meetings allowed me to understand patients' experiences as fully as possible; it also introduced me to a larger network of patients. It was with these patients that I began to conduct in-home interviews. I also recruited patient interviewees through email listservs and at Lyme disease fundraisers and patient advocacy events. These interviews, of which I conducted thirty-four, were audio recorded and often lasted two to three hours, as patients' stories often stretched back decades and included the stories of multiple family members.

As I gained traction with Lyme patients, I also reached out to physicians and scientists. Their response was equally positive, even if, like patients and advocates, they were also cautious. After explaining the nature and aims of my project—and particularly if I had been introduced by a colleague whom they trusted—mainstream and Lyme-literate physicians invited me to observe their practices, and scientists agreed to let me observe their activities. Only a handful of physicians and scientists did not respond to my email inquiries. In total, I observed seven physicians' practices on either side of the standard-of-care divide, as well as the meetings and activities of four scientific laboratories. In addition to asking me about my project, mainstream physicians and scientists were particularly interested in learning about what it was like to spend time with chronic Lyme patients and Lyme-literate physicians. I told them what I told Lyme patients and Lyme-literate physicians: that we talked a lot about Lyme disease and that each side wondered how I could spend so much time in the company of the other side.

To make sense of the antipodal perceptions that characterize the Lyme controversy, I began, during my fieldwork, to assume an ethnographic stance inspired by quantum mechanics that I call "quantum ethnography."[28] A physics term, quantum mechanics hinges on the discomfiting idea that one thing can be in two or more places at once. Unlike the familiar model of multisited ethnography, quantum ethnography is not a spatial practice but a conceptual one. That is, when conducting research, no matter where I was or with whom I was speaking, I tried always to occupy multiple perspectives within the parameters of my project's field and, in doing so, attempted to map out relations between these perspectives and between myself and these relations. Unlike methodological relativism, which requires the suspension of one's own perspective to understand another perspective, quantum ethnography required that I *fully and simultaneously inhabit* every perspective of which I was aware. In this way, quantum ethnography draws from "a feminist epistemology that insists that all claims to truth must be located," but it also attempts to push this work further by creating an ethnographic roadmap to capture and represent a range of situated perspectives *across* lines of difference (Myers 2015, 15; see also Harding 1986; Haraway 1988). For the purposes of this book, quantum ethnography enables an analysis that inhabits Lyme's multiplicity of meanings and holds them in productive tension.

Learning Lyme

During early conversations with Lyme patients, physicians, and scientists, I described my project as value neutral to assure them that I had no interest in "who was right" and "who was wrong." I soon learned, however, that in the Lyme world, not taking sides is its own form of taking sides. A year into research, the individuals with whom I had spent a significant amount of time would still make the microgestures of someone suspicious of infidelity: a surreptitious sideways glance to gauge my reaction or a pause before responding. Early on, I was often asked, "What's your hypothesis?," which was an indirect way of asking, "Which side do you agree with?" It was a question that also unveiled two interesting social facts: (1) the hegemony of the hypothesis-testing model inside and outside the academy, and (2) the suspicion that academic inquiries are premised on preconceptions. For example, one of my first interviews with a mainstream scientist began with a heated and unexpected reverse interview: "Do you have Lyme disease?" No. "Have you ever had Lyme disease?" No. "No one gets involved in this without having some connection to Lyme. Who is it? Your mom, your dad, your cousin, your friend?" I promise, before I began this project, I did not know anyone who had had Lyme disease. "Well, you better not get Lyme," he declared. "You'll ruin the credibility of your project."

Mainstream physicians and scientists, like the one above, worried for my safety and warned me that "Lyme crazies" might try to hurt me; Lyme patients, advocates, and Lyme-literate physicians expressed concern that just being part of an academic institution that was populated with "chronic Lyme deniers" spelled doom for my project. Irrespective of whether they trusted me or my intentions, they worried that once individuals in administrative positions caught wind of my project, they would put restrictions on what I would be able to say or, at the very worst, make me toe the "party line" that chronic Lyme disease does not exist. For example, even after we had shared two meals together, the leader of a prominent advocacy group declined to be interviewed simply because of my academic affiliation. And one mainstream physician declined to be interviewed because he had Googled me and saw that I had given a presentation at a community event that was cosponsored by the local health department and a Lyme advocacy group. When one of his colleagues later introduced me to him at a conference, he exclaimed with surprise, "If I had known you were with him, I would have let you interview me! I just figured you were a Lymie!"

Lyme time is measured by these wary advances and retreats. To protect my informants and to preserve the integrity of my project, anonymity was the golden rule. But even under conditions of anonymity, physicians and scientists often felt uncomfortable having our meetings audio recorded, which meant that I relied on my increasing typing speed to capture our conversations. At the end of one interview with a mainstream scientist, the scientist confided, "I'm glad you did it this way [not recording interviews]. I imagine that people were more honest with you." At project's end, I, too, had the sense that, by not recording these interviews, what I lost in accuracy, I gained in depth and "honesty" of disclosure. I also became vigilant about the consistency of my engagement with individuals across the divide to ensure that the way I approached, described, or responded to an idea in conversation was the same irrespective of context. Each time someone asked me whom else I had spoken to or spent time with, I explained why I could not tell them. When I caught myself entertaining the thought that my vigilance was just a self-imposed neurosis, I quickly remembered that these ethnographic parameters were an original function of individuals' nearly ubiquitous concern for their privacy and safety. This concern was most apparent on a day when I conducted multiple interviews at a public health office. The scientist I had just interviewed offered to lead me through the building's labyrinthine structure to my next interview with his colleague. On the way over, we eased into the familiar social territory of benign personal exchange but stopped abruptly before we reached his colleague's open door so that he would not be seen with me. "I'll have to leave you here," he said as he shook my hand and turned quickly on his heels. It was at moments like these that the line between ethnographer and intelligence agent seemed tenuously thin.

The steepest part of the learning curve, however, was becoming proficient in Lyme's language. Because I did not have a natural science or medical background, there was, of course, the new frontier of antibodies and antibiotics, epitopes and proteomics, SPECT scans and PET scans. But more difficult still was maneuvering through the intricacies of how the words used to describe Lyme disease index the speaker's positionality. During an interview with a mainstream physician, I used the word "Lyme literate" to describe the physicians who diagnose and treat Lyme disease according to the alternative standard of care. This term—or LLMD (Lyme-literate medical doctor)—has become so commonplace that, like "pro-life," its referent displaces its actual meaning. The physician I was interviewing, however, winced as if in pain and told me that he would end the interview if I used the term again. Another physician would not participate in my project until he had clarified how I was using the term "Lyme patient." Was I referring to acute or chronic Lyme patients? I told him that I was referring to anyone who identified as a Lyme patient. He agreed to participate but feared that my eventual audience would not be able to distinguish between "real" and "fake" Lyme patients. Finally, during an interview with a scientist who was new to the field and reluctant to ruffle feathers, we spent a significant amount of time discussing the implications of using the term "post-treatment Lyme disease" versus the term "post-Lyme disease syndrome." At the time of our interview in 2011, mainstream physicians often used the term post-Lyme disease syndrome (found in the 2006 IDSA guidelines) to describe what they believed was a small number of patients who continued to experience symptoms (unrelated to an active bacterial infection) after treatment for acute Lyme disease. Given that much of the debate hinges on whether the bacterium that causes Lyme disease can persist after standard antibiotic treatment, some argued that "post-treatment Lyme disease" was a preferred term because it left open the possibility that persisting symptoms after treatment might be due to persistent infection, while "post-Lyme disease syndrome" foreclosed it. Although, as of this writing, the CDC uses post-treatment Lyme disease syndrome on its website, the use of post-treatment Lyme disease syndrome versus chronic Lyme disease is still understood to reflect implicit support of the mainstream versus Lyme-literate standard of care (DVBD, NCEZID 2019). More than just nosological preoccupation, anxiety over Lyme terminology and its semantic ambiguity is deeply connected to allegiances to particular ways of knowing the body.

During my fieldwork, I found that the division between these ways of knowing the body was reinforced by how Lyme news travels. Time-space compression technologies like Twitter, Facebook, and Instagram have made the idea that news travels fast a banal tautology. But news *does* travel fast across Lyme's electronic etherscape. For example, during my fieldwork, I participated in a panel discussion on the documentary film *Under Our Skin*, which, in following the stories of several chronic Lyme disease patients, has provided a cinematographic loudspeaker for the Lyme community's rallying cry. The panel discussion was hosted at an institution that is widely understood to support Lyme disease's mainstream standard of care. No sooner was an article about the panel posted to the institution's website than it was absorbed by the rhizomatic tangle of Lyme disease listservs, forums, websites, and blogs, and, within hours of having participated on the panel, I had emails waiting for me in my inbox. This example nicely conveys the paradoxical intimacy of enemy lines. For many mainstream physicians and scientists, "support group" is a four-letter word, a breeding ground for conspiracy theories and antiscience sentiments. For many Lyme patients, mainstream Lyme physicians and scientists are inhabitants of the "dark side," obdurate obstacles to patients' recognition as legitimate sufferers, if not the source of their suffering. But, as the response to the panel discussion reveals, each side is also attuned to the other's Lyme-related activities.

Given this familiarity, it is striking how little communication—let alone personal interaction—actually takes place between Lyme's camps. This was made apparent at a scientific conference I attended. The first evening, I had dinner plans with a Lyme-literate physician. While I waited for him in the hotel's restaurant, a group of mainstream physicians arrived and asked me to join them. I explained that I already had plans and asked if it would be OK for the Lyme-literate physician to join us. "Yes," they replied, before their eyes widened and they looked at each other as if they were only then processing the implications of their answer. When the Lyme-literate physician joined our table, the conversation slowed, and the room felt heavy with the details that had gone unnoticed: the metronomic pulse of the clock on the wall, the edible flower perched on the butter square, the perspiring water glasses, the waiters talking in the corner. One of the mainstream physicians introduced himself, and the Lyme-literate physician replied, "I know who you are," which was to say, "We all know who we are." The conversation haltingly progressed with caution, circumlocution, and subtle jabs. When the check arrived, we rose quickly to leave. The Lyme-literate physician and the mainstream physician who had initially introduced himself walked silently toward the restaurant door, as if neither wanted to be the first to break stride. Upon entering the lobby, the mainstream physician veered off to another section of the hotel, and the two physicians separated, only to return to the tracks of their virtual intimacy.

In the end, the patients and Lyme-literate physicians that mainstream physicians described as dangerous were generous and supportive and welcomed me into their fold. I took it as quite a compliment when one advocate finally exclaimed, "She's practically a Lymie!" And the physicians and scientists whom Lyme advocates feared would silence me were equally generous, supportive, and welcoming. After I completed my research, I continued to receive emails from individuals across the divide who were curious about the progress of my work and when my book would be published. I am confident that there will be a range of reactions to this text: disappointment and interest, clarity and confusion, validation and exclusion. Any flaws in this book, of which I am sure there are many, are wholly my own. My only hope is that individuals across the divide come away feeling that, at the very least, I attempted to understand and communicate their ideas and experiences as fully and fairly as possible.

Representing Lyme

Even before I finished my research, I became acutely aware of the representational challenges that my project posed. I knew that to maintain the project's integrity—and to avoid the fate of it becoming a casualty of Lyme's controversy—I would have to use utmost care in how I chose my words and represented the ideas and experiences of the individuals with whom I had spent time. In this book, I am interested in knowledge as it is understood and practiced by Lyme patients, physicians, and scientists; I am less interested in knowledge as something that *is*. My interest in facts—scientific and social—only extends as far as individuals perceive or act on them. The choice to represent ideas and experiences in this way is neither an endorsement of certain practices and opinions nor a superficial attempt at evenhandedness for the sake of evenhandedness; rather, it is an intentional and intimate engagement with the complicated, interactive, and relational processes of meaning making in individuals' lives.

Of course, one of the implications of a "knowledge as practice," "constructivist," or "genealogical" approach is that it precludes the possibility of being able to answer questions such as, "Does chronic Lyme disease exist?," in any way other than, "It depends on whom you ask."[29] Although this approach is consistent with anthropological and other "explanatory and descriptive" approaches more generally, it nevertheless runs the risk of raising concerns among readers, particularly in the context of contemporary American politics, where conversations about fake news and alternative facts have provoked anxiety about an emergent social reality in which boundaries between facts and beliefs—if not between truths and lies—are blurred (Smith 2006, 3).[30] I hope to convince the reader that what is at work in this book is not false equivalency but an attempt to dig deep enough to reveal the textured and entangled roots of Lyme's bifurcated trunk, to show how, in the spirit of philosopher of science Ludwik Fleck, the "specific features" of what Lyme patients, physicians, and scientists engage with as "reality" do not precede their engagements but, across time and space, "emerge and acquire their specificity through them" (Smith 2006, 51). In other words, as anthropologist Allan Young suggests, "the ethnographer's job is to stick to reality, its sources and genealogies; that should be enough" (1995, 10).

In this way, I take part in an anthropological tradition of what João Biehl calls the production of "different kinds of evidence," a tradition that is less interested in making normative claims about research participants' ideas and practices and more interested in what happens when these ideas and practices are grounded within a meaningful theoretical framework (Biehl and Eskerod 2007, 405). As a result, I do not hierarchize or take a stance on the different kinds of evidence under analysis but, instead, describe them as fully as possible and, more critically, put these kinds of evidence in conversation with each other. The goal of the book is not to draw conclusions about controversial issues related to Lyme disease but to describe how individuals across the divide understand, experience, and act on these issues to shed new light on the relationship between contested illness, evidence-based medicine, and biopower in the United States.

Along these lines, interlocutors' stories are conveyed as they were told to me. These stories have not been fact-checked or cross-referenced with medical records; rather, they are intended to be read as representations of individuals' lived experience. Furthermore, the terms I use are the terms that individuals use to describe themselves. For example, I use "Lyme patient" to describe any patient who identifies with having or having had Lyme disease, irrespective of their medical history, and I use the term "Lyme-literate physician" to describe any physician who identifies with being a Lyme-literate physician. Although most of the patients I interviewed and observed described experiences with Lyme disease marked by chronicity, I do not make a distinction between chronic Lyme disease and Lyme disease when referring to the ideas and experiences of these patients because most patients and Lyme-literate physicians understand chronic Lyme disease to be one point on the timeline of the Lyme disease experience and not a qualitatively different disease state from acute Lyme disease. Moreover, although patients often refer to themselves as chronic Lyme patients, they also perceive the use of this term by mainstream physicians as a means to distinguish them from what mainstream physicians perceive to be "real" Lyme patients. Because I am only interested in the ideas and experiences of my project's participants, the terms I use in this book reflect the positionality of the individuals who use them, as well as the social contexts in which they are used.

In addition to term use, two other distinctive features of this book are its quotation and citation styles. When quoting project participants, I often include the entirety of participants' thoughts in block quotations. Block quotations, of course, run the risk of diminishing a text's readability; however, because individuals on either side of the divide often felt that their stories had been partially or poorly represented in the past, the importance of keeping participants' voices intact outweighed my writerly impulse to keep quotations short. On the other hand, because this book will likely be read by a range of readers, some of whom will be familiar with Lyme's controversy and some of whom will be learning about Lyme for the first time, I also aim to enhance readability and accessibility by endnoting citations—in addition to discussions about citations—that are related to particularly detailed and esoteric issues. This is the case, for example, in chapter 1, where, in mapping the Lyme disease controversy, I describe and analyze the extensive scientific and medical literatures related to Lyme, a significant portion of which is endnoted.

Finally, in keeping with anthropological representational practices, but particularly because Lyme disease is such a sensitive topic, I have gone to great lengths to ensure participants' anonymity. All names used in this book (with the exception of public figures who did not participate in my project or individuals who were not directly connected to the controversy) are pseudonyms, and I have anonymized stories by removing identifying information, including the locations of most interviews and all observational sites.[31] Because of my commitment to participant anonymity, I chose not to write about some stories and events because I worried that their telling risked exposing participants' identities. And unlike some ethnographies, this one does not include composite characters, a character that comprises features of two or more characters. Although the composite character does offer an ethnographic solution to the problem of participant anonymity, I found that this project's need for transparent representation outweighed the benefits that a technique like the composite character confers. That said, in sections of this book where I quote participants but do not also describe them, I randomly switch participants' gender to provide enhanced anonymity.

Despite the range of representational techniques I use to meet the needs of such a controversial project, it was clear from the outset that these measures alone would be insufficient. Throughout my research, Lyme patients, physicians, and scientists continually expressed concerns about how I would represent the Lyme disease controversy, and some confided in me that they worried that the end product would be quite different from how I described it. In response to these concerns, and in an attempt to make this project as transparent, participatory, and collaborative as possible, I decided to invite participants to review the dissertation on which this book is based and to provide feedback prior to its submission to the Yale Graduate School of Arts and Sciences in 2014.

The review process occurred in two stages. To ensure that I had protected participants' identities as fully as possibly, I first asked any participant who could be potentially identified in the manuscript to review and approve the section of the manuscript in which they appeared. After this was accomplished, I invited a representative sample of the 145 individuals I interviewed to review and provide feedback on the manuscript, which I uploaded to a private and secure website designed solely for the purpose of participant review. These individuals included ten patients (including patient advocates), ten physicians (half of whom were Lyme literate and half mainstream), and ten scientists. To further protect the privacy of project participants and to ensure that the manuscript was not copied and distributed prior to submission, I required each participant to sign a confidentiality agreement. In total, four patients, six physicians, and four scientists registered to review my manuscript, with the knowledge that, although I would take all feedback into full consideration, I would only be obligated to make changes that were related to concerns about personal identity.

Although inviting one's interlocutors to participate in the representation of their ideas and experiences is becoming an increasingly common anthropological practice, it still gives many anthropologists pause. When I told one of my colleagues about the review process I had undertaken, he replied in an email that he suspected that "transparency" would "serve a diluting rather than an enhancing function." I am happy to report that for this project, the experience was an enhancing one. During both stages of reviews, participants across the standard-of-care divide were eager to help, provided incisive comments and suggestions, and, in their feedback, were notably cautious about suggesting that I change parts with which they disagreed. For example, one mainstream physician, after reading a section in which he anonymously appeared, wrote, "It gave a better appreciation of the anthropological perspective. I don't necessarily entirely agree with you, but then we might not entirely agree about whether George HW Bush was a good president. I found everything to be mostly clear, well written and interesting." Another Lyme-literate physician, after reviewing the entire manuscript, wrote, "Not always 'pretty' (to me) representation of what is going on in 'LymeWorld'—however—honestly reports what your research encountered." He continued, "Like I had hoped of your thesis: honesty & integrity. I'll be interested to learn (eventually) of the 'feedback—or even push-back' you get." I am grateful for the feedback that my interlocutors provided at all stages of this project, but I am particularly grateful for their collaboration with its written form; in the end, it helped to ensure, as much as possible, the accurate representation of their range of ideas and experiences.

Anatomy of a Book

The chapters in this book describe and analyze how Lyme disease is prevented (chapter 2), lived (chapter 3), diagnosed and treated (chapter 4), and biopolitically regulated and legitimated (chapter 5) in the United States. Chapter 1, "Mapping the Lyme Disease Controversy," sets the stage for this discussion by providing an in-depth exploration of the specificities of the Lyme disease controversy and by examining how the controversy is much more complex than a disagreement over diagnosis and treatment. Here, I argue that the controversy can be better understood as the sum of the interaction between Lyme's individual nodes of contestation, which include bacterial species and strains, geographic distribution, vectors and mechanisms of transmission, co-infections, signs and symptoms, pathophysiology, immunization, diagnosis and laboratory testing, and treatment. Drawing from Deleuze and Guattari ([1980] 1987), I use the idea of the rhizome to capture the entangled and contingent nature of the Lyme controversy and to circumnavigate the most common pitfalls—such as teleological assumptions and binary accounts—of representing controversy more generally.

Chapter 2, "Preventing Lyme," fleshes out the environmental dimension of living Lyme disease by examining how individuals across the standard-of-care divide attempt to prevent themselves and their loved ones from getting tick bites. In doing so, the chapter more broadly explores the relationship between individuals' understandings of "nature" and the ways in which they understand and act on their health. As vector-borne diseases like Lyme become an increasing threat in the United States as a result of climate change (Sonenshine 2018), individuals who live in Lyme-endemic areas face the difficult task of negotiating the competing demands between their attraction to nature and their fear of environmental risk. As a result, I suggest that the experience of Lyme disease can be better understood through what I call an "epidemiology of affect." That is, who gets Lyme disease and why has just as much to do with how individuals *feel* about their natural environment as it has to do with traditional epidemiological factors of risk.

After tracing the historical emergence of Americans' affective relationship with nature, I continue to examine what individuals in Lyme-endemic areas understand to constitute their environment and which part of that environment they find risky in the context of their broader "environmental privilege" (Park and Pellow 2011, 14). I suggest that, for many Lyme disease patients, Lyme disease is just one risk in a constellation of risks that can be broadly defined as a "toxic environment," and I conclude by exploring the range of practices that individuals engage to prevent Lyme disease. I also argue that the incidental effects of tick-borne disease prevention practices—for example, quality time spent between parents and children, intimate time spent between partners, and a collective feeling of greater safety—become just as important to individuals as their perception that the practices they engage *actually work*.

Chapter 3, "Living Lyme," tells the stories of five Lyme patients: a mental health practitioner, a business professional, a teacher, a college student, and a self-described "homemaker." Their stories reveal the striking range of bodily possibilities that being a Lyme patient—and particularly a chronic Lyme patient—entails. In telling their stories, I also analyze what I found to be the most salient themes related to the experience of living contested illness in the context of evidence-based medicine: suffering, survival, and surfeit. By shifting suffering's metric from "mortality to morbidity," this chapter explores the experience of bodily discomfort in the context of social disbelief, disbelief that is compounded by perceptions that Lyme disease is more common among women and that it is an illness of the mind and not the body.[32] In response to their discomfort, patients also enact a range of practices, including the use of complementary and alternative medicine (CAM), which many patients describe as key to their survival. In light of this, I suggest that many patients are attracted to CAM therapies because they perceive these therapies to offer the possibility of *being healed* over and above the possibility of *being cured*. This chapter ends by exploring how individuals in Lyme-endemic areas understand the relationship between wealth and ill health in the United States.

Chapter 4, "Diagnosing and Treating Lyme," explores the experiences and practices of four physicians—two mainstream and two Lyme literate—who diagnose and treat Lyme disease. These stories bring to light the com-

peting and overlapping ways in which mainstream and Lyme-literate practitioners understand and treat the Lyme body; through them, I examine the
broader relationship between biomedicine and CAM in the United States
and the epistemic significance of medically unexplained illness as a diagnostic category. In this chapter, I suggest that biomedicine makes a fundamental distinction between symptoms and signs as legitimate bases for
clinical diagnosis and that this distinction simultaneously generates—and
holds in tension—biomedical explainability and unexplainability. In contrast, because CAM does not delineate between symptoms and signs as legitimate bases for diagnosis, illness, by way of symptoms, always has the
potential to be explained, a reality that offers some patients with contested
illnesses the satisfaction of having their full range of symptoms recognized
and therapeutically responded to. I ultimately suggest that, despite their
perceived marginality, medically unexplained illnesses are not incidental to
biomedicine but intrinsic to it.

Finally, chapter 5, "Lyme Disease, Evidence-Based Medicine, and the
Biopolitics of Truthmaking," draws on the example of Lyme's controversy
to shed light on both the biopolitical and the biolegitimizing dimensions
of evidence-based medicine. I begin the chapter by tracing the historical
emergence of evidence-based medicine in the United States and by investigating its relationship to the controversy over whose truths about Lyme
disease get to count. Drawing from interviews and conversations with
Lyme physicians and scientists, and by closely examining two significant
Lyme-related political events, I suggest that evidence-based medicine can
be more fully understood as a technology of biopower that organizes and
regulates bodies in the pursuit of more "effective and efficient" medicine
and as a form of biolegitimacy whose power is located in the democratic
reach of its affirmation and hierarchization of biological life. I also reinforce the overarching argument of this book, which is that, in addition
to standardizing medical practice, evidence-based medicine has had the
unintended consequence of amplifying differences in practice and opinion by providing a platform of legitimacy on which all individuals—from
patients and physicians to scientists and politicians—can make claims to
medical truth.

In exploring Lyme disease at the intersection of biomedicine, biopower,
and the environment, this book's five chapters make a case for why the rise
of evidence-based medicine in the United States has made contested illnesses like Lyme disease even *more contested*. They do so by suggesting that
evidence-based medicine has further marginalized contested illnesses

through the formal categorization of medically unexplainable illnesses at the same time that it has opened up a new space in which a range of truths about contested illnesses get to count. If this argument bears weight, it is only because it has been constructed by listening to the stories and observing the practices of those who live Lyme's controversy every day: Lyme patients and the physicians on either side of the standard-of-care divide who diagnose and treat them.

MAPPING THE LYME DISEASE CONTROVERSY

Although I chose this project in part because it was controversial, I did not realize until my research had already begun that Lyme disease is so controversial that even *describing* it as a contested field is controversial. Because many
contend that there is as little to be contested about Lyme disease as there is
about a round Earth, the controversy's mere mention is often interpreted
as a willingness to entertain "nonscience" as "science." Of course, eighteen
months of research proved that even within the rather amorphous layers
of what could be described as the "mainstream" and the "Lyme-literate"
camps, caveats, exceptions, and points of difference abound. Learning
to converse in Lyme—being able to anticipate what might strike a nerve
or send a conversation into a spiral of misfires—requires understanding
where nodes of contention lie. These rhizomatic nodes span the wide
range of species and strains, geographic distribution, vectors and mechanisms of transmission, co-infections, signs and symptoms, pathophysiology, immunization, diagnosis and laboratory testing, and treatment. In
this chapter, I review each of these nodes in an attempt to map Lyme's
controversial subterrain and to provide footing sturdy enough to support
and lend relevance to the ethnographic analysis that I engage in the chapters
that follow.

The framework of this chapter takes its cue from Deleuze and Guattari's
([1980] 1987) conceptual intervention of the "rhizome." As both a quality of
being and a way of thinking, the rhizome is characterized by unpatterned
connectivity, in addition to a perpetual and dynamic "becoming" that has
no beginning or end but only a middle (25). In this way, the rhizome is a
corrective to the classificatory temptation to "tame the wild profusion of
existing things" and to reorder a world in which, for example, the oblique

might be intimately connected to each other and the proximal might be of tangential relevance (Foucault [1966] 1994a, xv). By framing the multiplicity of contested topics related to Lyme disease as mappable rhizomatic nodes, this chapter recognizes that each topic is infinitely connected to other topics and that, far from a sedentary point, each node is a position on a "line of flight" that extends *across* domains of ideas and practices that are of both general and specific relevance to Lyme disease (Deleuze and Guattari [1980] 1987, 21). Through this chapter's rhizomatic structure, I also hope to disrupt the tendency to describe controversy in binary terms that are couched within a cohesive master narrative. Instead of organizing the chapter into corresponding sections about Lyme's two camps and their respective "party lines," I move through the nodes of Lyme's controversy in no particular order. I also let them "interfere" with each other and refer back and forward to other nodes to approximate how, on the ground, learning about Lyme disease—and becoming proficient in navigating its controversial terrain—is a process as random and unordered as it is, at times, overwhelming (Haraway 1997). In doing so, I aim to enact the process by which ideas, practices, and materialities related to Lyme disease aggregate and collect in "offshoots" rather than "filiation" (Deleuze and Guattari [1980] 1987, 24–25).

Finally, a note about this chapter's content and approach. It might appear to the reader that parts of this chapter—particularly the scientific literature reviews—are beyond the purview of an anthropological analysis and are better suited to a footnote discussion. However, the extent to which I explore and elaborate on these topics is deliberate. Lyme's controversy is often in its details and, even more importantly, in the sum of its details. Conversations that I observed among patients, as well as among physicians and scientists, often hinged on the scientific fine print of Lyme disease, and it is only in discussing them here that I am able to fully convey what the Lyme controversy is really about. Furthermore, because this book will be read by Lyme patients and by physicians and scientists across the standard-of-care divide, this chapter's depth and focus are both an engagement with conversations that are important to many of my readers and a further attempt to demonstrate the genealogical nature of my project's intervention. The aim of this chapter is to describe the perspectives that relate to each of Lyme's controversial nodes. These varying perspectives are bound up with a range of scientific "evidence" (from "personal anecdote" and "expert opinion" to case reports and randomized controlled trials), and my intent is not to differentiate between these evidence forms but to describe them and, for the first time, put them in conversation with each other. Because Lyme's scientific conversations continue to expand and change, those featured here are only as current as they were at the time of this book's writing.

Of Species and Strains

The bacterium that causes Lyme disease is a spiral-shaped organism known as *Borrelia burgdorferi*, named after Willy Burgdorfer, the microbiologist who, in 1982, discovered it in the midgut of ticks collected from Connecticut and New York (Burgdorfer et al. 1982). Since then, *Borrelia burgdorferi*'s singular sensation has proved to be a genetic plurality. Although the phylogenetic schema is continuously expanding to accommodate emerging data, *Borrelia burgdorferi* has been and is currently divided into two broad categories: *Borrelia burgdorferi* sensu stricto and *Borrelia burgdorferi* sensu lato. Sensu stricto includes only *Borrelia burgdorferi*, the species initially pinpointed as the causative agent of Lyme disease. It is found in North America and Europe. Sensu lato includes a growing range of related species, some of which cause Lyme disease, and some of which do not; some of which are found only in North America, Europe, or Asia, and some of which are found on multiple continents. As of this writing, there are twenty recognized *Borrelia burgdorferi* sensu lato species (Golovchenko et al. 2016). Of these, twelve are known to exist in Eurasia (*B. afzelii*, *B. bavariensis*, *B. finlandensis*, *B. garinii*, *B. japonica*, *B. lusitaniae*, *B. sinica*, *B. spielmanii*, *B. tanukii*, *B. turdi*, *B. valaisiana*, and *B. yangtze*), five are known to exist in North America (*B. americana*, *B. andersonii*, *B. californiensis*, *B. carolinensis*, and *B. mayonii*), and three are known to exist in both North America and Europe (*B. burgdorferi* sensu stricto, *B. bissettii*, *B. kurtenbachii*), with the possibility of a fourth to be included in this group (*B. carolinensis* [Cotté et al. 2010]) (Margos et al. 2011; Pritt et al. 2016; Rudenko et al. 2011a, b; Schotthoefer and Frost 2015).

It had been long assumed that *B. burgdorferi* sensu stricto, *B. afzelii*, and *B. garinii* were the only species to cause Lyme disease in humans, with *B. burgdorferi* sensu stricto understood to be the only species that causes Lyme disease in North America. Although many seem to agree that these three species still account for the majority of Lyme disease cases, there are discrepancies in the emerging literature over which species, even if only occasionally detected in patients, are also associated with Lyme disease. For example, while Stanek et al. (2012, 461) report that *B. afzelii*, *B. garinii*, *B. burgdorferi*, *B. spielmanii*, and *B. bavariensis* are now recognized to cause Lyme disease in Europe, with B. *bissettii*, B. *lusitaniae*, and B. *valaisiana* being "very occasionally" detected, Schotthoefer and Frost (2015, 725) list B. *americana*, B. *andersonii*, and B. *bissettii* as possible causes of Lyme disease in North America based on "molecular analyses" case reports. Discrepancies aside, what is no longer up for debate is whether B. *burgdorferi* sensu stricto is the only species that causes Lyme disease in North America. In 2016, scientists from the Mayo Clinic made headlines with the report of a new species, *Borrelia mayonii*, that "causes Lyme borreliosis with unusually high spirochae-taemia," and the CDC's website now lists B. *mayonii* as "the only species besides B. *burgdorferi* shown to cause Lyme disease in North America" (Pritt et al. 2016, 445).[1]

Of further clinical relevance is the fact that the three primary *Borrelia* species that cause Lyme disease are also known to have different disease courses and physiological manifestations. For example, while B. *burgdorferi* sensu stricto is associated with inflammation of the joints, B. *garinii* is associated with neurological manifestations, and B. *afzelii* with skin manifestations. What complicates clinical matters even further is that each *Borrelia burgdorferi* sensu lato species also has different strains that are correlated with varying degrees of disease virulence and pathogenicity, in addition to the *Borrelia* species known as "relapsing fever" that are not part of the *Borrelia burgdorferi* sensu lato complex but whose geographic range is coextensive with it. These borrelial species cause disease in humans and have overlapping clinical manifestations with *Borrelia burgdorferi* sensu lato but require a different course of treatment. In recent years, a relapsing fever *Borrelia* known as *Borrelia miyamotoi* was "detected in all tick species that transmit Lyme disease," discovered to be present in all "areas of the United States where Lyme disease is endemic," and shown to infect humans in the United States (P. Krause et al. 2013, 291).

For some patients and physicians, knowledge that (1) more than three species of *Borrelia* are now known to cause Lyme disease, (2) new *Borrelia* species have yet to be discovered, and (3) species and strain types affect disease presentation has not only become an increasing source of concern but has also provided a possible explanation for patients with Lyme-like symptoms who do not have serological or microbiological evidence of Lyme disease. For example, some hypothesize that patients with atypical symptoms who have been told that they do not have Lyme disease might be infected with a yet-to-be-recognized *Borrelia* species or strain (this is especially true for patients in states in which Lyme disease is not recognized as an endemic infection). Others wonder if an infection with an unrecognized or regionally mismatched strain or species will not be picked up on available diagnostic tests in a particular region.

Ideas like this have become so widely circulated that at a grand rounds on Lyme disease I attended, a mainstream physician asked, "I get a lot of questions from patients. They say that Lyme disease tests aren't accurate because they use a European strain of Lyme disease. Is this true?" The idea framed in this question is actually slightly different from the idea that tends to circulate among Lyme patients and Lyme-literate physicians, which is that the *criteria* for determining whether someone has Lyme disease in the United States are based on a *study* done with a European strain. The study under question, however, states that it used a strain called G39/40 to determine its Western blot pattern (one of two assays [laboratory procedures] that comprise Lyme's two-tiered test) (Dressler et al. 1993), and a subsequent study reveals that strain G39/40 was isolated from a tick collected in Guilford, Connecticut (Fung et al. 1994). Nevertheless, some mainstream scientists recognize the possibility that a Lyme infection acquired in Europe or Asia might not appear positive on a North American Western blot assay because this assay would not also include the strains found in these regions (Makhani et al. 2010).

Geographic Distribution

Named after Lyme, Connecticut, Lyme disease is most commonly associated with the shoreline and suburbs of New England. According to the CDC and the entomologists I interviewed, Lyme disease is endemic throughout the northeastern, upper midwestern, and mid-Atlantic regions of the United States and Northern California (Schwartz et al. 2017).[2] Individuals across the spectrum agree, however, that since the late 1970s, when cases were first reported, Lyme disease in the United States has spread and increased to "epidemic" proportions (Eddens et al. 2019).[3]

In the United States, patients and Lyme-literate physicians often argue that "Lyme disease is everywhere." And, in fact, Lyme disease *has* been reported in all fifty states. But what this means to individuals is highly variable. For many mainstream physicians and scientists, Lyme disease cases that are reported in states not known to be endemic for Lyme disease are chalked up to misdiagnosis or instances of patient travel (i.e., the patient acquired the disease while visiting a Lyme-endemic area). Furthermore, these cases, and the existence of Lyme disease support groups and networks in non-Lyme-endemic states, are often interpreted as further evidence that chronic Lyme disease is a *constructed* illness. For many patients, however, the fact that Lyme disease is reported in fifty states—and, perhaps more importantly, that patients report tick attachments followed by Lyme-like symptoms in non-Lyme-endemic states—highlights the limits of scientists' knowledge and reveals the magnitude and extent to which individuals suffer from Lyme disease.[4] This difference in understanding becomes critical in clinical settings because physicians are less or more likely to entertain a diagnosis of Lyme disease depending on the location of the patient's exposure.

Another issue that complicates understandings of Lyme's geographic distribution in the United States is the existence in the southern and south-central United States of southern tick–associated rash illness (STARI), or Masters disease, named after Ed Masters, a Missouri primary care physician who spent much of his career attempting to bring STARI into the "Lyme light." In the 1990s, physicians and clinical investigators reported cases of Lyme-like illness (an EM-like rash accompanied by flu-like symptoms such as fatigue, headache, and arthralgia) with contested serological or micro-biological evidence of *Borrelia burgdorferi* infection.[5] These cases were associated with the bite of *Amblyomma americanum*, or the Lone Star tick, which is understood to be responsible for the majority of tick bites in the southern United States.[6] Debate over STARI, and whether it should be treated with antibiotics in the absence of *consistently* confirmed bacterial etiology, continues. Some suggest that it should; others suggest that antibiotic therapy is premature and that the illness is likely to resolve without it. In the early stages of this writing, I received an email from a Lyme advocate in the southern United States. She had heard from another Lyme advocate that I was doing a project on Lyme disease and wrote with urgency, hoping to reach me before I completed my project. In her email, she described the added anguish that patients in the southern United States endure because, in addition to not feeling well,

> the existence of Lyme is denied and dismissed here . . . and, despite our having more Lyme species (7) and strains (hundreds) than any other region in the country, authorities urge medical providers here to dismiss our cases as "false positives," often even in patients with a history of a tick bite, erythema migrans, all compatible history and positive serology.

As this advocate's experience makes clear, on the ground and in clinical settings, the near indistinguishability of Lyme disease and STARI rashes—and the fact that EM is early Lyme's most specific sign—blurs the boundaries of Lyme's perceived geographic limits.[7]

Finally, some attention should be given here to ideas and understandings about the origin of Lyme disease in the United States. DNA evidence suggests that Borrelia burgdorferi has existed for millions of years and has been infecting humans for as long as ticks and humans have crossed each other's paths. In 2012, a 5,300-year-old man found frozen in ice in the Alps was shown to be infected with Borrelia burgdorferi (Perry 2012).[8] The first American case report of an EM-like rash (referred to as erythema chronicum migrans [ECM]) was published in 1970 (Scrimenti 1970), and it described the history of a Wisconsin physician who developed an ECM, in addition to a "low-grade fever, headache, malaise, and hip pain" three months after a tick bite (Aronowitz 1991, 86; see also Mast and Burrows 1976). However, the first case reports of ECM in northern Europe were published much earlier, in 1910 (Afzelius 1910) and 1913 (Lipshutz 1913), by a Swedish dermatologist and an Austrian "dermato-venereologist," respectively, both of whom described "an expanding ring-like rash that developed at the site of a tick bite" (Aronowitz 1991, 82–83). In the years that followed, European physicians and scientists came to widely recognize the association between ECM and tick bites, and a "prominent hypothesis" embraced the idea that ECM was caused by a spirochetal (spiral-shaped) agent (83). Although the spirochetal etiology was not confirmed until Willy Burgdorfer's discovery in 1982, Burgdorfer writes that "by 1955, clinical and epidemiological evidence was fully provided that ECM is caused by a penicillin-susceptible bacterial agent transmitted by the ixodid tick, I. ricinus" (1986, 8; see also Hollstrom 1951; Weber 1973).

Some patients and practitioners, however, maintain that the origin of Lyme disease in the United States is not so natural and much more recent. The most popularly held idea, speculated about in texts such as John Loftus's Belarus Secret (1982, republished in 2010 as America's Nazi Secret), Michael Christopher Carroll's Lab 257: The Disturbing Story of the Government's Secret Germ Laboratory (2004), and Kris Newby's Bitten: The Secret History of Lyme Disease and Biological Weapons (2019), as well as the documentary Under the Eight Ball (Grey and Russell 2009), is that Borrelia burgdorferi was either created or manipulated by the US government to be a weapon of biological warfare. This theory maintains that after World War II, the US government began exploring tick-borne disease as a potential weapon and used Plum Island as its testing ground.[9]

Plum Island, which lies off the easternmost tip of Long Island in the Long Island Sound, is home to a controversial high-security federal research facility called the Plum Island Animal Disease Center, the described aim of which, since its creation in 1954, has been the study of highly patho-genic animal diseases, such as foot and mouth disease. Originally under the auspices of the Department of Agriculture, the center has been managed by the Department of Homeland Security since 2002, and, in the near future, it will be relocated to Kansas State University, where Homeland Security is constructing a biosafety level 4 (BSL-4) laboratory that is "expected to be operational by 2022–2023."[10] Advocates of the Plum Island–Lyme disease connection suggest that ticks reared on the island and infected with various diseases were either covertly dropped on Plum Island as part of an experi-ment or accidentally dispersed to the mainland on the backs of birds.[11] As a result, among advocates of the Plum Island–Lyme disease connection, perceived resistance by American medical and government authorities in responding to the Lyme disease epidemic can be explained, in part, as a government cover-up.

Among mainstream physicians and scientists, however, and within mainstream media more generally, accounts of Plum Island tend to be quite divergent. While there have been reported outbreaks of foot and mouth disease that were contained on the island in 1978 and again in 2004, micro-biologist Marvin Grubman, who worked at the Plum Island Animal Disease Center for more than three decades, told CBS News, "There is no scientific basis for suggesting that Lyme disease originated on Plum Island. In fact, the scientific evidence indicates that it did not."[12] And in a 2012 interview with the New Haven Register, Luis L. Rodriguez, the center's "research leader" as of this writing, said, "We take a lot of pride in what we do here. . . . We do science. We do vaccines."[13] In an effort to further "dispel rumors," parts of the research facility were opened first to journalists in 1992 and then to the public in 1994, only to be discontinued in June 2018 because of "current litigation over the island's future, the increasing activities related to DHS's ultimate departure and the need to ensure proprieties of the future sale."[14]

In my own limited research into Plum Island and its history, I was struck by how little public information is available, particularly in relation to the question of whether biological warfare research was conducted there. There appear to be no academic historical accounts of the Plum Island Animal Disease Center, and the center's website provides little related information other than asserting that it does not conduct research on "human or prion diseases," avian influenza, Lyme disease, and West Nile virus, and that its researchers "do not perform classified research."[15] Similarly, a newsletter published in October 2003 by the US Animal Health Association, The Na-tion's Plum Island Laboratories, with a special section devoted to "1669–2003:

A Partial History of Plum Island," contains no mention of biological warfare research.[16] Publicly accessible archives of major news publications also seem to house few illuminating details, aside from a handful of articles, like one that appeared on CNN.com on April 2, 2004, in which, in a review of *Lab 257*, its author writes, "When it was founded, just after World War II, the lab was a research center for biological warfare." Or another that appeared in the *Hartford Courant* on September 8, 2012, in which its author writes, "The US government steadfastly denied the existence of biological warfare experiments on Plum Island during the Cold War era. In 1993, *Newsday* unearthed documents suggesting otherwise, and in 1994, Russian scientists inspected the facility to verify that any such experiments had ended, according to various reports on Plum Island."[17]

It is easy to see how someone interested in learning about the Plum Island Animal Disease Center might Google it, only to stumble on the first hit, which is a Wikipedia article. This article states that "during the Cold War a secret biological weapons program targeting livestock was conducted at the site, although it had slowly declined through the end of the century. This program has for many years been the subject of controversy."[18] To support this statement, the article cites Michael C. Carroll's *Lab 257* and an article titled "An Overview of Plum Island: History, Research, and Effects on Long Island," which was published in the *Long Island Historical Journal* in its fall 2003/spring 2004 issue and written by Alexandra Cella, a then junior in high school whose essay had been accepted for publication as part of a secondary school essay competition. In this document, Cella writes that, at Plum Island, "research on foreign animal diseases was originally done with the intent of developing biological weapons. President Richard Nixon stopped this research program in 1969." To support her statement, she cites a 1998 article published in the Long Island newspaper *Newsday*, in which journalist Robert Cooke writes,

> Documents suggest that some of the early animal disease research was done with biological warfare in mind. The "intended" targets of the bioweapons being studied were the livestock on which the former Soviet Union was very dependent, the Army wrote in 1951. All offensive biowarfare research in the US was halted in 1969 by President Richard Nixon, however. The major center for America's biowarfare research was at Ft. Detrick, Md.

This article, however, is only accessible with a library or university subscription to a database like ProQuest because it is no longer available through *Newsday's* online archive. The documents that Cooke refers to were declassified army documents, which form the basis of the available credible information about Plum Island Animal Disease Center and biological warfare research that might have happened there. These documents were first obtained through a Freedom of Information Act request by journalist John McDonald, who, on November 21, 1993, published an article in *Newsday* titled "Plum Island's Shadowy Past; Once-Secret Documents: Lab's Mission Was Germ Warfare." In this article, McDonald writes, "Documents and interviews disclose for the first time what officials have denied for years: that the mysterious and closely guarded animal lab off the East End of Long Island was originally designed to conduct top-secret research into replicating dangerous viruses that could be used to destroy enemy livestock." McDonald notes that army documents from the summer of 1953, a year before Plum Island Animal Disease Center's creation, revealed that the "mission" of Fort Terry (a former military base on Plum Island) had been changed from one that studied both the "offensive and defensive potentialities" of a range of animal diseases as "biological warfare agents" to one concerned only with the "defensive aspects." However, McDonald also quotes an interview with Dr. William Hess, a scientist who worked for the Department of Agriculture and "directed research on African swine fever at Plum Island during the 1950s," in which Hess said,

> A lot of the work was, well, we were doing things like studying how to produce quantities of the virus and so forth. . . . When it changed from offensive to defensive, well, we were not interested in the delivery system of how to get this material off as a weapon or deliver it as a weapon. It changed to study vaccines that might help us protect against the spread of disease.

In a personal email communication with John McDonald, he wrote that his November 21, 1993, article "document[s] that research begun under the Army's germ warfare program continued into the 1990s and likely up to the present," and that the de-classified documents he obtained showed "remarkably the government's intention to turn the lab over to the Agriculture Department as a cover for the ongoing germ warfare research." He also wrote that the "lab folks" he spoke with "contend that the absence of a[n] agent delivery system kept their work from violating the countries [sic] germ warfare prohibition." In contrast to McDonald's account, the former director of the Plum Island Animal Disease Center, Robert Breeze, in an August 28, 1994, *New York Times* article, claimed that, of all the rumors that have circulated about Plum Island, none "had any basis . . . except that the Army once had a germ warfare laboratory on the island that was never used, and moved to Fort Detrick, Md." Breeze also added that "the United States has never made any germ-warfare weapons, although some people absolutely refuse to believe this."[19] In the end, what seems to hang in the balance is not whether there was a "germ-warfare laboratory on the island" but whether it was used as the US Army intended and, if it was used, whether it was used for defensive *and* offensive biological warfare research or defensive research alone. Consistent with former Plum Island scientist Marvin Grubman's account, however, McDonald, in his email to me, emphasized that he "never developed any evidence that Plum Island conducted any research on Lyme Disease, at leas[t] not up to 1995 [the year McDonald left *Newsday*]."

Because ideas about Plum Island and its connection to Lyme disease continue to circulate and find new platforms for production, many mainstream physicians and scientists perceive chronic Lyme patients and Lyme-literate practitioners to be conspiracy theorists. During my conversations with mainstream physicians and scientists, this perception often led them to doubt the claims of chronic Lyme disease patients more generally. However, during my conversations with patients, I found that they seemed to be positioned along a continuous spectrum in relationship to ideas about Plum Island. Many had never heard of the connection, some had but were not convinced one way or the other, and others had pored over documents and had amassed collections of annotated references that they were eager to show me. Like all controversial issues related to Lyme disease, but particularly in the case of Plum Island, ambiguous or absent knowledge produces and sustains contestation.

Vectors and Mechanisms of Transmission

According to the CDC and the entomologists I interviewed, *Borrelia burgdorferi* sensu stricto is transmitted by the bite of *Ixodes scapularis* in the eastern United States and by that of *Ixodes pacificus* in the western United States.[20] As for the numerous other species of ticks in search of a blood meal in the United States and whether they, too, can transmit Lyme, one entomologist I interviewed made the distinction between whether a tick *could* transmit *Borrelia burgdorferi* and whether it *does*. For example, some ticks might harbor *Borrelia burgdorferi* but do not seek out humans as hosts, while some might seek human blood meals, but do not or do not often carry *Borrelia burgdorferi*. This entomologist continued to explain that there is a tick in Colorado,

Ixodes spinipalpis, that has been found to be infected at low rates with *Borrelia burgdorferi* but that this tick rarely seeks blood meals from humans. "I'd have to sit on a rock near a woodrat's nest all day just to get one or two to climb on me," he explained. In addition to host-seeking habits and infectivity rates, vector competency also depends on a constellation of other factors such as the ecology of a region, the life cycle of the tick, and whether the natural hosts that ticks seek are competent reservoirs for the infection. For example, on the west coast of the United States, the primary host for *Borrelia burgdorferi* is the lizard. Unlike the white-footed mouse on the east coast, the lizard is not a vector-competent host, which means that it does not become infected with *Borrelia burgdorferi* and does not infect ticks that feed on it. Until recently, the assumption had been that the presence of an infection-clearing host would decrease infectivity rates of *Borrelia burgdorferi* in ticks. But one study found that its *absence* from an environment actually decreased the bacterial burden (Swei et al. 2011).

For many patients, literature volleys like the one above create a sense of distrust in the stability of current knowledge and heighten their concerns that, because "whatever we know now is probably just going to be proven wrong," there is perhaps more to fear about ticks like *Ixodes spinipalpis* and *Amblyomma americanum* (Lone Star tick) than scientists currently recognize. When it comes to the likelihood of being bitten by an infected tick that is not an *Ixodes scapularis* or *pacificus*, or of being bitten by an *Ixodes scapularis* or *pacificus* in what have been determined to be non-Lyme-endemic regions, another entomologist I interviewed made a distinction between what he described as "risk" and "real risk." "Is there some risk? Sure! But is it real risk?" he asked. "Probably not." For many patients and physicians, however, statistical significance is only as real as it *feels*. This idea is brilliantly fleshed out by anthropologist Ryan Sayre in an essay where he muses about the likelihood of running into his ex-girlfriend on the Tokyo train. He writes,

> Is it really so ridiculous to think that I might [bump into her]? Sure, it may be a city of nearly twelve million, but the odds of meeting my ex-girlfriend on the train or passing her on the street can't really be that low, can they? By my calculations, it's an even fifty-fifty: either I see her or I don't. At least that's how it feels. (Sayre 2010)

For many individuals, irrespective of tick infection rates, the possibility of crossing paths with a tick that happens to be infected with *Borrelia* but rarely bites a human at least feels like a "fifty-fifty" possibility.[21]

Beyond ticks, testimonies and firsthand accounts about mosquitoes and biting flies as vectors of transmission also circulate among patients and physicians. For example, one patient I interviewed reported that she developed a physician-identified EM rash after she was bitten by a black fly on her property in Connecticut. And a keyword search on many Lyme forums will uncover queries and concerns about having been bitten by a biting fly only to develop Lyme disease or Lyme-like symptoms. One early report documented Lyme disease after a known fly bite (Luger 1990a), and two early studies explored the possibility of biting flies as vectors of transmission for *Borrelia burgdorferi* (Magnarelli, Anderson, and Barbour 1986; Magnarelli and Anderson 1988). One of these studies detected *Borrelia burgdorferi* in horse and deer flies, but it did not try to demonstrate whether they could transmit infection (Magnarelli and Anderson 1988). The authors recommended that further studies be done, but as of this writing, none have been.[22]

In addition to contestations over which vectors transmit Lyme disease, there is also contestation over how long it takes for Lyme disease to be transmitted. A much-cited early study showed that it takes between twenty-four and forty-eight hours for *Ixodes* ticks to transmit *Borrelia burgdorferi* to their host (Piesman et al. 1987). Six studies published after this confirmed these findings (Eisen 2018). Because of this, mainstream physicians do not often recommend prophylactic treatment for ticks that are not fully engorged or that have been attached for less than thirty-six hours (Cook 2015). Some patients and physicians argue, however, that if a tick were detached prior to attaining a full blood meal, it might seek another host to feed to repletion, in which case spirochetes might already be present in the tick's hypostome (mouthpiece) and transmit the infection in less than thirty-six hours. At an annual scientific Lyme conference that I observed, a Lyme-literate physician made a case for more rapid transmission by describing a scenario in which a mother removed a tick from her daughter within hours of attachment, only to watch her daughter develop Lyme disease. Entomologists are aware that this issue remains an active question among some patients and physicians. During an entomology lab meeting that I observed, one of the entomologists reported that during tick collections, she occasionally finds partially engorged ticks, but that it occurs rarely enough that the likelihood that ticks would transmit Lyme disease in less than twenty-four hours is low. One study (Shih and Spielman 1993) found that partially fed nymphal ticks can reattach and infect a host with *Borrelia burgdorferi* after twenty-four hours, but it appears that no further studies investigating whether partially fed ticks can transmit *Borrelia burgdorferi* in less than twenty-four hours have been conducted.

In addition to how long it takes for *Borrelia burgdorferi* to be transmitted, *what time of year* it can be transmitted is also a point of confusion. While physicians, patients, and scientists seem to agree that May through July is peak nymphal tick season and represents the period of greatest risk, they are in less agreement about whether individuals are at risk for Lyme disease during the winter. Based on my observations, mainstream physicians often tell patients that they do not have to worry about Lyme disease risk when temperatures fall below forty degrees. Because of this, physicians are more likely to question a Lyme disease diagnosis if it occurs in the winter months. But one entomologist has gone to great efforts to educate the public about winter Lyme disease risk. "Ticks don't die when it gets cold," he exclaimed during our interview. "Even my mother-in-law asks when it will be safe enough to go in the yard to feed the deer, and I have to remind her that it's never safe. You can freeze ticks, down to four degrees, and they'll come back to life." Many entomologists have assumed that in the winter when it is drier, ticks, in search of more moisture, will burrow down through the snow into the leaf litter. But when this idea was presented at scientific conference, I watched as another entomologist in the audience shook his head. I approached him after the talk to follow up on his reaction, and he exclaimed, "It's all conjecture! We actually don't know what ticks do during the winter because it hasn't been studied!"

Finally, the most contested area of Lyme disease transmission is maternal-fetal and sexual transmission. The CDC and the mainstream physicians and scientists I interviewed argue that *Borrelia burgdorferi* does not cross the placenta and cannot be transmitted through breast milk or other bodily fluids. In the years after Lyme disease's discovery, there were several case reports of adverse fetal outcomes in pregnant women diagnosed with Lyme disease.[23] Of these, Weber et al. (1988) was the only one to report fetal infection despite maternal antibiotic treatment. Schutzer, Janniger, and Schwartz (1991) describe a patient with a favorable outcome but warned that this is not the case for all patients, an experience that many patients have also described. In fact, the woman who founded one of the first patient advocacy groups claimed that her infant son contracted Lyme disease in utero and suffered fatal disabilities because of it; a similar story is true for another woman who later founded another advocacy group. Since then, patients, advocates, and Lyme-literate physicians have continued to amass anecdotes related to congenital Lyme. However, studies have not been able to consistently corroborate these reports.[24]

Like maternal-fetal transmission, reports of venereal Lyme disease emerged on the heels of Lyme's discovery. Given Lyme disease's close genetic relationship to syphilis, mainstream physicians and scientists initially entertained the possibility of venereal Lyme but now disavow it.[25] Many mainstream physicians and scientists often perceive patients' continued reports of sexual transmission of Lyme disease to be humorous. For example, at a grand rounds meeting I observed, mention of the fact that some patients believe that Lyme is sexually transmitted incited a wave of giggles throughout the audience. Later in the year, at a scientific conference I observed, the hosting scientists surprised—and delighted—many attendees by staging a mock late-breaking presentation on the sexual transmission of Lyme. Begun in silence, as attendees tried to discern whether the presenter was being serious, the presentation ended with audience members doubled over in laughter and some standing in applause. One physician approached me afterward and told me that she thought the presentation was in poor taste; even those who were amused by the presentation were concerned about how I would represent this event in my book. The fact that physicians and scientists felt comfortable mocking patients (irrespective of the cause of their suffering or the accuracy of their suffering's attribution) highlights how antagonistic—and how personal—the relationship between some physicians and patients has become over the last four decades.

Co-Infections

The same tick that is understood to transmit the bacterium that causes Lyme disease is understood to cause two other infections in humans in the United States: babesiosis (caused by *Babesia microti*, a malaria-like protozoan parasite) and anaplasmosis (caused by *Ehrlichia chaffeensis* and *Anaplasma phagocytophilum*, gram-negative bacteria that infect peripheral blood cells). Individuals across the divide appear to agree on this. Although rates of babesiosis and anaplasmosis in the United States are far lower than Lyme disease, prevalence is rising and geographic distribution expanding. Among patients, awareness of the risk of co-infections (the possibility that a tick can transmit more than Lyme disease and that a patient can be sick with multiple infections at once) is so acute that, during conversations and at advocacy events, patients often clarified for me that when they use the term "Lyme disease," they are actually referring to the condition of being infected with a plurality of tick-borne diseases. "It's no longer just about fighting Lyme disease; it's about fighting tick-borne disease," one woman explained. Many patients and Lyme-literate physicians also contend that the *severity* of patients' sickness and the failure of standard treatment are the result of patients fighting off what are perceived to be multiple and often undiagnosed infections.

Mainstream physicians and scientists agree that patients can be simultaneously infected with multiple tick-borne diseases, but they disagree about how often this occurs. And within the mainstream community, there is some disagreement about whether, when this occurs, multiple infections make the course of Lyme disease worse. One study suggests that patients who are co-infected with *Borrelia burgdorferi* and *Babesia microti* experience more symptoms and a more protracted period of illness than patients infected with babesiosis alone (P. Krause et al. 1996). In interviews with mainstream physicians and scientists who were familiar with this study, some expressed concern that the study was not well designed and that its authors jumped too quickly to its conclusions. A later retrospective study reported that, in cases of subclinical babesiosis, "prior Lyme disease and serological exposure to B. *microti* are not associated with poorer long-term outcomes or more persistent symptoms [than with] Lyme disease alone" (Wang et al. 2000, 1149).

What patients, physicians, and scientists across the divide do not agree on is how common co-infection is and the extent to which co-infection *chronicity* becomes a problem. Unlike Lyme disease, there is an operating understanding among mainstream physicians that babesiosis can persist despite treatment, particularly in immunocompromised patients.[26] Nonetheless, ideas about how often this occurs in tandem with Lyme disease—and how to interpret corresponding symptoms—vary dramatically between mainstream and Lyme-literate physicians. For example, during my observation of physician practices, I never observed a mainstream physician ask about or test for babesiosis or anaplasmosis in the context of a Lyme disease diagnosis, but most Lyme-literate physicians I observed asked questions related to both diseases in their patient intakes and often followed up by ordering laboratory tests.

More contested, still, is whether *Ixodes* ticks can transmit *Bartonella henselae* (a gram-negative bacterium that causes cat scratch disease) and a variety of *Mycoplasma* bacteria (intracellular organisms whose treatment is controversial because their ubiquity makes some individuals question whether they should even be considered pathogenic).[27] Many Lyme-literate physicians routinely test for *Bartonella henselae* and are actively involved in its treatment. Mainstream physicians and scientists, however, are adamant that ticks do not transmit *Bartonella* to humans.[28] When mainstream physicians hear that a patient is being treated for bartonellosis in conjunction with Lyme disease, they often interpret it as a sign that the patient is receiving unconventional care at the hands of a Lyme-literate physician, an interpretation that is no less frequently accompanied by concerns that patients are being treated for conditions that they do not have.

The short distance that is often traveled between mention of *Bartonella* and a volatile eruption of Lyme's territorial strife is nicely demonstrated in a story that was relayed to me by a medical student. This medical student recounted how, during a lecture on Lyme disease, a fellow student asked a question regarding the scientific legitimacy of *Bartonella* as a tick-borne infection in humans and was met with a stern rebuttal by the physician-scientist giving the lecture. To the surprise of the students, this rebuttal quickly turned into an impassioned lesson on the "quacks" and "snake oil charmers" of the Lyme world. That a topic as seemingly oblique to Lyme disease as *Bartonella* could simultaneously stand in for and represent the Lyme controversy is a telling example of just how densely rhizomatic the field is.

Signs and Symptoms

Lyme disease has two origin stories. One is told by the physicians who first investigated reports of a mysterious illness in Lyme, Connecticut, in the early 1970s. In this version, the mysterious illness was a cluster of rheumatoid arthritis–like illnesses among children, often manifesting in swollen knees and preceded by a strange red rash in the shape of a bull's eye. The other story is told by Polly Murray, one of two mothers who reported the illness cluster to public health officials. In her book, Murray (1996) describes a mysterious illness that expanded beyond a cluster of arthritis cases and encompassed a range of disabling chronic symptoms, including, among others, fatigue, malaise, muscle and joint pain, fevers, blurred vision, irritability, and chills. Polly's experience—a protracted period of unwellness in which one symptom followed on the tail of another—and the way in which Lyme disease came to be defined through its objective signs highlight a critical dimension of how biomedicine knows the body. This tension between signs ("objective" and measurable by a practitioner) and symptoms ("subjective" and articulated by a patient) continues to define Lyme disease. For example, while Lyme's signs include EM, arthritis, carditis, and Bell's palsy, its recognized symptoms differ depending on whom you ask. Whereas many mainstream physicians and scientists argue that

Lyme disease is most often associated with symptoms of "fatigue, fever, headache, mildly stiff neck, arthralgia, or myalgia" *in the presence* of an objective sign, Lyme-literate physicians argue that Lyme disease often exists in the absence of objective signs, and diagnosis must be made based on an attentive evaluation of all available symptoms.[29]

Lyme-literate physicians and advocates also make the case that the way in which symptoms are categorized—and the legitimacy that this categorization adds or takes away—has changed over time. For example, Pamela Weintraub (2008), a journalist and one of the leading voices in the Lyme advocacy movement, argues that this shift in symptom categorization happened shortly after researchers realized that Lyme disease had a bacterial basis (not viral, as originally assumed). As Weintraub observes, in a 1983 study in the *Annals of Medicine*, what had previously been categorized as "late manifestations" were now divided between "major" and "minor" late manifestations (92; see also Steere, Hutchinson, et al. 1983). Where major manifestations included "meningoencephalitis (severe headache, stiff neck on physical examination, and a spinal fluid pleocytosis), myocarditis (greater than first-degree atrioventricular nodal block or evidence of left ventricular dysfunction), or recurrent attacks of arthritis (pain on motion and swelling of at least one joint, ascertained by physical examination)," minor manifestations included "facial palsy alone, supraventricular tachycardia, brief arthritis (one episode for less than 2 weeks), or headache or joint pain without abnormal physical findings" (Steere 1983, 23). Although "nearly 50%" of the patients in this study went on to experience minor late manifestations, major late manifestations were "unusual" (26). Ultimately, Weintraub argues that redefining symptoms—and which symptoms mattered—allowed researchers to redefine what "treatment success" meant, even if, as Weintraub argues, "the so-called minor late complications were far more disabling to many Lyme patients than the major ones, and rarely resolved with time" (2008, 92–93).

In the absence of Lyme's objective signs, another point of much debate is what Lyme disease can *look like* or be *mistaken for*. Patients and Lyme-literate physicians argue that Lyme disease can easily be misdiagnosed as fibromyalgia, chronic fatigue syndrome, depression, multiple sclerosis (MS), Alzheimer's disease, Parkinson's disease, amyotrophic lateral sclerosis (ALS), and, in children, autism. Of these, the idea that Lyme disease can be misdiagnosed as autism is perhaps the most controversial. Among some Lyme-literate physicians, however, the idea is a growing part of clinical practice. For example, I observed a Lyme-literate physician tell the story of "Henry," a young boy who arrived at his office with classic symptoms of autism-spectrum disorder and, most significantly, an inability to verbally communicate. Upon making a diagnosis of Lyme disease, this physician recounted how he looked into Henry's eyes and told him, "We're going to give you the key to unlock your brain." Four weeks later, after a round of IV antibiotics, the physician described how Henry walked into the office, grabbed the physician's face between his hands, and said, "Thank you for giving me the key to unlock my brain." While this story impressed the large audience to which it was told, it is likely that a mainstream Lyme physician might identify it as a telling example of the manipulative potential of the anecdotal story in clinical practice.

Many mainstream physicians who are actively involved in the treatment of Lyme argue that what is often diagnosed as Lyme disease is, in fact, fibromyalgia, chronic fatigue syndrome, or depression but is rarely, if ever, confused with or the source of other neurological diseases such as MS, ALS, Parkinson's disease, or Alzheimer's disease. Part of the confusion also stems from the fact that publications by mainstream physicians and scientists (of which many Lyme patients and Lyme-literate physicians are aware and, in some cases, have cataloged) initially described and continue to describe Lyme disease as one that can be misdiagnosed as a range of other disorders.[30]

There have been case reports and studies on each of the abovementioned neurological conditions and their association, lack of association, or symptom overlap with Lyme disease.[31] In light of or irrespective of these conversations in the literature, most mainstream physicians and scientists I interviewed were adamant that these points of clinical confusion are rare occurrences and do not apply to the majority of patients. As one neurologist explained, "Because physicians and patients are more aware of Lyme disease and treat it earlier, I just don't see advanced cases like I did in the early days." Beyond changes in incidence, however, part of the confusion over whether Lyme can look like other neurological disorders seems to stem from a more general lack of consensus across biomedical specialties about what is specific to MS. Two neurologists I interviewed said that MS is characterized by oligoclonal banding (inflammation-related proteins in the cerebrospinal fluid) and that this is usually absent in Lyme disease; an immunologist I interviewed said that the primary difference between MS and Lyme disease is demyelination (a process by which the myelin sheaths of neurons are damaged). Either way, the persistence of clinical confusion over how to distinguish between Lyme and MS was borne out in my observations of physician practices, where on several occasions a patient would arrive with a pending diagnosis of MS and would have in hand an MRI report whose impression would read: "Pattern consistent with MS or Lyme disease."

Again, anecdotal stories and personal experiences play an important role in lending gravity to the lived reality of Lyme disease as a "great imitator." One of the most powerful examples for patients and Lyme-literate physicians is the case of a primary care physician who was diagnosed with ALS only to begin IV antibiotic treatment for Lyme disease and experience improvement in his symptoms (a journey that he documented on video). Although his own health could only reportedly be maintained through continuous treatment with antibiotics, the physician claimed to have eventually progressed enough to open—and become the director of—a clinic devoted exclusively to the antibiotic treatment of patients diagnosed with ALS. For mainstream physicians, stories like these provide another example of how patients might gravitate toward a Lyme diagnosis in the face of a disease that cannot be cured. As one mainstream physician reflected, "If I were given the option between having a curable or incurable disease, it seems pretty obvious which one I might be inclined to cling to."

Pathophysiology

Little is controversial about the idea that, as an *untreated* infection, Lyme is a chronic disease. (Although some—and especially those who first conducted research on Lyme when it was assumed to be a viral infection and patients were observed without being treated with antibiotics—argue that it is ultimately self-limiting and will eventually, with fewer and fewer episodes, resolve over time.) What *is* a matter of great controversy is whether spirochetes persist and are pathogenic after antibiotic treatment.[32] Of increasing interest have been studies on *Borrelia burgdorferi* persistence in animal models after antibiotic treatment.[33] Criticisms in response to these studies include lack of evidence that surviving spirochetes are pathogenic; use of suboptimal antibiotics and a lack of regard for the "pharmacokinetic-pharmacodynamic properties" of the antibiotics used (Wormser et al. 2012, 389); lack of correlation between the detection of *Borrelia* DNA/mRNA and the viability of spirochetes, in addition to the prediction that surviving spirochetes are in the process of dying; and the expectation that *Borrelia burgdorferi* would behave differently in mice than in humans because mice are an evolutionarily adapted natural host (Bockenstedt and Radolf 2014; Iyer et al.

2013; Wormser et al. 2012; Wormser and Schwartz 2009). Among patients, advocates, and Lyme-literate physicians, however, these persistence studies have generated substantial enthusiasm, in addition to cautious optimism, that they might provide enough of the right kind of evidence to convince the mainstream of the existence of chronic Lyme disease.

A microdomain of debate related to persistence is *how* (or the mechanism by which) *Borrelia burgdorferi* persists. The idea that *Borrelia burgdorferi* is pleomorphic (capable of modifying its shape and size in response to environmental stimuli) and can form dormant cysts is the most polarizing. This was demonstrated at a scientific conference on Lyme disease in which a medical student, unaware that what he would present would be controversial, gave a presentation on the interaction of *Borrelia burgdorferi* with skin fibroblasts and reported having observed structural changes that included the formation of granules, tubules, and cysts. Immediately following the close of his talk, hands were raised and comments made regarding the implausibility of his laboratory's observations. One of the leading voices among mainstream Lyme disease physicians insisted that "bacteria do not form cysts; what you saw were cyst-like structures." Another scientist in the audience argued that the bacteria were dying or degenerating, not changing form in a metabolically significant way. Later that night, over drinks and peanuts in the hotel lobby, cysts, again, found their way to the center of conversation among a small group of physicians and scientists. The discomfort among them was palpable (the result, perhaps, of the visceral sensation generated by the heterodoxy to which the word "cyst" has become inextricably linked), and the conversation moved forward in distracted tangents and noncommittal asides, only to return intermittently to the familiar refrain of "bacteria don't form cysts."

That there appears to be so much at stake for Lyme disease in whether bacteria form cysts is linked to the idea that cyst formation might be a way in which *Borrelia burgdorferi*, in a metabolically inactive state, evades the immune system and survives antibiotic therapy. Outside the academy, cysts matter because their treatment has become a well-established part of Lyme-literate practices. In addition to antibiotics, Lyme-literate physicians also prescribe medications like Flagyl and Plaquenil, which they and their patients refer to as "cyst busters." And explanations for why patients feel better on antibiotics and then relapse weeks to months later often center on cysts, the idea being that antibiotic therapy creates a hostile environment in response to which Lyme spirochetes convert to a "dormant stage" only to return to their spiral-shaped form after antibiotic therapy is over.[34]

In pursuit of an answer to why knowledge about cysts is so fractured, I posed questions to a range of scientists (e.g., microbiologists, immunologists, and entomologists) and was left with a range of answers. One scientist responded that *Borrelia burgdorferi's* many forms have long been observed but that they are metabolically insignificant and are merely snapshots of the transformation the bacterium undergoes as it is dying. In response to the statement made at the abovementioned scientific conference on Lyme, a microbiologist I interviewed was incredulous that anyone could deny that bacteria form cysts. "This is basic microbiology—I can name a bunch of bacteria that, for lack of a better word, form cysts!" Which he proceeded to do. He continued to postulate that the only explanation for why the idea of bacterial cysts is not embraced among scientists in the mainstream Lyme community is a knowledge gap, that most either have a conventional medical background or a highly specialized scientific background in spirochetal biology but not a broad background in microbiology. And, indeed, one of the most popular microbiology textbooks for college students, *Microbiology: A Human Perspective*, lists several genera of bacteria that form a resting or dormant cyst stage, including *Azotobacter* and *Myxobacteria* (Nester et al. 2012, 266–68). Of course, whether bacteria can form cysts does not answer the question of whether *Borrelia burgdorferi* can also do so, but it does conflict with the often-repeated statement among mainstream Lyme physicians that *bacteria in general* cannot form cysts. Above all, this case is a revealing example of the power of "word-of-mouth" knowledge production inside and outside the academy and the way in which patterned phrases reveal the extent to which, among patients *and* physicians, knowledge is often inherited.

After my research ended, Lantos, Auwaerter, and Wormser (2014) published a review on morphological variants of *Borrelia burgdorferi*. This article marks a shift in mainstream acceptance of bacterial cyst forms because it recognizes that "a few bacterial genera, such as *Azotobacter*, *Azospirillium*, and *Rhodospirillium*" form "true encystment" (Lantos, Auwaerter, and Wormser 2014, 664). However, Lantos et al. distinguish these bacterial genera from *Borrelia burgdorferi*, which, they argue, does not form a "true" encystment. They continue, "As this has become recognized, less specific descriptors such as 'round bodies' have come into more common use regarding chronic Lyme disease" (664). In recent years, use of the terms "round bodies," "persisters," and even "aggregated biofilm-like microcolonies" (Feng et al. 2014, 2016; Feng, Auwaerter, and Zhang 2015) to describe a "minor population of non-growing bacterial cells that are not killed by bactericidal antibiotic treatment" has become increasingly common among scientists across the divide (Feng, Weitner, et al. 2015, 398; see also Meriläinen et al. 2016; Sapi et al. 2012), and a range of in vitro studies aimed at determining the antibiotic susceptibility of these "persisters" has been published (Caskey and Embers 2015; Feng, Shi, et al. 2015a, 2015b; Pothineni et al. 2016; Sharma et al. 2015).

Less volatile than cysts but still contested is whether Borrelia burgdorferi are intracellular organisms (organisms that exist within its host's own cells).[35] Like cyst formation, intracellularity matters for patients and Lyme-literate physicians because it also provides a mechanism for why spirochetes might persist despite antibiotic therapy. Intracellular organisms are broadly recognized as more difficult to treat than extracellular organisms because they require an antibiotic that can cross the cell membrane, and even then, the host cell often offers some degree of protection (Imbuluzqueta et al. 2010). As with cysts, the treatment of Borrelia burgdorferi as an intracellular organism is already a well-established part of Lyme-literate practice and a patterned feature of patient vocabulary. For these patients and physicians, the strongest evidence that Lyme persists—regardless of mechanism—are the reports and stories of patients who continue to feel unwell after standard antibiotic treatment. That patients with EM-documented or seropositive Lyme disease can continue to experience symptoms after treatment is well described and fairly well agreed on.[36] What is up for debate is how many Lyme patients go on to experience persistent symptoms and the severity and cause of those symptoms. Some studies report 10 to 20 percent;[37] other studies report 35 to 53 percent.[38] Some studies suggest that the symptoms experienced by individuals with persistent symptoms are no more than the "aches and pains of daily living" (Wormser et al. 2006, 1115), while others suggest that they are equivalent to the experience of an individual living with congestive heart failure (Klempner, Hu, et al. 2001), and that individuals with persistent symptoms have affected sleep quality (E. Weinstein et al. 2018), "mild cognitive decline" (Touradji et al. 2019), and are "highly and clinically significantly symptomatic, with poor health-related quality of life" (Rebman et al. 2017, 1).

Finally, ideas about what causes persistent symptoms after antibiotic therapy are wide ranging but generally include (1) active infection, (2) an autoimmune reaction, and (3) inflammation incited by the residual antigens of dead bacteria. Over the past decade, there has been a flurry of publications within the mainstream literature demonstrating a localized autoimmune reaction in Lyme arthritis specifically,[39] but, more recently, there have also been several studies that, in isolating a set of inflammatory biomarkers not also found in controls, point to the possibility of systemic autoimmunity in Lyme disease patients after antibiotic treatment.[40] These studies have been received with mixed reviews. One immunologist I interviewed commented on how hard it is to pinpoint causality in autoimmunity. "This study is an observational study," he explained. "It showed that there are markers, but are they pathogenic? Having antibodies doesn't necessarily mean you have pathologies. For example, if you draw the blood of someone four weeks after they've had a heart attack, they'll be making antibodies to their own myocardium." And for patients, the possibility that their discomfort is related to an autoimmune reaction is also a difficult pill to swallow, not only because it offers no cure but also because they perceive it to distract from the real issue at hand, which, for many, is the persistence of *Borrelia burgdorferi* in their bodies.[41]

The Lyme Vaccine

In an article titled "Antiscience and Ethical Concerns Associated with Advocacy of Lyme Disease," its authors write that "advocacy for Lyme disease has become an increasingly important part of an antiscience movement that denies both the viral cause of AIDS and the benefits of vaccines and that supports unproven (sometimes dangerous) alternative medical treatments" (Auwaerter et al. 2011, 713). During my research, the mainstream physicians I spoke with often made comparisons between chronic Lyme patients and "antivaccine" individuals, citing similarities in their perceived willingness to entertain anecdote over scientific evidence and their susceptibility to a fear-mongering culture. However, in addition to Lyme advocacy groups' early support of a Lyme vaccine, stories relayed to me by patients indicate that, prior to the entry of LYMErix (the Lyme vaccine) on the market, demand for and interest in a Lyme vaccine within Lyme-endemic communities were also relatively high.[42] For example, Meredith, a chronic Lyme patient I interviewed, explained how her husband, a firefighter, elected to get the Lyme vaccine *because* of her experience with Lyme disease and his desire to avoid her fate. She described being shocked, then, when he developed arthritic symptoms after getting the vaccine.

The experience of developing symptoms after vaccination with LYMErix is one that soon became the basis for class action lawsuits filed against the vaccine's manufacturer, SmithKline Beecham (now GlaxoSmithKline GSK), in the years following the FDA's approval of the vaccine's use in 1998.[43] In response to accumulating reports by physicians in Lyme-endemic areas that individuals who received the vaccine were experiencing debilitating joint and muscle pains, the FDA convened public hearings in February and November of 2001, during which experts and individuals who had received the vaccine gave testimony. While the director of the CDC and the FDA's cosponsored Vaccine Adverse Event Reporting System (VAERS) said that, despite the system's recognized "limitations," "reports of arthritic events reported to date do not provide clear evidence of a causal association," others described experiences and concerns to the contrary (Edlow 2003, 232–34).[44] For example, in "The Bitter Feud over LYMErix: Big Pharma Takes on the Wrong Little Osp," Pamela Weintraub (2001) describes how, at the second hearing, patients took the stand and detailed a life of disability after vaccination, including a woman who spoke on behalf of her husband, who had once been an "active outdoorsman" but had entered the hearing with the aid of a walker. Physician Jonathan Edlow also describes how "more than one investigator" demonstrated that vaccination with LYMErix confounded the accuracy of Lyme diagnostic tests and that one study documented four individuals (two adults and two children) who developed arthritis after vaccination (2003, 237). After taking into account this evidence, the FDA decided to take no further action regarding the vaccine, but in February 2002, GlaxoSmithKline, citing poor sales, pulled the vaccine from the market and, shortly after, released the license.

In the wake of the vaccine's discontinuation, a sticking point for some patients, physicians, and scientists has been the fact that concerns about the vaccine's safety were voiced in advance of the vaccine's approval. As early as 1993, researchers began to publish studies that suggested that the production of a particular type of antibody to one of Borrelia burgdorferi's antigens, outer surface protein A (Osp A), might trigger an autoimmune arthritis in genetically susceptible individuals (specifically, individuals with a genetic variation called HLA-DR4, which is also found in those predisposed to rheumatoid arthritis).[45] During the clinical trials leading up to the vaccine's approval, one of the clinical investigators, who had also been involved in the research linking Osp A antibodies and arthritis, reported that some patients in the study were complaining of joint pain following vaccination.[46] These concerns were also voiced at the 1998 FDA hearing prior to the vaccine's approval. Although the FDA committee went on to unanimously approve the vaccine because these concerns were considered theoretical and the clinical trials had shown sufficient safety, the chair of the advisory board confessed that "it's rare that a vaccine is voted on with such ambivalence and such a stack of provisos" (Edlow 2003, 230).[47]

In retrospect, critics argue that the design of the clinical trials should have included and tracked a subgroup of individuals with the HLA-DR4 genetic variation. Representatives from GlaxoSmithKline defended their study design by arguing that, because one-third of the general population is HLA-DR4 positive, these individuals would automatically be represented in a large-scale clinical trial. In an interview with a physician involved in one of the vaccine's clinical trials, I learned that this physician drew one hundred blood samples from a subset of patients in view of the possibility that the samples could be analyzed "to see if any potential symptoms were related" to the HLA-DR4 subtype; the analysis, however, was never done because it was not part of the original study design. Nevertheless, this physician was confident that the vaccine "did not cause an autoimmune phenomenon." He explained,

> My office has administered many vaccines, and I never saw any pattern. That's what happens in a large group of people: you get tunnel vision, and it's easy to link it to the Lyme vaccine. I got a flurry of phone calls. People would say, "I got the vaccine four months ago and now my knee hurts." That's around the time when the lawsuits started to occur. I thought I was going to have to leave town. . . . I was able to say to people who asked, "People get joint pains. We in the vaccine study meticulously followed individuals for 36 months, and there was no difference between vaccine and placebo." Out of curiosity, I also conducted my own highly unscientific study. I asked patients in my practice [who were not also enrolled in the study] if they had any joint pain in the last week and 44 percent of the people said, "Yes."

Twelve years after the vaccine's discontinuation, the debate over whether it triggered autoimmune arthritis continues. Shortly after the vaccine was approved, scientists developed a mouse model with an HLA-DR4 gene and demonstrated that, when these mice were exposed to Osp A, they developed an inflammatory response that mice without the gene did not (Iliopoulou, Alroy, and Huber 2008; Iliopoulou, Guerau-de-Arellano, and Huber 2009). Two relevant publications followed. The first was a study that recruited HLA-DR4 positive individuals who had complained of arthritic symptoms after receiving the LYMErix vaccination and compared them with controls (Ball et al. 2009). This study determined that "the Lyme disease vaccine is not a major factor in the development of arthritis" in individuals with

HLA-DR4 subtypes (Ball et al. 2009, 1179). When I interviewed one of the scientists on this study, however, he reluctantly communicated that he did not agree with the results and did not want to comment on the study. Interestingly enough, this study *did* find a significant correlation between arthritis and vaccination in individuals with one particular allele variation, which was the same allele described in the abovementioned mouse study. The second was a review article that determined that while the vaccine does not cause antibiotic-refractory Lyme arthritis, it remains possible that, through a "vigorous inflammatory response," it may "uncover latent autoimmunity in genetically susceptible individuals, as might happen with other types of vaccination or with certain infections" (Steere, Drouin, and Glickstein 2011, s264).

Like many controversial vaccines, the debate over LYMErix is plagued by—and in part produced by—the specter of elusive causality. Difficult to determine in general, causality in the case of LYMErix is even more confounding because, as its proponents argue, arthritis is a common affliction among older but healthy adults, who were disproportionately represented among individuals who received the LYMErix vaccine. For this reason, and from the perspective of LYMErix proponents, patients who developed arthritis after being vaccinated with LYMErix will always bear the burden of never being able to prove that they were not going to develop arthritis irrespective of whether they had the vaccine. Unlike other controversial vaccines, such as the one for measles, mumps, and rubella (MMR), in which the vaccine continues to be used after "an 8-year court process in the US federal vaccine injury compensation court ended in 2010 with rulings that autism was not an adverse reaction to vaccination," LYMErix's shelf life was uniquely short (Kirkland 2012, 237).

As I discuss in the next section, the controversy over the vaccine is also bound up with the controversy over the accuracy of diagnostic tests and the criteria by which they are interpreted. In the early stages of vaccine development, researchers identified which of Borrelia burgdorferi's outer surface proteins would make ideal vaccine candidates, and these included Osp A and Osp B. Because the Lyme diagnostic test measures antibodies produced against different Borrelia burgdorferi proteins, researchers also realized that an individual vaccinated with an Osp A protein would test positive on an assay that included Osp A as one of its diagnostic markers. Although Osp A, unlike other outer surface proteins, is specific to Borrelia burgdorferi, many felt comfortable removing it from the diagnostic criteria because it is expressed only in late disease.[48] As one pathologist who has been actively involved in

Lyme disease research explained in an interview, "Osp A and Osp B are not expressed in the organism in the early stage of the disease, so there was no reason to include them in the criteria. The only time that they are expressed is late in the arthritis stage."

Given this, when the CDC convened a meeting to standardize laboratory tests and to develop diagnostic criteria for epidemiological surveillance in 1994 (commonly referred to as the Dearborn meeting), Osp A and Osp B were not included in anticipation of the possibility that they might be used for vaccines.[49] In the absence of a vaccine that uses Osp A or Osp B as its antigens, many patients and Lyme-literate physicians argue that these antigens should be reintroduced into the diagnostic criteria, and that their continued absence is one reason that chronic Lyme patients fall through the diagnostic cracks. It is also an argument that has limited support among mainstream scientists, two of whom agreed during my interviews with them that, while it would not make a substantial difference for the population as a whole, the inclusion of Osp A and Osp B could determine the difference between a positive and a negative diagnosis among a handful of patients, and that that alone might be significant enough.

Like all things Lyme disease, the explanation for the short and troubled trajectory of LYMErix depends on whom you ask. For many patients and Lyme-literate physicians, the removal of the vaccine from the market was interpreted as tacit admission by GlaxoSmithKline of the vaccine's risks. For many mainstream physicians and scientists, LYMErix's discontinuation was perceived to be yet another casualty of a misinformed Lyme advocacy movement. I also observed how, among mainstream physicians and scientists, the mere mention of the Lyme vaccine during our interviews often drew tight lips and stilted conversation. One scientist, who was involved in the vaccine's development, said that he preferred not to comment and abruptly ended our interview; another, when asked about factors that contributed to the vaccine's downfall, mentioned the expense of booster shots and poor sales. When I followed up by asking about reports of vaccine side effects, he responded, "Well, and there was that." Some, citing the fact that it only ever offered 76 percent protection and could not be used in children, suggested that the vaccine's limitations made it destined for failure; others directly criticized their colleagues for not looking into the possibility that the vaccine could stimulate an autoimmune reaction in genetically susceptible individuals. As one scientist exclaimed, "If I were working on a vaccine and also coming up with data on a potential autoimmune reaction, I would pull my hair out."

Opinions about the vaccine also vary according to individuals' research interests and their proximity to the vaccine's development. Perhaps not surprisingly, those I interviewed who were at the time working on a non–Osp A vaccine suggested that an Osp A vaccine was never going to be successful. On the other hand, one scientist who was involved in the Osp A vaccine's early development argued that, despite its problems, it is the only one that has the *potential* to work because, once inside the body, the bacteria's ability to shift outer surface proteins provides it with too many options to evade a vaccine-enhanced immune system. As one such scientist responded, "After all this time, they still don't have a vaccine for syphilis. Shouldn't we infer something from this?" Finally, several physician-scientists who were involved in the vaccine's clinical trials prior to its approval spoke to the trauma of being part of the fallout. As one physician explained, "It's one part of Lyme disease that I've really blocked out. Here we are being slapped with million dollar lawsuits, and the company that was supposed to protect us abandons us!"

Although an Osp A vaccine for Lyme disease continues to be used in dogs, the development of another Lyme vaccine for humans remains a holy grail for some scientists and public health officials. In 2011, *Clinical Infectious Diseases* published a special issue, "The Need for a New Lyme Disease Vaccine," which featured commentaries by public health officials, physicians, and scientists. In 2013, Baxter Pharmaceutical published the successful results of a phase I/II clinical trial on a recombinant Osp A vaccine for use in Europe (Wressnigg et al. 2013). Although it, like LYMErix, is an Osp A vaccine, it was formulated without the part of Osp A that is purported to be correlated with the development of arthritis. For unknown reasons, Baxter is "no longer developing this vaccine" (Plotkin 2016, 912). On March 19, 2018, however, Valneva, a French biotech company, announced that its multivalent Osp A vaccine candidate had cleared its phase I trial and that it would begin a phase II trial in late 2018; on August 22, 2019, a writer for STATnews also reported that another product called "Lyme pre-exposure prophylaxis (Lyme PrEP)," which "delivers a single defensive antibody" and is under development at the University of Massachusetts Medical School, will be put through a phase I clinical trial in 2020 and "could be available as soon as 2022."[50] Nevertheless, some wonder whether any Lyme vaccine will be able "to overcome the financial and social obstacles that led to LYMErix's demise" (Willyard 2014, 699). Most patients I spoke with remain leery that a new vaccine would not be burdened with the same perceived risks of the first vaccine. And many scientists, aware that patients and would-be consumers feel this way, are reluctant to go through the effort of bringing a Lyme vaccine to market again.

Diagnosis and Laboratory Testing

If topics such as co-infections and pathophysiology are the appetizers of Lyme's controversial meal, then diagnosis and treatment are its main courses. When it comes to diagnosis, several challenges present themselves. The first, which links back to the previous section, "Signs and Symptoms," is that, aside from an EM rash, symptoms of early Lyme disease (e.g., fever, chills, fatigue, and headaches) are understood to be nonspecific and, depending on whom you ask, easily misdiagnosed. Nonetheless, because it is generally understood that it takes three to six weeks for an individual's immune system to mount an antibody response to *Borrelia burgdorferi*, diagnostic tests are often incapable of diagnosing early Lyme disease (Moore et al. 2016; Schutzer and Luan 2003; Szczepanski and Benach 1991). For this reason, emphasis across the standard-of-care divide has long been placed on the importance of clinical diagnosis in the treatment of early Lyme disease. And because EM is the only specific sign in early Lyme disease, much is at stake for patients and practitioners in determining how common it actually is.

Although mainstream and Lyme-literate physicians tend to agree that EM does not often look like a bull's-eye rash and can be uniform in appearance, they do not agree how often it occurs. While mainstream practitioners and the sources they cite suggest that 70 to 80 percent of early Lyme disease cases present with EM, Lyme-literate practitioners and the sources they cite argue that "the EM rash may be absent in over 50% of Lyme disease cases" (ILADS Working Group 2004, S6).[51] More confounding still is the fact that while EM was once widely embraced as Lyme's pathognomonic sign, the indistinguishability of EM from the STARI rash and the fact that STARI is now being reported in the northeastern United States (Feder et al. 2011) has, for some mainstream physicians, made clinical diagnosis based solely on an EM rash less foolproof than it was once understood to be.

In light of early Lyme disease's relative nonspecificity and the perceived limitations and challenges of a clinical diagnosis at any stage of Lyme, laboratory testing has become a much-relied-on component of Lyme's diagnostic machinery. Although individuals from both the mainstream and Lyme-literate camps often criticize laboratory testing, criticisms from the mainstream are often directed at how laboratory testing is *used* and *inter-*

preted, and those from the Lyme-literate camp are often related to *accuracy*. Because *Borrelia burgdorferi* is notoriously difficult to culture and its DNA equally difficult to isolate from patients' bodily fluids, laboratory diagnostics rely on an antibody test, which, in measuring the immune system's response to the bacterium, cannot reliably distinguish between *having* the disease and *having had* it.[52]

Beyond use and interpretation, Lyme diagnostic testing has long been criticized for problems with consistency and accuracy. The origin of these criticisms can be traced to the early frontier days of Lyme's diagnostic development, when diagnostic criteria were not standardized, and scientists were still tweaking the test's antigen preparation. One scientist I interviewed who was among those who developed and used the early Lyme tests told me, "I never had a problem getting consistent results, even with the early tests!" On the other hand, mainstream physicians and scientists who were more recent arrivals to Lyme disease research were often quick to point fingers at the unreliability of early tests.[53] The abovementioned Dearborn meeting in 1994 was meant to correct this variability, although mainstream scientists acknowledge that the ELISA test continues to suffer from lack of standardization across laboratories because, unlike the antibody test for HIV, Lyme ELISA tests "have not been standardized against a panel of well-characterized sera," and "variations exist between assays in terms of antigenic composition and in the detection of specific immunoglobulin classes, particularly in the detection of IgM antibodies" (Aguero-Rosenfeld et al. 2005, 494).[54]

Following the Dearborn meeting, the most common test for Lyme disease has been two tiered, comprising a more sensitive ELISA assay, which, if positive, is meant to be followed by a more specific Western blot assay. Where the ELISA measures all bacterial antigens, the Western blot separates antigens by molecular weight. The Western blot is itself divided into two types of immune responses: IgM and IgG. IgM (immunoglobulin M) measures the immune system's response to *Borrelia burgdorferi* during early infection, while IgG (immunoglobulin G) measures the immune system's response to *Borrelia burgdorferi* during late infection.[55] The criteria that resulted from the Dearborn meeting (which the CDC quickly adopted) were criticized by patients and Lyme-literate practitioners not only for the limitations of the tests themselves but also because certain antigen bands were left out (as I mentioned in the previous section) and because what was intended to be a set of surveillance criteria became the template for Lyme's diagnostic criteria.[56] For example, to be considered positive for Lyme disease, a patient must have a positive or equivocal ELISA test, as well as two out of three positive IgM bands and five out of ten positive IgG bands on the Western blot. Lyme-literate physicians and patients are often quick to point out that Western blot tests for other diseases often provide three categories of results (positive, equivocal, and negative), whereas the FDA-approved Western blot for Lyme disease most commonly offers only positive and negative. Because an individual who has one positive IgM band and three positive IgG bands is considered to be negative and not equivocal for Lyme disease, many Lyme-literate physicians and patients argue that the absence of an "equivocal" category translates to the possibility that patients are falling through the cracks.

How Lyme disease tests have been standardized—and the implications of standardization for diagnosis—is a slightly different conversation than that of the accuracy of individual tests, which is an equally salient one had by individuals on both sides of the divide. Among Lyme patients and Lyme-literate practitioners, phrases such as, "Lyme disease tests aren't accurate," or "They're only accurate 50 percent of the time," or "A negative test doesn't mean that you don't have Lyme" are common. To support these statements, patients and physicians often refer to studies like the one published by Bakken et al. in 1997, which reported a sensitivity range of 75 to 93 percent (contingent on the laboratory conjugate used), and that by P. Coulter et al. in 2005, which demonstrated that, in early Lyme disease, two-tiered serological sensitivity is 45 percent, 77 percent when combined with serology from convalescent serum, and 78 percent when combined with skin PCR. More recent publications within the mainstream Lyme literature often describe two-tiered serological sensitivity in early Lyme disease to be as low as 30–40 percent (Moore et al. 2016) and 40 percent (Marques 2018), a trend that has led to increasing mainstream interest in alternatives, such as "modified two-tiered testing" that relies on the "second generation" c6 and VlsE antibody tests as a solution to increased sensitivity in early Lyme disease (Branda et al. 2017, 1074; see also Marques 2018; Molins et al. 2017; Pegalaiar-Jurado et al. 2018).

However, mainstream physicians and scientists distinguish between the importance of serological sensitivity in early and late disease, especially as it relates to the issue of chronic Lyme disease. While many mainstream physicians and scientists readily acknowledge that Lyme serology has very low sensitivity in early disease, they argue that the same test in untreated late disease is highly sensitive, with close to—if not—100 percent sensitivity (Bacon et al. 2003; Branda et al. 2011; Steere et al. 2008). In light of this, they argue that while early cases of Lyme disease in the absence of typical signs might very well be missed, it would be difficult to overlook a patient with late Lyme disease, which puts into question, for many mainstream physicians and scientists, the pathophysiological legitimacy of chronic Lyme disease patients who do not also have positive serology.

Of even more debate is the existence and use of what mainstream physicians and scientists call "unconventional," "specialty," or "alternative" laboratories. These laboratories, whose services are not covered by insurance and can often result in high out-of-pocket expenses, offer tests not available through mainstream laboratories.[57] One particular "alternative" laboratory has been the target of much mainstream criticism, including the concern that it applies "nonstandard interpretation criteria" and produces "false positive results" (Moore et al. 2016, 1175; see also Dattwyler and Arnaboldi 2014). For example, a mainstream physician whose practice I observed would often warn patients that this laboratory is not FDA approved and that it has been the target of a series of investigations. In response to claims like these, which are well circulated in the Lyme world, this laboratory and its supporters explain that the FDA does not approve laboratories but, rather, approves the diagnostic kits that laboratories use. Because this laboratory uses a Lyme diagnostic kit that is not mass produced, it does not require FDA approval. Laboratories, on the other hand, are licensed by state regulatory agencies, and the laboratory in question has active licenses in five states.

Like mainstream Lyme physicians and scientists, this laboratory has also been accused of conflicts of interest, including the practice of giving presentations at patient support group meetings and maintaining a too-cozy relationship with ILADS. Beyond claims of conflicts of interest, which I explore in more detail in chapter 5, it is more interesting to note that the intimacy between unconventional diagnostic companies and the physicians who use them is not unlike that between mainstream physicians and their diagnostic companies, who fund and have tables at the conferences and events that mainstream physicians and scientists attend. Indeed, for all of their proclaimed differences, mainstream and Lyme-literate practitioners both fall victim to the corporate connections that are the reality of practicing any type of medicine within a capitalist framework and the reason why each side can say that the other has conflicted interests.

Finally, above and beyond contestation over the consistency and accuracy of past and present tests and the integrity of unconventional laboratories, some patients and practitioners also have persistent concerns about two extenuating factors that might defy the "best test" from the "best laboratory": seronegative Lyme disease and mismatched strains. While the idea of seronegativity in early Lyme disease is well accepted, that of seronegativity in late Lyme disease is not.[58] Nevertheless, mainstream physicians and scientists *do* disagree about the possibility of seronegativity in late Lyme disease. For some mainstream physicians, beyond what is perceived to be the rare case of an individual with a severely compromised immune system who would be unable to mount an antibody response, the most agreed-on reason for seronegativity in late Lyme disease is the abrogation of an antibody response by a suboptimal course of antibiotics in early disease. In response to this, Halperin et al. argue, "There is no precedent in the scientific literature—with respect to Lyme disease or any other identified infection—of noncurative antibiotic treatment transiently suppressing an already-existing antibody response, nor is there a plausible biologic explanation of why this might occur" (Halperin, Baker, and Wormser 2013, 264.e2). They also argue that in studies in which there is a "minority" of patients with "culture-confirmed EM" who received "early, effective treatment" but never seroconverted, these patients "clearly had been treated and cured of Lyme disease before a measurable antibody response had developed" (Halperin, Baker, and Wormser 2013, 264.e2–3; see also Aguero-Rosenfeld et al. 1993; Aguero-Rosenfeld et al. 1996; Nowakowski et al. 2001; Steere et al. 2008).[59] However, two mainstream physician-scientists I interviewed said that, although it rarely happens now because patients typically receive curative doses, seronegativity due to a suboptimal course of antibiotics "does happen."

As I mentioned in the first section, *Borrelia burgdorferi* species and strain diversity are also perceived to present real and theoretical challenges for diagnostic testing. Studies have shown that testing is less sensitive in serum infected with a different species of *Borrelia burgdorferi* than that used in the antigen preparation of the diagnostic kit (Assous et al. 1993; Bunikis et al. 1995; Dressler et al. 1994; Hauser et al. 1998; Makhani et al. 2010; Norman et al. 1996; Strle et al. 1997). Whereas most mainstream scientists argue that antigens within a species are conserved enough that strain heterogeneity within a region would not have a significant effect on the sensitivity of diagnostic tests, some patients and Lyme-literate physicians question whether certain strain variations of a particular species *would* decrease the sensitivity of a species-matched test. Of greater concern across the divide is whether individuals infected in regions and countries with different *Borrelia* species would test positive when they return home, and more critically, how the discovery of species not known to exist in a region or not previously known to cause disease in humans would ultimately affect the performance of diagnostic tests (Girard, Fedorova, and Lane 2011; Makhani et al. 2010; Schutzer et al. 2012).

Treatment

When it comes to the Lyme disease controversy, treatment is often the issue that first comes to mind. Perhaps it is because treatment is one of the most visible and memorable aspects of Lyme. During my interviews with mainstream physicians and scientists who participated in the early scientific conferences on Lyme disease that chronic Lyme patients also attended, several recounted how patients walked around with intravenous antibiotic drip bags or set up makeshift beds in the aisles so that they could watch the proceedings from a more comfortable position. During my interviews with patients, some would carefully show me the port or PICC line (an intravenous catheter) where they connected the catheter to administer antibiotics; others would display the pharmacopoeia of medicines and supplements they were taking and explain them to me one by one. One patient, whom I interviewed at his office in a county government building, took a discreet break in the middle of our conversation to set up his antibiotic drip. As visible as they are, however, intravenous antibiotics are just one part of a complex debate over Lyme disease treatment that includes, among others, which type of antibiotics to administer, when and how long to treat, risks and benefits, insurance coverage, and out-of-pocket expenses.

Much of the research conducted in the years following Lyme's discovery was focused on determining the type and duration of antibiotic that would lead to treatment success (Dattwyler et al. 1987; Luft et al. 1989; Nadelman et al. 1992; Strle et al. 1993, 1996). These studies provided the foundation for the current and much contested mainstream recommendations, which are standardized in the IDSA's diagnosis and treatment guidelines (originally published in 2000 and updated in 2006, with a draft of new guidelines released in June 2019). As of this writing, the 2006 IDSA guidelines, stripped to their skeletal form, recommend ten to twenty-one days of oral doxycycline for early Lyme disease, twenty-eight days of oral doxycycline for Lyme arthritis (to be followed by two weeks of intravenous ceftriaxone in patients with persistent swelling), and fourteen to twenty-eight days of intravenous ceftriaxone for late Lyme disease with neurological involvement (Wormser et al. 2006).[60]

The diagnosis and treatment guidelines that were formulated by ILADS in 2004 and updated in 2014 are strikingly different (Cameron, Johnson, and Maloney 2014; ILADS Working Group 2004). Arguing that the "guidelines of the Infectious Diseases Society of America (IDSA) fall short of meeting the needs for diagnosis and treatment of individuals with chronic Lyme disease," and that they "fail to take into account the compelling, peer-reviewed, published evidence confirming persistent, recurrent and refractory Lyme disease and, in fact, deny its existence," the ILADS guidelines recommend an open-ended, "individualized" approach to treatment that provides no specific duration other than whatever is deemed necessary by the practicing physician based on patient response (ILADS Working Group 2004, S4, S7). In addition, the ILADS guidelines recommend the option of increasing standard antibiotic dosage and employing "sequential treatment," a sequence that begins with intravenous antibiotics and is followed by oral therapy for "persistent or recurrent Lyme disease" (S9). In the updated 2014 version of the ILADS guidelines, the authors focus on "three clinical questions" in the treatment of Lyme disease—"the usefulness of antibiotic prophylaxis for known tick bites, the effectiveness of erythema migrans treatment and the role of antibiotic retreatment in patients with persistent manifestations of Lyme disease"—and conclude that, because the available evidence related to these three clinical questions is of "very low quality," "clinical judgment is crucial to the provision of patient-centered care" (Cameron, Johnson, and Maloney 2014, 1103, 1129).

In an attempt to settle the debate over whether extended antibiotic treatment has benefits for patients who continue to have symptoms after standard therapy, four randomized, double-blind, placebo-controlled trials have been conducted in the United States and their results published (B. Fallon et al. 2008; Kaplan et al. 2003 [an analysis of subsets of data from Klempner, Hu, et al. 2001]; Klempner, Hu, et al. 2001; Krupp et al. 2003).[61] As science studies scholarship has revealed, however, because of the "'interpretive flexibility' built into scientific findings" and the fact that "experiments do not, in the simplest sense usually understood, 'settle' scientific controversies," "uncertainty is often not just the cause of scientific controversy but its consequence" (Epstein 1996, 333). In his work on AIDS activism, sociologist Steven Epstein observes that "a study's 'definitiveness' is not given but is a negotiated outcome and one that may be actively resisted by some parties to the controversy" (334). In the case of Lyme disease, mainstream physicians tout the results of these four clinical trials as a victory and argue that they demonstrate that there is no clear evidence that long-term antibiotic therapy provides any benefit for patients with post-treatment Lyme disease syndrome. Lyme-literate physicians and patients disagree. Their primary criticisms are that (1) the trials were underpowered, (2) the patient enrollment criteria were too strict, (3) antibiotic therapy in the Klempner study was discontinued earlier than proposed, and (4) the decision in the Klempner study not to use combination antibiotic therapy foreclosed the possibility that investigators would be able to replicate the success that Lyme-literate practitioners report in their practice. In the case of the Krupp and Fallon studies, Lyme-literate physicians and patients argue that the Krupp study *did* show significant improvement in fatigue and that the Fallon study also showed significant but not sustained improvement in fatigue. Finally, Lyme-literate physicians and patients point out that, despite their disagreement with its design, the Klempner study at least *recognizes* that the experience of living with "persistent symptoms" is equivalent to the experience of living with congestive heart failure.[62] Speaking to the "interpretive flexibility" of scientific findings, one Lyme-literate physician I interviewed reflected, "We [Lyme-literate and mainstream physicians] often quote from the same studies. It's how you interpret it."

Given the climate in which these trials were conducted, it is not surprising that many of the investigators, advocates, and patients who participated in these trials are still nursing battle wounds. In an interview with a scientist who had been involved in one of the trials, he exclaimed in disbelief how the person who was appointed to chair the trial's independent oversight committee disapproved of the implications of his findings and, as a result, asked to be removed as the oversight chairperson. And one patient advocate I interviewed described the betrayal she felt when, after being invited to participate in the design of one of the trials, her comments and suggestions were ignored. This response, in particular, reflects the critical role that patient participation in both the design and analysis of clinical research now plays in the contemporary production of medical knowledge, the pathway to which was, in large part, paved by the work of AIDS activists in the 1980s and, according to Epstein, "transformed how biomedical knowledge gets made" (336).

The chasm between mainstream and Lyme-literate approaches to treatment is filled with a tangled morass of ideas, experiences, and realities that interrupt and compete with one another. Lyme-literate physicians and patients claim that mainstream physicians' disapproval of extended antibiotics for Lyme disease is inconsistent with the approach that mainstream physicians have more generally toward the use of antibiotics in other diseases.

For example, several parents of teenagers being treated for chronic Lyme disease made comments to the effect of, "I can't get doxycycline for my child's Lyme but I could walk into a doctor's office today and get a month of doxycycline for his acne." While Lyme-literate practitioners and patients recognize the risks of antibiotic use, they also argue that these risks are dwarfed by the perceived risk of living a life of disability and discomfort, and that, while real, the risks are far less extreme than mainstream physicians make them out to be. Mainstream physicians and scientists, on the other hand, argue that the risks of potentially lethal resistant bacteria and opportunistic infections like *Clostridium difficile* are not to be underestimated.[63] And finally, where Lyme-literate physicians and patients argue that the benefit of extended antibiotic use is "in the pudding," mainstream physicians argue that anecdotal reports of "feeling better" can instead be attributed to the placebo effect and the fact that some antibiotics, including doxycycline, have anti-inflammatory properties.

In exploring each of the Lyme controversy's nodes of contestation, this chapter has provided a foundation for a textured and nuanced understanding of the rhizomatic complexity of Lyme disease. More critically, this chapter reveals that, from geographic distribution to pathophysiology, Lyme's controversy is much more complicated than a simple disagreement over diagnosis and treatment and that it can be more fully understood as a dynamic and unwieldy sum of its many interrelated parts.

PREVENTING LYME

Susan is an artist who lives with her family in a farmhouse in Connecticut. Her studio is located in a barn that is adjacent to the house. From the windows of both buildings, the windswept fields and surrounding woods create verdant tableaux that are her art's inspiration. When I interviewed Susan at her home in 2010, she had been undergoing treatment for Lyme disease since 1994, when she discovered a "bull's-eye" rash on the back of her neck. In addition to the toll that sixteen years of ill health had taken on her, Susan described being haunted by the fact that she continues to live in an area where she and her family are at risk for getting more tick bites. She explained,

> A part of me would like to just get the hell out of here; part of me would like to move where there are no ticks. That's just the worst thing about being here. It's awful. It's like a scourge. It has definitely changed how I understand nature. I love the country so much, but I'm not going to walk out in those fields. I only walk on mowed lawn. There's no careless running through the forest anymore.

Like Susan, many individuals who live in Lyme-endemic areas of the United States are increasingly concerned about tick encounters in their everyday lives. And for good reason. On May 1, 2018, the CDC announced that, between 2004 and 2016, "illnesses from mosquitoes, ticks, and fleas [had] tripled."[1] Driven in large part by climate change's warming temperatures and increasing humidity, the rapid rise of the tick has led public health officials and entomologists to issue warnings about the importance of taking vigilant preventive measures to avoid contracting Lyme disease.[2] These warnings are often accompanied by warnings about other emergent vector-borne diseases, ranging from more familiar ones about West Nile virus to newer ones about dengue fever, chikungunya virus, and, in particular, Zika virus. As changing climate patterns shift and transfigure ecological boundaries, the globality of vector-borne disease has become a plurality of local realities. For this reason, the task of examining these diseases through an anthropological lens has never been more timely nor more urgent.

Despite Lyme's controversy, the prevention of tick bites is exceptionally *uncontroversial*. This is likely to due to humans' nearly universal dislike of ticks. For example, physician and medical science writer David Scales describes how one Cape Cod entomologist begins his Lyme-prevention presentations with a purported quotation by the Dalai Lama, an individual celebrated for his love of and respect for all life: "I love everything in the world . . . except for ticks."[3] And really, what is there to love? To feast on blood, a tick can take up covert residence on human bodies for as long as a week by anesthetizing and then anchoring its barbed weapon-like mouthpiece into the skin of its chosen host. Once anchored, and as it swells and grows taut and green like a small grape, a tick can transmit a range of bacteria and viruses, most notable among them *Borrelia burgdorferi*.

As one of the few areas related to Lyme that is not rife with disagreement and contestation, the prevention of Lyme disease invites an exploration of how individuals across the standard-of-care divide understand and interact with their environment in an attempt to avoid ticks. As a tick-borne disease, Lyme disease's viability depends on an ecology suitable to the habitat preferences of the blacklegged tick, small rodents, and deer. And because the transmission of Lyme disease to humans requires exposure to this landscape, Lyme and other vector-borne diseases draw unique analytic attention to contemporary ideas about—and practical engagements with—nature. More critically, by exploring the complicated relationship between how individuals like Susan understand (and feel about) their natural environment and the ways in which they understand and act on their health, this chapter sheds light on an important dimension of how Lyme disease is lived in the United States (the focus of the following chapter). To do this, the first part of this chapter provides a broad historical context for the production of an aesthetic of nature in the United States. Here, I suggest that because an American aesthetic of nature encompasses the affective spectrum between attraction and repulsion—nature is beautiful, in part, *because* it is frightening—the contours of Lyme disease can be better understood through what I call an "epidemiology of affect."[4] That is, who gets Lyme disease and why is more than just a matter of demographic and geographic correlations of risk; it is also about how Americans in Lyme-endemic areas understand and act on their competing feelings toward their natural environment.

The second part examines the underbelly of an aesthetic of nature in the United States: environmental risk. The task here is to identify what constitutes "the environment" and what part of that environment individuals in Lyme-endemic areas find risky. I suggest that, for some Lyme disease patients, Lyme disease is just one risk in a constellation of environmental risks that can be broadly described as a toxic environment. That this is so points to a reality in which the environment is not confined to the "outside," and where individuals perceive environmental risk—in a broader context of "environmental privilege"—to exist on an almost indistinguishable continuum between the inside and the outside (Park and Pellow 2011).

Finally, the third and last part ends with an exploration of the practical consequences—in this case, prevention practices—produced by the tension between an attraction to nature and an awareness of environmental risk in Lyme-endemic areas. Drawing from Saba Mahmood's Aristotelian-inspired work on "exteriority as a means to interiority" (Mahmood 2005, 134), I explore a range of emerging "bodily practices" related to tick-bite prevention and how they shape ideas about nature and environmental risk (Lock 1993a; see also Brotherton 2012). Here, I argue that, in the lives of the people who enact them, the *effects* of tick-bite prevention practices— what they incidentally happen to produce across relations—become more important than their efficacy, and that these practices constitute the active building of new individualized environments, or what biologist Jakob von Uexküll terms "environment-worlds" (Agamben 2004, 40).

An American Aesthetic of Nature

It is not a coincidence that, during his 2012 presidential campaign, candidate Mitt Romney often quoted lines from "America the Beautiful," a song that celebrates "spacious skies" and "purple mountain majesties above the fruited plain": in the United States, nature has become inextricably linked with ideas of beauty *and* with what it means to be an American. Environmental historian Roderick Nash observes that as "the basic ingredient of American culture," nature has been understood as "beautiful, friendly, and capable of elevating and delighting the beholder" since the late nineteenth century ([1967] 2001, xi, 4). But this was not always the case. Prior to the 1800s and the emergence of Romanticism in Europe, nature was considered to be unsightly, without moral merit, and a threat to "civilizing" tendencies. As environmental historian William Cronon observes, "To be a wilderness then was to be 'deserted,' 'savage,' 'desolate,' 'barren'"; rather than a place of beauty, "wilderness" was often used to "refer to places on the margins of civilization where it was all too easy to lose oneself in moral confusion and despair" (1995, 70).

One of the most compelling examples of nature's cultural and historical transformation is that of the mountain.[5] Now emblematic of natural splendor—reaching the peak of which is, for many, the true test of a nature-compatible constitution—mountains in the seventeenth century were, as Nash describes, "generally regarded as warts, pimples, blisters and other ugly deformities on the earth's surface" and were, fittingly, given such names as "Devil's Point"([1967] 2001, 45). However, under the Romantic's eye, and with an "enthusiasm for the strange, remote, solitary, and mysterious," the boundless unruliness of forests, crevasses, and mountainscapes became a means to transcendence (47).[6] More critically, philosopher Kate Soper argues that although nature had been represented as a duality between terror and serenity since the days of Homer, the Romantics' representations differed in that, in them, the "chaos" of nature became "endowed with its own aesthetic appeal" (1995, 222).

Like their European counterparts, American pioneers and frontiersmen also perceived nature to be "cursed" and "ungodly" (Nash [1967] 2001, 36–37). As journals and other narratives attest to, living in proximity to the wilderness was perceived not to be a source of pleasure or inspiration but, rather, a forced necessity. However, as Nash also describes, the ideological momentum generated by the Romantic movement in Europe gradually translated to changing understandings of nature in America. And for a former colony like America, nature and the unique features of the American landscape quickly became a means by which to distinguish itself from Europe. This was especially true for Henry David Thoreau, who saw in American wildness a clean slate for national moral growth. Political theorist Jane Bennett observes that from Thoreau's perspective, "the milk of [American] Wildness flows freely, and this is, as we know, crucial to recrafting the self. The Wildness of the American wilderness is the condition of possibility of a new man, a 'new Adam'" (2002, 114). In the eyes of Thoreau, what America once had too much of it now had in enviable quantity and in kind conducive to moral advantage: a new "wilderness" that, galvanized by the influential "cultural constructs" of the "sublime" and the "frontier," had become "a place not just of religious redemption but of national renewal, the quintessential location for experiencing what it meant to be an American" (Cronon 1995, 72, 76).

The rise in appreciation for an untamed wild that could be morally edifying was also helped along by a shift in Christian spirituality, which, Nash argues, was influenced by European deism ([1967] 2001, 46–47). A product of the Enlightenment, deism was a cosmological movement that was closely linked with contemporaneous scientific development. Scientists' rapidly expanding discoveries of the universe provided a platform—and material narrative—for the possibility of divine engineering, and links made between the celestial solar system and earthly wonders infused in the natural world a not-until-then appreciated insight into "God's handiwork" (45). As environmental historian Carolyn Merchant writes, "Looking at mountains—seeing God's action in the land through thunderstorms and lightning—was now looked upon not as the work of the devil but as evidence of God's power and goodness" (2004, 88). In this way, the linking up of nature with God as something uniquely American sowed the seeds for the development of American nationalism.

In addition to an expansive wilderness, environmental historian Daniel J. Philippon (2005) argues that toward the end of the nineteenth century, the suburban garden came to assume an equally important place as a natural refuge. Just as the Romantics saw the wilderness as a site for moral instruction, early suburban architects saw in the proximity of suburbs to nature the possibility of social uplift. Philippon also credits the rise in early twentieth-century Americans' appreciation for suburban nature—and their recognition of suburban nature *as nature*—with the work of writer, conservationist, and president of the Connecticut Audubon Society Mabel Osgood Wright. Unlike the orderly and ornate gardens of European royalty and aristocrats, the suburban gardens of the late nineteenth and early twentieth centuries that Wright encouraged fellow Americans to cultivate still had inflections of the "wild" within them. Wright's work not only offered Americans a more accessible place to commune with nature than the wilderness (as "field and forest often hold one at bay") but conscientiously opened it up to women, for whom "nature" was often still inaccessible (72). That American suburbs are still identified with feminine domesticity and fastidious attention to lawn and garden care can, according to Philippon, be largely credited to how Mabel Osgood Wright's writing and conservation work "appeal[ed] to the patriotic sentiments and untapped energies of suburban women" *through* nature (73). This is no more true than in the case of Lyme disease, where the confluence of Lyme's peridomestic risk and "Connecticut housewives'" domestic exposure reinforces the perception that women are particularly susceptible to languishing in Lyme's lengthy grip.

In the twenty-first-century United States, the historical link between the wilderness and wooded suburbia has continued to be reinforced by deer. Since the frontier days, deer have been a linchpin of American hunting. According to historian Daniel Herman (2001), hunting was consciously crafted as a dimension of American identity by nineteenth-century writers and explorers like Davy Crockett and Meriwether Lewis. More recently, however, deer have also become the totem of the American suburbs. Once hunted to near extinction, deer were reintroduced to rural areas in the northeastern United States, and in the absence of natural predators and as hunting has declined, deer populations have grown to unsustainable sizes (Côté et al. 2004). As most residents of small towns in the northeastern United States have come to know, deer overpopulation is not only a threat to local ecosystems but also causes extensive property damage. One county in Connecticut, where I observed the meetings of a tick-borne disease prevention task force, contracted two scientists to study the economic impact of deer overpopulation and found that, for their county alone, the cost ran upward of $180 million per year.

Within the Lyme community, deer are a particularly rich conversation piece because, over and above their threat to property, they are also tick carriers whose presence in a landscape is understood to directly correlate with Lyme disease risk. But even those individuals most concerned about Lyme risk are often conflicted about what that risk should mean for the lives of deer. For many suburban residents, the deer seems to most fully capture nature's best qualities. Quiet, meek, and elusive, deer add wildlife to a backyard tableau without also imposing the threat of the wild. One patient I spoke with described the calm and serenity she felt every morning as she gazed at deer in her backyard while she drank her coffee. But more than just an unwillingness to alter the aesthetic surroundings of their home environments, individuals' reluctance to have deer populations reduced seems to stem from the conflation of deer with innocence, an idea cultivated in no small part by the Disney cartoon classic Bambi. Again and again in my conversations with Lyme patients, physicians, scientists, and public health officials, the topic of deer would often elicit Bambi's mention. One individual who was opposed to controlling deer populations qualified her rationale with, "I don't know, maybe I've seen Bambi too many times, but I just can't bring myself to support killing deer." Similarly, in a September 5, 2009, New

York Times article, residents of Nantucket expressed feeling torn between reducing the incidence of Lyme disease and preserving their natural environment. A woman whose husband had been sick with Lyme disease but was nevertheless opposed to reducing the deer population said, "I really love the deer, and I can't help it. My mother took me to see *Bambi* when I was little."[7] Whether for their nature appeal or their innocence, the deer has, for many residents, become a synecdoche for both, and as a result, what deer represent often becomes more important than the risk they present.

But, of course, Bambi does not pull at everyone's heartstrings. The reason so many local communities are locked in a standstill over how best to manage their deer population is that there are just as many individuals who would be thrilled if they never saw a deer again. Dr. Fields, a physician who feels strongly that deer populations should be completely eliminated, described the obstacle course of community decision-making over the issue of deer. "You would think that Lyme patients would be natural allies," he said. "But maybe they're worried that being against deer is politically incorrect, and they want to keep politicians on their side so that they get insurance benefits." He continued,

> The other group you would think would be a natural ally is hunters. But the natural extension of deer elimination is that there would be no more hunting. . . . How important is it to have the deer? Important enough to have a disease just so you can see them? Me personally, I don't think it's that important to see them every day. People have a vested interest in deer. They like them, they think they're beautiful animals and would rather they not be hunted. The anti-hunters, i.e., the humane society and PETA, all figure that Lyme disease is a plot by hunters to hunt deer and exterminate Bambi. So they say it's evil and oppose it. It's been a very effective campaign.

A Lyme patient I interviewed echoed Dr. Fields's thoughts. He exclaimed,

> The humane society? The pro-rights animal groups? Bambi lovers is what we call them! I grew up on a farm. No deer, no ticks. . . . That's a common thing in this country. Everything that's argued is political, it's an opinion. Well, that's the problem: Mother Nature doesn't solicit an opinion. Mother Nature runs things here, and ticks are one of her masterpieces.

Differences in opinion over how to manage deer populations are not only politically charged but are often perceived to fall on either side of the liberal-conservative divide. As Dr. Fields explained, "I see this in the political world as a whole. Certain types of people tend to adopt certain positions. If you're anti-abortion, you're conservative and tend to support other conservative causes. I think the people that support deer are liberal, and the pro-hunting are conservative." Dr. Fields's perception is not surprising, given that liberal and conservative political sensibilities often lend themselves to different approaches to nature and the environment.

Sociologist Robert Brulle has traced the nuance and complexity of American environmentalism and describes how, as the largest and oldest social movement in the United States, the environmental movement is far from monolithic and comprises, in his estimation, eleven "distinct communities," each of which is founded on a "particular world view" and distinguished by a unique "discursive frame" (Brulle 2009, 211–12). Of most relevance here are the "wildlife management," "conservation," "preservation," and "reform environmentalism" frames (213–16). While the "wildlife management" and "conservation" frames, in their emphasis on conserving wildlife and natural resources to "meet human needs," tend to align with conservative sensibilities, the "preservation" and "reform environmentalism" frames, in their emphasis on "preserving wilderness in a pristine state, untouched by humans" and "protecting earth's ecosystem and human health," respectively, tend to align with liberal sensibilities (213–16). As a result, where liberals have been cast as—and have embraced the image of—"tree huggers," conservatives, through hunting, fishing, and outdoorsmanship, have cultivated the image of a "man" at home in the wild.

Among the Lyme disease patients I interviewed, all of whom live in suburban or rural environments, the majority identified as politically conservative and Christian. This fact gives critical texture to popular understandings of *who* American nature lovers are, understandings made even more popular through the books of a self-professed "PhD dropout" named Christian Lander (2008b, 2010). In these books, Lander satirizes upper-middle-class, liberal-arts-educated, left-of-center individuals who, while characterized broadly as "White people," actually constitute a small segment of them. On his *Stuff White People Like* blog, Lander lists as #9, after organic food and film festivals, "making people feel bad for not going outside" (2008a). It is important to note here that emphasis is not placed on spending time outside but on the judgment of those who do not spend time outside. This is an important distinction, as it underscores the moral weight that inheres in an American aesthetic of nature. As much as nature is an aesthetic, it is also a morally imbued dimension of a way of life, a means to the "good life," and one of a set of criteria that often constitute what are perceived to be American "family values." But for whom is this true? As *New York Times* journalist Dwight Garner observes in a November 15, 2010, review,

> The white people under Mr. Lander's microscope are emphatically not those who enjoy NASCAR, Sarah Palin, bratwursts, deer hunting, Metallica or "Ice Road Truckers" in any way except ironically. People who do gravitate toward these sorts of things, he warns, sotto voce, might be "the wrong kind of white person."[8]

In my experience, however, the nature lovers of Connecticut's suburbs often do not fit the stereotype of a person outfitted in a Patagonia fleece, a gear-laden backpack, and hiking shoes who eats organic food and attends film festivals. Instead, they often are those "White people" who enjoy "NASCAR, Sarah Palin, bratwursts, [and] deer hunting" but for whom the aesthetic and morality of nature are no less salient than they are for those to their political left.

More critically, in addition to the political nuance of humans' affection for nature, it is important to emphasize that, from its earliest days, the construction of nature's aesthetic *and* the conservation and preservation of natural spaces in the United States have been accompanied by the deliberate and coordinated exclusion of people of color. As a result, "nature" continues to be broadly perceived and experienced as a "white space," a reality that has spawned a range of popular articles, such as "The Unbearable Whiteness of Hiking and How to Solve It," "Why America's Parks Are So White," and "Hiking While Black: The Untold Story" (Anderson 2015).[9] Sociologist Dorceta Taylor writes, "Despite the fact that people of color helped to build and maintain national and state parks and forests, these were—at times—segregated entities that barred blacks and other people of color from using all or parts of the facilities" (2016, 372). For example, although members of the US Army's all-Black regiments, commonly referred to as "buffalo soldiers," were among the first backcountry rangers and built Yosemite's "first national marked trail," African Americans were systematically excluded from "national parks, preservation sites, and national forests," even though "African Americans were also drawn to and actively participated in the back-to-nature movement" (373–74).[10] In addition to being excluded from these natural spaces, individuals of color who attempted to visit them often faced harassment and bodily harm. In an earlier article, Taylor describes a range of racial incidents that occurred in the 1930s and 1940s when African Americans "attempted to use recreational facilities" and concludes that "in the interest of preserving their lives, and because of widespread, institutionalized, *post-slavery segregation*, blacks were limited in their outdoor recreation pursuits" (1989, 187).

Today, the legacy of the violence and exclusion that occurred in the creation of America's natural spaces is that many Americans of color continue to perceive these spaces as threats to their safety. In a *New York Times* opinion piece titled "Why Are Our Parks So White?," Glenn Nelson reflects on his college experience of leading outdoor adventures for minority student groups:

> There was always nervous banter as we cruised through small rural towns on our way to a park. And there were jokes about finding a "Whites Only" sign at the entrance to our destination or the perils of being lynched or attacked while collecting firewood after the sun went down. Our cultural history taught us what to expect.[11]

A survey conducted by the National Park Service in 2000 also found that "nonwhites were more than three times as likely as whites to say that the parks provided poor service and were not safe to visit."[12] Given these sentiments, it is not surprising that individuals of color would be reluctant to visit parks. In a 2009 survey by the University of Wyoming and the National Park Service, while Hispanics, African Americans, and Asian Americans comprise approximately 37.6 percent of the total US population, they made up only 19 percent of the country's national park visitors from 2008 to 2009.[13] At Yosemite during the same time period, only 1 percent of the park's visitors were African American. In addition to efforts by the National Park Service to correct this, grassroots action within communities of color has manifested in organizations like Outdoor Afro, whose mission is to help "more people, especially African Americans, equitably connect with the natural world through Outdoor Recreation," including "activities" that not only promote "a healthy lifestyle" but also "help communities find healing" and "connect to black history found in many natural areas."[14]

In recent years, nature and one's exposure to it have become not only about a good and beautiful life—irrespective of political affiliation and through the continued exclusion of people of color—but also about a healthier one. Of course, ideas about the health benefits of nature are long-standing. In the late nineteenth century, physicians began to advocate for pure mountain air as a treatment for tuberculosis and other lung diseases.[15] And as early as the mid-nineteenth century, suburban architect Andrew Jackson edited a gardening book for women in the hopes that it "would increase, among our own fair country women, the taste for these delightful occupations in the open air, which are so conducive to their own health, and to the beauty and interest of our homes" (Philippon 2005, 77). But contemporary understandings about the health benefits of nature—whether that nature is located in the wilderness of Alaska or in the suburbs of Fairfield County, Connecticut—are myriad and range from obesity prevention and the abatement of neurological conditions to the reduction of childhood behavioral disorders. As a result, a movement has coalesced around concerns that individuals—and children in particular—are suffering from nature deprivation. One of the most vocal advocates for this movement is journalist and author Richard Louv, who coined the term "nature deficit disorder." Louv argues that increasing diagnoses of childhood behavioral disorders, such as attention deficit disorder, are a result not of increasing pathology but of the absence of the biophysical benefits of nature in individuals' lives. To support his argument, he cites a range of studies that show that children who live and play closer to nature are, for example, better able to concentrate and less obese (2005, 31–54).

In the case of Lyme disease, however, Louv's means to health—nature—is also a threat to it. Because of the ecology of Lyme disease, individuals who tend to contract Lyme are either those who prefer to live near the woods or those who like to spend time in the woods. This fact lies at the heart of my argument for why tick-borne disease, and Lyme disease in particular, can only fully be understood through an epidemiology of affect. As a cornerstone of public health, epidemiology can be defined as "the study of how often diseases occur in different groups of people and why" (Coggon, Rose, and Barker 1997). Traditionally, epidemiological explanations for disease incidence among particular populations are based on statistical analysis of demographic and socioeconomic factors, including age, racial and ethnic background, and income status. However, Lyme disease makes a strong case for the role of affect in the incidence and distribution of tick-borne disease. Understanding how people navigate the tension between their competing feelings of affection for and aversion to nature helps to shed light on who gets Lyme disease and why; it also helps to explain why Lyme disease prevention proves to be so challenging, as the primary risk for acquiring Lyme disease—exposure to nature—is simultaneously and collectively valued as a personal and cultural benefit. Following an epidemiology of affect, then, an aesthetic of nature—and feelings of love toward nature—tend to be particularly strong among patients who end up having Lyme disease.[16] Although many individuals have a dramatically estranged relationship with nature after their experience with Lyme disease, for just as many, the aesthetic, affective, moral, and health benefits outweigh its risks.

Take, for example, Regina and Mary, two women who founded and led a Lyme disease support group that I attended almost every month for eighteen months. Both Regina and Mary describe enduring long struggles with Lyme disease. They, as well as their children, have been treated for Lyme disease over the years, and although they report that they have recovered, they explained to me that their children, at the time, continued to struggle with symptoms. For Regina and Mary, however, the importance of living near the outdoors continues to be paramount, so much so that Regina moved her family from Texas back to Connecticut when her three children were young so that they could "grow up near nature." "I wanted them to have what I had," she explained. "Horseback riding and fields to run in. If only I knew that moving here is what would make my children sick." During our interview together, Mary echoed the same sentiments: "We were always big outdoors people. We loved to camp and stuff. And I struggle with, I just can't live in a house. I need to be outdoors, you know, so I just can't live in a vacuum, and I think my kids are the same way. I wouldn't let them go running in a field, but . . ." her voice trailed off. It was clear from Mary's expression that, as much hardship as her family had gone through *because of* nature, the thought of living *without it* was impossible to imagine.

For individuals like Regina and Mary, how they feel about nature—and the importance they ascribe to it—influences how they choose to navigate environmental risk. Indeed, the salience of nature's aesthetic, affective, moral, and health dimensions makes possible the idea of risks worth taking and transforms (what in other contexts would be perceived as) irresponsible and reckless behavior into noble and courageous action. This idea is consistent with psychologist Paul Slovic's trailblazing work on risk perception, affect, and "acceptable risk" (2000, 2010). For example, one of Slovic's early studies demonstrated that "the inverse relationship between perceived risk and perceived benefit was linked to an individual's general affective evaluation of a hazard" (2000, xxxii). That is, if individuals "liked" or had affection for an activity, they perceived it to offer high benefit and low risk; however, if individuals did not "like" or had little affection for an activity, the activity was perceived to have "low benefit and high risk" (xxxii). Slovic and his colleagues' related concept of "risk as feelings" (2010) (that is, how affect influences the way in which individuals perceive risk and their response to that risk) is nicely captured in the blog entry of one Lyme patient, who writes,

I hope that you may take heart and continue to explore wild, wooded places free from concern about menacing, infectious ticks and vector-borne illnesses. Just rock the pants-tucked-into-socks look and have an OCD friend check you for unwanted guests afterward. No illness, or threat thereof, should keep you from enjoying the breathtaking beauty and majesty of nature.

Another revealing example is that of Dr. Childs, a mainstream Lyme physician whose practice I describe in chapter 4. Dr. Childs is a self-identified nature enthusiast who wakes up early before work to row on the Connecticut River and spends weekends bird watching with his wife. He loves to hike, and during the time I spent with him, he was often busy planning his next outdoor adventure in a country that he had never visited. One of the few photos in his office is of him and his children triumphantly astride the peak of a mountain range. Dr. Childs found it hard not to share his enthusiasm for the outdoors when he discovered that his patient was also an outdoors enthusiast; and he seemed particularly pleased when a patient was determined to continue their outdoor activities. One patient described how much he loved hiking in the woods and how he was excited to get back in the woods when his knee got better. "That's the spirit!" Dr. Childs chimed in. Another patient exclaimed, "I've hunted and fished all my life. And nothing, not even Lyme disease, is going to keep me from hunting and fishing!" Dr. Childs nodded approvingly in agreement.

Even those who continue to love and admire nature, however, often recognize that they no long feel comfortable in it, a recognition that is met with a certain degree of sadness and nostalgia. A physician I interviewed named Dr. Reed explained,

> I like the outdoors, always have. I love to camp. I'm also an assistant scout leader. I used to feel safe, but now I don't. I'm constantly worried that a bug will bite me. Now when I go into the woods, I have gaiters that I put on. I lay them down and spray them with permethrin. And then I put DEET on my skin, and I still don't like to go into the woods. My family looks at me like I'm nuts, but so far, knock on wood, we haven't found a tick on any of our family members.

The regime of bodily practices that Dr. Reed engages just so that he can feel safe enough to enjoy the woods that he still loves is discussed in the final section of this chapter. What is important here is the difficulty that individuals like Dr. Reed face in navigating the gap between their love for and fear of nature. In 2010, the *New Yorker* published a cartoon depicting Adam and Eve in the Garden of Eden. As Adam inspects a lifted leg, Eve says, "It's Eden. You don't have to keep checking for ticks."[17] For Thoreau, American nature was a prospect more hopeful than the actual Garden of Eden because "it remained to be seen" how the "backwoodsman in America"—the "Adam in the wilderness"—turned out (Bennett 2002, 114). Thoreau, it seems, could not have anticipated that, for some, the rise of Lyme disease would be a fall from nature as disillusioning as that which followed the original eaten apple.

Environmental Risk Inside Out

As the previous section makes clear, ideas of nature are intimately linked to perceptions of environmental risk. Sociologists Alan Petersen and Deborah Lupton observe that the limitation of the "discourse of nature," or what I describe as an American aesthetic of nature, is that nature is also "responsible for death, destruction, [and] disease" (1996, 103, 106). More critically, as sociologists Lisa Sun-Hee Park and David Naguib Pellow have shown, the "flip side" of environmental risk is that it is always accompanied by "environmental privilege" (2011, 3). "For Park and Pellow, environmental privilege is "embodied in the fact that some groups can access spaces and resources, which are protected from the kinds of ecological harm that other groups are forced to contend with every day" (4). As a result, Park and Pellow observe, "while some people are forced to live next door to a paint factory, a landfill, or an incinerator and breathe air that contributes to asthma and various respiratory disease, others have the luxury of spending time in second homes in semirural environs" (4–5). For many individuals in Lyme-endemic areas, however, it is precisely the environmental privilege of being able to live in or close to "nature" that makes possible the environmental risk of Lyme disease. The case of Lyme disease, then, builds on and complicates Park and Pellow's work by exploring how the emergence of tick-borne disease has created an environmental risk for individuals that is a *function* of their simultaneous *environmental privilege*.

Within the Lyme world, identifying what actually constitutes environmental risk is no easy task.[18] For example, ticks and the pathogens they carry might appear to be the most obvious environmental risks for Lyme patients. But as I came to learn, in Lyme patients' everyday lives, Lyme disease is just one part of a larger constellation of environmental risks that can be described as "toxins," and in general, individuals' concerns tend to be more broadly centered around environmental *toxicity*, whether chemical (e.g., pesticides) or microbial (e.g., tick-borne pathogens). In this way, many perceive environmental risk to be located less in the wildness of nature and more in the diffuse and ubiquitous quality of a toxic environment. In light of this, I suggest that ideas and practices surrounding Lyme disease help to shed light on a broader emerging relationship between the body and the environment among the environmentally privileged in the United States, in which the risk of the environment is not a matter of the "outside" but of an immanent environment that individuals engage with—and in— irrespective of whether they are inside or outside.

For example, during one of my conversations with a mainstream Lyme physician-scientist named Dr. Elway, she asked,

> Did I tell you what I find so interesting about chronic Lyme patients? In general, they tend to be really concerned about toxins—about the potential harm of what they're putting in their bodies—and yet they seem to be perfectly fine with exposing their bodies to years of antibiotics.

While it is true that chronic Lyme patients are often concerned about exposure to toxins, their concerns are not unique. In the last couple decades, many Americans have come to perceive toxins—both inside and outside the home—as an increasing menace to health and wellness. Among the most effective vehicles for the construction and operationalization of the body as a site of toxicity have been government-sponsored biomonitoring studies. The first, conducted by the CDC and published in 2001, confirmed the presence of 27 chemicals in American bodies.[19] A fourth report in this series was published in 2009 and expanded the list of chemicals to 212.[20] No longer theoretical, the traffic between the outside and the inside of the body is now variously visualized and responded to in everyday practice. As one woman observed at a Lyme disease support group meeting, "The skin is the largest organ on the body. [Why wouldn't I be] afraid of chemicals getting inside of me?"

Sociologist Andrew Szasz describes individuals' response to what they perceive as an increasing toxic threat—and the porousness of the boundaries between toxins and their bodies—as the "inverted quarantine" (2007, 4). The inverted quarantine describes a shift from a popular understanding of the "classic" quarantine, in which the underlying "assumption" is that "the overall collective environment is basically healthy," to one in which the "whole environment is toxic, illness-inducing" (5). Practices that proceed from this shift include a range of behaviors centered around "isolating" the body from "disease-inducing surroundings," including installing water and air filtration systems, purchasing organic produce, wearing organic clothing, using toxin-free cosmetics and cleaning supplies, and ensuring that building materials adhere to the strictest regulations for toxicity (5). In a move that mirrors trends in public health toward a greater emphasis on individual responsibility, the inverted quarantine operates under the assumption that individuals can circumvent failures in mass regulation by protecting themselves and the ones they love. Szasz argues that it is not only impossible to "shop our way to safety" but that the illusion of doing so translates to further neglect of mass regulation (see MacKendrick 2010).

For many, an increasing awareness of the risk of environmental toxins translates into the individual consumer practices that Szasz describes, but for some, the ubiquity of toxins has produced a condition known as multiple chemical sensitivity, or environmental illness, the symptoms of which sometimes overlap with those of chronic Lyme disease (Kroll-Smith and Floyd 1997). What makes these patients particularly difficult for others to decipher (and, for some, to have sympathy for) is that the contexts that make them sick are not the asbestos-laden interiors of navy ships or the debris-infused air of Ground Zero but the inner sanctums of houses, malls, and office buildings. As another compelling example of the way in which environmental risk has moved inside, multiple chemical sensitivity, like all bodily conditions, has a range of phenomenological possibilities, the less acute end of which includes patients who might not identify with multiple chemical sensitivity but who do identify with having particular chemical intolerances. This is sometimes where Lyme patients find themselves. Some Lyme patients I spoke with explained that they are more sensitive to certain products after having had Lyme than they were before they had Lyme. As one woman commented, "I'm too sensitive to chemicals to use DEET, so I have to use natural alternatives. And if I do take a hike or walk, I just make sure to shower and check myself."

I would push Szasz's arguments one step further and suggest that even as many individuals create barriers to toxin exposure, many also recognize the limitations of these barriers; that is, they recognize that there is only so much they can do. The result of this understanding is an emerging and focused attention on toxin removal. Accordingly, while the consequence of a diminishing gap between the inside and the outside is that no place is safe anymore, the solution is that, once toxic, the body can often be detoxified. This is particularly true for Lyme patients. When I began observing Lyme patient support group meetings, I soon discovered that a significant part of most meetings was occupied by strategies for how to eliminate toxins from the body. This reality is rooted in an idea shared by many Lyme patients and Lyme-literate practitioners that Lyme disease is particularly pernicious, not merely in and of itself, but in its synergy with other ailments of the body, most notable among them, toxicity. At support group meetings, seasoned members often tried to communicate to newcomers that addressing Lyme disease is addressing only one piece of the unwellness puzzle. One woman explained, "If you have a toxic swamp in your body, that's what Lyme prefers. You have to get rid of toxic soup." For many Lyme patients, heavy metals are perceived to be a frontrunner of toxicity, but toxins like "xenoestrogens," "yeast," "bacterial die-off," and the antibiotics that many patients credit as critical to their recovery are close behind. When it comes to removal, what has worked and what has not worked for patients span the spectrum: loofah scrubs, Epsom salt baths, sweating out toxins by sitting in saunas or exercising, colloidal silver, chelation, colonic enemas, diets and fasts, and herbs like milk thistle and dandelion root.

For many mainstream scientists and physicians, the range of "detoxification" therapies that Lyme patients use is a subject of particular concern, as evidenced by the mainstream publication of "Unorthodox Alternative Treatments Marketed to Treat Lyme Disease," in which the authors identify thirty alternative treatments, review the corresponding medical literatures, and conclude that "the efficacy of these unconventional treatments for Lyme disease is not supported by scientific evidence, and in many cases they are potentially harmful" (Lantos et al. 2015, 1776). Among these therapies, chelation—the ingestion or injection of a chemical compound that binds with metal ions to form a chemical complex that is water soluble, enters the bloodstream, and is excreted in the urine—is often the target of mainstream physicians' most vociferous criticism. While chelation therapy is approved by the FDA for use in acute lead poisoning and iron overload, its use among some CAM and integrative practitioners for subacute heavy metal toxicity, in addition to its off-label use for ailments such as cardiovascular disease, Alzheimer's disease, and autism spectrum disorder (ASD), is often decried by mainstream physicians and scientists because of "weak" or absent scientific evidence (T. Davis et al. 2013; S. James et al. 2015) and reports of side effects ranging from fatigue and rash to nephrotoxicity, gastrointestinal distress (S. James et al. 2015; Kosnett 2010; Morgan, Kori, and Thomas 2002), and even death (M. Brown et al. 2006).

The controversy over chelation therapy offers an illuminating example of what sociologist Scott Frickel and colleagues describe as "undone science," or "areas of research that are left unfunded, incomplete, or generally ignored but that social movements or civil society organizations often identify as worthy of more research" (Frickel et al. 2010, 444). In recent years, as the science around chelation therapy has begun to be "done," the outcome of "science's doing" has done little to quell chelation's controversy. For example, to address the knowledge gap of whether chelation therapy provides benefit for patients with cardiovascular disease, a team of scientists undertook a ten-year NIH-funded double-blind placebo-controlled study called Trial to Assess Chelation Therapy (TACT). In 2013, the results of this study led its authors to conclude that "among stable patients with a history of MI [myocardial infarction], use of an intravenous chelation regimen with disodium EDTA, compared with placebo, modestly reduced the risk of adverse cardiovascular outcomes, many of which were revascularization procedures" (Lamas et al. 2013, 1241). Although the authors cautioned that the results were not "sufficient to support the routine use of chelation therapy for treatment of patients who have had an MI" (1241), the study was met with a wave of criticism, including claims of "possible ethics violations" and concerns about the "safety of the chemicals used in the research" (Watson 2013). As science journalist Karen Weintraub observes, "Despite the time, effort, and money, the initial trial hasn't had much of an impact. Few mainstream doctors have changed their minds about chelation, and alternative medicine therapists apparently haven't stopped using it in patients without diabetes" (K. Weintraub 2016). Although, as Weintraub emphasizes, "no single scientific study can be considered the truth" and "findings should be repeated to be confirmed," the case of chelation also reveals how, as Frickel et al. observe, "even when 'undone science' is completed, the knowledge may become stigmatized and the credibility and standing of scientists who produce it may suffer" (2010, 446).

For Lyme patients, however, the diversity of detoxification options—chelation included—is as promising as it is overwhelming. In response to patients' questions and confusion over the right way to detox, one integrative physician, who was invited to a support group meeting to give a presentation on his approach to treating Lyme disease, offered a streamlined detoxification solution. "You know what detoxing is?" he asked a captive audience. He continued,

> Detoxing is drinking three liters of water a day. Eat a diet high in vegetables; 50 percent of those should be raw vegetables. Eat as much fruit as you want, as long as it's 50 percent less than the veggies you eat. And

exercise thirty minutes a day. If you do this and you still feel toxic, we can discuss other options.

Another illuminating exchange about toxins occurred while I was observing the practice of a Lyme-literate physician. As the Lyme-literate physician's nurse practitioner began the patient intake, the patient immediately declared, "I have toxins in me, and I want them out!" Although the patient knew that he would most likely be prescribed chelation therapy, he was concerned about what good things he would also be losing. "I don't want to be getting rid of minerals I need," he continued. In response to the patient's concerns, the nurse practitioner admitted that the process of detoxification is a messy one. At the outset, she explained, the challenge is to determine whether the root of the patient's symptoms is a tick-borne disease or a toxin. Once this is established, the next challenge is to recognize that, in the same way in which antibiotics kill both good and bad bacteria, chelation also removes good things. What is worse, she continued, it is impossible to know which toxins have been removed. "If only we knew!" she exclaimed. Although it would be easy to assume that this explanation would not be the sort to inspire confidence, the patient found it greatly reassuring, not only because the nurse practitioner admitted what she did not know but also because the patient was given the responsibility of becoming his own barometer of cure. In the end, as this interaction so helpfully made clear, detoxification therapy (like treatment for chronic Lyme disease more generally) is one that often proceeds by trial and error and whose success can often only be measured by whether the patient feels better or not.

The validity of using patients' self-reports as an end-point criterion is itself a subject of much dispute. While helping patients feel better would appear to be a reasonable goal of medicine, the idea of feeling better in the absence of "objective" data makes some scientists and physicians skeptical. In an article in the New Yorker, "The Power of Nothing: Could Studying the Placebo Effect Change the Way We Think about Medicine?," Michael Specter describes the work of Ted Kaptchuk, an acupuncturist turned senior scientist at Harvard Medical School who conducts research on the placebo effect (Specter 2011). Among his many publications, Kaptchuk published a study of an asthma drug in the New England Journal of Medicine in which he and his colleagues found that "although placebos had no impact on the chemical markers that indicate whether a patient is responding to therapy, patients nonetheless reported feeling better" (Specter 2011). Kaptchuk and his colleagues concluded that although "objective physiological measurements are important," "other outcomes such as emergency room visits and quality-of-life metrics may be more clinically relevant to patients and physicians" (Wechsler 2011, 125). As Specter observes, alarmed critics quickly responded. "'Other outcomes' besides objective measures of disease severity may be 'more clinically relevant?'" one physician asked incredulously on a blog (Gorski 2011). But for Kaptchuk and many others, the primary goal is that "people feel better."[21]

This is certainly true for many Lyme-literate practitioners and, of course, for Lyme patients, who, like most individuals who feel unwell, just want to feel better. For some Lyme patients, detoxing is perceived to work because they feel better but only after having felt worse during the actual process of detoxing. As one woman explained, "It's so hard to tell the difference between my Lyme symptoms and my detox symptoms that sometimes I don't even think I have Lyme, that I've cracked! But, no, I know that there are real things going on." Another woman at a support group meeting described how, when she was going through detox, "I couldn't get out of bed." Upon hearing this, another woman responded, "I can't be sick for weeks! I have people to take care of. I have mercury in me, and I'll just have to deal with it." In general, the idea that you have to feel worse to feel better is one that many chronic Lyme patients are accustomed to—and in many cases have come to embrace—because it is the main principle of the Herxheimer reaction. For Lyme-literate practitioners, the Herxheimer reaction is an important diagnostic tool in the treatment of Lyme disease, whereby the elicitation of external symptoms is just as important for assessing "what's getting better" as it is for assessing "what's wrong." First described within conventional medicine as the release of toxins into the bloodstream from the antibiotic treatment of spirochetal organisms, the Jarisch–Herxheimer reaction, in conjunction with an increase in inflammatory cytokines (molecular proteins), produces fevers, headaches, fatigue, and muscle pain—symptoms that are also understood to be characteristic of Lyme disease. For Lyme-literate physicians, a limited period in which symptoms worsen is a sign of progress because it is interpreted as the successful killing of Lyme spirochetes. For chronic Lyme patients, the experience of the Herxheimer reaction is so universal and so identifiable that it is colloquially referred to among patients as "herxing."[22] While distinguishing between detoxing and a Herxheimer reaction (symptoms due to toxin removal versus symptoms due to bacterial death) can be a challenge, patients and practitioners describe the end result as worth the discomfort. As the integrative physician mentioned above exclaimed, "It wakes you up and makes you feel alive!"

If a toxin can be biological and chemical, can be found inside and outside, and can cause bodily discomfort in both its exposure to and removal from a body, it also happens that one substance can be toxic or beneficial depending on its context. The subtle distinctions that constitute when and where something is or is not a toxin play out, for example, in the case of mold. As one Lyme patient explained, "After we detox, I can come home and smell mold. I smell the mold from the ground, which isn't a problem, because it's outside, and I don't have a problem. You can't stop living outside; you can remedy it in your home." Perhaps most striking here is the rationalization for why outside mold, unlike inside mold, is not a toxic threat. The issue is not that one type of mold is more toxic than the other: they are perceived to be the same mold. The issue is that the ability to control outside mold is perceived to be out of one's hands, while inside mold is perceived to be controllable. The extent to which something is perceived to be controllable is a good barometer for how it will be perceived as a toxin. As one patient explained, "I like to focus on the things I can control."

Another good example of the environmental toxin's inherent ambivalence and contextual nature can be found in chronic Lyme patients' use of the Rife machine and the seemingly contradictory actions they take to limit their exposure to other electromagnetic frequencies. The Rife machine, a contraption that emits electromagnetic frequencies, was developed in the 1930s by a researcher named Royal Rife. A subscriber to the school of thought that cancer has a bacterial or viral basis, Rife created a machine that he believed targeted bacteria and viruses at their own unique frequencies and, in doing so, "devitalized" them (Hess 1996, 664). Initially taken seriously by medical institutions, the machine was tested in clinical trials conducted at the University of California, San Francisco (UCSF) and the University of Southern California (USC), only to become the center of a heated lawsuit and meet the fate of being banned by the California Department of Health (664–66). As of this writing, the Rife machine has yet to be approved by the FDA. Patients and alternative practitioners have continued to use the machine for a range of maladies, and they have done so in an underground fashion by purchasing the machine in parts and assembling it on their own. Because the machine costs upward of a couple thousand dollars, patients often collectively purchase one and alternate use among its owners.

Among chronic Lyme disease patients, the Rife machine is increasingly used in conjunction with antibiotics or on its own. However, as they are with antibiotics, Lyme patients appear to be acutely aware of the Rife machine's potential risks. Several patients I spoke with or observed brought up the possibility that it could be causing long-term DNA damage. Others articulated concerns that the device had not been fully evaluated by the scientific community. But like antibiotics, claims of efficacy outweigh fears of risk. Take, for example, a woman named Nancy who, at a support group meeting, explained that she had just begun using a Rife machine. "My sister had a bad experience with it," she said. "It's never been approved by the FDA, and there's been little research on it. Plus, there are concerns that it's affecting DNA. But I've heard through the grapevine that it's working well. So I'm going to take it slowly."

At the same time, patients like Nancy, who are willing to expose themselves to the Rife machine for the promise of its benefits, are also concerned about the risks of their exposure to everyday electromagnetic frequencies. Like concerns about toxins in general, concerns about an electromagnetically toxic environment are not unique to Lyme patients. As questions about the potentially harmful effects of everyday electronic devices have become more common in popular media, some Americans have begun to take precautionary action, such as using cell phone headsets to create a perceived safe distance between the phone's output and the ear or using a lap guard under a laptop. But for many Lyme patients, even these efforts taken by some concerned consumers are not sufficient. Several support group meetings I attended were spent strategizing about how to best limit exposure to electromagnetic frequencies. Some members suggested removing all electronic equipment from one's bedroom. Others thought that just turning off the wireless router at night would be sufficient. Still others, like Nancy, suggested more aggressive action, recommending that filters or nodes be applied to all electromagnetic devices that a person owns in their home, office, and cars. "I have electromagnetic sensitivity," she explained. "All I do is read. I can't sit in front of the computer or the television." To protect herself from what she believes are the harmful effects of electromagnetic radiation, Nancy has installed technology throughout her home that is purported to interfere with frequencies and "renaturalize" them so that they are no longer harmful. "It's expensive, but it works," she said. "I can feel all my cells open up. It makes me feel more open." Another support group member agreed. "I'm so much less sleepy when I drive," the woman exclaimed. "I can tell immediately when the node is not in place."

The tension in this example turns on the fact that while Nancy goes to great lengths to accommodate "electromagnetic sensitivity" and to prevent herself from being exposed to electromagnetic frequencies, she is nevertheless willing to use an electromagnetic frequency machine to target the bacterium that causes Lyme disease. The difference, of course, is that Nancy's everyday exposure to electromagnetic frequencies is not on her terms and is beyond her control. With the Rife machine, however, the exposure is on Nancy's terms and *within* her control. And unlike everyday exposure, the Rife machine has a targeted and expected health effect. In the end, the toxicity of electromagnetic frequency is not gauged according to dose—on how much or how little is used—but on the intent and outcome of its use.[23]

If Lyme patients often perceive their health predicament as one of choosing *between* toxic environmental evils (i.e., strategically accommodating one toxin to mitigate the toxic effect of another), it makes sense that when it comes to pesticides, the environmental toxin par excellence, Lyme patients are often its greatest proponents. During a conversation with a mother of two daughters, all three of whom were being treated for chronic Lyme disease, the mother exclaimed, "We're almost completely organic except that we spray the most horrible toxins on the yard. We also spray ourselves like crazy!"[24] Another woman I interviewed had made it her year's mission to persuade her local drugstore to provide a continuous supply of an insecticide called permethrin to its customers. For these Lyme patients, even in the face of their concern about toxin exposure, there is no such thing as being too careful when it comes to tick eradication. As the woman above explained, "We try to have our lawn sprayed at least six times per year." Another patient admitted,

> Of course I spray my lawn! I'm a nut job—I'm very careful. I also take permethrin, spray it on cotton balls, and stuff it in paper tubes. Squirrels and chipmunks nest in there, and it kills the ticks. Ever since I began spraying, I haven't found one tick on my property.

For most patients with whom I spoke, the decision to use pesticides was a choice between two personal health risks: the risk of pesticide exposure and the risk of Lyme disease infection. As one patient explained, "When it comes to applying repellents, some people believe that it's dangerous to them. I respect that because that's pretty much where I was coming from, too. But you get neurological Lyme and you have Lyme long term and you start reevaluating your opinions." Some individuals also considered the environmental impact of pesticides when making their decision. For example, one chronic Lyme patient I interviewed, a twenty-five-year-old college student, reasoned, "It might be horrible for the environment, but of course I'm going to spray pesticides. What's the point of having a world if you can't live in it?" Another patient, a middle-aged government employee, exclaimed,

> I've always been a really ecological [sic] friendly person. But there wasn't hesitation when it came to my health and protecting my family. That outweighed the possibility of the effects of it leaching into the Farmington River. The immediacy of Lyme disease, that made the difference. When it comes to ticks, I don't care what I have to do.

In both cases, the risk of Lyme disease was almost always prioritized over the risk of pesticides to the health of humans and the environment.

Given that an aesthetic of nature tends to be strong among residents of Lyme-endemic areas, it might seem surprising that individuals often dismiss their own concerns about the impact of their pesticide use on the nature they love. But a scientist who strongly advocates for pesticide use succinctly suggested, "Human health will always prevail. Before the West Nile scare happened, who could have imagined that helicopters would be flying over New York to spray pesticides? New Yorkers are the most toxic paranoid outside of San Francisco." "The decision is easy," he says. "Either spray pesticides or get Lyme disease." Interestingly enough, this scientist admitted that he does not spray his own yard because he is not worried about ticks. But he also does not collect ticks because he does not want to know what his risk for acquiring Lyme disease is, since knowing what his risk is might change the fact that he is always in his yard. "If I had children, it would be different," he reflected. Whether made by a patient or scientist, decisions about when to use pesticides for personal use follow the unpredictable but always rationalized internal logic of every individual.

During my research, disagreement over how and when to use pesticides was best demonstrated at the monthly meetings of a precariously assembled committee composed of public health officials and Lyme advocates. The purpose of these meetings was to discuss and plan tick-borne disease prevention strategies in a particular region of that state. One of the most contentious meetings I observed centered on a tick-borne disease prevention acronym that had been created in collaboration between health officials and patient advocates. While it had been given a seal of approval by state officials who deemed it sufficiently based on credible scientific evidence, the acronym came under attack when it began to circulate locally because more than half of the prevention directives encapsulated in it were related to pesticide use, an issue that proved controversial among residents less concerned about exposure to ticks and more concerned about exposure to pesticides. Although support of pesticide use among Lyme patients appeared to be relatively high, support of pesticide use among the general population in affluent suburbs of that state appeared to be much lower. In the end, several health officials (each of whom represented separate townships) responded to or anticipated the concerns of their constituents by changing the acronym directives related to pesticide use, which meant that the Lyme disease prevention equivalent of "Stop, drop, and roll" recommended different tick prevention practices depending on where and by whom it was used.

Although individuals in Lyme-endemic areas who are concerned about Lyme disease often choose what they perceive to be the risks of pesticide use over those of Lyme disease, it is also important to recognize that, for all those who weigh the "two evils" of ticks and pesticides and choose pesticides, there are still those who are acutely concerned about tick exposure but cannot bring themselves to spray pesticides (either for health or environmental reasons) and look to other creative solutions. This was the case with an experimental "green school" in Maryland, a representative of which spoke at an EPA conference held in Washington, DC, in the spring of 2011. The representative explained how, when planners chose the seventeen-acre forested site on which the school was built, they were not aware that it was infested with ticks. Upon realizing that it was, the school unanimously agreed not to spray. Because they were a Quaker school, the representative explained, they considered themselves "stewards of the earth" and, given their proximity to wetlands, were concerned about the effect their actions would have on local amphibians. Among the tick-management solutions they had put in place were free-range guinea hens, duct taping the pant legs of every child who went outdoors, and limiting recess play to the black top. In the end, the representative concluded, she was not sure if any of it was effective, but the school consoled itself in recognizing that they had at least created "quite a discussion piece." Of all the stories I heard over the course of my research, the example of the Quaker school was an exception. As I learned, when individuals make a decision at what they perceive to be a crossroads between personal and environmental health, the health of the environment rarely comes out on top.

As the above examples have demonstrated, one answer to the question posed by Dr. Elway in the beginning of this section is that the simultaneity of Lyme patients' use and avoidance of substances that they recognize as toxic is not contradictory. Rather, toxin avoidance is merely an attempt to limit further exposure to a toxic environment of which, through their antibiotic and pesticide use, Lyme patients are an inextricable part. From ticks and mold to electromagnetic frequencies and pesticides, the case of Lyme disease makes clear that what constitutes the "environment" in environmentally privileged areas of the United States is often much more than just the "outside," and that, for many people in Lyme-endemic areas, ticks are just one risk in a range of environmental risks that are perceived to be "toxic."

The Practice of Lyme Disease Prevention

While the previous two sections examine how individuals in Lyme-endemic areas navigate the tension between their attraction to nature and their fear of environmental risk, this section concludes by examining the practical consequences of that tension—more specifically, bodily practices that individuals enact to keep ticks off them. Here, I argue that, through individuals' engagement with an environment whose salience to the self is constantly changing, tick prevention practices become less about whether they actually work and more about what they incidentally happen to produce across social relations. As I demonstrate in the example of the tick check, a personal prevention practice that often requires the help of someone else, it is the effects of these practices—for example, quality time spent between parents and children, intimate time spent between partners, and a collective feeling of greater safety—that individuals come to value over the efficacy of the practices themselves.

Described by first-century Roman naturalist Pliny the Elder as the "foulest and most vile creatures that be," ticks have long made humans uneasy (Edlow 2003, 84). In 1749, Pehr Kalm, a naturalist from Sweden who documented the experience of traveling through the United States, wrote of ticks, "To these I must add the wood-lice [ticks] with which the forests are so pestered that it is impossible to pass through a bush or to sit down, though the place be ever so pleasant, without having a whole swarm of them on your clothes" (Stafford 2007, 1). The dense "annoyance" of ticks that Kalm experienced in 1749 changed at the turn of the twentieth century when forests were cleared for farmland and tick-carrying deer were hunted out of the landscape. Entomologist Kirby Stafford describes how an entomologist in 1872 declared ticks to be "nearly or quite extinct" along the path that Pehr Kalm had traveled one hundred years before (2007, 2). It was not until after WWII that the perfect storm of reforestation, deer reintroduction, and the expansion of suburbs into forested areas allow for the return of the tick. As a result, Americans, often preferring to live close to the woods but not in them, became increasingly familiar with and wary of tick encounters.

Pamela Weintraub (2008) describes how this threat of tick encounters estranged her from the nature she had always loved. She writes,

> Before I realized our environment was making us sick, I viewed the natural beauty around me as a gentle, beneficent luxury, a reward for my success. . . . After Lyme, I hesitated even stepping on the grass in Chappaqua without high socks and boots, my suburban version of the Hazmat suit. What had once seemed pristine now felt toxic and ruined. (105)

Like Weintraub, many of the individuals I spoke with during the course of my research moved to or remained in forested suburbs to be "close to nature." But "after Lyme," many described an experience of becoming "prisoners of their own paradise." As one patient exclaimed, "I don't go out. I used to always go out. I love nature, and I love animals. Now I don't like grass or walking through the woods. If I see people walking through the woods, I want to say, 'You're going to get sick!'" Another patient explained,

> The deck outside is my world. It's way above the ground. I don't go on the lawn. I don't go to picnics. My life is totally changed. I used to be outside camping, hiking, hiking eighty miles per week. Now I walk on the pavement and come back. That's it. I'm afraid to go on any grasses. Also, I heard that a tick came in on someone's Christmas tree, so I've been putting up artificial ones for the past couple years.

Still another patient, a television producer in his early forties who continues to venture outside, explains that he does so with great unease. "Now I'm freaked out," he admits. "Even when I take the dog for a walk. And now that it's summer, I see a tick waiting to jump off every leaf. My perception of where ticks are has changed—ticks are totally on my radar screen."

Because the greatest risk for tick exposure often occurs in one's backyard, Lyme disease has transformed mundane domestic objects—like lawns, playgrounds, and stone fences—into frightening and difficult-to-decipher menaces. One father I met, whose children were not allowed to walk on the lawn without permission, recounted how his young son, in reaction to a pile of leaves he had raked together, exclaimed, "Look, Dad, a pile of ticks!" Upon later seeing a cartoon depicting children playing in leaves, his son asked, "Why would their parents let them do that?" Another woman described a recent Christmas-shopping-in-July outing when she had passed over some deer-themed Christmas cards because the sight alone had made her cringe. In a similar instance, another woman explained,

> When I see kids playing in the grass or people walking dogs in the grass, I grimace. We hear stories about Lyme every day. I feel bad because kids want to go out in the backyard, but my granddaughter will never go in my backyard. It's a shame. I love the woods!

Some families, overwhelmed by the idea of living in such close contact with ticks, have moved to non-Lyme-endemic areas (and many have at least contemplated it). But most stay, for a variety of reasons. One woman explained, "I've lived my whole life in Connecticut. My family is here, and my husband's whole family is here. So I just can't imagine. I've heard that people have moved to California, though." Other patients I spoke with, like Regina and Mary, who led the support group meeting I described in this chapter's first section, gestured to their constitutional incompatibility with city life: "We could move to New York City and not have grass, and that's not the kind of life I want. I like grass. It's nice." Another woman echoed this sentiment:

> I know that there are enough things that you can do to prevent Lyme disease without moving to the concrete jungle. We would never move. But I also don't let my kids go in the woods. Isn't that crazy? I live in a rural area and don't want to go in the woods!

In making the decision to stay, many turn to what they describe as the only thing at their disposal: prevention. Tick-bite prevention includes an ever-expanding range of emerging bodily practices, such as tick checks, repellents, knee-high socks, wearing socks with sandals, tucking pants into socks, light-colored clothing, wearing a hat, avoiding grass, avoiding leaf litter, keeping animals outside (or at least not letting them in bed with you), only having pets with white fur, spraying the yard with pesticides, putting clothes in the dryer after coming inside, and bathing after coming inside. Some individuals and families conscientiously engage in as many of these practices as they can. As Sue, a stay-at-home parent with two daughters, explained,

> When we're in the garden, we wear khaki pants with white socks. We also wear hats and socks on our hands. And, of course, we spray ourselves like crazy. When we come inside, we take our clothes off in the garage and then shower. We also try to find other things we like to do, like bike riding and skiing. And we try to spray six times per year.

In a similar vein, another woman explained,

> I cannot get bitten again. I have to take all the precautions that I can in order not to get bit: tick checks, repellents, pesticides, you name it. We even have a protocol for washing clothes: we take off clothes in the garage and then put them in a garbage bag until they go to laundry. They also get twisty tied.

Others find focusing on just one or two prevention practices more manageable. For instance, one woman explained how if she walks through her yard, she wears rubber boots. Another man, who lets his dog sleep on his bed, pulls down the covers every night and looks for ticks. He added, "And I insist on only solid sheets. It's the only way you can see the ticks."

In general, some prevention practices are rarely done. As one patient rhetorically asked, "Who's going to wear long pants on a hot summer day?" But some, like tick checks and remembering to shower after coming indoors, have, for many, become part of the daily repertoire of bodily hygiene. Eileen, a woman in her forties who used to work at a factory, explained, "Am I using permethrin? No. Am I using DEET? No. Just last weekend I was outside just doing a very little bit of yard work, and then I was inside taking a shower. My husband's also following me saying, 'Take a shower.' That's one of the most effective things." Echoing Eileen, Judy, a woman in her sixties who works as a freelance writer, explained, "I have two sons, and we all take showers immediately when coming back in. We also use loofahs. It's basic hygiene really. Some people I look at and think, 'Hello, you haven't taken a shower for a week; no wonder you're crawling with ticks!'"

That tick checks and showering after coming indoors have become part of some individuals' "basic hygiene" is notable given that personal hygiene as a means to a disease-free life has, over time, become a less urgent priority for many Americans. Beyond handwashing, which remains a touchstone of "sanitary citizenship" (Briggs and Mantini 2003), everyday attention to and care for the body as a functional barrier between the contagion of the outside and the health of the inside has, for many, become the stuff of outdated parental expressions like "Don't forget to wash behind your ears." Broadly speaking, public health measures, such as waste management, municipal drinking water, and vaccines, have dramatically reduced the menace of communicable diseases that produced vigilant inspection of the body's planes and folds up until the middle of the twentieth century. Medical historian Nancy Tomes observes how, in the early 1900s, "revelations that skin, hair, and body cavities harbored millions of germs provided abundant material for heightening anxieties about bodily hygiene" (1998, 165). For women, germ anxiety took the form of a nationwide campaign to wear shorter dresses and skirts, so that hemlines would not become petri dishes of contagion. For men, it meant a new aesthetic that valued shorn, beardless faces (159). This broader shift in public health from collective to individual responsibility in the form of personal hygiene behaviors became institutionalized through public education. For example, historian Suellen Hoy describes how schoolteachers in the mid-twentieth century conducted toothbrush drills and required daily inspections of hair, hands, ears, and necks (1995, 128).

Unlike tooth brushing and hair washing, which, for some, have become habits of an aesthetic nature associated with little conscious attention to health, tick checks are bodily practices explicitly enacted in health's pursuit and with a keen attention to risk of disease. But they are also a new breed of bodily practices in that they are acts of personal hygiene that are inherently social. This is, in large part, because of the habits of ticks themselves. Built for moist environments, ticks leave leaf litter to often make their way to the floral equivalent of the human body: armpits, the bra line, around the anus, and tucked within the creases of male and female genitalia. The irony is that these most intimate places, which most would prefer to inspect in privacy, are not easily inspectable to their bearer and require the help of another set of eyes and hands. In this way, the sociality of tick checks is always already linked to questions of intimacy, sexuality, and the obscene.

For example, at the abovementioned tick-borne disease prevention conference in the spring of 2011, an entomologist stepped up to the microphone during a question-and-answer session. Frustrated by the gap between concept and practice and working on a hunch that most people do not do thorough enough tick checks, the entomologist said, "Without someone to check me, a tick guy like me needs a tick-guy-sized mirror." He proceeded to bend over, so that his rear faced the panel, and then mimed spreading his cheeks open, his head peering around his body as if looking into the imaginary mirror before him. The discomfort in the audience was palpable. One could only imagine that it was a discomfort operating on two levels: discomfort with the idea of checking one's own body in that way and discomfort with the idea of having to check someone else's body in that way. The entomologist's simple mime also reinforced the idea that ticks prefer hard-to-reach intimate places and that tick checks are better performed by intimates than by the self, even if both practices are, at times, perceived to be unpleasant.

Consistent with the theme of this chapter, however, revulsion and attraction are two sides of the same coin. Helped along in no small part by country legend Brad Paisley's song "Ticks," which seeks to persuade a woman to walk into the sticks so that he can check her for ticks, the term "tick checks" has also become a sexual innuendo with the same clinical valence of something like "Let's play doctor." The salience of this term was confirmed during an interview with a male Lyme patient. After talking at length about hunting and camping and other outdoor activities, I asked the patient whether he performed tick checks, and transitioning from an until-then serious tone to one that was markedly mischievous, he responded with a knowing smirk, "Only for fun." And in a letter penned in support of a Lyme advocacy group by a famous Hollywood actor who also happens to have been a Lyme patient, the actor wrote, "Tick checks are great foreplay. Enjoy them!" Vector-borne disease health officials had hoped to capitalize on ticks checks' emerging colloquial traction by coining the prevention message "Get Naked," but I was told by a health official at another conference in the fall of 2010 that this idea was only too quickly given the kibosh by STD health officials, who warned that anything having to do with nudity and sexuality was infringing on their public health marketing territory.

Given all this, it is easy to see how tick checks can quickly become a sensitive subject between parents and children. As one patient I interviewed explained,

> When my son was a baby, we used to have what we called "tick patrol," and I would bring him in and strip him down every night, and we would check every area of his body, and I can tell you, I took a tick off his penis. I mean that's, I remember that, but I would check him constantly. But he's eighteen now. I'm hoping—well, I tell him he has to check himself.

Like this mother, parents I spent time with often complained that once their children reached a certain age, they and their children no longer felt comfortable doing certain types of tick checks with each other. Even though they had taught their children to check themselves, they worried that they would not do them thoroughly enough or, more likely, that they would forgo the check completely. As another mother asked, "Can you imagine getting a twelve-year-old boy to take a tick check seriously?" On the other hand, limited tick checks (of the hair, back, and shoulders) very much remain within the bounds of family intimacy. One physician explained how his children, now teenagers, still asked to be checked for ticks because they just liked it. "It's one of the things that they grew up doing with me," he explained. In the end, the intimate tick checks that families enjoy and the more sexual tick checks that Brad Paisley croons about are not as thorough as the miming entomologist would like them to be, while the thorough tick checks that the entomologist advocates for are not the ones that most people want to do.

In addition to the limitations of when and where tick checks are considered appropriate, tick checks are also plagued by the problem of ticks' small size. The juvenile, or nymphal, stage of the blacklegged tick is the size of a period. As demonstrated by the boy in the example above who conflated leaves with ticks, ticks *are* so small that they could be any-where and anything, and for all intents and purposes, they might as well be leaves. As one mother admitted,

> We're very religious about checking them for ticks, but I'm also, you know, they still roll around in the grass and hike in the woods, and I have two boys. They both have long hair. If my older one gets a tick, I'm not going to find it, you know, he's got curly, long hair.

More disconcerting still is when the ambiguous *there* of the outside be-comes the ambiguous *here* of the body. For example, several informants de-scribed the experience of watching a mole grow, only to discover too late that the mole *was* a tick. By then, the tick had already had a full blood meal and was given plenty of time to transmit infection, its removal no longer an act of prevention but a mere detachment. Central to the experience and practice of tick checks, then, is the idea of *the one you do not find*. Because most Lyme disease cases are the result of a tick that was not found (or found too late), tick checks are haunted by the specter of their own inefficacy. That is, irre-spective of how many ticks are found during any given tick check, they are always a reminder of the one tick that might not have been and, therefore, the one tick that might have mattered. As one woman I interviewed explained,

> I mean, I know people getting Lyme now, and no one, the majority of these people are not finding ticks. They're just being diagnosed and they're saying, "You know, I never took a tick off my kid. I don't re-member ever seeing it." And most of the parents around here are aware enough that they're checking their kids, so the only place they're going to miss it is their scalp.

Oddly enough, the inefficacy of tick checks is the very thing that leads to their continuation, for the limitation of realizing that a tick might not have been found is simultaneously the acceptance of the infinite possibility that there is *always* a tick to be found. It is a cycle propelled by absence rather than presence. Failure also inheres in the rest of the things that people do to keep ticks off them. A public health official I interviewed explained that although most tick prevention practices seem to be commonsensical, "we really don't know if most of them work." For example, regarding the application of pesticides to lawns, this official said that, in the absence of relevant studies at the time of our interview, the recommendation to do this merely operated on an assumption that lower tick populations translate to lower Lyme disease infection rates.[25] Among the patients with whom I spent time, I was not surprised to hear that, irrespective of outcome, many felt that they would rather do something that *might not work* than *nothing at all*. If not everyone likes tick checks or believes that they are effective, then many, at least, have gotten used to doing them and, in doing them, have come to value their effects.

In 1909, biologist Jakob von Uexküll coined the term Umwelt, or "environment-world," to give expression to the idea of a "surrounding world" (Agamben 2004, 40; Buchanan 2008, 7). Uexküll argued that, when it comes to the relationship between organisms and their environment, attention should be paid to "subjective universes," whereby each organism creates its own environment through interaction and, in doing so, has the potential to create "as many environments as there are organisms" (Buchanan 2008, 7, 22). By examining how an environment that is increasingly immanent is *also* produced in and through individuals' practical engagement with it, I have suggested that the bodily practices of tick-bite prevention constitute the active building of new environment-worlds. And the environment-world of tick-bite prevention practices is one in which protecting the self is also a matter of knowing the other, and where tick checks, whether or not they work, and although exacted on the individual body, are increasingly, if not incidentally, made meaningful across human relations.

Together, this chapter's three sections more broadly explored why a Lyme patient like Susan, who lives in nature and is inspired by its beauty, is also terrified of it. As tick-borne diseases like Lyme disease become an increasing threat in the United States, individuals face the difficult task of negotiating the competing demands between their attraction to nature and their concerns over the health risks of a "toxic" environment, an environment that crosses the boundary between inside and outside and of which Lyme disease is just one small part. In doing so, and in the context of their relative environmental privilege, these individuals must also navigate and make choices about which toxins—from bacterial pathogens to antibiotics to pesticides—are less risky than others. In light of this, I have suggested that the experience of preventing Lyme disease can be better understood through the construct of an epidemiology of affect, whereby individuals' feelings about nature inform their engagement with it and produce an emerging range of disease prevention practices that are characterized by affective social relations.

3

LIVING LYME

At the end of a two-hour intake at a Lyme-literate practice, the patient, reflecting on everything he had heard, asked, "So what is Lyme disease?" The nurse practitioner answered, "It's like Alice in Wonderland: it means different things to different people." This response pithily captures the range of ways in which Lyme disease is lived and known. For some patients, Lyme disease is a quiet but memorably shaped rash that clears up after a round of antibiotics and quickly becomes part of the summer's collection of stories. For others, it is hour-by-hour turned year-after-year discomfort and disorientation. It is numbness and tingling or headaches and light sensitivity or getting lost on the way to work. This irreconcilability of experience and meaning among patients is also true for physicians. For some physicians, Lyme disease is one of many diseases that is often or rarely seen but either way requires little attention. For others, it is the sole object of their practice, a disease whose complexity is only outmatched by an algorithm of therapeutic concoctions and combinations.

This chapter examines how Lyme disease is known through being *lived*; the following chapter explores how Lyme disease is known through being *diagnosed and treated*.[1] Together, these chapters analytically bridge the often presumed gap between illness *experience* and disease *knowledge* by examining how patients *and* physicians "do" and "know" disease (Mol 2002, 12). In doing so, these chapters flesh out the embodied and epistemic dimensions of contested illness's "divided bodies" by exploring themes related to disputes over the biological legitimacy of patients' experiences, in addition to competing claims to knowledge *about* those experiences. In this chapter's attention to patients, I examine three interrelated themes related to living a contested illness in an era of evidence-based medicine: suffering, survival, and surfeit. For patients with contested illnesses, a common source of suffering beyond that of the body is the experience of not being believed, as often by loved ones as by strangers. And for these patients, survival is as much a question of social survival and adaptation as it is about the bodily imperative to "just get through a day." This chapter, then, expands on a well-developed social scientific literature that has described illness experiences but has yet to explore how the perception and experience of relative privilege affects those experiences.[2]

Woven into my exploration of suffering, survival, and surfeit is the related topic of sex and gender. Because many contested illnesses, like chronic fatigue syndrome (CFS), fibromyalgia, and chronic Lyme disease, are also understood by many to be more common among women, Lyme disease is, in part, constituted in and through assemblages of practices and ideas related to sex (commonly understood as biological difference) and gender (commonly understood as the "social expressions" of biological difference) (Lock and Farquhar 2007, 383). In this way, Lyme disease provides an illuminating analytical perspective on how practices and ideas related to sex and gender are produced and operationalized in tandem. For example, questions that circulate within the Lyme community are not only about how women interact differently with physicians than men do but also about how differences in women's biology affect the way that women experience Lyme disease. How, then, does attention or lack of attention to sex-specific differences affect the way that individuals understand gender and vice versa? And how does thinking about disease in the context of sex and gender change the way individuals understand disease?

My analysis of this chapter's themes is interwoven with stories of patients living with Lyme disease. Having formally interviewed and followed up with thirty-four patients (of whom nine were men and twenty-five were women) and having informally spoken with hundreds of patients, the task of choosing which ones best represent the spectrum of these patients' experiences was not easy. And, of course, pinpointing what Lyme disease is is an even more difficult task. For the purposes of this book, my interest in Lyme disease extends only as far as what people variously perceive Lyme to be. This might be a well-worn anthropological intervention, but it nevertheless troubled many mainstream physicians and scientists who participated in my research. "How will you distinguish between 'real' Lyme patients and chronic Lyme patients?" one physician worried. The answer is: I do not. In this book, Lyme disease is as Lyme disease is experienced, and I use the term "Lyme patient" to refer to any patient who identifies with having Lyme disease. However, in the same way that someone who falls sick with influenza or strep throat is unlikely to identify as a flu or strep patient unless complications arise, patients are unlikely to identify as Lyme patients unless there is a certain degree of chronicity. For this reason, the patients I met at support group meetings, fundraisers, and conferences and the patients who responded to my recruitment announcements were those who have been inhabited by Lyme for long enough that they identify with it. And for this same reason, the voices of patients with acute Lyme disease or those who had acute Lyme disease but did not experience persistent symptoms are largely absent from this book.[3] Rather than a limitation, this absence reflects the conditions of possibility for how Lyme's discourses and practices are produced; it also throws into relief the consequential chasm between the experience of *having* a disease and the experience of a disease that *becomes part of the self.*

In the end, I chose to tell the stories of five patients: a mental health practitioner, a business professional, a teacher, a college student, and a self-described homemaker. Their stories contain striking similarities and differences. Between and among them emerges a range of bodily experiences—from cognitive difficulties to diffuse and migrating pains to anxiety and other neurological symptoms—as well as a range of ideas and opinions related to the experience of living a contested illness. As an unwieldy whole, these five stories convey the multiplicity of ways in which the experience of Lyme disease is lived over time, through contestation, and in the context of evidence-based medicine. As literary scholar Elaine Scarry observes, "It is not surprising that the language for pain should sometimes be brought into being by those who are not themselves in pain but who speak *on behalf* of those who are" (1985, 6). It is my intention, however, that, as much as possible, these patients speak for themselves.

Madison, "Wish You Were Here"

Entering Madison's home in Connecticut was like arriving at a party soon after it was over. The furniture and walls seemed heavy with fatigue, and the air was still. Even the clock on the wall seemed to tick to an expended beat. Like many Lyme patients' homes, the curtains were drawn at midday, trying their best to hold the sunlight at bay.[4] The interview took place on the couch, where it was evident that Madison spent much of her time. Near the couch and under a small cross were photos from Madison's wedding.

For her, the photographs were not only a testament to a life that had been lived but also a *reminder* of that life, as it was one that she could no longer remember. "I don't remember our wedding," Madison said as she shook her head, her eyes slightly widened as if even she could not believe what she was saying. "[My husband] tells me I did things, but, I mean, I could barely walk. I remember holding on to the walls, because I couldn't tell where I was in space. I was so dizzy, you know, the pain was so bad." For this reason, Madison said she did not like to look at videos or photographs from her wedding because it was too disorienting to see photos of herself that betrayed the reality of her pain. But not having the wedding was not an option. She explained, "I didn't want [my husband] to not have a life, so I probably would have gone, even if it killed me, just so that he could have a memory, even if I didn't."

Madison's story began long before what she now recognized as Lyme disease entered the picture. According to Madison, it is a story filled with pain. Although she did not remember much of her own wedding, she did remember being bitten by a tick when she was six years old, an event that she now understood as the cause of her present pain. Now in her late twenties, Madison described how her mother tried to remove the tick from the back of her neck, using an arsenal of tick removal strategies that are no longer recommended, including lighting a match and applying Vaseline. "The whole nine!" she exclaimed. When none of the methods worked, her mother took her to the emergency room, where they removed the tick and told her she was fine, even though they had not been able to remove the tick's head. Madison explained,

> They said, "The head's still in. It doesn't matter, go back to school." So I went back to school. About a year later, well, I still had that—it was a raised, angry, angry, painful bump on the back of my neck. It stayed there until about fourth grade.

Soon after the tick bite, Madison experienced a pain "in [her] bones"—first in her neck and then throughout her arms and legs and, finally and most painfully, in her back. Her parents took her to a chiropractor because, at the time, she said, "We didn't know any better." The choice to see a chiropractor was also informed by the fact that her mother, according to Madison, is more of a "naturopath," a label that for Madison means that, when given the choice, her mother leans toward "natural" remedies over conventional ones. She explained, "We did go to other MDs and stuff but mostly when we had the flu or something."

What first appeared to be growing pains turned into a constant companion. "By the time I was in seventh grade," she reflected, "I would come home from school so dead exhausted." She continued,

> Sometimes I'd just be on the couch, my neck was hurting so bad, couldn't get up, really hard to move my legs. . . . But then there were days I didn't. We were a very active family, so we would kayak and bike and hike and all that, and, you know, they were pretty good about, "Oh, I need to stop and rest," so we kind of compensated for each other all the time.

Madison eventually stopped telling her parents about her discomfort because there was nothing anyone could do to help the pain: "I decided that I was just going to keep moving until I was paralyzed." Despite what Madison described as her worsening pain, she continued to be an active child and young adult. For Madison, moving was the only thing that kept her pain at bay. That and swimming in very cold water, which she described as having the effect of numbing her body. Relying on these methods of self-help, Madison was able to finish college and, after graduating, began to work as a teacher for autistic children, a job that she described as her dream job. But it was here that her health precipitously declined. Growing more fatigued, and in more pain than she had ever been, she one day, in the fall of 2004, collapsed in the classroom while performing an evaluation. After her collapse, she returned to work part time, but it was clear within a couple months that even part-time work would be too difficult for her. With the scope of her disability finally sinking in, her fiancé and family moved her out of her apartment and into the home that she and her now husband shared. Reflecting on this time in her life, she said, "I just ceased to have an identity. It just took me over completely. I was pretty much housebound."

In addition to debilitating headaches, full-body fibromyalgia-like pain, and blackouts like the one that she experienced in her classroom, Madison's most significant symptoms had been cognitive impairment and memory loss. At her lowest point, no longer able to work and alienated from "the world" (although not from her family members and friends, who, according to her, had always been supportive), Madison described being alone in her dark basement (the best refuge from headache-triggering sunlight) and unable to recognize her surroundings. The only reason she knew that she was in a place where she belonged was that the dog by her side appeared to know her; she knew that she had not been kidnapped because she was not tied up.

Madison and her family continued to seek answers from neurologists and other medical specialists, many of the appointments for which she and her husband had to pay "hundreds of dollars" because the physicians' practices were out of network. But further CT scans, MRIs, and blood tests revealed nothing. Each physician told Madison the same thing: there was nothing objectively wrong with her, and there was nothing that could be done to help her. In addition to being told that she could not be helped, Madison also remembered the frustration of physicians not believing her. For example, after hearing Madison describe her headaches, one neurologist told her that she was lying and that she should seek the help of a psychiatrist. It was not until February 2006 that her husband heard about—and made an appointment at—a clinic that specializes in the treatment of fibromyalgia. And it was here, under the supervision of a physician that describes himself as Lyme literate, that Madison was finally given a diagnosis. As is often the case in the world of chronic Lyme disease, the diagnosis ended up being as complicated as the search for it had been. Madison recalled, "I know I had a ton of infections besides the Lyme, but I don't remember all of them. There were a ton, a ton, a ton of stuff that had been lying dormant in my body for a long time." Her new physician told her that in addition to Lyme disease and the other infections that Madison cannot remember, she also had a problem with her thyroid.

For almost a year, Madison tried a pharmacopeia of medications, all of which made her feel worse. Madison exclaimed,

> Oh God, he tried all kinds of stuff and, again, I don't remember a lot, but I was so tremendously ill from every single pill he gave me. I could just take one pill, and I could be vomiting for twelve hours. Couldn't get out of the bathroom, or I was just gone. I was completely not here.

At year's end, and unable to determine any appreciable improvement in her health (aside from a positive response from Lyrica for her fibromyalgia pain), Madison switched to another physician at the clinic and adamantly insisted that something was wrong with her "head." Not, she clarified, that her problem was "all in her head," but that the problem was *rooted* in her head. Upon hearing this, the physician decided to test her for heavy metals and, according to Madison,

> That's where they found that I had a lot of lead in my body. A lot of lead in my body. And I'll tell you, it took them about eleven months, I think, to get it out. And that was the first relief I had felt in years. The pain from that was just tremendous.

Madison's encouraging response to chelation therapy (she described her pain after it as half the amount that it had previously been) led her to hope that her ill health might not be related to Lyme disease after all. But this hope was fleeting. Soon after her chelation therapy, a neurologist recommended that she have a SPECT scan, in addition to a neuropsychology evaluation. For the first time in her medical odyssey, neurological testing indicated abnormalities. Her SPECT scan, according to Madison, "lit up," and her neuropsychology evaluation revealed severely compromised cognitive ability. From then up until the time that our interview took place in May 2010, Madison had been under the care of this neurologist. She had tried the range of oral antibiotics that are used by Lyme-literate practitioners to treat chronic Lyme disease but was not able to tolerate any of them. What worked best for her pain and brain fog was a combination of Bicillin (an injectable form of penicillin) and ONDAMED sessions (an electromagnetic frequency machine similar to the Rife machine). When this combination seemed to run its course in its ability to control Madison's pain, her neurologist suggested that she have a PICC line inserted in her arm so that she could be treated intravenously with an antibiotic called Rocephin (the brand name for ceftriaxone), which is the most common intravenous antibiotic used in the treatment of Lyme disease among mainstream and Lyme-literate practitioners.[5]

Barring a few setbacks (including a low white blood cell count and lapses in treatment due to her husband's employer switching to an insurance company that briefly denied her coverage), Rocephin, according to Madison, was the most successful intervention that she tried. Her pain was reduced, and her cognitive function increased to the point that she was cleared to return to work as a part-time tutor. The one significant problem, however, was that the effects of Rocephin were not lasting: her symptoms returned when she stopped treatment. For this reason, she said, "It's devastating when they talk to me about not doing the IV. Because that's the one that's helping me, you know, even if it hurts." Three weeks before Madison and I met, she and her neurologist had discussed how, after a year of intravenous Rocephin, her symptom relief had plateaued, so they made plans to begin a new intravenous antibiotic, the name of which she could not remember but had written down somewhere. She did remember, however, that "it's supposed to be really potent, which, to me, translates to it's going to hurt like hell, get ready." After three weeks without any antibiotics, Madison explained, "I'm only starting to get nervous now because I can feel everything coming back. I can feel the Lyme now coming back."

Madison's story (which took three hours to tell) shares commonalities with those of many Lyme patients I spoke with: it was long, complicated, and difficult to piece together; involved scores of physicians; and included a smorgasbord of protocols and treatments. For physicians in conventional practices, who, for a variety of reasons, often have no longer than fifteen minutes to see a patient, Madison's story exceeds the time they have to listen and brainstorm a plan of action. This is one of the reasons that Lyme patients like Madison often describe having such a positive experience with Lyme-literate physicians. Because the practices of Lyme-literate physicians are not encumbered by the requirements of insurance reimbursement (that is, patients typically pay out of pocket and in the range of several hundred dollars for each appointment), these physicians have the financial and institutional freedom to offer initial sessions that last an hour to an hour and a half. And in addition to having enough time to tell their full history and feel listened to, patients like Madison describe being further comforted by the fact that, under the care of Lyme-literate physicians, there is almost always something that can be done.

Madison's story is also similar to the experience of many Lyme patients in the financial toll that her pursuit of health had taken on her family. Madison and her husband earn just over thirty thousand dollars a year; since 2004, Madison had spent around twelve thousand dollars a year on medical expenses. Few patients I interviewed who had been treated for chronic Lyme disease reported spending less than ten thousand dollars on antibiotic treatment and physician fees, and many said they had spent upwards of a hundred thousand dollars. Although Madison believed that she was better than when she fell ill in 2004, she did not believe that she was better than she had been before that time. Looking ahead, Madison hoped that she would be able to work more than part time, but she did not think that she would ever be well enough to work with autistic children again. She was also unsure that she and her husband would be able to have children. She wanted to be a mother, but based on her illness experience, she did not believe that she would be able to carry a child. And after seeing the documentary Under Our Skin, she also worried that she might transmit Lyme to her child. If that were to happen, Madison explained, "I [couldn't] handle the guilt."

Dan, "A Palsy in Time"

I met Dan at his office in Connecticut on a sunny May afternoon in 2010. As soon as I parked, Dan strode out to meet me, his long legs arriving just before his outstretched hand. In his mid-forties with energetic eyes and salt-and-pepper sideburns, Dan had a handshake that was as confident as the way he spliced first names into a turn of phrase to create a welcoming sense of familiarity. As we began our interview, Dan joked that he only traveled or spent time in places where there are ticks and Lyme disease. He exclaimed, "I kid you not, Abby. My mom's family has a place in East Hampton, my wife's mom has a place in Nantucket, we've lived on the shoreline of Connecticut for twenty-five years, and my dad's retired to Sag Harbor." And it was there in Sag Harbor, in a "cool private garden with beautiful long grasses," that he believed a tick bit him.

Like many Lyme patients I spoke with, Dan had no recollection of seeing a tick or a rash, only that a couple weeks after visiting his father he began to feel like he was coming down with a cold. By the next day, fatigued and achy, he left work early and, over the course of his two-hour commute, stopped to take two hour-long naps along the side of the road. "I'm not a whiner," he assured me. "But this was the most tired I've ever felt in my life." The next day found him at his internist's office, seeing a new physician, who gave him a strep test and told him he most likely had a cold. When Dan returned home, however, and looked in the mirror, he was shocked to find that half of his face was drooping. A trip to the emergency room confirmed that he was not having a stroke. Instead, his physician felt confident that it was Lyme disease and recommended that he begin taking a three-week course of doxycycline, since blood tests would not be reliable for at least another two weeks.

Dan's response to the antibiotics was "dramatic." Within three days, he felt "100 percent better." But Dan's Bell's palsy remained. Although he was aware that the Bell's palsy symptoms could last anywhere between thirty and ninety days, he began to have the feeling that they were not resolving quickly enough. "I had trouble with my eye closing and, of course, it drying out, so I taped it with a big X. I looked like a World War I vet, but it worked." By month four, still having to tape his eye closed at night, Dan sought the advice of an ophthalmologist, who expressed concerned and sent him to Dr. Childs, "the guy to see when it comes to Lyme disease." Interestingly enough, Dr. Childs also happened to be one of the mainstream physicians I observed over the course of my research.

For many chronic Lyme patients, Dr. Childs is the embodiment of the mainstream approach to Lyme disease. For example, one patient who was being treated for chronic Lyme disease by another physician traveled from New Jersey to get a second opinion from Dr. Childs before she switched from oral to IV antibiotics. When Dr. Childs informed her that he did not believe her symptoms were related to Lyme disease, she responded, "This is what pisses me off because what you're saying is so different from what my other doctors have said." When Dr. Childs maintained that he did not know what the source of her suffering was but that it was not Lyme disease, she continued, "They told me not to bother coming to you. How you don't believe in Lyme disease, how you're a bunch of jerks up here." The patient then grabbed her purse and stormed out of Dr. Childs's office.[6]

Of course, interactions with patients were not always so heated. Another patient, who had been treated for Lyme disease based on persistent symptoms of fatigue, sweats, and arthritic pain in her hands, feet, and knees, accompanied by a positive IgG and IgM, arrived at Dr. Childs office asking, "I want you to tell me: do I or don't I have Lyme disease?" When he suggested that her symptoms were not related to Lyme disease but, instead, to the "wear and tear" of osteoarthritis and that she could benefit from low-impact exercise and nonsteroidal anti-inflammatories, she responded, "I was scared to come see you. But I'm very happy. You're not at all like what I've heard. I've heard that you have a bad bedside manner, but I think you're a perfect gentleman, and I like your manner."

During office examinations, I observed Dr. Childs listen to patients' complaints of fatigue, migrating muscle aches, and joint pains in the absence of a positive Lyme test (or one that Dr. Childs found to be convincingly positive) and respond, "I don't believe that Lyme disease causes chronic fatigue," or "In your situation, additional antibiotics have not been shown to be effective." Dr. Childs also did not refrain from using choice words to describe practitioners who describe themselves as Lyme literate. But, during one of our conversations, Dr. Childs clarified what, from his clinical experience, he understood "chronic" Lyme disease to mean. "There is, of course, chronic Lyme disease. But that is only in very particular cases. When you've been treating it for more than three months without success, that's what I call *resistant*." For Dr. Childs, these cases—"real" Lyme cases—also meet the objective criteria of Lyme disease: pattern-specific arthritis and/or certain well-defined neurological symptoms. A month later, Dr. Childs further revealed the nuance of his understanding of chronic Lyme disease when he explained, "We'll be getting real Lyme cases soon. Since I saw you last, I saw two Lyme arthritis cases. One of them is not getting completely better and is about to go on IV antibiotics. Real cases can be somewhat stubborn, somewhat chronic. Maybe that's what underlies all this anxiety."

In the end, what Dan did not realize is that he happened to fit into a category of patients whose persistent symptoms are related to what Dr. Childs believes is ongoing infection and can be helped with additional antibiotics.[7] For this reason, Dan's understanding of Dr. Childs's perspective on Lyme disease was at odds with, for example, the first patient mentioned above. Instead, Dan described Dr. Childs as "bright" and "forthright" and left his visit with the impression that Dr. Childs was sympathetic to the idea of chronic Lyme disease. Dan explained,

> Dr. Childs basically told me that there are two camps. One says take thirty days, and any side effects are an autoimmune response. The other camp says that it sticks with you, and you're still infected. And he's in the latter camp. He said, "What I can tell you is that, pretty consistently, when I have patients do a second course of antibiotics, sometimes six months later, sometimes a year, sometimes years later, I find they get results from it. What it means to me is that the infection is still lingering, and it's not an autoimmune response."

Dan's experience with Dr. Childs demonstrates the complexity of how Lyme disease is understood both *across* the standard-of-care divide and *by* individuals themselves. After his appointment with Dr. Childs, Dan took the extra course of antibiotics that Dr. Childs recommended (which he described as helpful but "not off-the-charts helpful") and then stopped seeking further treatment because both he and Dr. Childs believed that they had done all they could do. At the time of our interview, Dan still "felt" his palsy (for example, he could not "spit or smoke a cigar properly"), but he took comfort in knowing that the only people who noticed were those who knew him really well.

Although Dan, unlike many patients I spoke with, did not experience symptoms that significantly disrupted the quality of his life, he wanted me to know that he considered his experience *exceptional*. He confessed,

> On balance, I feel very lucky: I was diagnosed within four days of first presenting. I'm not going to say that never happens, but going to venture to say that that rarely happens. The point is I got help right away, and I didn't have any long lingering issues with it.

At the same time, even though I recruited him at a patient-organized Lyme fundraiser (the first one he had ever attended), Dan was quick to clarify that he had ambivalent feelings about forums like patient support groups. He explained,

I should say, this isn't nice, but it is what it is: I don't care to be around people who are complainers. And Lyme disease is very tricky because it can persist for a long time. That's very real, and I accept that. It can make someone who is a really huge whiner or someone who's not into a whiner. I can't stand it. I want to be clear about the fact that I'm not saying that people with Lyme disease aren't sick, I'm not saying that. I just don't like the emotional baggage that goes with it.

Instead of turning to the support of other Lyme patients or to Lyme disease advocacy, Dan had devoted himself to fitness. Admitting that his experience with Lyme disease made him feel more "vulnerable," he had begun competing in Olympic distance triathlons and felt healthier than he had ever been.

Suffering

The degree to which Lyme patients perceive themselves to suffer is wide ranging. Some patients, like Dan, perceive their suffering to have been minimal. Others, like Madison, would describe their suffering as incapacitating. It is clear, however, that suffering—and an awareness of what suffering *means* in the context of Lyme disease—is a common thread among Lyme patients. Moreover, how Lyme patients' suffering is perceived by the mainstream community is a critical component of the way in which Lyme disease, as a contested illness, is experienced. When, over the course of my research, I would ask mainstream physicians about chronic Lyme disease patients, they would often tell me, "There's no doubt that these people are suffering; they're just not suffering from Lyme disease."[8] More importantly, as I was told on multiple occasions, "no one dies from Lyme." One of the most-cited publications during my conversations with mainstream physicians and scientists was a then recently published study by the CDC that reviewed several hundred death certificates that listed Lyme disease as the cause of death and found only one to be consistent with Lyme disease.[9] Reference to this article or to the fact that Lyme disease is rarely fatal was often followed by the argument (made in this case by a neurologist) that "in developing countries, where there are real problems, people don't have time to have things like chronic Lyme disease."

The tendency to qualify suffering—and to assign it legitimacy accordingly—is commonplace. Likewise, survival is often talked about in terms of death's immanence rather than in terms of quality of life. Whether in popular or academic discourse, suffering and survival are rarely explored within the context of affluence. And often for good reason: those with more resources have better access to the means that reduce suffering and increase survival, and systemic structural inequalities exacerbate suffering and make survival more difficult. But what happens when we expand the metrics by which we measure suffering and survival?

An important clue might be found in an article by Didier Fassin inspired by philosopher Jacques Derrida's last interview, in which Derrida describes survival as "not simply what remains" but also "the most intense life possible" (2010, 82). For Fassin, this is a welcome move away from the binary distinction between "bare life" and "qualified life" to an understanding in which survival is both "the 'unconditional affirmation' of life and the pleasure of living" and "the hope of 'surviving' through the traces left for the living" (83). This approach also enacts a more ecumenical understanding of suffering because it does not measure life in relation to others but according to one's individual potential for pleasure and intensity. For example, rather than crudely equate Madison's suffering with that of others, I suggest that suffering be understood on its own terms, as a quality measured against "the most intense life possible" of each individual person. Building on an understanding of survival that recognizes the inextricability of one's physical and existential body, as well as how a life is lived (not just that it is lived), how does a qualitative shift from mortality (end of life) to morbidity (compromised life) change the way we think about survival? And how, in the case of Lyme disease, does situating survival within a context of affluence change the way we think about suffering in the absence of health?

First and foremost, a shift from mortality to morbidity means that the face of suffering looks different. Individuals with chronic Lyme disease, in company with those who suffer from other contested illnesses, often suffer the fate of "not looking sick enough." Take, for example, when I participated in a panel discussion on the documentary film Under Our Skin. After showing segments of the film, the moderator began to ask questions about the veracity of the illness experiences of the characters featured in the documentary. A fellow panelist and physician answered that one of the characters could not be suffering because she was smiling. "Patients in pain don't smile like that," he said. This observation raises important questions: What does a person in pain look like, and how is that pain best communicated?

Perhaps not surprisingly, the answers to these questions are elusive. As Elaine Scarry suggests, this is because the experiences of the "person in pain" and the person who bears witness to that pain are fundamentally "incommensurate" (1985, 4, 60). She continues, "For the person in pain, so incontestably and unnegotiably present is it that 'having pain' may come to be thought of as the most vibrant example of what it is to 'have certainty'" (4). However, for the person who bears witness to that pain, pain "exist[s] as the primary model of what it is 'to have doubt'" (4).[10] Necessarily linked with the experience of pain and discomfort, then, is the "social suffering" of being doubted by others—a critical feature of the divided experience of contested illness (A. Kleinman, Das, and Lock 1997). As one member of a support group meeting so succinctly explained, "I couldn't have understood if I didn't have it!" That the pain of patients who identify with chronic Lyme disease is compounded by the experience of being doubted is not unique. As Arthur Kleinman observes, "If there is a single experience shared by virtually all chronic pain patients it is that at some point those around them—chiefly practitioners, but also at times family members—come to question the authenticity of the patient's experience of pain" (1988, 57). Following Scarry and Kleinman, then, "being doubted" is an experience shared by all who suffer from pain, but it is particularly true for those who suffer from chronic illness and even more so for those (and especially women) who suffer from or identify with *contested* chronic illness.[11]

Scholars who have written about other contested illnesses provide ample examples of this. Anthropologist Norma C. Ware (1992), in her research on chronic fatigue syndrome, argues that one of the most salient experiences of individuals who suffer from CFS is that of "delegitimation." Drawing from interviews with fifty individuals who identified with CFS, Ware suggests that patients experience delegitimation in two primary ways. The first is that patients' symptoms are trivialized because they are perceived to be insignificant; the second is that their illness is categorized as psychosomatic, or "all in [their] head[s]" (350). In their work on multiple chemical sensitivity (MCS), sociologists Stephen Kroll-Smith and Hugh Floyd also highlight how the physical suffering of patients with contested chronic illnesses is compounded by social suffering in their exploration of the efforts of the "chemically reactive" who must "persuade some members of their interpersonal worlds to accept MCS as a legitimate, albeit strange, disease" (1997, 65).

The Lyme patients I interviewed and spent time with described social experiences similar to those of CFS and MCS. One woman described the challenge of not being believed by her family:

My family still didn't totally get it—that I had Lyme disease and that that was like a legitimate illness. And I was trying some really out-there treatments that they had a hard time with. My mother had this friend who kept telling her that she was enabling me by not charging me rent when I was still living at the family house, and my mother fell prey to that kind of influence.

In the same vein, another woman reflected, "Part of the healing is to have someone tell you you're not crazy. It's hard because even your family doesn't believe you." And still another declared, "I don't want anything for nothing. I want someone to recognize that I'm sick and to believe me." At the root of why even members of Lyme patients' families sometimes doubt Lyme patients' suffering is the dissonance between "looking fine" and "feeling terrible." For example, one patient recalled how her doctor said, "I think you're a good actor, because you look a lot better than you describe." She continued, "You should have seen me in November and December—I just wanted to cry. I couldn't get dressed. I couldn't take a shower every day. I've got to do something, and I figure that I have nothing to lose." Another patient explained, "You look normal, so people don't know what's wrong with you. Everybody looks normal. The healthy person that sees you, they don't know what your problem is; they don't try to understand. Even my parents aren't open minded." While another patient, a postal worker, explained,

> Like people said at the support group, people say, "Those people look like they're fine! They don't really look like they're sick; they don't look drawn and haggard." I just want to turn away and want to cry. I do have my pains and my issues, too. It's very depressing.

Because not being believed by intimates, strangers, and doctors is such a central feature of the chronic Lyme experience, commonly shared responses include (1) rhetorical attempts at legitimacy through comparison to cancer and AIDS (two diseases perceived to be universally legitimate) and (2) self-doubt. For example, in the case of illness comparison, one woman at a support group meeting gave the example of her good friend who had been diagnosed with breast cancer. She explained,

> When my friend was diagnosed, she got hooked in with Sloan Kettering, a wonderful place in that they support the whole person. There wasn't anyone that wasn't supportive. . . . No one questioned whether she should be on treatment; no one said that it wasn't cancer. Talbots does a fashion show for cancer and makes money for cancer. What do we have

in Lyme land that helps us with that? It's far more complicated than a terminal illness. How do we live our lives despite the fact that we don't feel well?

Another woman echoed this thought when she said, "Lyme is a tough illness. There is no easy answer about anything. People say, 'You look fine by me.' And I respond to them, 'Do you diagnose cancer by how you look?'"

Still, efforts at persuading others that their illness is legitimate are not mutually exclusive with doubt, and being doubted by others can lead some to self-doubt. While many of the patients I spoke with or observed at support group meetings or in the examination room of physicians' offices described feeling confident in their diagnosis in the face of differing opinions, others expressed having had moments of uncertainty about whether what they were experiencing was Lyme. For example, one woman, who at one point thought she might have fibromyalgia instead of Lyme disease, explained to other members of her support group meeting that "the best gifts were the herxes because fibromyalgia doesn't have a herx. Doubt can be a problem. But change your belief system, and you'll change your feelings." Another woman looked to the perceived clarity that objective evidence can provide when she asked, "Do you ever doubt it yourself? Absolutely. That's why tests are good." Against the assumptions of some mainstream physicians who explained to me that chronic Lyme patients are wedded to Lyme disease and unwilling to consider other diagnoses, many patients I spoke with said that they did not care *what* illness they had, they just wanted to *feel* better. As one member of a patient support group meeting exclaimed,

> I'd be more than happy if it's not Lyme and you can fix me, great. I'm more than happy to be wrong, as long as you can tell me what it is and that it's not in my head. Or that I like attention. Trust me, there are better things I can do with my time.

As I explore in the section on survival, the perceived solution to the doubt *and* self-doubt that many Lyme patients experience can often be found in the everyday and ritualized practices of complementary and alternative medicine.

Gender, Sex, and Lyme

In the *New Yorker*'s 2018 Summer Fiction issue, journalist Lidija Haas reviews *Sick*, a much-anticipated memoir by novelist Porochista Khakpour about living with Lyme disease, and asks, "Is Lyme disease a feminist issue?" (Haas

2018). It's a striking question because, as Haas notes, there is little that is obvious about the relationship between Lyme disease and women. As some of the Lyme patients I spent time with were quick to remind me, "Lyme doesn't discriminate." Like other contested illnesses, however, a salient feature of the chronic Lyme experience is that it is perceived by Lyme patients, Lyme-literate physicians, and mainstream physicians alike to be more common among women. (Because chronic Lyme disease is not epidemiologically surveilled, one can only make assumptions about its demographic distribution.) Lyme disease is also, in part, a story about women because it was put on the map by two Connecticut "housewives" who, after observing unusual symptoms in their community, plied the medical establishment with questions until they were taken seriously. As one of these women, Polly Murray, wrote in her memoir,

> I may have been one of the first to start asking questions back in the mid-1970s, but since then I've been joined by a chorus of voices from the field, most of them belonging to women. . . . And these women have tremendous power, for they are often driven by a primal instinct to protect their young. (1996, 292)

Since Murray's early advocacy work, most of the leaders in the Lyme advocacy world continue to be women.

Like Murray's gendered explanation for why Lyme advocates are primarily women, gendered explanations for why chronic Lyme disease might be more common among women abound. For example, Mary, the Lyme patient and support group leader who had spent much of the past decade seeking care for her two daughters who had also been diagnosed with Lyme disease by a Lyme-literate physician, explained that because doctors are more likely to believe men's complaints, men are treated more quickly for Lyme disease and have fewer complications. She had come to this conclusion after observing her husband's experience with Lyme disease. She explained,

> Men are a pain in the neck. They don't like to admit [they're sick], and my husband was getting really, really sick and got nasty. . . . Men complain a lot. They do complain a lot, but they don't do anything about it. If they do get into a doctor, I think they get more attention paid to them, but they won't go. I mean, still now, he's relapsed and needs to go. He's starting to get really stupid again.

Tina, a member of another support group whose meetings I attended, expressed a similar sentiment that men are louder complainers and less tolerant of discomfort, traits that are also perceived to lead to quicker treatment. She reasoned,

> Men do not seem to suffer the way that women do. Women do seem to get it more. I've seen plenty of men with chronic Lyme disease over the years. They're not immune to it. It may be that women are proactive about it and not willing to suffer through it. And men complain a lot sooner, and are listened to, and get faster treatment up front.

Following Mary and Tina's line of logic, women, who are understood to be accustomed to sacrificing sleep and well-being to nurture their children and their careers, refrain from complaining about the same symptoms that, in men, would be addressed sooner and more quickly by physicians. And when women do see a physician for their symptoms, Mary and Tina reason, their symptoms are not taken seriously. In a similar vein, several women described how it took multiple appointments to be diagnosed with Lyme disease because, according to them, physicians assumed that their symptoms were a function of being "depressed," or "a busy Fairfield County mom," or "a mom that stays home with her kids and needed to find something worthy." One mainstream physician I spoke with came to the conclusion that a couple of his patients (whose reasons for their visits were "suspected Lyme disease") did fit the profile of a "busy, sleep-deprived mom" more than they did a Lyme patient.

Like patients themselves, many mainstream physicians I spoke with provided gendered rationales for sex differences in chronic Lyme disease. For them, however, the fact that more women appear to have chronic Lyme disease—when acute Lyme disease affects men and women in equal numbers—substantiates the fact that chronic Lyme disease does not have a biological basis.[12] As two physicians reasoned in an article that appeared in the *Journal of Women's Health*,

> If chronic Lyme disease is directly related to ongoing infection with B. *burgdorferi*, one might expect that the proportion of men and women who have this diagnosis would be similar to the proportions among persons diagnosed with Lyme disease in the general population, as well as among those with post–Lyme disease syndrome. On the other hand, if there is a substantial difference in the gender of patients with chronic Lyme disease, it is additional evidence that this disease is unrelated to infection with B. *burgdorferi*. (Wormser and Shapiro 2009, 832)

Like these physicians, some mainstream physicians postulate that because the proportion of men and women who have chronic Lyme disease does not match the proportion of men and women who have *acute* Lyme disease, chronic Lyme disease must be "unrelated to infection with B. *burgdorferi*." For them, it seems more likely that what is diagnosed as chronic Lyme disease is actually fibromyalgia, CFS, or depression, disorders without a clear biological basis that also happen to be more prevalent among women. As one mainstream physician suggested at a grand rounds presentation, "The majority of these women are just depressed." In a similar vein, another mainstream physician explained,

> The other argument that I've heard that seems to feed the conception that it's all in their head, that these people are just depressed, that these should be grouped under medically unexplained symptoms, is that, well, when you look at it you see the gross percentage of them are women, and women tend to be more depressed. And when they're depressed, they actually, they somaticize their depression and so, of course, this would confirm our hypothesis anyway.

Because mainstream physicians contend that chronic Lyme disease does not have a biological basis and, as a result, is not correlated with sex differences, chronic Lyme disease's unexplained nature can sometimes be explained by unflattering stereotypes: women perseverate on negative details, have overly anxious personalities, are more easily frightened, or crave attention, all of which are consistent with the "age-old charge that women psychosomaticize their distress" (M. Murphy 2006, 152) and with "a long history of nonorganic 'women's diseases,'" such as hysteria and neurasthenia, "that have been named, diagnosed, and treated by masculinist medical science" and that have been perceived to be particularly common among affluent women (Greenhalgh 2001, 318). For example, in a section of a pamphlet published by the Feminist Press in 1973 titled "The 'Sick' Women of the Upper Class," feminist authors Barbara Ehrenreich and Deirdre English describe how a "cult" of "female invalidism," which started in the mid-nineteenth century and lasted through the late 1910s, created a space in which "it was acceptable, even fashionable, to retire to bed with 'sick headaches,' 'nerves,' and a host of other mysterious ailments" (17–18). These persistent stereotypes also continue to circulate within the mainstream medical literature, most notably in a satirical 1991 opinion letter to the *Annals of Internal Medicine*, "From the Centers of Fatigue Control (CFC) Weekly Report: Epidemiologic Notes and Reports," in which the author writes that, unlike Lyme disease, the "attack rates" of "Lime disease" are "highest in adults of upper middle to upper socio-economic class, with a female-to-male sex ratio of approximately 3:1" (Lettau 1991, 602). This letter was later followed by a 2005 commentary in which the authors, in response to a study that concluded that "ongoing infection has not been excluded," caution, "We hope that misinterpretation of their report will not exacerbate the anxiety and misattribution that are probably at the root of much of the PLDS/CLD [post–Lyme disease syndrome/chronic Lyme disease] predominantly limited to females in the North-east" (Sigal and Hassett 2005, 1346).

As these examples demonstrate, long-held gender stereotypes about women's "neurological weaknesses" and "hysterical tendencies" are often used to "make sense" of chronic Lyme disease. However, as Tina observed, the perception of "being unwomanly" can equally delegitimize women's illness experiences: "I'm always getting into trouble with my big mouth. We like big mouths, but we get labeled as pushy, bitch, and demanding. When a man is like that, he's taking charge." One physician I spoke with pointed to the broader dynamics of gender relations as a factor that contributes to the chronic Lyme disease phenomenon. He observed that in affluent areas, men often marry younger "trophy wives" only to find that they cannot keep pace with them. He exclaimed, "A sixty-year-old executive can't keep up with a thirty-year-old babe!" As a result, he continued, these men psychologically corner their wives into playing the "sick role" of chronic Lyme disease to attain a better fit. Irrespective of whether they construct women as *agents of* or *victims to* their own suffering, however, the shared effect of gendered rationales is the delegitimization of the biological reality of chronic Lyme disease.

In addition to attributing the perceived prevalence of chronic Lyme disease among women to gender, the reflections of these patients and physicians also highlight what anthropologist Susan Greenhalgh has described as the "asymmetrical character of the doctor-patient relationship" between women and male physicians (2001, 307). Because of this asymmetrical character, Greenhalgh argues, women patients often enact "self-silencing, other-centered routines of femininity" of being "compliant" and "pleasant," but they also have the power to reject them (308). In the case of Lyme disease, only eleven of the fifty-six physicians I interviewed were women. Yet, as feminist author Maya Dusenbery suggests, "gender bias in medicine runs much deeper than the gender of its practitioners"; that is, "it is largely unconscious and systemic, and women doctors are not immune to it" (2018, 11).

In this way, Lyme patients' experiences with their predominantly male physicians also reflect the broader institutionalization of gender bias in medicine, the effects of which exceed the impact that physicians' gender has on patient care. As Dusenbery observes, what little research there is "paints a fairly consistent picture: women are often not taken as seriously as their male counterparts when they enter the medical system" (4). For example, she continues, "women wait sixty-five minutes to men's forty-nine before getting treatment for abdominal pain in the emergency room," "young women are seven times more likely be sent home from the hospital in the middle of having a heart attack," and "women experience longer diagnostic delays in comparison to men for nearly everything, from brain tumors to rare genetic disorders" (4). Similarly, a 2012 review of the medical literature on gender disparities in health care concludes that "despite the fact that women are more proactive in the use of preventive care, disparities between men and women exist in the diagnosis and treatment options that are recommended to them" (Kent, Patel, and Varela 2012, 555). Together, these observations point to a reality in which "women's accounts of their symptoms are too often not believed" (Dusenbery 2018, 11), a reality that is particularly pertinent to chronic Lyme patients, who often present with a range of symptoms in the absence of clinical signs.[13]

Given mainstream physicians' claim that chronic Lyme disease does not have a biological basis, it is not surprising that narratives to explain its prevalence are often cast in terms of gender. But in light of Lyme patients' quest for medical legibility through the recognition of the biological basis of their suffering, it is striking that very few of the patients, advocates, and Lyme-literate physicians I interviewed offered a sex-based explanation.[14] For example, Lyme-literate physicians' retorts to the idea that women were more likely to have chronic Lyme disease were often couched in gendered terms, even if they also entertained the idea that there might be a biologically based difference. During my interview with a Lyme-literate psychologist who also happens to be a woman, she exclaimed,

> It's more common in women than men? That's just disgusting. Women are more willing to recognize it than men. Men aren't willing to go to the doctor. It's a biased sample. Women are more willing to acknowledge that they're struggling, more likely to be multitasking, more likely to run into trouble. Women are much more comfortable with their feelings. All you have to do is be in a relationship to see this. Much of this relates to how we're socialized. It's also the brain. There are studies that show that there are differences between male and female brains.

Another Lyme-literate physician reflected,

> Being a woman, more women come to me. In response to the idea that more women have Lyme disease: that's very sexist. Women tend to have fatigue, but men also have fatigue. Connecticut housewives do tend to be more needy, but you can discern those kind. In general, women are more expressive; women need to be loved a lot. We are nurturers. I think Lyme affects and aggravates autoimmunity more than other infectious diseases.

Although both practitioners briefly considered the possibility of sex-based differences (e.g., differences between male and female brains and a predisposition toward autoimmunity in women), their primary emphasis—like that of Lyme patients—was on gender. The question, then, is why? In addition to the fact that attention to sex-based differences might be perceived to distract from the broader goal of gaining recognition for the persistence of bacteria within the bodies of *all* chronic Lyme patients, another compelling answer is the historical impact of the movement within social scientific and feminist scholarship to work toward social equality in the face of biological difference. Initiated in the 1970s and 1980s as an important corrective to early scientific discourses that justified social inequality through biological determinism, meaningful sex differences across fields of inquiry were bracketed in favor of analytical attention to gender. As anthropologists Margaret Lock and Judith Farquhar observe,

> To account for the many empirical variations in the social practice of gender, . . . it was useful for mainstream social scientists to hold sex constant—usually seeing it as biological and consequently unproblematic—while focusing on the social fields in which variable gender roles—men, women, homosexuals, etc.—were determined. (2007, 383)

As a result, anthropologist Elizabeth F. S. Roberts suggests, "the sex/gender distinction prevented the conflation of biology with social, psychological, and cultural attributes, countering the biological determinism that equated women with their reproductive and domestic capacities" (2016, 111; see also Herrmann and Stewart 1994; Rubin 1975; Vogel 1995).

The sex/gender binary has been vigorously theorized and critiqued in subsequent years, and the continued salience of this framing is particularly notable within academic and popular understandings of infectious disease. For example, infectious disease prevalence and severity are often correlated with geography, demography, and social behaviors, but they have rarely been correlated with sex. And as I previously mentioned, the Lyme patients I spent time with affirmed the perception of infectious disease's democratic nature by telling me on several occasions that "Lyme doesn't discriminate." For Lyme patients and Lyme-literate practitioners alike, the imperative to emphasize equality in the context of biological difference often seemed to exceed the impulse to claim biological legitimacy through the perceived sex differences at the root of chronic Lyme disease.

That Lyme patients and Lyme-literate practitioners at the time of my research often refrained from drawing on sex differences to make claims to biological legitimacy is notable, particularly in the context of recent scholarship by Melissa Creary, who, in her work on sickle-cell disease in Brazil, argues that, through what she calls "biocultural citizenship," patients draw on "cultural ties" and "biology thought to be inherited directly from Africa" to "gain access to fuller citizenship" (2018, 124). However, the implications of these claims for social justice remain to be seen. In Steven Epstein's work on "inclusion and difference" within biomedical research, he worries about the possibility that "'calling attention to [difference] in order to ameliorate inequality has the unintended effect of perpetuating social divisions one wishes to eliminate'" (2007a, 296). That is, Epstein suggests that biologically based claims to inclusion through what he terms "biomulticulturalism" run the risk of "re-essentializing" biological difference and ignoring the broader structural causes of health inequalities (278).[15] Bridging these two scholars, medical anthropologist Duana Fullwiley anticipates the exclusionary and emancipatory possibilities of increasing attention to biological difference when she argues that, within genetic science, "the new synthesis" (the blending of "old [racial] concepts" with "new attitudes") "holds the possibility of reinvigorating racism, while simultaneously possessing the potential to promote antiracist science education, disease awareness, and social justice efforts" (2014, 803).

And yet, while many Lyme patients and Lyme-literate practitioners at the time of my research resisted the possibility of Lyme's sex-based differences, feminist scholars and biomedical scientists were beginning to pay more attention to sex-based biology. For feminist scholars, the shift from "social constructionism" (in which gender is understood to be a flexible social construction, and sex is understood to be a fixed biological constant) to "constructionism" ("where the material world or what has been framed as nature is also understood as contingent") has been accompanied by an interest in "new materialism" (E. Roberts 2016, 115).[16] Also referred to as the "biological turn," new materialism is characterized by an attention to the "entanglement, a non-separability, of biology with/in sociality" (N. Davis 2009, 76) and the "processes and activities" whereby the "ongoing mutual shaping of the biological and the social" produces "encultured biological organisms" and "biocultural creatures" (Frost 2014, 322–23). This approach is exemplified by the work of feminist biologist Anne Fausto-Sterling, who, through the example of bone development, suggests that the body is "simultaneously composed of genes, hormones, cells, and organs—all of which influence health and behavior—and of culture and history," the result of which is that we are "always 100 percent nature and 100 percent nurture" (2005, 1495, 1510). Like feminist scholars, biomedical scientists have also become increasingly interested in sex-based biology, particularly in the context of infectious disease (even if, as Fausto-Sterling observes, much biomedical research "seems strictly to deal with *sex* in the 1970s feminist meaning of the word" and there remains "a lot of confusion about the terms *sex* and *gender*" [1497–98]). In the feature article of the Spring 2011 issue of *Johns Hopkins Public Health*, "Science of the Sexes: Why Hasn't Infectious Disease Research Reflected Fundamental Differences in Women and Men?," Maryalice Yakutchik describes the work of scientist Sabra Klein, which demonstrates that women mount a stronger immune response to the flu than men. As Klein explains, "[Women] don't just feel worse. They don't just visit doctors more or complain more. They literally experience worse disease than males" (Yakutchik 2011, 25).

Klein's work is one of a series of tectonic shifts in the field of sex-based biology, which includes, among others, the founding of an academic society called the Organization for the Study of Sex Differences, the formation of centers for the study of sex-based biology, and calls for the reevaluation of the dosage of viral vaccines administered to women. At the time of my research, some Lyme-literate physicians, whose approach is tied to the biological reality of chronic Lyme disease, had also taken an interest in Klein's work and were hopeful that future clinical studies might shed light on the relevance of sex differences in the disease they treat. As a researcher who collaborates with a Lyme physician concluded in the article above, "These are people who were told by their physicians that they are just depressed. . . . Well, if they weren't depressed before the rash, then there's got to be more to it. That can't be the end of the story" (Yakutchik 2011, 29).

But as is often the case with Lyme disease, it is unclear whether further scientific inquiry will resolve uncertainty or sow the seeds of more uncertainty. Although one study conducted by scientists who position themselves between Lyme's two camps found "evidence for sex-based differences" in "the magnitude of ELISA and IgG serologic response to early Lyme disease" (Schwarzwalder et al. 2010, 310), and another study by some of the same scientists found "clear sex-based differences in initial and later CCL19 reactivity [immunological response] to early Lyme disease" (Rebman et al. 2014, S1), a study conducted by mainstream scientists concluded that "males and females with culture-confirmed early Lyme disease had similar clinical features, rates of seropositivity, and long-term outcomes" (Weitzner, Visintainer, and Wormser 2016, 493). Either way, it is clear that there is growing attention to the relationship between Lyme disease and sex-based differences among Lyme advocates and Lyme-literate practitioners. For example, on January 6, 2020, a Lyme advocacy organization published a blog post, "Lyme Disease Prevalence: Does Sex Matter?," that included a video presentation by a Lyme-literate physician to explain "how males and females with Lyme disease might differ" and announced the "launch" of a study on this topic using data from the organization's patient registry.[17]

Furthermore, from an analytic perspective, the field of sex differences and disease invites a social scientific engagement that simultaneously takes into account sex *and* disease. As Annemarie Mol observes, while it "may seem that 'studying perspectives' [of disease] is a way of finally attending to 'disease itself,' . . . the body's physical reality is still left out," and "the disease *recedes* behind the interpretations" (2002, 11–12). As a corrective, Mol calls for an ethnography of ontology that, in "foregrounding practicalities, materialities, *events*," attends to the ways in which disease is "done" (12–13). Taking its cue from Mol and the new materialists, social scientific attention to sex and disease would require that we move beyond Judith Butler's (1993) intervention of examining the *materialization* of the body through the performative enactment of linguistic signification to the materiality of the body *in interactive practice*.[18] Where Butler asks, "How is sex materialized?," an attention to sex and disease pushes us to ask, "How does materiality enact sex?" If, as the *Biology of Sex Differences Journal* observes on its website, "the function of cells and organs depends on their sex, determined by the interplay among the genome and biological and social environments," then sex is neither located in the predetermined status of genitals, chromosomes, and hormones, nor merely in linguistic formation, but, as philosopher of science Georges Canguilhem observes, in the continuous and contingent *interaction* of the nonbinary materiality of the "living" with the social and historical "signals" and "excitations" of its "milieu" ([1965] 2008, 111).[19] What dimensions does the relationship between sex and gender gain or lose when sex is understood to be produced by the interactive materiality of the living within a particular "time and space" (E. Roberts 2016, 120)? And, as knowledge about the implications of sex differences in Lyme disease continues to cross the porous boundary between laboratory and life, how will it inform the way in which individuals understand sex and gender in the context of disease, and which emancipatory and/or exclusionary experiences and ideas will it enable or foreclose?

Hints of answers to these questions can be found in the way that some physicians I interviewed were already entertaining the simultaneity of sex and gender in their approach to Lyme disease. For example, one Lyme-literate physician spoke at some length about the relationship between sex and gender in Lyme disease. She explained,

> If it means anything, I would say—and I'd be kind of guessing—but I would say for every male Lyme disease patient I used to see in my office, I would see four or five females. So there's definitely a good ratio of four or five to one. There are definitely a lot more women.

And as for why this is true, she explained,

> I think, well, gee, it's probably multifactorial. I think a lot of women are so busy that they may not be paying attention to a tick bite or a rash or some vague symptoms. And so it may take them longer to get to the doctor only because we know that women tend to multitask a lot more than men. From a pure biological standpoint, I think that men may actually feel—as much as they say you can't feel the ticks and you can't feel them bite because they have the local anesthetic in their saliva and da, da, da—I think the hair, the extra hairiness of men may be protective. Or there may be some type of pheromone that's not attracting the ticks to a male as opposed to a female. We know it's the CO_2—I don't know if there's a difference in CO_2 content between men and women. But anyway, so that's that.

She continued,

> And then another biological aspect is that hormones and estrogen play a big role in symptomatology. The reason I say that is that little girls who are diagnosed with Lyme and treated before puberty tend to be cured, for all intents and purposes. But if they have Lyme disease, and they're not completely treated, and they've already entered puberty, and they start with all their cycles, it's a lot more difficult to treat them afterward.

So there's got to be some link with estrogen and progesterone. And I think, just speaking frankly, a woman going to a male physician, many times the male physician doesn't take the woman's symptoms seriously. I mean look at what happens with heart attacks and chest pain. And that's because women tend to have atypical symptoms when it comes to heart disease. I mean they're not going to have the typical angina-type symptoms that a man would have. So that's why they have a higher mortality rate, too, because it takes them so much longer to get attention. So I think that's part of it with the Lyme.

Another physician echoed these thoughts when he exclaimed,

It comes down to gender differences and immune responses! It's the perfect storm: there's something biological happening in which women are developing a different immune response to infectious disease and are prone to bad outcomes. It's the way that they're wired that predisposes them to feel this way. And then, socioculturally, society tells them they're goofy and makes them neurotic because the system treats them like garbage. That's not the cause; that's the result.

In their observations, these two physicians gesture to the processual, interactive, and mutually constituted possibilities of sex and gender in the formation of Lyme patients' illness experiences; together with the ethnographic insights of these patients and physicians, they also reveal how the sex/gender binary is practically and discursively disrupted *and* reinforced in everyday life.

Renee, "From Practitioner to Patient"

Renee, a mental health practitioner, asked to be interviewed at her office in the northeastern United States, where our interview was scheduled between appointments.[20] In contrast to the brightly lit waiting room, her office was quiet and still, the shades slightly drawn. Well-tended plants, framed photos, and decorative objects lined the periphery of her office, and the bookshelves were stacked with medical texts. It was in this space, Renee noted, long before her own experience with Lyme disease, that her patients would often mention their struggles with Lyme disease, and Renee would chalk it up to a psychological condition. After her own experience with Lyme disease, however, she described having a strong sense of when someone had Lyme disease and would preemptively mention it to them or recommend that they see a doctor. She explained,

I didn't believe in chronic Lyme actually. I was very dismissive of people who had a lot of the memory and the cognitive stuff. But I've actually diagnosed a few people with chronic Lyme's based on symptoms they've said to me which don't completely add up or that don't make sense.[21]

Interestingly enough, memory loss was not one of the symptoms that Renee experienced. Her symptoms began with numbness and tingling, first in one foot and then in all of her extremities. She also began to have regular headaches, five to six per week. Although the headaches were a new symptom, she had experienced numbness and tingling three years before in 2005. She had initially consulted a neurologist, who, after a battery of tests, diagnosed her with a seafood poisoning called ciguatera. But in 2008, the tingling and numbness had returned, accompanied by headaches. She again returned to the neurologist, who decided, this time, to test her for Lyme disease. She explained,

> He called me back and said, "It's very strange. You have Lyme disease, but it is acute." Basically, I had IgM bands but not IgG bands. So he said that he was going to treat me with three weeks of doxycycline anyway because I hadn't yet been treated with antibiotics.

Renee began, but was unable to complete, the antibiotic regimen that her neurologist prescribed for her. Her reaction to the medication was severe. She vomited, suffered "the worst headaches" she had ever experienced, and was unable to get out of bed. In addition, Renee reflected, "I didn't know what my illness was so it made it sort of impossible to function day to day." Renee had a sense that her reaction to the medication was something more than not being able to tolerate it, but she did not know what that "something more" might be. It was only after one of her patients overheard her describing her symptoms to another colleague that she describes having insight into what she was experiencing: a Herxheimer reaction. She explained,

> My colleague said, "You're having Herxheimer reactions." And I said, "What's that?" And she said, "It's when you have Lyme. You take the antibiotics; you don't just get better right away. You get these reactions," which, you know, is a good thing in a way. So, I went online, I looked it up, and it seemed like I had a lot of those symptoms.

Renee continued to describe these Herxheimer-like reactions to her neurologist and her internist, but "no one knew what was going on." Although Renee felt that what she was experiencing sounded similar to what one might experience with Lyme disease, she was unsure if what she had was Lyme, or "Lyme plus something else," or just something else entirely.

As Renee described getting "sicker and sicker," with symptoms including dizziness, extreme fatigue, and disrupted sleep, she underwent more testing. One test revealed that she had small fiber neuropathy; a repeat MRI showed the same "five to six hyper-intensities" that an MRI in 2005 had revealed. Her spinal tap was clear. Propelled by the urgency of her diminishing health, Renee sought the advice of an infectious disease specialist and a neurologist who specializes in neuropathies. Both doctors, neither of whom described themselves as "Lyme literate," confirmed that her symptoms might be related to Lyme disease. According to Renee, the infectious disease doctor said, "You have Lyme disease. It's a clinical diagnosis. The blood tests, you know, are not always accurate. I'm going to repeat the blood tests and send them to a different lab, but in the meantime, you've got to stay on the antibiotics." And according to Renee, the neurologist said, "Well, it could be Lyme-related neuropathy. It could be something else, but you should stay on the antibiotics, and it will get better, and then we'll know it's Lyme disease." It was only at this point, with the combined weight of these two doctors' opinions, that Renee was convinced that she had Lyme disease (even though her internist was adamant that she did not); it was also at this point, having struggled with poor health for nine months, that she sought the help of a Lyme-literate physician whom people she knew had recommended.

Renee was aware of other Lyme-literate physicians, but she liked that the Lyme-literate physician she chose was an internist who did not just see Lyme patients. She explained, "I wanted someone who was sort of more like a regular doctor but who knew a lot about Lyme, so that's why I went to see him." She also appreciated that his practice seemed efficient and organized. And unlike her experience with her neurologist, she was comforted by the fact that, when she described her symptoms, the Lyme-literate physician confirmed that they fit a coherent clinical picture. Finally, and perhaps most importantly, Renee liked that he had a "plan" for her, that he was able to offer her a protocol of action.

Renee's new plan began with another round of doxycycline, which, this time, she handled much better. She responded so well that she was discharged from the practice after two months of treatment. Unfortunately, her neuropathy returned two months later, and this time, her doctor recommended intravenous antibiotics. She took the gravity of an intervention like intravenous antibiotics seriously. She again consulted with the neurologist who specializes in neuropathies and with another Lyme-literate physician. This time, the neurologist thought that Lyme might no longer be the cause of her symptoms, since she had been on a dose of antibiotics that far exceeded standard recommendations; the Lyme-literate physician thought otherwise. He supported the recommendation that she begin intravenous antibiotics. Renee was happy that she followed this recommendation because, according to her, IV antibiotics finally made her feel better. After three months of IV treatment, Renee's energy had returned, her headaches had gone away, and she was no longer having interrupted sleep.

Renee has a slim frame and an energetic step. Like many Lyme patients I spoke with, she described herself as someone who never got sick and was very active. "I've always been a very fit person," she said. "And up until I got sick, I was running regularly. I was going to the gym. I was playing tennis. I was, you know, very outdoors." Her illness was particularly hard on her two young children. "I was spending days in bed and they'd never, ever seen that before," she explained. "I couldn't do, I mean the entire household schedule was like in disarray because I wasn't functioning, and I was canceling patients the day of because some days I just couldn't get into work." Compounding the frustration of not feeling well—and the "chaos" her illness was creating in her home and work life—was the challenge of navigating her doctors' competing opinions. She explained, "There was just a lot of bad mouthing of each other to me. Everyone had such strong opinions, so when you were in the middle of it, it was just hard. You didn't know which way to turn because people were coming out with very, very strongly held beliefs." When she sought the opinion of a second neurologist, who happened to be a Lyme-literate physician, her primary care physician exclaimed, "He's a quack! I don't like that you're seeing him!" Having been a practitioner who questioned the veracity of her patients' Lyme stories, Renee also found it difficult to experience not being taken seriously. She described the experience of a doctor who diminished what she was feeling by telling her that Lyme was not going to kill her and that her condition was not a matter of great urgency. She explained, "I mean, the neurologist told me to calm down and that I'm getting myself all worked up and maybe, you know, that I should take some Ativan. He said I'm just sounding hysterical to him. He said, 'You're not dying. You know, we'll figure this out. Calm down.'"

In the end, Renee considered herself lucky. Although she still experienced neuropathy and fibromyalgia-like pain and did not consider herself to be the healthy person that she once was, she also understood her symptoms to be residual and not persistent Lyme. She explained, "You know, I guess I'm lucky that I responded to antibiotics because some people don't respond to antibiotics, or they have a lot of residual symptoms, or they really have major, ongoing pain meds. And I don't I fall into that category." While at one point, Renee was consumed by thoughts of Lyme disease, she no longer liked to talk about it. "You know," she reflected, as the interview wrapped up, "I've really kind of avoided the whole subject. Some part of me thinks if I dwell on it, I'll get sick again. I just have this feeling that I really should not talk about it too much."

Dylan, "Lyme Rage"

Dylan and his family live in Connecticut. Their house is wrapped in a cocoon of trees and brush, a landscape so green that it blocks out all sunlight and seems to hold the house in a perpetual dusk. When I knocked on the door at midday, I wondered whether anyone was home. When Dylan's mother opened the door to invite me inside, it was almost as quiet and dark inside the house as it had been outside. In the kitchen, where our interview took place, Dylan and his mother sat side by side, both facing me. His mother was tensely upright; Dylan, in his late twenties, sat slightly slouched in his chair with the brim of his baseball cap pulled low to his brow. They rarely looked at or talked to each other during our interview, but the painful intimacy of what they had shared was an invisible tether between them. As our interview progressed, it became clear that Dylan's mother, who responded to as many of my questions as Dylan did, was present not only as a memory aid but also to help Dylan in the event that he became upset. An hour into our conversation, Dylan and his mother confided in me that only recently was Dylan well enough to participate in an interview. Not long before, his rage had been so imminent and his temper so unpredictable that probing questions would have set him off like a detonated land mine.

Discussing Dylan's violent behavior was difficult for both Dylan and his mother. At one point, Dylan's mother turned to Dylan and said, "You know I love you," before describing a violent incident that had occurred at home. They also took turns finishing each other's sentences when the other paused or hesitated to describe Dylan's behavior. Both Dylan and his mother explained how, most days, they tried not to think about Dylan's violent past, the trauma of it too painful to think about too long. But sometimes it was unavoidable. Dylan's mother explained how, during the years of Dylan's Lyme rage, she developed a habit of covering the holes that Dylan made in the wall with wall hangings and paintings. Recently, she decided to reorganize the paintings and, in doing so, revealed the damage that Dylan had made during his Lyme rages. Where the sight of the damage alone would have sent Dylan into a spiral of rage two years ago, he was now able to make a joke about it. She explained one instance in which she had come home to find Dylan struggling with his laptop, which seemed to be broken. He told her that it was not working, and she responded that she was going to set down the groceries to come help him. Something about what she said "set him off," and according to his mother, Dylan proceeded to "tear the entire house apart." Dylan's violent outbursts also included taking doors off cars and breaking doors and windows. Neither Dylan nor any of his family members suffered injuries from Dylan's outbursts, but both his sister and the family dog came very close to getting hurt. And Dylan, unable to remember anything about the episodes once they were over, would be so exhausted from them that it would take him days to recover.

In the world of chronic Lyme disease, two phrases capture some of the experiences most common to Lyme patients. One is "Lyme brain," which refers to the memory loss, inability to concentrate, and cognitive difficulty that many Lyme patients describe experiencing. The other, which is often spoken about less openly, is "Lyme rage." As it is described by those who experience it, Lyme rage is a heightened state of anger and irritability, often characterized by violence. Because many Lyme patients are aware that the mainstream community often perceives their symptoms to be psychiatric, they are often hesitant to fully embrace the perceived psychiatric features of Lyme disease.

Dylan's experience with Lyme rage began in January 2001, when he had a serious snowboarding accident. Both Dylan and his mother remembered this date because it was "the year of 9/11." Dylan was knocked unconscious and suffered a concussion, a broken jaw, and a dislocated shoulder. After a significant recovery period, he was able to return to college, and aside from the shoulder, which he was planning to have surgery on in the summer, all seemed to have returned to normal—until April, when he went on a fishing trip with one of his friends. He returned from the fishing trip with severe flu-like symptoms. He went to the hospital and was told that he was dehydrated; the next day, feeling worse, he returned to the hospital and was given a spinal tap, which, according to his mother, did not go well. He proceeded to get migraines that, according to Dylan, incapacitated him to such an extent that his school suggested he finish the semester from home. Dylan returned to school in the fall, still experiencing migraines.

His family and friends also started noticing changes in his behavior, including labile affect and severe "ups and downs." His mother described how he was "really happy one minute and very angry the next minute." Some days, she would receive as many as "fifteen to twenty" calls from him in one hour. "You just had to agree with him, you know?" his mother said. Dylan's unpredictable behavior continued through the end of the school year and into the next. Prior to this, Dylan had not only been what his mother described as even-tempered and happy but also very active. A former athlete, Dylan was also a volunteer at a local community organization, something he signed up for as soon as he graduated from high school. He described having a robust social life.

Dylan remained at school through the following year. When he came home for the holidays, he confided in his parents that he was unable to shake his depression and that he "hated his life." Dylan's family and doctors continued to assume that his migraines, behavior changes, and depression were caused by "organic brain damage" from his snowboarding accident. He was prescribed antidepressants for his depression and antianxiety medication for his anger. Following the logic of organic brain injury, his family switched him to the care of a neurologist who also happened to be recognized as Lyme literate, although Lyme disease was not yet on Dylan's family's radar screen. Everything came to a head, however, in January 2003 when a fellow student hit Dylan's car at school. Having had continuing behavioral problems, unable to find the right dose of antidepressants, and in increasing pain (Dylan described his pain as one that hurt his bones), this incident seemed to be the last straw. Dylan called his mother and told her that he had had enough. He hung up the phone and proceeded to drive his car into a snowplow. Persuaded not to arrest him at the scene of the crash, the police took him to the same hospital where he had initially sought treatment when he had returned home ill from his fishing trip. His parents and neurologist, who met him at the hospital, were discussing the prospect of having Dylan committed to a psychiatric hospital when the emergency physician who had first treated Dylan asked, "What are you going to do about his Lyme disease?"

Dylan's neurologist and parents were soon shocked to discover that the spinal tap performed two years previously had been positive for Lyme disease but that this information had not been communicated to them by Dylan's pediatrician.[22] Dylan was sedated with powerful medication and brought back to a hospital near his parents' home, where he began a long and winding road of Lyme disease treatment. In addition to receiving the intravenous antibiotic Rocephin, he also underwent a range of tests, including a SPECT scan and a neurological work-up. According to Dylan's mother, "The frontal lobe was basically 95 percent gone. The auditory processing was gone. So we had a lot of work to do." Once Dylan returned home, he was on Rocephin for another six months before he had an anaphylactic reaction and had to discontinue it. He slept so much, sometimes twenty hours a day, that his mother described putting a finger under his nose to make sure he was still breathing. After Dylan's anaphylactic reaction to the Rocephin, his neurologist experimented with other antibiotics, none of which seemed to work as well. According to Dylan's mother, the doxycycline made him more depressed, and the other antibiotic combinations seemed to have no effect at all. It was at this point that his neurologist began treating him with an intravenous infusion of immunoglobulin (IVIG) to "build up his immune system."[23] These infusions were time consuming and, initially, required Dylan to go to the neurologist's office three times a week for up to five hours a day.

Very slowly, and over stretches of time marked by setbacks (the most significant one being a life-threatening pulmonary embolism caused by the IVIG infusions), Dylan and his family began to notice a positive response to the pharmacopeia of medications with which Dylan was being treated. He became less angry, less irritable, and his cognition improved. For example, he could again spell well enough that he could play Scrabble with his grandmother. Most importantly, Dylan's violence "disappeared." According to Dylan's mother, a repeat SPECT scan confirmed that "his frontal lobe had returned." But like many Lyme patients, Dylan's story had become about more than just Lyme disease. Further tests ordered by his neurologist and performed by a conventional laboratory revealed that he had positive antibodies for *Bartonella* and *Babesia*, two other controversial tick-borne pathogens discussed in chapter 1. Another test performed by his general practitioner was interpreted to mean that Dylan's adrenal glands were no longer working properly, so he began a regimen of steroids to help with his energy level. And still another test was positive for a subset of antibodies correlated with systemic lupus erythematosus (an autoimmune disorder), so Dylan was prescribed Plaquenil to alleviate associated symptoms.

As Dylan's health improved, he began to reach out to others for support, including a Lyme-literate psychiatrist. He briefly joined a support group for young adults suffering from Lyme disease. And, most importantly, according to Dylan, he began to volunteer again, which he described as his "biggest medication." At the time of my interview with Dylan in 2010, nine years after he had returned from his fishing trip with flu-like symptoms, and seven years after his treatment for Lyme disease had begun, he was still on an impressive list of medications: strong pain medication delivered every forty-eight hours through a patch, Plaquenil for his lupus, and occasional rounds of antibiotics when symptoms interpreted as relapses of Lyme, bartonellosis, and babesiosis emerged. His mother wondered out loud during our interview whether it was time to try to wean him off some of his medications, but she and Dylan both agreed that the prospect of "upsetting the apple cart" made them nervous.

Like other patients I spoke with, Dylan's family is one in which multiple members have had Lyme disease. Unlike Dylan, however, Dylan's mother, father, and sister all responded quickly to standard antibiotic treatment. Dylan's story is also a revealing mirror up to discussions that take place across the standard-of-care divide over the risks of intravenous antibiotic treatment. Among mainstream physicians, the use of intravenous antibiotics is one of the most common examples given to highlight the dangers of treatment for chronic Lyme disease. Even many Lyme-literate physicians are not willing to take on the risks of intravenous treatment, which include pulmonary embolisms, low platelets, and opportunistic infections like C. difficile, and prefer to treat chronic Lyme disease with a combination of oral antibiotics. The use of intravenous antibiotics is further complicated by the fact that most insurance companies in Connecticut will not cover intravenous antibiotic treatment unless is it prescribed by a cardiologist, neurologist, or rheumatologist. Most Lyme-literate physicians, however, are primary care physicians, most likely because primary care is the first place that patients with perplexing nonspecific symptoms end up. And because Lyme-literate physicians are often primary care physicians, the path to getting a prescription for intravenous antibiotic treatment—and having its cost paid for by the patient's insurance company—can be one with many hurdles. Even so, when faced with what is understood to be the choice between the risks of IV antibiotics and the risk of continuing to feel unwell, many Lyme patients choose the risk that is understood to offer them the possibility of getting better.

At interview's end, Dylan told me that he believed he would never fully recover. He and his mother both worried that he had suffered irreversible brain damage from his untreated Lyme disease. However, he was also quick to acknowledge that his health was "night and day" compared to what it had been. While he continued to daydream about pursuing a career, he was, for the moment, content to volunteer and was fulfilled by the positive impact that his presence seemed to have.

"It's All in Your Head"

Renee's and Dylan's stories nicely highlight one of the primary differences between the suffering of those who identify with chronic Lyme disease and the suffering associated with other contested chronic illnesses: the tension between the perception of being "crazy" and the understanding that Lyme disease has psychiatric manifestations. While mainstream Lyme physicians recognize that untreated Lyme disease can, in rare cases, lead to central nervous system involvement and manifest in "memory and cognitive difficulty," they do not recognize that Lyme disease has psychiatric manifestations (Halperin, Baker, and Wormser 2013). For example, in "Common Misconceptions about Lyme Disease," the authors describe how, despite case reports of Lyme patients developing a "range of psychiatric disorders," "no epidemiologic study has ever demonstrated a statistically meaningful association," and "no biologically plausible mechanism for such an association has ever been proposed" (Halperin, Baker, and Wormser 2013, 264.e5).

On the other hand, many mainstream physicians and scientists *do* believe that patients who identify with chronic Lyme disease often have psychiatric disorders that are not related to Lyme disease. During my conversations with and observations of mainstream physicians and scientists, the topic of mental health as it relates to Lyme disease was often expressed in two different ways: the first is the perception that patients who claim to have chronic Lyme disease are actually somaticizing depression and anxiety; the second is the perception that many Lyme disease patients are irrational, unstable, and potentially dangerous.[24] For example, one mainstream physician I spoke with described Lyme disease as "a socially acceptable definition for psychosomatic illness." During an observation of a Lyme-literate physician's practice, the physician showed me a physician's letter given to him by one of his patients, in which the physician, writing to a referring physician, concludes after the patient's physical exam that the patient has "waxing and waning, self-controlled Bell's palsy on right side of face," that "this woman has a somatization disorder or another psychogenic illness," and that "she probably needs some counseling regarding her obsession with this disease." It was also not uncommon for mainstream physicians and scientists I spoke with to use the phrases "Lyme crazies" or "Lyme loonies" when describing Lyme disease patients.[25] One scientist used the phrase "when wackos come to Rome" to describe the phenomenon of Lyme disease support groups. And several physicians and scientists mentioned fearing for their personal safety, often referring to the well-known story of a prominent mainstream Lyme physician who reported receiving death threats from patients.

On the other side of the standard-of-care divide, however, Lyme-literate physicians claim that Lyme disease can be an infection "in the brain" that has clearly defined psychiatric features. One Lyme-literate psychiatrist I interviewed, Dr. Lang, described the nature of the disagreement over Lyme's psychiatric features:

> A lot of the literature says it doesn't exist. But in this literature, there are overgeneralizations, data is taken out of context, and people make outrageous statements. Dr. Fisher [a well-known mainstream physician] has said that there is no evidence that Lyme is associated with psychiatric illness. I have 240 journal articles that show an association. One from the Czech Republic that went into a mental hospital and compared to healthy patients. It was a well-controlled study of hundreds of people. That's compelling. But there are still people that say this isn't Lyme; this is psychiatric!

A Lyme-literate neuropsychologist agreed. During our interview, this practitioner exclaimed, "These are kids who are sick, who have an infectious disease process that is affecting their brain!" He continued, "The children I see typically have a lot of emotional problems, but it's totally related to Lyme. These are together kids that have a physical illness that has just devastated them."[26] He described how, in his experience, Lyme disease affects his patients' "memory and processing speed"; he said that it also causes "rages, anxiety, depression, and OCD, any one of which could cause oppositional defiant behavior disorder," in addition to having a "huge overlap" with attention deficit disorder.

Another Lyme-literate neuropsychologist I interviewed described how she differentiates between Lyme rage and psychosis: "The person with a rage reaction becomes quite apologetic for what has occurred. This is not true of someone who is psychotic." Because this subtle distinction is easily overlooked, and because Lyme rage is not generally recognized by mainstream physicians, Dr. Lang described how there is resistance among Lyme patients to openly talking about the psychiatric side of Lyme disease. He explained, "When I say that it can make people homicidal and suicidal, I get resistance from the Lyme community because they don't want to be mislabeled." And he admits that part of the problem is that because some patients *are* "encephalopathic," "it makes us look bad and crazy."

For these Lyme-literate practitioners and for Lyme patients who experience the myriad psychiatric symptoms mentioned above, the psychological effects that they associate with Lyme disease are of the body and not of the mind, a line that is easily blurred and, for them, easily misrecognized by mainstream physicians and society at large. More critically, although Lyme-literate practitioners and Lyme patients disrupt the long-standing biomedical distinction between body and mind by disentangling psychiatric symptoms from the mind and anchoring them *within* the body, it is important to note how, in their claims to the biological legitimacy of Lyme's psychiatric symptoms as a function of the body, Lyme-literate practitioners and Lyme patients also *reproduce* this distinction. Although as early as 1928, physician William Osler predicted that "in the medicine of the future, the interdependence of mind and body will be more fully recognized within biomedicine," in the case of chronic Lyme disease and other contested illnesses, the idea of a "divided body"—a body set apart from its mind—persists (Kirmayer 1988, 59).

As this brief discussion makes clear, psychiatric conditions are important to both mainstream and Lyme-literate understandings of Lyme patients' suffering, but for most mainstream physicians, psychiatric features are a reality *despite* Lyme disease, and for most Lyme-literate practitioners and patients, psychiatric features are often a reality *because of* Lyme disease. In linking the topic of suffering with experiences related to the practical and discursive distinctions between sex/gender and body/mind, I have explored how, beyond the range of physical suffering that Lyme patients experience, living Lyme's "divided body" is also about not being believed and the experience of "being sick in the wrong way." And like other contested illnesses, the experience of being sick in the wrong way with Lyme disease is further complicated by the sociohistorical binaries of sex/gender and body/ mind that are both deconstructed and reproduced in patients' quests for biological legitimacy.

Barbara, "Nervous Conditions"

I met Barbara at her home in Connecticut, a big but not ostentatious house nestled in verdantly green woods and with enough distance between the next house that it gave the impression of seclusion. Barbara opened her front door, and I stepped across its threshold from a humming, sun-filled porch to a quiet, still, and sparsely decorated foyer; half-packed boxes signaled a home in transition. With her shoulders arched slightly forward and one hand holding her cardigan together, Barbara led me to her living room, where we sat on a floral-patterned couch surrounded by photos of her family and her three daughters. Her face was pale, made paler by the highlighted bangs that framed it, and her cinched lips and taut skin gave her the appearance of being at once aged and youthful. Unlike other interviews, ours unfolded slowly and tentatively, as Barbara, soft spoken and quick to avert her eyes, established her narrative's rhythm.

Barbara's story began eleven years prior to our interview with a summer flu and sore throat that did not get better. When it got to the point of being unbearable, she went to her primary care physician, who prescribed her antibiotics. The antibiotics made her feel "really sick and achy with vomiting and diarrhea." But then she got better and remained better for a year, until she started to experience a range of what she described as neurological symptoms, including panic attacks, anxiety, depression, insomnia, and tingling on her head. She again returned to the doctor, who this time prescribed her antidepressants. She recalled, "But I got home, and I thought about it, and I said, 'Nothing in my life has changed. Something is wrong with me.'" Barbara spoke to her neighbor who "had been sick with Lyme for ten years," and her neighbor told her that "all her symptoms were Lyme." It was a conversation that changed her life. On the recommendation of her neighbor, Barbara sought out "Lyme-literate treatment." Under the care of two successive Lyme-literate practitioners, she took oral antibiotics for two years, which intermittently upset her stomach and also exacerbated her symptoms through what she was told was a "Herxheimer reaction."

In 2002, Barbara transferred to a third Lyme-literate physician, who, after hearing Barbara's history, immediately put her on nine months of intravenous antibiotics. Unlike her previous antibiotic treatments, these antibiotics made her feel "99.9 percent better," until 2003 when she had to discontinue them because of a "clogged line." Since 2003, and having never again felt as good as she did then, Barbara had been on a combination of oral antibiotics. In 2006, she transferred to a fourth Lyme-literate physician whose approach she described as similar to her previous physician except that "he uses natural protocols, so that's kind of nice to get away from antibiotics." Recently, however, because of financial difficulties and facilitated by her current physician's expanded toolbox of medical modalities, she had switched to an herbal regimen known as the Cowden Protocol. Used by Lyme patients who prefer "more natural methods," by those with fewer financial resources, or by those who can no longer tolerate antibiotics, the Cowden Protocol was developed by an allopathic physician to treat chronic Lyme disease and includes fourteen herbal tinctures that are taken in a highly regulated manner for no less than two months but often for as long as four to six months. Barbara explained, "My husband's in construction, and work is slow. We pay our own health insurance, and when we go to the Lyme doctors, you have to pay out of pocket. And then we have a high deductible, so my daughter and I are just doing herbal stuff right now."

Like many Lyme patients I spoke with, Barbara felt better when she was on antibiotics; for example, she was able to sleep through the night, had fewer panic attacks, and experienced reduced joint pain. But the relief was neither permanent nor sustainable, and her symptoms began to return when she stopped taking them. After eleven years of treatment, Barbara continued to be plagued by disabling panic attacks. During our interview, she described a recent one that was so severe that she had to pull over at a gas station on her drive home. Her anxiety and her susceptibility to fatigue also made it impossible for her to work. She explained,

> I am very sensitive to stress, like if I would try to work a job, the stress of just working the job, I would come home all achy. I haven't worked since I got sick, and I need to work, and I want to work, and it's frustrating because I don't know if I will ever be able to work. Like sitting at a desk all day, you think that you are just sitting there not doing anything, but just the stress, just wipes your whole body out.

As bad as her own struggle had been, however, she said that it did not match the suffering of watching her daughters struggle with Lyme disease. Like many patients I interviewed, Lyme disease had, for Barbara, become a family affair.[27] Within a couple years of beginning treatment for her own illness, Barbara's daughters began developing symptoms that ranged from brain fog to fatigue to intermittent fevers. Her eldest daughter had been the sickest and had recently transferred to a local community college from a state university so that she could live at home. Although her daughter felt better than she had the year before, both she and Barbara worried how the stress of college would continue to affect her, since, in the past, it had taken such a toll that "she has to just stop because she feels like she is going to die, like her body can't go on anymore."

Together, Barbara and her daughter were an important source of support for each other. But aware that she was a stereotype of what many mainstream physicians envision when they refer to chronic Lyme patients (female, anxious, depressed, with no history of having had objective signs of Lyme disease and with repeated negative serology), Barbara not only felt misunderstood but was also fearful that she and her daughter would never be cured. For the moment, she was just looking forward to moving out of her "too big" house that she no longer had the energy to care for.

Survival

Having fleshed out the multidimensionality of the suffering that chronic Lyme patients experience, I now, following Barbara's story, turn to the question of survival. As one of the patients previously quoted asked, "How do we live our lives despite the fact that we don't feel well?" For many patients, support groups provide an answer to that question by offering antidotes to the social suffering that many of them experience: support, companionship, understanding, validation, information, and identity, among others. For example, one monthly meeting I observed was founded by two women, Reba and Lydia, both of whom had had experiences with chronic Lyme disease. The meetings were typically attended by ten to fourteen people, but sometimes as few as four or five. Most of the members were women. All the meetings began with a round of introductions, with members taking turns to introduce themselves to the group and to provide updates on the progress of their health. At the second meeting I attended, the group members became involved in a discussion about the experience of being perceived as "crazy." One man exclaimed, "That doctor told me I'm crazy!" Another woman chimed in, "Because I cried a lot, my doctor said that I was manipulative and trying to get attention." In response to this discussion, Lydia reassured them,

> We know everything that people are feeling. You're not hypochondriacs; you're not making it up. We know that everything you say is true. Don't let them think you're crazy, because you're not. We've been to a lot of these meetings, and I don't think we've ever met someone that is crazy, that hasn't been sincere in their symptoms. You can be depressed, but it doesn't mean that you're crazy. It can be a reaction to being so sick, but it can also be an effect of the organism in your brain that generates anxiety, depression, and psychosis. It can also affect your neurotransmitters. Or there really is a neurotransmitter imbalance because your body really is trying to fight something off.

The validation and comfort that these words provided were palpable. Members looked around and smiled at each other; one woman confided at the end of the meeting, "I knew the tone of this meeting was going to be different!" Several patients I spoke with in other forums credited Lyme disease support groups with having saved their lives. As one patient exclaimed, "I went from victim to survivor to thriver!"

When it comes to surviving the *physical* suffering that many patients experience, one common theme was eloquently captured by a patient when she explained, "It all comes down to mindfully living with your pain. Resistance is what makes you suffer. You have to turn your ghosts into ancestors." But what does it mean to turn your ghosts into ancestors? For this patient, it meant that the challenge for many Lyme patients is to recognize that one's illness, pain, or discomfort is part of oneself but not all of oneself, that Lyme disease is part of who you are but does not define you. One Lyme advocate echoed this thought when she said, "Unfortunately, [Lyme] has defined our lives in a lot of ways. I have always said to our children, we are not Lyme disease, and Lyme is not us. I've really tried hard." Another support group member explained, "I try not to blame everything on Lyme, to say that everything's Lyme. When I first got this, I believed everything my doc said. But now I see that it's not just Lyme, but all aspects."

Closely linked to the challenge of turning one's ghosts into ancestors—or reconciling oneself with the reality of Lyme disease but not becoming consumed by it—is the imperative to "know your body" and its limits. One advocate explained, "My children know their bodies really well. They're so in tune with their bodies. Sometimes they will nap for two days if they think they need it. Where they lack in social exposure, they have inner strength and character." Another patient echoed this thought when she said,

> You have an illness. You're in pain sometimes. Take some time to rest. I'm going to sit for the day, and that's OK. Give yourself permission and stop fighting. I taught my kids to listen to their bodies. In fact, my nine-year-old said the other day, "I'm going to listen to my body. Can I watch some TV?" We're programmed to power through, but we need to rest.

Following historian Barbara Duden (1991), to "have" a body is a thoroughly historical phenomenon, to "know" a body, as these patients' observations reveal, is still another. To know a body requires that those who "have" a body become students *and* clinicians of that body—that they learn about their bodies and then act on that knowledge of their bodies.

As students of their bodies, many Lyme patients have a strong interest in learning everything they can about Lyme disease, to become, as one patient put it, "their own advocates." Their sources of knowledge are wide ranging. Many read books (*Cure Unknown* [P. Weintraub 2008] is the most cited), medical articles, and internet sites; they ask questions at support group meetings and of one another about which remedies have worked and which ones have not worked.[28] As one patient I interviewed explained, "I Google a lot. I read a lot in the *Lancet* and go online to read some articles. Germany has produced some really great articles." Another patient described himself as "the kind of person that doesn't like to give an answer without knowing all the information." He continued, "I'm very research based. You don't make a decision based on what you think. You look at numbers, raw numbers."[29] Because the experience of Lyme disease, for many patients, also includes tick-borne co-infections *and* the requirement that they be able to distinguish Lyme disease from other disorders that are perceived to manifest in similar ways, many patients also have a distinct working knowledge of Lyme's "overlapping" disorders.

Over the course of my research, I was continually struck by the attention that many Lyme patients give to the *details* of Lyme disease. For example, support group meetings sometimes feature presentations by Lyme-literate practitioners. One particular meeting featured a Lyme-literate physician who, in his twenty-year career of treating Lyme disease, described having treated twenty thousand patients.[30] The meeting was well attended, and the room was small. Within a half an hour, as the physician discussed the nuances of how he determines the doses of the antibiotics that he administers, the room had heated up to a temperature that would have invited an unintended nod from even the most alert listener. But the patients in attendance remained transfixed. Many were taking notes and asking engaged questions, following up on, for example, the biochemical difference between natural cat's claw (an herb) and TOA-free cat's claw (cat's claw stripped of the compound known as tetracyclic oxindole alkaloids) in the treatment of Lyme disease. This level of attention and involvement was also on display at conferences hosted by Lyme-literate organizations. Unlike conferences hosted by mainstream organizations, medical conferences hosted by Lyme-literate organizations are well attended by patients, some of whom, unable to sit up for the duration of presentations, use cots to recline in the auditorium aisles. In addition to attending conferences, many patients also keep meticulous records of their health, logging their symptoms and keeping track of which remedies they have tried and their responses to them. Lyme patients I spoke with described how their medical binders were not only a way to keep their physicians more informed but also a means to help their "Lyme brains" keep track of the complicated histories of their Lyme bodies. One of the Lyme advocates I interviewed explained how she used her medical record binder to help choose her doctors. She continued, "The doctors who weren't interested, I would walk away. The ones who wanted to read the book, I would keep."[31]

If being students of their own bodies leads many Lyme patients to be as informed as possible, being clinicians of their own bodies leads them to act on their knowledge. And in acting on their knowledge, many Lyme patients are drawn to the accessibility and everyday structure of complementary and alternative medicine (CAM).[32] Although the allopathic intervention of antibiotics is an important part of many Lyme disease patients' experience, the everyday practices of CAM are, for many, just as important. Of the thirty-four patients I formally interviewed, twenty-seven had tried some form of CAM therapy or had sought help from a CAM practitioner. From herbal tinctures and teas to nutritional supplements and hyperbaric oxygen chambers, many patients seamlessly integrate medical modalities that are often described as diametrically opposed. The reasons for using these therapies are myriad. Some believe that CAM therapies support immune systems that have been taxed by antibiotic use. Some no longer find (or never found) benefit from antibiotics and are looking for another solution. Others see medicine as only fully effective when multiple approaches are used simultaneously. And still others use CAM therapies only to discover that they do not work for them. Irrespective of what they thought of CAM before they got sick, almost all express a willingness to try anything to feel better.

The question remains: What is CAM? The National Institutes of Health (NIH) National Center on Complementary and Alternative Medicine, which was created in 1999, simply defines it as what it is not: "any group of diverse medical and health care systems, practices, and products that are not generally considered part of conventional medicine."[33] In the United States, these "diverse medical and health care systems" and "practices" are commonly understood to include chiropractic medicine, naturopathic medicine, Chinese herbal medicine and acupuncture, Ayurvedic medicine, homeopathy, herbalism, bodywork, mind-body medicine, "religious healing systems," and "folk medical systems" (Baer 2004, xviii).[34] Although these therapies are often perceived to be as different from one another as they are from biomedical therapies, they are also understood to be bound by a common episteme characterized by, among other features, "holism" (the practice of "treating the whole person—mind, body, and sprit—not just isolated physiological systems"), "vitalism" (the body's ability to "heal itself"), and the idea that disease is not merely the result of an invading organism but also the result of an internal bodily imbalance that can be diagnosed and explained through corresponding external symptoms (I. Coulter 2004, 112–13; Pizzorno 2008, 406; see also Micozzi 2001).[35]

Lyme patients are not unique in their engagement with CAM. In the United States, "alternative medical knowledge systems" have continued to "gain legitimacy" (A. Clarke et al. 2010, 15). While hypotheses to explain why patients in the United States appear increasingly interested in CAM are varied, my argument here is that, for many Lyme patients, the "habitus" of CAM's "gentle interventions" is an important part of their survival, of their "being able to live despite not feeling well."[36] This argument is informed by anthropologist Judith Farquhar's illuminating work on Chinese medicine. In "Eating Chinese Medicine," Farquhar coins the phrase "aesthetics of habitus" to argue that, beyond "symptom relief," the practice of medicine in China is itself a source of "empowerment" and "pleasure" (1994, 471). For many Lyme patients, the practiced ritual of using CAM therapies in the pursuit of better health meets a demand common to sufferers of many difficult-to-diagnose disorders, which is the desire to be able to do something about the way they feel. Throughout my research, I heard phrases to this effect again and again, phrases such as, "I just want to do something to feel better," or "That physician told me that there was nothing that he could do for me" (emphasis added).

In addition to making some patients feel better, CAM is also well suited to the chronicity and symptomatic ambiguity of chronic Lyme disease because, in its sheer inexhaustibility of options, it provides a limitless source of being able to do something. One text that nicely illustrates this is *Insights into Lyme Disease Treatment*. Published in 2009 and written by Connie Strasheim, *Insights* features chapters written by thirteen Lyme-literate providers who discuss their personal approaches to treating Lyme disease. The following is an excerpt from one practitioner's herbal protocol for Lyme disease:

> I have formulated an herbal blend remedy called Dr. Nicola's Lyme Formula. This product contains samento, teasel, smilax (sarsaparilla), guaiacum (an anti-spirochetal herb used in Europe but which is not very well known in the United States), and astragalus (which is used to boost

the immune system). . . . I also use Transfer Factor Multi-Immune from Researched Nutritionals as part of my protocol, which is an excellent formula. I may start my patients on this product, then add teasel root tincture to their regimen. I will usually do this prior to administering antibiotics, and depending upon the patients. (291–92)

Another practitioner describes a different approach to treating Lyme disease with herbs:

A typical protocol might involve patients taking the two or three herbs that they test best for energetically, and administering these on a rotational basis so that they only take one herb at a time. Typically, they would take the first microbial defense herb for twelve and a half days, then take thirty-six hours off, during which time they don't take any herbs. They would take the second microbial defense herb for twelve and a half days, and then take another thirty-six hours off before going back to the first herb again. They would then continue with that rotational protocol for several months. (152)

The remedies described in these short excerpts represent just a small portion of the myriad, ritualized, and time-intensive CAM remedies that are used for Lyme disease. Although they differ in content, they share commonalities in the specificity and intensity of their form. As one patient I interviewed reflected about his own use of CAM therapies, "I have found quite a bit of benefit from [the herbals]. Not that it [Lyme] goes away, but it helps me manage things. It walks me through my day."[37] More interesting still is the combination of approaches that patients use to tailor remedies to their own specific needs. One support group meeting that I observed provides a particularly good example of this. It was a small meeting, with only four people in attendance, but these members described in detail their daily engagement with CAM therapies and how these therapies were interwoven with other strategies to "walk them through their days." For example, one woman explained,

I've been reading a book called the *Lyme Disease Solution* by Singleton. Seventy-five percent of your immune system is in your stomach. Also, dandelion root stimulates bile production. Detoxing is important. I use milk thistle for my liver. It's important to know that eighty-five percent of the online stuff that you get is not accurate. I think we have to take it with a grain of salt. Olive oil and lemon is also good.

Another woman responded,

> I'm on Lymenet constantly. I've learned that they don't even have tests for half of the *Babesia* that's out there, so the test doesn't work for everyone. I use cat's claw, colloidal silver, and oregano oil. All of these modulate your immune system and reduce inflammation. But resveratrol raises CD57. It's supposed to help *Bartonella*. You know this bug can change into different forms, right? The question is: How do you kill the bug? Antibiotics and Rife. Some people don't think Rife kills the bugs. But when you feel a herx, you know you're killing a bug. There are some people that disagree with that as well. Some say that it's hurtful to the body, that you can push yourself too far.

And a third member shared,

> I use herbal antibiotic tea, salmon oil, and probiotics are huge. I also try to follow Dr. MacFadzean's diet. She wrote *The Lyme Diet*. You have to avoid dairy, sugar—it's a whole-food-based diet. It's a slow and steady progress. The body on this person is getting very worn out. I only have a slight herx with it. You have to approach lifestyle as part of healing.

Mirroring the elaborate prescriptions of the practitioners who treat them, the everyday health routines that these patients describe are complex, healing focused, and ritualized. And in detailing how these patients describe their experiences, I have highlighted how some Lyme patients' practiced use of CAM therapies constitutes a "lifestyle" that enacts "healing," a means to, as one support group leader explained, "build some structure into your day, down to the little things, like putting on your shoes." My argument diverges from Farquhar's argument, however, in that for Lyme patients, the key to the everyday mundane rituals of CAM remedies is less about the aesthetics of these therapies (that is, how they engage or excite the senses) and more about how, in contrast to conventional medicine, they offer the possibility of *healing* the body over and above the possibility of *curing* it. Within this framework, while a "cure" might eliminate a disease, it does not necessarily return a body to "good" health. Healing, in the understanding of those who use this term, offers the possibility of a return to "wholeness" and the alignment of the body, mind, *and* spirit. That being healed—irrespective of cure—is often Lyme patients' most desired outcome was reflected in an email exchange with a Lyme advocate who, eight years after my research ended, wrote: "[My daughters] both are doing well and living normal healthy lives. I like to say we are 'healed.' Every so often someone complains of being soo tired or having a headache that won't go away which causes me some anxiety but nothing that stops anyone from moving forward."

The cure/heal binary is a common trope in the field of CAM and one that is often criticized by mainstream physicians, but it is a real distinction for many of the Lyme patients I spoke with. As I discussed in chapter 2, Lyme patients often feel ambivalent about antibiotic use. While many perceive antibiotics to be the most viable option for a cure, they also perceive them to be "hard on the body," interventions that make the body "fragile." As one advocate asked, "Do you really think that these parents who feed their children organic milk and only spray their backyard for bugs when they must, really want their children to ingest antibiotics that are unacceptable to even them for months or years?" The answer for many is to combine the evil necessity of antibiotic use with the perceived healing properties of CAM to "rebuild" the immune system.

For example, one woman I interviewed described how she took a break from antibiotics for an entire year. "I went on a homeopathic protocol," she explained. She continued,

> I did a lot of detox, a lot of chelating therapy. My naturopath said to me, "Let's support your liver and get you on a healthy regimen. Let's reverse the things that antibiotics have done to you after all these years. We're still dealing with what the antibiotics were doing to you."

Another woman explained,

> Fortunately for me, because I've done naturopathic remedies, it's not as bad as some patients. I've taken supportive stuff, for the adrenals. The immune system is your ability to fight off diseases, bacterias [sic], all that. My immune system was really good for ten years, until I had the physical trauma, and my immune system went right down the tubes.

Still another patient described how antibiotics were her "last resort," and that the combination of CAM therapies she had researched would help her "get strong." But perhaps most illuminating was an insight from a woman at a patient support group meeting who explained, "What was helpful for me was worms and tea, a Lyme tea recipe from *Healing Lyme*. You need to reclaim responsibility for healing your life and *have knowledge of what strengthens you*" (emphasis added).

This last quotation nicely captures much of what I have tried to outline in this section on survival and the question of how to achieve "the most intense life possible," not at the edge of mortality but in the midst of everyday morbidity. For many Lyme patients, achieving the most intense life possible becomes a matter of first *knowing* the body and "what strengthens it" and then *acting* on that body through the practiced and healing regimens of CAM therapies.

Surfeit

On the way to a restaurant with a Lyme scientist, we took a short detour through the storied neighborhoods of a town in western Connecticut. As we drove past sprawling estates, each one ensconced in expertly manicured woods, the scientist described how, when he had recently hosted some foreign colleagues, he had given them a tour through these same neighborhoods to show them how "America's other half lives." There, in the heart of one of the wealthiest counties in the United States, the perception that Lyme disease affects America's most affluent citizens is one shared inside and outside the Lyme community. Lyme advocacy events, such as annual fundraising galas, are held at high-end hotels and feature auctions that offer expensive art and luxury travel packages. In 2013, a panel discussion featuring several Lyme-literate physicians was hosted at a Mercedes-Benz dealership. And, in 2013, the wife of a well-known fashion designer, whose family has publicly described their experience with chronic Lyme disease, began designing and selling handbags to support Lyme disease research. As I have already mentioned, Lyme disease is understood to primarily affect those "above" and "well above" the national poverty level. But this does not represent the full range of patients' experiences with Lyme disease, as the stories of the patients in this chapter attest to. Of the thirty-four patients I formally interviewed, thirteen were low to middle income, struggling to pay their medical bills and making difficult household decisions about whether to continue or discontinue treatment. Nevertheless, the *perception* that Lyme disease, and chronic Lyme disease in particular, is a disease of the wealthy is perhaps just as important as whether it actually is because it directly affects how those inside and outside the Lyme world perceive the experience of Lyme disease. In this brief section, I explore ideas about wealth and health as they relate to Lyme disease and the conditions of possibility for the emergence of these ideas.

Across the disciplines, from anthropology to public health to economics, much attention has been devoted to the deleterious health effects of poverty.[38] For example, a high-profile study showed that the stress of poverty requires so much cognitive "bandwidth" that it results in a "concurrent shortfall of other cognitive resources," or the effect of losing "~13 IQ points" (Mani et al. 2013, 980). In contrast, aside from the emergence of the colloquial term "affluenza," which refers to the "stress" and reckless behavior that result from having grown up "too privileged," little quantitative or qualitative data suggest that wealth can have negative biosocial impacts.[39] This is the case for disease prevalence and burden, since more resources translate to better preventive care and better access to higher quality health care (Pickett and Wilkinson 2015).[40] And it is especially true for environmental health, because, as decades of critical environmental justice scholarship has shown, "access to a healthy and clean environment is increasingly distributed by power, class, and race" (Pellow and Brulle 2005, 2).[41] As Pellow and Brulle observe, "Where one can afford to live has a major effect on the nature and extent of one's exposure to toxic pollutants" (2005, 2).

Resource inequality is no less consequential when it comes to Lyme disease, and individuals with fewer resources face greater diagnostic and treatment challenges. However, of particular interest here is how persistent ideas about the relationship between wealth and health also negatively affect perceptions about the biological legitimacy of the ill health of individuals with a *surfeit* of resources. For example, during my research, I was contacted by a reporter writing an article on Lyme disease who asked me by email,

> Do different populations (i.e., suburban vs. urban, wealthy vs. poor) have different attitudes about Lyme disease? It seems to me (and this could just be me) that the most concerned are affluent White suburban women, for their children and themselves. I've never heard such concerns expressed by inner city people in New Haven.

A mainstream physician-scientist I interviewed made a similar remark:

> Chronic Lyme disease is a disease of the entitled. People who are very busy and working hard and they have other problems don't have time to get sick with Lyme. It's a disease of the privileged. Another side of the story is that the suburbs have more deer and people that are living in sterile environment, their immune system is perhaps weaker. Perhaps they are more prone to allergies in general, more prone to illnesses.

For two mainstream scientists, both of whom had been born and raised in countries other than the United States, chronic Lyme disease was not an affliction unique to the affluent but to Americans in general who, relative to citizens of some other countries, are privileged whether or not they are affluent. "A lot of it is America," the first scientist said. He continued, "You don't see this in developing countries. You never see chronic fatigue, and when you do, it's only in the upper echelons. Individuals who struggle day to day, they don't have time for this crap." The other scientist exclaimed,

> Is it something uniquely American? Oh god, yes! I visited Sweden, twice. I remember vividly being in the office when a farmer came in. The farmer was dragging himself, because his knees were like this. Does a man like this go to the doctor for an EM? You have to be kidding. You do not have suburbia in Europe. Farmers tend to be tough and not readily induced to go to doctor. If Lyme were a disease of farmers, we wouldn't have this. Instead, it's a disease of suburbia. You're an anthropologist; you figure that out.

The perception that chronic Lyme disease is more common among the affluent (or among Americans more generally) appears to have two primary implications for mainstream physicians and scientists. The first is that, like gender, it provides a social explanation that delegitimizes the perceived biological reality of chronic Lyme disease. The second is that it provides a rationale for diminished compassion. It also highlights frustrations conveyed to me by some physicians about "problem patients." For these physicians, chronic Lyme disease patients are the quintessential problem patients because, as a function of their perceived privilege, they are also perceived to have a propensity for intentionally subverting physicians' authority and knowledge. For example, one mainstream physician confided, "Many times when you treat them from the inner city, they're grateful for helping you. When they're from places like Greenwich, you have people feel entitled, they don't accept what you have to say. Occasionally you have parents that are overbearing, and that becomes very unpleasant."

Like the mainstream physicians I spoke with, Lyme patients and Lyme-literate physicians also conveyed perceptions that chronic Lyme disease is more common among the affluent. But for them, that this is so does not diminish the biological reality of chronic Lyme disease but merely highlights the critical role that resources play in access to health care. As one advocate explained, "People think we're all histrionic suburban women. It's all true. Who's going to advocate for children more than moms? But if you think of this as a yuppie disease, it's not. It's just that we're more aware: we have more time on our hands and more education." A Lyme-literate physician echoed this distinction when he explained, "Lyme disease is the disease of the privileged. How many of the patients that you've met are landscapers? Arborists? You don't see them in doctors' offices as much. In a way, it's a disease of the people that can afford to get treatment." And still another reflected, "You can speak to families where, in less affluent areas, they talk about ticks. They'll say, 'We always have ticks. It's a way of life.' You accept it that way. The push to achieve academically is not there. There's a different acceptance of what you should tolerate."

In this statement and others, we see a troubling conflation between access to education and intelligence. For example, one Lyme-literate practitioner explained,

> Lyme disease is affecting the well-to-do. It hits them where they live in the suburbs. They're well educated, and they are doing less well than they were used to doing, but they're still higher functioning compared to the general population. You get used to smart people, and then everyday people start seeming like dolts.

The complicated history of how individuals understand the relationship between intelligence and class and how these understandings affect perceptions of low-income individuals, although relevant, is not a thread that I was able to follow during my research. I mention it, however, because, like some of the ideas about gender that I discuss above, I found it—and the veiled sentiments about race and ethnicity, captured by coded words like "inner city"—to be thorns in the side of the bodies of thought I encountered. Indeed, race and ethnicity are two of Lyme disease's specters. All thirty-four patients I formally interviewed were White, and in all of my interactions with patients at advocacy events, conferences, and physicians' practices, I cannot remember meeting a person of color.[42] Although the topic of race did not arise at these sites, a 2014 MDJunction.com public discussion on the topic of "Black People and Lyme" reveals an interesting discussion among eighteen forum members.[43] The first member begins the discussion with the question, "Hi everyone, I was just wondering is there anyone on here in mdjunction who is black and has lyme disease. If not do you know anyone who has been diagnosed with lyme disease that is black?" To which the next member responds, "I don't know anyone personally, but have heard of black people who were diagnosed with lyme. Why?"

The discussion that follows includes one member who observes that "rarely do you see" profiles featuring African Americans within Lyme groups on Facebook, another who wonders about a potential biological difference between Black and White bodies that makes White bodies more susceptible to Lyme, and others who hypothesize that perceived racial differences could be due to the fact that "caucasians spend more time than african-americans in the outdoors doing activities like hunting, fishing, hiking etc." or because it would be "different or harder to see [erythema migrans rashes] on darker skin." Of the four members who reveal that they are African American, one writes that she has Lyme despite not being an "outdoorsy type"; another writes that her son, who has been diagnosed with Lyme, "is the only one that I have know [sic] to have the disease, let alone on this level"; the third explains how "none of my relatives or peers really know much and most have asked 'do black people get Lyme?'"; while the fourth reflects, "I didn't think my race got it either. . . . In my personal opinion, our race wears a lot of lotions and don't do 'as many' outdoor activities."

Even though these types of conversations did not occur during my research, it is clear that the striking absence of people of color within online and in-person support forums is nevertheless a topic of intrigue in some corners of the Lyme world that coincides with a shared perception that Lyme disease is less common among African Americans. This perception is also consistent with a CDC study that analyzed 2002 data from the Nationally Notifiable Diseases Surveillance System and found that the incidence rate for Lyme disease among White Americans is "approximately 11 times greater" than it is for Black Americans (Adekoya 2005). The MDjunction .com discussion further reveals the salience of the perceived and experienced "whiteness" of outdoor recreation (a phenomenon, as explored in the previous chapter, that was historically produced by the intentional exclusion of Black Americans from outdoor spaces) and the idea that bodily differences (particularly skin tone) affect Lyme patients' visibility. This idea was similarly expressed when I observed a meeting of a scientific laboratory that provides images of Lyme rashes to the CDC, and the laboratory's members described the difficulty they have encountered in finding images of rashes on the skin of individuals of color. Together, these ideas form the tip of an iceberg whose submerged body holds a range of structural conditions of possibility for Lyme's racial disparities.

A prevailing assumption within the medical literature has been that Lyme's racial disparities can be "attributed to differences in risks of exposure, primarily due to area of residence" (Fix, Peña, and Strickland 2000, 756). The one study that explicitly examined Lyme's racial disparities, however, sampled a rural Lyme-endemic area in Maryland with a larger than national average representation of African American residents and found that, although there was a "diminution in the differences in incidence of

Lyme disease between Whites and African Americans in a rural area of endemicity," there were also discrepancies that could not be explained by area of residence risk alone (Fix, Peña, and Strickland 2000, 758). These authors proposed "difficulty in recognizing the rash [because of skin color]," "lack of awareness of the significance of the rash," "poor access to health care," and "bias of diagnosis by health providers who believe that Lyme disease is relatively rare in African Americans" as other possible causes (758). Furthermore, in the almost two decades since the Fix, Peña, and Strickland study was published, American suburbs have undergone substantial demographic changes, with minorities representing "at least 35 percent of the suburban population" in "36 of the 100 largest metropolitan areas" (Frey [2015] 2018, 159). This trend further complicates the assumption that Lyme's racial disparities are due to differences in area of residence risk alone.

What other explanations remain? Beyond acute Lyme disease, one can speculate that because most Lyme-literate physicians do not take insurance, and because long-term antibiotic treatment is often not covered by insurance, the prohibitive cost of being treated for chronic Lyme disease provides a significant financial barrier to identifying as a chronic Lyme patient or being diagnosed with chronic Lyme disease. Moreover, data on the impact of clinician bias on racial disparities in pain management—in addition to the impact of "medical racism" on clinical care more generally (D.-A. Davis 2019; see also Bridges 2011 and Rouse 2009)—support the idea that Lyme disease, whose clinical diagnosis often relies on patients' subjective reports of discomfort, might suffer the same fate (Hoffman et al. 2016; Singhal, Tien, and Hsia 2016).[44] Coupled with the assumption that "Lyme disease is relatively rare among African Americans," one can continue to speculate about the diagnostic failures that might occur when African Americans present with nonspecific symptoms in the absence of a rash that conforms to the "classic" bull's-eye rash typically seen on White bodies. As a result, it appears ever more likely that the invisibility of individuals of color within the Lyme landscape—in both the CDC's statistics and at chronic Lyme support groups—is due in large part to the enduring "structural violence" of, among others, reduced access to health care, insufficient information dissemination, and medical racism within the healthcare system (Galtung 1969; see also Farmer 2004).

Finally, a related question that was posed several times during my research was the extent to which migrant workers, whose occupations often expose them to tick-infested landscapes, contract and silently suffer from Lyme disease. In 2010, a Lyme advocate forwarded me an announcement about a "beautiful and (much needed) website" that had been created "in Spanish by a volunteer patient advocate" and wrote, "Don't forget the Hispanic Community—day laborers, landscaping, etc. . . . Very vulnerable group. If the rest of us get misdiagnosed and undertreated, I can't imagine trying to get help if you are illegal, don't speak English or go back to your home land not knowing you're sick." In an attempt to address this problem, this patient advocate had begun providing Lyme prevention information in Spanish and had distributed materials at a booth at a local "Hispanic health fair." Even celebrity and chronic Lyme disease spokeswoman Ally Hilfiger, in a 2016 *Women's Health* article about her memoir, *Bite Me: How Lyme Disease Stole My Childhood, Made Me Crazy, and Almost Killed Me*, notes, "The people who are more likely to be infected with Lyme disease are the migrant workers who spend most of their time outdoors" (Heiser 2016). One 2002 epidemiological study investigated whether individuals who work outdoors in Lyme-endemic areas are at increased risk for contracting Lyme disease and did not find "an increased risk of symptomatic, clinically confirmed Lyme disease" (Piacentino and Schwartz 2002, 82). In this study, however, the occupations under analysis, such as state and federal park rangers, were ones that more likely had greater access to Lyme prevention knowledge and practices but were also not occupations that migrant workers were likely to have.

Only two studies have focused specifically on Lyme risk among new— and often undocumented—immigrants in the United States. In the first study, which tested the efficacy of an educational tool in increasing Lyme disease awareness among eighty South American immigrants in Peekskill, New York, the majority of whom worked in landscaping and construction, the authors found that "none of the new immigrants were aware of Lyme disease"; they also observed that the ten diagnosed cases of EM at the authors' immigrant medical care facility during the summer months of the study's operation, in addition to the three hundred immigrants who sought care during the same months, "underlined the need for education in this population" (Jenks and Trapasso 2005, 158–59). Similarly, in the second study, which examined behaviors and attitudes related to Lyme disease among 103 Brazilian immigrants in Martha's Vineyard, the authors found that "while a small majority of the Brazilians surveyed on MV reported general knowledge of LD, few expressed confidence in their ability to recognize symptoms or understanding of the seriousness of LD" (Heller et al. 2010, 381). Moreover, because only 2 of the 103 participants reported having been diagnosed with Lyme disease, and because of Lyme's "cumulative presence of 10–30%" on Martha's Vineyard, the authors suggest that "this low self-report likely indicates a lack of diagnosis among Brazilian residents, a lack of understanding of the diagnosis or a reticence to admit having been diagnosed" (381–82). In light of these studies, and the broader global reality that factors such as "language/cultural barriers, access to health care, documentation status, and the political climate of the host country" produce "higher rates of adverse occupational exposures and working conditions" for migrant workers (Moyce and Schenker 2018, 351), what little "done science" there is suggests that Lyme disease among migrant workers is a significant problem that is severely underrecognized and underaddressed.

Within the social landscape of Lyme disease, these limited but still revealing observations highlight the expansive inequalities of race, ethnicity, and class that undergird access to and biases within health care, prevention education, exposure to the outdoors, and suburban development, which geographer Laura Pulido describes as "a form of white privilege" that "allowed whites to live in inexpensive, clean, residential environments" and which was "denied to most people of color" (2000, 16). By contrast, these inequalities also throw in relief the uniqueness of how individual and collective ideas about health and wealth simultaneously—and counterintuitively—underscore Lyme patients' experience at home, with friends, and in physicians' offices that their illness is not as legitimate as other illnesses and that their suffering is not as severe because they have more resources. In short, these ideas reveal that even those with a surfeit of resources, like all who suffer, often receive a shortfall of compassion.

To better understand this observation, it is helpful to review political theorist Hannah Arendt's ([1963] 2006) work on what sociologist Luc Boltanski calls the "politics of pity" and the "spectacle of suffering" (1999, 3). For Arendt, the politics of pity emerged during the French Revolution and hinges on "a distinction between those who suffer and those who do not" (3). In contrast to a "politics of justice," a politics of pity is anchored in the "observation of the unfortunate by those who do not share their suffering, who do not experience it directly and who, as such, may be regarded as fortunate or lucky people," hence, a spectacle of suffering (3). Important here is that for the observation of suffering by those who do not suffer to induce pity, this suffering must take place at a distance. As Boltanski, building on Arendt's work, argues, "It is inherent in a politics of pity to deal with suffering from the standpoint of distance since it must rely upon the massification of a collection of unfortunates who are not there in person" (12–13). Boltanski continues, "For when they come together in person to invade the space of those more fortunate than they and with the desire to mix with them, . . . they no longer appear as unfortunates and, as Hannah Arendt says, are transformed into '*les enragés*' [enraged ones]" (13). In this way, indifference to the experience of chronic Lyme disease patients can, in part, be explained by the fact that Lyme patients are neither distant nor perceived to be unfortunate, since, despite not feeling well, they are perceived to have the good fortune of resources.[45]

It is equally true that for those who suffer from a distance, a politics of pity usually proves impotent. There are many ethnographic examples of this, but few more provocatively capture pity's impotence than Didier Fassin's ethnography *When Bodies Remember: Experiences and Politics of AIDS in South Africa* (2007). In the introduction to this text, Fassin writes, "We are no more interested in the almost six million persons infected with HIV in South Africa than we are in the three million men, women, and children killed over the past decade in the African Great Lakes region" (xii). He continues, "We know that they exist because the press tells us so and television shows them to us, but we feel no need to know more" (xii). Compelled by the idea that "it is never superfluous to demonstrate interest in the Other," Fassin wrote *When Bodies Remember* with the modest but meaningful hope of "interesting" his readers in South African history (xii–xv). Together, the case of Lyme patients in the United States and that of AIDS patients in South Africa reveal that whether local or distant, perceived to be more fortunate or less fortunate, aporias of interest in and compassion for others abound. At the very least, anthropological analyses can localize the distant and historicize the present and, in doing so, might, if they do not succeed in seeding compassion and enacting justice, pique even the most intransigent interest.

In this chapter, I explored Madison's, Dan's, Renee's, Dylan's, and Barbara's experiences with Lyme disease to give texture to the nuances and multiplicity of ways that Lyme disease—and, in particular, chronic Lyme disease—is lived in the United States. Their stories show that Lyme disease is as Lyme disease is lived; that, like all illnesses, Lyme disease is made manifest in its practice. For these patients, Lyme disease is irritability, rage, headaches, muscle and joint pain, neuropathy, dizziness, forgetfulness, and light sensitivity, among other symptoms—it is all these things because it is lived this way. Even more importantly, like other contested illnesses that are described as medically unexplainable within an evidence-based framework that privileges signs over symptoms, chronic Lyme disease is distinguished by the "divided experience" of being lived as a biologically rooted disease, even though it is often perceived to be an illness that lacks a biological basis.

I have also engaged a critical approach to the ideas of suffering and survival. I first argued that Lyme patients' suffering is intimately tied up with ideas of legibility and legitimacy ("What should a person in pain look like?") and with the sociohistorically constructed binaries of sex/gender and body/mind, binaries that are both disrupted and reinforced by Lyme patients, physicians, and scientists in their everyday lives. I then argued that, for many Lyme patients, survival, understood as "how to live despite not feeling well," is a matter of "knowing" and "acting on" their bodies, and that, for many Lyme patients, the practiced regimens of complementary and alternative medicine provide a path toward healing even if they do not enact a cure. Finally, I concluded with a brief exploration of ideas of wealth as they relate to the experience of suffering and surviving Lyme disease and in the context of racial and economic inequalities. Here, I suggested that, at the same time that structural violence perniciously erases individuals of color from Lyme's landscape, the perception of Lyme disease as an affliction of the affluent also has the effect of calling into question the authenticity of Lyme patients' experiences and provides a rationale for diminished compassion.

The topic of suffering and survival in the context of suburban affluence is a difficult and sensitive one. I was told in the early stages of my writing that using the lenses of suffering and survival to better understand Lyme disease was inappropriate. However, I continue to maintain that it is not, precisely because it is not an exercise in comparison. Rather, I suggest that suffering and survival should be engaged on their own terms, anchored in a particular time and a particular place and always within their broader sociohistorical context. The analytical challenge with Lyme disease is to capture the tension between patients' embodied suffering and the fact that, in the context of a "politics of life," these same bodies are typically those that are privileged above others (Fassin 2018b). In this chapter, I use the word "suffering" because that is the word that patients and physicians across the standard-of-care divide used to describe the experience of chronic Lyme disease; I use the word "survival" because that is how many patients described their response to being ill. Recognizing Lyme patients' experience as suffering and their response to their suffering as survival— while at the same time recognizing the violence of the suffering of those who, across lines of race and class, do not get counted in Lyme's abacus, and the deep injustice of health inequalities that exist across lines of race, gender, class, and nationality, more broadly—is an important first step in opening up space for unqualified compassion and conviviality and dissolving the ossified boundaries that divide Lyme's two camps.

DIAGNOSING AND TREATING LYME

Before my research began, I was unfamiliar with the allegorical tale of the elephant and the blind men; by research's end, it was a story so familiar—told to me by both mainstream and Lyme-literate physicians—that I wondered how I had never heard it before. The tale, which originated in India and gained popularity in the nineteenth-century United States in the form of a poem by John Godfrey Saxe, begins with a group of blind men who are asked to inspect an elephant and describe what they find. Each man feels a different part of the elephant and, in doing so, arrives at a different conclusion. For example, the man who feels the elephant's leg exclaims that an elephant is like a pillar, while the man who feels the elephant's tail cries that an elephant is more like a rope. The tale's ending is as varied as its many versions. In some tellings, the men agree to collaborate so that they can reconcile their disparate findings; in others, the men continue to disagree, each convinced that their partial truth is the whole truth.

Endings aside, the telling of this tale by Lyme physicians is ethnographically significant because it captures one of medicine's often vision-centric tasks, which is to know a body and interpret its symptoms and signs. It can be taken for granted that patients and practitioners understand bodies differently, but many find it perplexing that practitioners, irrespective of their epistemic positioning, could differently interpret something as seemingly objective as a sign. Few scholars have more thoughtfully examined this phenomenon than Shigehisa Kuriyama (1999). Through an introduction to his subject via the blind men and the elephant tale, Kuriyama explores how, in performing what appeared to be the same gesture of pulse taking, seventeenth-century European and Chinese medical practitioners actually *perceived* two very different things. Drawing from this example and others,

Kuriyama suggests that signs are not "timeless" but "results of historical change" (12, 272). Something similar is at play when it comes to Lyme disease and practitioners' disagreement over how to understand and treat it; however, the primary tension lies not in interpretive differences over the same sign but in the diagnostic validity of interpreting Lyme's symptoms *as signs*. In this way, mainstream and Lyme-literate approaches to determining which symptoms matter in the diagnosis of Lyme disease can often "entail perceptions as disparate as grabbing the elephant's tail and rubbing its stomach" (22).

This chapter tells the stories of two mainstream Lyme physicians and two Lyme-literate physicians and the observations I made of their practices. Over the course of my research, I formally interviewed fifty-six physicians and observed the practices of seven. The stories told here convey the range of ways that a contested illness like Lyme disease is medically understood, a range strikingly characterized by a disagreement over the relative importance of symptoms versus signs. The telling of these stories is more broadly situated within an exploration of the historical and epistemic underpinnings of the two medical paradigms—biomedicine and CAM—that reinforce the division between Lyme-literate and mainstream approaches to Lyme disease but also exceed it. In exploring how Lyme disease is understood across its standard-of-care divide, and by attending to differences between how biomedical and CAM practitioners approach symptomatic suffering in the absence of signs, I highlight the epistemic tensions that characterize the "divided bodies" of contested illness, illnesses that biomedical physicians often perceive to be unexplainable. Because CAM is diagnostically aligned with patients' symptomatic experience, explanations for the experience of suffering are nearly limitless, and medically unexplained illness as a diagnostic category is noticeably absent. However, because biomedical practitioners often prioritize a patient's pathophysiological signs over that patient's symptomatic experience, there is always a limit to which biomedical practitioners can explain the experience of suffering. This limit, an epistemic delineation between symptoms and signs as legitimate bases for diagnosis, simultaneously generates—and holds in tension—biomedical explainability *and* unexplainability.[1] That is, illnesses such as chronic Lyme disease, which often present with a range of symptoms in the absence of identifiable signs, function as the "constitutive outside" of biomedically explainable illnesses, such as acute Lyme disease, which are understood to be biologically substantiated by, for example, the sign of an EM rash. As biomedical explainability's constitutive outside, medically unexplained illnesses are, to quote Judith Butler, "the excluded and illegible domain that haunts the former domain as the spectre of its own impossibility, the very limit to intelligibility" (1993, xi). In this way, I argue, medically unexplained illness is not a biomedical anomaly but, rather, a fundamental feature of biomedicine.

The Lyme Veteran

Tall and sturdy with graying temples and a habit of wearing a bow tie, Dr. Childs is a rheumatologist who attended prestigious universities and has been practicing medicine for more than thirty years. He is part of a small rheumatology practice that sees a range of rheumatological conditions, including rheumatoid arthritis and lupus. Scattered among these more typical visits are appointments with patients with Lyme-related questions who have been referred to the practice by another physician. Some patients have been diagnosed with Lyme arthritis and are being prescribed antibiotic treatment for the first time; some patients have already been treated for Lyme arthritis and are seeking a second opinion about further treatment. Others have had a positive Lyme test in the past or have been treated for acute Lyme disease and are curious about whether the symptoms they are experiencing are still related to Lyme.

From our first meeting, Dr. Childs was enthusiastic about my project and generous with his time. To make the most of the days I observed his practice, Dr. Childs would schedule all of his Lyme-related appointments on one day so that I could observe as many Lyme patients as possible. It was these days that Dr. Childs referred to as "all Lyme all the time." From the corner of his office where I sat in a chair with my notebook in my lap, I would observe his interactions with patients, from the moment they sat down to give their patient histories until the end of their physical examinations in the adjacent room. After the physical exam, it was often my job to prepare the room for the next examination while Dr. Childs dictated his notes into an audio recorder in his office. When the practice got busy, I would check to see if Dr. Childs had any messages or retrieve his patients' charts. In between patient appointments, Dr. Childs would review the case we had just seen and reflect on any other issue that seemed related. He would often ask for my opinion during and after an exam, a habit seemingly borne out of years of having been shadowed by medical students. At lunchtime, we would walk to a nearby restaurant and continue our conversation about Lyme disease.

On the first day that I observed Dr. Childs, which started cold and overcast, he saw twelve patients, and each appointment lasted anywhere between fifteen and thirty minutes. His first patient was a woman who had been treated with thirty days of oral antibiotics for an EM rash in 2000 and had had trouble with her "arthritic knee" since 2007. When her primary care physician ordered a Lyme test for her at that time, it was interpreted as negative. Three years later, she was again tested for Lyme disease; this time, her physician told her that her test was positive. Based on this result, her physician decided to treat her with another round of antibiotics. Although the antibiotics had not resolved her knee pain, she described feeling less tired when she was on them. Even before her physical examination, and unlike many of the other patients I would later see in Dr. Childs's office, this patient insisted that she no longer had Lyme and that her problematic knee was an effect of aging.

During the physical examination, Dr. Childs validated this patient's assessment. He told her that her exam was consistent with "wear and tear" osteoarthritis, that Lyme arthritis typically caused more swelling than she had, and that further antibiotics would not relieve her discomfort; he also told her that repeat testing a month later would still be positive, and he explained the mechanics behind antibody testing, which included a phrase that I would hear many times over the course of my observation: "The war is over, but the troops haven't gone home." "These tests don't test for the germ," he explained. "They only tell us about your response to the germ, which can continue even after the germ is gone." When he asked her whether she had any questions, she mentioned that she had noticed some twitching and wondered, after doing some reading online, whether it might be neurological complications. She was also curious how, as someone who "didn't go outside or work in the garden," she could have been exposed to Lyme disease twice in a relatively short amount of time.

For Dr. Childs, this case and others like it had convinced him that misguided diagnoses made by family members, other physicians, and patients themselves were to blame for most of the Lyme-related cases that he saw, cases he distinguished from "real Lyme." He echoed this idea on another day when he exclaimed, "I really feel like primary care docs aren't testing properly and informing people properly." In cases where Dr. Childs believed that Lyme disease was not the reason for his patient's ill health, he described having had some success at "convincing [his patients] to the other side," which he found "gratifying." There were other times, however, when Dr. Childs realized that nothing he could say would change the patient's mind. For example, after seeing one patient, he concluded that there was "enough of a psychological and cultural barrier to really get to her." After seeing another, he exclaimed, "The world has sent me patients like her before. I'm not going to change her value system in five minutes."

In these cases, Dr. Childs described how, in the cautious dance of the patient–physician encounter, he often had to compromise his own medical opinion to make the patient happy. As he had learned over the course of his career, "The option of doing nothing is not an option." He continued, "If I take something away from a patient, I also have to give something to that patient." Sometimes that "something" was just the assurance that the patient would no longer be seeking what Dr. Childs perceived as dangerous treatment options from Lyme-literate practitioners. In such an instance, Dr. Childs explained, "[This patient] wants Lyme; she wants to feel better. The only thing I gave her was keeping her from going down a path." Sometimes what Dr. Childs had to offer a patient was a low-risk solution like aquatic therapy. "Within reason," he explained, "I want to give people what they want. If that patient had asked me why I wasn't treating him, he could have walked out with antibiotics."[2] In a similar instance, he explained, "I don't believe that Lyme disease lingers, I don't believe her feeling better has anything to do with antibiotics. But have I ever treated someone like this with antibiotics? Yes, if they're worried about it." Dr. Childs described these encounters as "not very elegant."

In the absence of a convincing physical exam and laboratory evidence, explanations for the range of symptoms that Dr. Childs's patients experienced—dizziness, numbness in extremities, hand tremors, swollen lymph nodes, fatigue, muscle weakness, joint pain, vertigo—were case specific. In several cases, Dr. Childs attributed symptoms to underlying psychiatric conditions. Take, for example, a man in his twenties who had recently graduated from college and had a history of depression. Several years before his appointment with Dr. Childs, he had developed an EM rash after a known tick bite. He was immediately prescribed doxycycline but had to discontinue it after four to five days because it burned his throat. He was then prescribed ceftriaxone (around which time he also switched antidepressants), and his rash disappeared, but his fatigue continued. Fatigue plagued him over the next four years, as he also developed other symptoms that included dry eye, chills, sore throats, and muscle aches. Further testing by a conventional laboratory revealed an ELISA interpreted as negative and a Western blot interpreted as positive (positive IgM but negative IgG), while further testing by a laboratory that is often criticized by mainstream Lyme physicians resulted in a test that was interpreted as positive for babesiosis. The patient had recently been diagnosed with an autoimmune disorder, but he explained that most of what he was experiencing had been chalked up to depression by his own physicians. When Dr. Childs had finished taking this patient's history, he explained to the patient that what he was experiencing was not related to Lyme disease. When the patient left his office, Dr. Childs concluded, "This is a case of depression expressed somatically."

As I discuss in the previous chapter, some mainstream physicians believe that, in the case of chronic Lyme disease, affluence is correlated with a higher likelihood of presenting with somatically expressed depression or with cases that are not "real Lyme." And Dr. Childs's clinical experience supported this correlation. During one of our conversations, Dr. Childs recommended that I pay attention to the demographic dimension of chronic Lyme disease because "chronic Lyme disease is skewered toward the privileged. It's a problem of expectations of the elite." During another conversation, he reiterated that chronic Lyme disease patients are often of "the same upper middle-class background as the depression group." And after an appointment with an elderly man who described himself first and foremost as a hunter and a fisherman, Dr. Childs surmised, "This is a blue collar guy who is not caught up in yuppie flu. Culturally it's different. He's saying, 'Fix me doctor!'"

Most appointments I observed in Dr. Childs's office were similar to the first appointment described above. That is, Dr. Childs concluded that the patients were suffering from fibromyalgia, depression, life stress, or aging, what some mainstream Lyme physicians have described as "the aches and pains of daily living" (Wormser et al. 2006, 1115). For these patients, Dr. Childs argued, Lyme disease had entered the equation because it was an "easy answer." But there were several notable exceptions. For example, I observed two cases in which Dr. Childs suspected that the patient might have ALS instead of Lyme, and one case in which Dr. Childs thought the patient had MS. In these patients, Dr. Childs argued, "Lyme looks a lot better to the patient than the alternative." In addition to three cases of Lyme arthritis, there were also, as Dr. Childs described, "good cases, tough cases."[3] These cases were difficult to decipher, and Dr. Childs found himself in the rare position of being unsure whether the patient did or did not have Lyme disease and whether to prescribe antibiotics.

Take, for example, the case of a professor in her late thirties. At the time of the appointment, she had recently begun to notice tingling in her arm and upper thigh. Although she did not report a problem with muscle strength, she described lacking sensation in some parts of her body and having extra sensation in others. Otherwise, she reported feeling "fine." She had no recollection of a tick bite or rash, but having grown up in a tick-endemic area and having spent time outdoors, she had had ample exposure to ticks. The first neurologist she consulted with suspected MS but first tested her for Lyme disease, both tests for which came back floridly positive. The results from a spinal tap and an MRI were also, according to her neurologist, "consistent with Lyme disease." Her neurologist immediately prescribed her thirty days of doxycycline. At the time of her appointment with Dr. Childs, she was waiting on the results of a second spinal tap. After hearing her story and performing a physical exam, Dr. Childs was perplexed. He explained, "I think you have MS and not Lyme." At the same time, he understood that, in the face of an MS diagnosis, neither he nor the patient would want to overlook a "curative strategy." He continued to explain,

> We could make an argument for giving you IV ceftriaxone. But let's hedge our bets and do thirty days of doxy. We'll leave it at doxy, which is risk-averse. We're sort of treating you as if you have central nervous system Lyme. I want to be an authority figure, but it's an area with some controversy.

After the patient left, we continued to discuss the case. Dr. Childs reflected,

> There are differences between MS and Lyme. For example, oligoclonal bands, which are more indicative of MS than Lyme. And white lesions on MRIs that are interpreted as Lyme, I think that's way overdone. But this patient, she has a very positive Lyme test. What do you do after that? Is it a big deal to give her ceftriaxone? Dr. Richardson [a mainstream colleague] thinks there is some MS caused by Lyme. This is a good case, a tough case. I don't think the puncture will show positive, but if it does, I would go for ceftriaxone.

In the case of another woman with persistent headaches after treatment with oral antibiotics for Lyme arthritis, he explained,

> Sometimes the world is shades of gray. What's the most risk-averse thing to do in this case? I can't say, "No way, José!" in either direction. I see a woman who has had several early Lyme infections. She has a positive spinal tap, which is significant because, if it's accurate, it means that she's producing antibodies in the brain. She has neurological symptoms, that has [sic] an MRI that shows evidence. I'm recommending the antibiotics

as an insurance policy. Am I thrilled about it? Not necessarily. These are possibilities and probabilities, not certainties.

And in still another difficult to decipher case, Dr. Childs explained, "Sometimes it's straightforward; sometimes it isn't. If I'm not sure, I should be humble and say that." Dr. Childs explained to me how, over the years, he had seen cases in which there was not a convincing clinical story but an unequivocally positive test, as well as cases in which there was a convincing clinical story in the absence of a positive test. He described how, in these scenarios, he has occasionally treated patients. He explained, "Medicine is an art, not a science. Am I a purist? No. The question remains: At what point do we stop trying to help?"

For all patients, whether they were perceived to be "real" Lyme cases or not, Dr. Childs insisted that the clinical picture—the physical exam—was paramount. As he explained to one patient, "Eighty percent of what I'm interested in is how you look. And I think all of this is mechanical." During an appointment with another patient, he explained, "The most important piece of evidence here is not the test but your clinical picture. Your test is the only piece of evidence going against us here." Dr. Childs's emphasis on the importance of the physical exam is a significant overlap with Lyme-literate physicians' approaches to knowing the Lyme body, many of whom were quick to repeat the catchphrase "Lyme disease is a clinical diagnosis." However, the difference between these approaches hinges on the clinical relevance of symptoms. Although biomedical practitioners like Dr. Childs often describe clinical care as an "art" as much as a "science," their willingness to entertain the diagnostic value of what cannot be measured generally does not extend to the "nonspecific" symptoms that they associate with individuals who suffer in the absence of "objective" signs. This tension lies at the heart of what many have called the "Lyme wars." For Dr. Childs, who has been in the Lyme trenches as long as any other physician, the battle lines were drawn long ago, and the possibility that they might be redrawn seemed very unlikely.

The Lyme Standard-Bearers

Like Dr. Childs, the mainstream physicians who founded the Lyme Clinic know the Lyme trenches well. Housed in a spare and aging building in a university hospital complex, the clinic was founded in the late 1980s and opened its doors to treat patients with early Lyme disease and other tick-borne illnesses. Thirty years later, the physicians who founded it continue to manage it and have come to be seen as emblems of the mainstream standard of care. Unlike Dr. Childs, however, these physicians were cautious about agreeing to be observed. It took several email queries to get a response, and even after I was personally introduced to them by colleagues whom they trusted, my presence was still cause for a high level of suspicion. This was no more apparent than during my second visit to the clinic. I was in an examination room observing Dr. Smith, the physician who had invited me to shadow him that day, when one of his colleagues, Dr. Frank, entered the room. Clearly made uncomfortable by my presence, he turned on his heels without a word and exited the room as quickly as he had entered. Dr. Smith, too, worried about the repercussions of his participation in my project; my promise that I would provide anonymity did not quell his concerns. "I have no idea what you'll write about!" he exclaimed. As a result, some of what Dr. Smith communicated to me was off the record.[4]

During my interview with Dr. Smith, the reasons for his and Dr. Frank's concerns soon emerged. The primary one was the perceived threat of ill-wishing chronic Lyme patients and Lyme-literate practitioners. Dr. Smith explained,

> I don't have a real big fear of getting hurt by these people, but it's in the back of my mind. After 9/11, I got calls in the office from people all over the country who said they had been called by someone masquerading as me. They were told that their blood test was positive and that they should call my office. . . . I remember at that time, my wife was petrified. I would check under my car to make sure there wasn't a bomb. When I got a package, I would always hesitate to open it. When I got a letter from someone I don't know, I would think, "This is going to have white powder."

Beyond concerns over personal safety, Dr. Smith described the toll that the legal dimension of the controversy had taken on his career and compared his and other mainstream physicians' experience to that of Galileo:

> Galileo had some science that went against the church doctrine, and the government put him in big trouble and put him on trial and house arrest. I look at these people, and they're persecuting these poor doctors that are trying to do good. They're well supported and well funded, and they're getting the government to go after us. . . . These people who are

accusing the academics of suppressing the truth, they're actually the ones who are re-creating the apparatus that Galileo had to face.

When asked whether he would have chosen a different career path, given the challenges he describes having encountered, Dr. Smith said that he would not have. He considers his career to have been marked by worthwhile accomplishments, not the least of which were publications in major medical journals. He reflected,

> When I was in medical school and an intern, if I just had one article published, it would have been the greatest thing. But I've done so much. I wouldn't give that up. When my article came out and CNN and the *New York Times* did stories on it, it was an amazing personal experience. It was incredible. I still have the newspaper, folded over and yellow. But it wears thin after a while. When people want to interview now, I say, "No."

While a feeling of personal accomplishment seems to have overridden what Dr. Smith described as the challenges of being a mainstream Lyme physician, he was insistent that, contrary to the claims of the "other side," financial incentive was not a factor in his decision to continue treating and conducting research on a controversial disease. He exclaimed, "They make it look like we're in academics and making tons of money on our research. It's sort of preposterous." He continued, "When I became a doctor, I thought, I wanted to help people, and I liked science. I wanted to make a living, but not for the money."

For Dr. Smith, Lyme's controversy is somewhat perplexing. Like most of the mainstream physicians I spoke with, Dr. Smith believes that the available evidence supports the mainstream position on Lyme disease, and he finds it "bothersome" that, in the interest of "fairness and balance," the media gives both sides "equal standing." "I'm a little surprised at how this has become a whole controversy." He continued,

> I understand how AIDS became a controversy. In that case, there were many on the fringe of society, and they had to fight to get funding from the government. Now, when we see somebody with HIV, the science is pretty much there, and you treat them. There's not a whole lot of people with HIV that want to have HIV. People don't want to get congestive heart failure; they don't want to be diagnosed with chronic obstructive pulmonary disease. But somehow, patients latch on to the chronic Lyme disease thing and get treatment forever. . . . It brings out the worst in a lot of people, especially junk science thinking.

I visited the Lyme Clinic two times during my research. During the first visit, my observations were limited to the waiting room of the clinic, where I was able to speak with Roseanne, a patient who had just had an appointment. Roseanne, elderly but spritely and accompanied by a younger friend, was eager to tell me her story. Although she had no recollection of seeing a tick in the recent past, she described having been unwell for three years leading up to her most recent diagnosis of Lyme disease, anaplasmosis, and babesiosis, with a range of symptoms including chills, headaches, and what she described as "evil spirits" in her body. Her symptoms were unpredictable: she would feel fine for a stretch of time, and then, after exercising or expending more energy than she was accustomed to, she would "crash."

A month prior to our conversation, Roseanne decided she wanted to see an "Asian-thinking doctor" and became the patient of an acupuncturist. A month into treatment, Roseanne, who described having had a low fever throughout the course of treatment, suddenly developed a high fever, chills, and excruciating back pain. (At this point in our conversation, Roseanne's friend interjected, "Don't forget to tell them about your headaches!") Soon after these symptoms emerged, she also developed what she described as a "red bull's eye," a "big one with two satellites." Only then did she begin to suspect Lyme disease, and on the recommendation of her friend, she decided to pay a visit to the Lyme Clinic. At the time of our conversation, Roseanne had returned to the Lyme Clinic for a follow-up visit, feeling dramatically better and having responded well to what she described as a "strong regimen" of antibiotics. "The first two days I had bad side effects, bad nausea," she said. "But by the third day, I was feeling like I had slept my whole life."

On my second visit to the Lyme Clinic, I was permitted beyond the waiting room. I observed six appointments that day, each of which took place in a small, unadorned examination room lit by fluorescent lights. These appointments were almost all related to acute Lyme disease. For example, I observed the appointment of a former firefighter in his sixties who was diagnosed with Lyme disease after presenting with an EM rash, headaches, and fatigue. Having had a well-documented case of EM, he had been asked to return to the Lyme Clinic for a follow-up visit. Dr. Smith first asked the patient how the antibiotics had made him feel and, in particular, whether he had felt slightly worse before feeling better. This question was striking because it indicated an interest in the Herxheimer reaction, which, in the treatment of Lyme disease, is typically of more interest to Lyme-literate physicians. However, where Lyme-literate physicians argue that the Herx-heimer reaction can occur at any time during treatment, mainstream phy-sicians who are interested in the Herxheimer reaction argue that it only occurs immediately following treatment. Still more interesting was how Dr. Smith and the patient navigated the patient's response. The patient first recalled feeling worse a couple days after beginning the antibiotics, which prompted Dr. Smith to question whether the patient was remembering cor-rectly. They went back and forth for some time, unable to pin down whether the patient, in Dr. Smith's opinion, had had a Herxheimer reaction.

Dr. Smith then asked whether the patient felt that he had made a full recovery. The answer to this question again elicited some confusion. The patient mentioned that his knees sometimes hurt when he was going up the stairs, following which Dr. Smith asked whether he had experienced knee pain prior to Lyme disease. The patient answered that he had had leg pain but did not recall having had knee pain when climbing stairs. This response prompted Dr. Smith to explain a phenomenon called "recall bias." At the end of this conversation, Dr. Smith asked, "So, you're back to baseline?," and the patient replied, "Yeah. Yeah, I guess so."

All but one of the remaining appointments were related to EM rashes: two of the patients presented with what Dr. Smith diagnosed as EM rashes and were being prescribed antibiotics for the first time, and one had re-turned for a follow-up appointment after having had a confirmed EM rash. The sixth appointment was a visit from a retired healthcare professional in her sixties. After having been diagnosed and treated for Lyme disease a couple of years prior to the appointment, she had felt fine until she had two hip replacements. Following her hip replacements, the patient described how her knee had become warm, swollen, and painful, several days after which she developed what she described as a bull's-eye rash. Dr. Smith con-firmed that her knee was indeed warm and swollen. This unusual case in-trigued Dr. Smith, and as we left the examination room and headed toward the clinic's common office, his step quickened in his eagerness to discuss it with his colleagues.

In the common office, where I had spent time in between appointments talking to medical students who were rotating through the clinic, Dr. Smith and I fell into a conversation that meandered across topics, from the peer review process to anthropological methodology to perceptions about chronic Lyme disease. At conversation's end, Dr. Smith again reiterated his concern about how I would represent the clinic in my book, and I again as-sured him of my commitment to anonymity. By that time, it was already past

7:00 p.m., and the clinic had closed to patients. I gathered my belongings amid a flurry of goodbyes and handshakes and headed to my car to begin the long drive home.

Biomedicine and the Medically Unexplainable

The way in which Dr. Childs and Dr. Smith approach Lyme disease—particularly their hesitance to make diagnoses based on the range of symptoms associated with chronic Lyme disease—is consistent with how biomedicine, more broadly, approaches the relationship between symptoms and signs in the diagnosis of disease. In contrast, as I explore in the next section, Lyme-literate practitioners' approach to Lyme disease is more consistent with how CAM, more generally, relies on symptoms to provide medical explanations. The historical emergence of this difference can be traced to the late eighteenth and early nineteenth centuries. In the United States, the coexistence of multiple medical systems—or "medical pluralism"—has been a long-standing social reality. In a comprehensive overview of the historical relationship between biomedicine and "alternative healing systems," anthropologist Hans Baer describes how in nineteenth-century America, "regular medicine" (biomedicine's predecessor) "shared the stage with a wide array of competing and sometimes complementary alternative medical systems, including homeopathy, botanic medicine, eclecticism, hydropathy, Christian Science, osteopathy, and chiropractic" (2001, 7). Baer attributes the emergence of nineteenth-century medical pluralism to widespread discontent with "regular" medical practitioners' use of "heroic medicine," which included "administering remedies such as calomel, antimony, emetics, purgatives, and opiates, and by bleeding, cupping, blistering, leeching, and prescribing a starvation diet" (9).

In search of a gentler and less interventional medicine, many Americans were drawn to alternative healing systems. But by the end of the nineteenth century, even regular medicine practitioners had denounced heroic medicine and had begun to actively "rebrand" regular medicine by calling it "scientific medicine" (31–33). Baer argues that this development, along with the "alliance" between a newly formed American Medical Association and the "emergent industrial capitalist class," paved the way for "regular medicine to transform itself into biomedicine and to establish political, economic, and ideological dominance over rival medical systems" (31). For scientific medicine practitioners and institutions, a shift to science-based medicine signaled the emergence of an epistemic framework that privileged internal pathophysiology and etiology over external symptoms and social determinants of disease (33).

Many characteristics that emerged to define "scientific medicine" as early as the late eighteenth century and into the early twentieth century continue to define biomedicine in the early twenty-first century. Most relevant, here, is the particular way in which practitioners of biomedicine have come to know the human body. In *The Birth of the Clinic*, Foucault describes how medicine transitioned from a practice in which the physician asked, "What's the matter with you?" to a practice in which the physician asked, "Where does it hurt?" ([1973] 1994b, xviii). The difference between these two questions hinges on the formative influence of anatomic pathology on the interpretation of external symptoms. As Annemarie Mol observes, Foucault suggests that prior to the nineteenth century, European and American physicians did not understand "disease" to be a "condition of the body" but a plural entity ("diseases") that could enter and "inhabit" the body (2002, 125). In this way, physicians' only option was to recognize diseases through what Mol calls the "transparency" of external symptoms. When disease became linked to "a pathological state of the tissues," however, access to the visualization of the interior by way of autopsy—as well other vision-based technological advancements such as microscopy and radiological imaging—made the transparency of external symptoms "opaque" (126; see also Armstrong 1983; Haraway 1989).

Understanding biomedicine's shift in interest to anatomically based pathology, in addition to its well-described embrace of the Cartesian division between mind and body, helps to shed light on why a medical system that is able to explain some bodily phenomena with a precision never before imagined simultaneously struggles to explain certain forms of chronic illness. For many biomedical physicians, physical symptoms in the absence of observable pathophysiology are often understood to have their genesis in the mind, to be outside the purview of biomedical intervention, and to be subsequently "medically unexplainable."[5] As the "most common disorders seen in primary care," medically unexplained illnesses are perceived to be "syndromes characterized by multiple symptoms, significant suffering, and disability that fail to show consistent pathophysiology" (S. Johnson 2008, 3). Although the first use of the term "medically unexplained illness" did not appear until 1980 (Nettleton 2006; Smith-Morris 2016), scholars seem to agree that the emergence of the *categorization* and *diagnosis* of disorders that could not be medically explained coincided with the emergence of biomedicine in the late eighteenth and early nineteenth centuries (Armstrong 2011; Fàbrega 1990; Shorter 1990).[6] Psychiatric anthropologist Horacio Fàbrega argues that the "concept of somatization"—physical symptomology in the absence of observable pathophysiology that is often assumed to have a psychological origin—is itself a "cultural and historical product of Western medicine" (1990, 653; see also Greco 2017). For many biomedical physicians, what came to be known in the twentieth century as medically unexplained illnesses have merely been repackaged by biomedical practitioners to reflect the medical "zeitgeist of the times" (S. Johnson 2008, 19). That is, what was understood to be neurasthenia from the mid-nineteenth century through early twentieth century came to be understood as hypoglycemia in the 1960s, Briquet's syndrome in the 1970s, chronic fatigue syndrome in the 1980s, and, in the late 1980s and early 1990s, multiple chemical sensitivity, Gulf War syndrome, and chronic Lyme disease, among others (19; see also Shorter 1992; Showalter 1997).

The idea that medically unexplained symptoms have been renamed over time to better reflect their cultural moment has become so entrenched within the biomedical community that it, like the anatomical basis of biomedicine, is perceived to be self-evident. This fact was made apparent in my conversations with mainstream Lyme physicians and scientists. For example, one physician-scientist I interviewed exclaimed,

> There's a whole history of claimed diseases to explain nonspecific symptoms, things that you can't prove. Some of them stick, and some of them don't. When I was a junior faculty member, people who were tired and not able to think too well thought they had hypoglycemia. And then it was chronic mono and candidiasis. When unprovable diseases take on this mantle of being significant to society, I'm interested in why do some stick and why do some go away?

Another physician explained, "Chronic Lyme disease is clearly a classic form of hysteria. It has spread like wildfire. It was hypoglycemia in the 1950s, and then chronic fatigue syndrome, multiple chemical sensitivity, and repetition strain injury after that. It's also typical of hysteria in that there are a group of patients with real disease who actually have infection, and this spreads waves of hysteria." And still another physician-scientist reflected, "The social business of chronic Lyme disease is very interesting. In every generation, there are people that don't feel well and latch on to things. For example, neurasthenia. Many people want to have something, and chronic Lyme disease is socially acceptable."

For these physicians, chronic Lyme disease's "aches and pains" constitute a medically unexplained illness because most of the patients they have examined present with what they perceive to be nonspecific symptoms. And to ensure that I understood what they meant by "symptom," several explained to me the difference between the subjective nature of the symptom and the objective nature of the sign. One mainstream Lyme physician-scientist explained,

> Most Lyme patients are not difficult to diagnose and treat. Do you know the difference between a symptom and a sign? It boils down to subjective symptoms and objective signs. For example, arthralgia is the subjective experience of pain, and arthritis is an objective sign. Chronic Lyme patients only have nonspecific symptoms that are chronic. There's so much evidence that this is related to psychological factors.

In another interview, a Lyme scientist began to read aloud a list of symptoms that he had found on a chronic Lyme disease website. He went through the symptoms one by one:

> Fevers, sweats, chills and flushing, unexplained weight loss or gain, unexplained hair loss, testicular or pelvic pain, irritable bladder, constipation, diarrhea, heart palpitations, muscle pain or cramps, headaches, neck stiffness, tingling numbness, Bell's palsy, double vision, floaters, buzzing, ringing, ear pain, difficulty reading, disorientation, irritability, depression.

He then stopped reading and continued to explain, "These are exaggerated, nondescript symptoms that people read about and think, 'Oh! They're due to chronic Lyme disease.' But a number of these symptoms should be put in the MUS [medically unexplained symptoms] category; they're not due to Lyme or any other infection."

For Dr. Childs, Dr. Smith, and the other mainstream physicians and scientists I interviewed, these symptoms are diagnostically *insignificant* because they are not also accompanied by an objective sign—a disease marker that can be visually verified, measured, and compared across cases. This assessment is more broadly consistent with the CDC's case definition of Lyme disease, which explains that EM is "the most common clinical marker for the disease."[7] To qualify as a sign, an EM must expand over a quantifiable period of time ("a period of days to weeks") and reach a measurably specific size ("greater than or equal to 5 cm in size across its largest diameter"). And for symptoms such as "fatigue, fever, headache, mildly stiff neck, arthralgia, or myalgia" to be diagnostically significant, they must be accompanied by a sign that meets these and other specifications. For these physicians, the disjuncture between the presence of patients' symptoms and the absence of their symptoms' pathophysiology is evidence of chronic Lyme disease's medically unexplainable nature. In the next section, I explore how Lyme-literate and CAM practitioners' recognition of the symptom as a legitimate basis on which to make a diagnosis opens up a space in which illness always has the potential to be explained.

Integrative Lyme

Dr. Johnson's practice is nestled between other businesses alongside a small highway in a quaint town in the northeastern United States. A bio-medically trained physician, Dr. Johnson combines CAM with conventional medicine in his treatment of Lyme disease. When I arrived at his practice for a day of observation in 2011, Dr. Johnson's physician assistant, Eve, took me aside and explained in a hushed voice,

> We're a different kind of practice. We're integrative. But we also ap-proach Lyme differently. We believe that Lyme hangs out in the body; we believe that Lyme can present without bull's-eye rashes. OK? I just wanted to give you a heads-up.

With that, and a quick nod from me to indicate that I had understood her, Eve opened the door to the exam room of the day's first patient.

A year prior to my observation of Dr. Johnson's practice, I had lis-tened to him give a presentation at a community health fair organized by a Lyme disease support group. During his presentation to a crowded gymnasium, Dr. Johnson had explained what first attracted him to medi-cine and, later, to the integrative treatment of Lyme disease. Although Lyme disease was not initially on his radar screen, his penchant for dif-ficult diagnoses found its niche when he was hired by a hospital that hap-pened to have the "highest rate of Lyme disease in [the area]." Once he opened his own practice, Dr. Johnson began to see a lot of patients with Lyme disease and noticed that some got better and some did not. He became intrigued by why some patients did not get better. "Twenty-three or four years later," he continued to explain, "I've seen over eleven thou-sand chronic Lyme patients—we see thirty to thirty-five chronic Lyme patients a day—so I wanted to tell you the reasons that many of you do not get better."

According to Dr. Johnson, the first obstacles are typically misdiagnosis and test inaccuracy. He described the common occurrence of patients coming to his office having been diagnosed with MS, CFS, fibromyalgia, and post-traumatic stress disorder. In the absence of what Dr. Johnson described as accurate testing, he explained that a correct diagnosis—or distinguishing between Lyme disease and other illnesses with overlapping symptoms—is fairly simple. "How do you know when patients have Lyme disease?" he asked. He continued,

> It's actually very easy: Lyme disease is a multisystemic disorder with a classic constellation of symptoms that include fatigue, headaches, muscle and nerve pain ([such as] tingling, numbness, burning and stabbing sensations), and memory and concentration problems as well as sleep and mood disorders. Also, people can feel better with antibiotics but then worse, [which is] called a Herxheimer reaction, when the bacteria is [sic] being killed off. And women often notice flare-ups of their disease with their hormonal cycle. One of the hallmarks of Lyme disease is that the symptoms come and go. You have good days; you have bad days. Your joint and muscle pain tends to migrate: one day it hurts in the elbow; two days later, it hurts in your shoulder. . . . And the tingling and numbness, if you had carpal tunnel, it stays in your hands, right? . . . So migratory tingling and numbness that comes and goes and moves around your body with these migratory muscle pains and joint pains, very specific for Lyme disease.

Once the diagnosis of Lyme disease is correctly made, however, Dr. Johnson described the conundrum of how, despite treatment, patients who have been chronically ill often continue to feel unwell. For Dr. Johnson, the answer to this conundrum is that chronic Lyme patients are often sick with a range of other "medical problems," including "different forms [of *Borrelia burgdorferi*]," such as "round body forms, persister forms, and biofilms." He exclaimed,

> Remember, the key to medicine is always get to the source of the problem. . . . What I'm gonna show you is twenty years of research of digging and digging and digging to figure out why so many people are so sick. So I'm gonna give you a list of differential diagnoses that can interfere with the illness, OK?

These differential diagnoses range from immune dysfunction and toxicity to nutritional enzyme deficiencies, food allergies, and "leaky gut." In

Dr. Johnson's practice, every patient is examined and evaluated within this disease matrix. Every patient is also treated with a blend of conventional and complementary therapies, because, in Dr. Johnson's opinion, there is a "certain group of patients" for whom "antibiotics are essentially ineffective." He explained, "If you're a doctor whose goal is to help people, and you don't give up, and you keep looking for answers, ultimately you're going to be led to the field of complementary and alternative medicine."

The approach Dr. Johnson described, although not necessarily representative of Lyme-literate approaches in the extent to which it incorporates CAM therapies, exemplifies Lyme-literate approaches in its holistic embrace of the diagnostic significance of symptoms, including their quantity, temporality, and qualitative specificity. For example, in contrast to the CDC, which lists six symptoms in its case definition for Lyme disease, ILADS, the Lyme-literate standard of care's professional organization, lists thirty-five, including

> fatigue, low grade fevers, "hot flashes" or chills, night sweats, sore throat, swollen glands, stiff neck, migrating arthralgias, stiffness and, less commonly, frank arthritis, myalgia, chest pain and palpitations, abdominal pain, nausea, diarrhea, sleep disturbance, poor concentration and memory loss, irritability and mood swings, depression, [and] back pain. (ILADS Working Group 2004, S5)

Here, the constellation of symptoms resists a universalizing classification that can be compared across cases and, instead, allows for variability across bodies.[8] Consistent with how CAM's epistemic framework refrains from delineating between symptoms and signs, more generally, the quantity of symptoms also reflects an approach that is expansively inclusive. This inclusiveness is reflected in how ILADS describes Lyme disease as "a multi-system infection, which can produce a wide range of symptoms and symptom clusters that can be difficult to distinguish from other illnesses."[9] While Lyme-literate practitioners describe individual symptoms as "difficult to distinguish from other illnesses," they also highlight how these symptoms can be differentiated through attention to, for example, their relationship to the entirety of other symptoms, the specificity of their temporality (e.g., "tingling and numbness that comes and goes" and "good days and bad days"), and their qualitative manifestations (e.g., "*migrating* arthralgias" and "*migratory* joint pain" [emphasis mine]).

Observing Eve and Dr. Johnson allowed me to better understand how Lyme-literate approaches play out in practice. Take, for example, Bette, one of the patients I observed Eve examine. Having grown up vacationing on Cape Cod and along the Connecticut shoreline, Bette described being hospitalized in the 1970s when she developed an EM rash accompanied by aches and a fever. Soon after, she developed difficulty reading and recalling words, in addition to cyclical body aches, strange sensations in her mouth and on her tongue, and debilitating fatigue. It was not until Bette read an article in her local newspaper around twenty years later that she began to think about Lyme disease. "The paper listed twenty symptoms," she explained. "And I had eighteen of them." Since then, Bette had seen two Lyme-literate physicians and had been on both intravenous and oral antibiotics. She described how her symptoms responded well to antibiotics, only to "plateau for eleven years" before she became one of Dr. Johnson's patients and discovered what she described as the benefit of herbal protocols. In particular, Bette had recently transitioned off chelation therapy, a combination of Chemet (a pharmaceutical conventionally used in pediatric lead poisoning) and chlorella supplements (composed of green algae and understood by many CAM practitioners to remove heavy metals from the body). She had also begun an herbal protocol taken in a highly regulated manner and was "working up to thirty drops a day." "I'm one of the lucky ones," Bette reflected.

The diagnostic importance of symptoms was also demonstrated in Dr. Johnson's examination of a patient named Dean. Dr. Johnson described Dean as one of the most "Lyme-treatment-resistant" patients he had ever treated. Dean exclaimed, "Before I came here, I had seen seventeen doctors! A lot of them said, 'Why don't you take antidepressants.' At least when I got here I was taken seriously. Anything that I come up with they're willing to entertain." Dr. Johnson explained that in complicated cases like Dean's, which included problems such as "inflammation" and "hormonal dysregulation" in addition to tick-borne disease, the healing process is often protracted, and despite improvement, the patient continues to feel unwell.

Prior to getting sick, Dean had worked full time. "I was in great health," he reflected. "I traveled, I was really outdoorsy." Dean described the decline in his health as "gradual." What began as morning fatigue in 2000 developed over six years into round-the-clock fatigue, drenching night sweats, and painful joints. Dean sought the opinion of the "best orthopedic specialist" he could find, who, upon examination, suggested that Dean be tested for Lyme disease. All of Dean's tests were interpreted as negative.

Having tried an impressive array and combination of conventional and alternative therapies since becoming Dr. Johnson's patient, Dean, who had recently received test results that indicated "low adrenals" and "exposure to pesticides," was prepared to try a new herbal remedy called SyDetox, a homeopathic remedy that Dr. Johnson had recently learned about at an "alternative Lyme conference" and had begun prescribing. Dr. Johnson handed Dean a copy of an informational pamphlet on SyDetox, and they reviewed it together. "A modulator?" Dean asked Dr. Johnson, seeking clarification for the term. "An immune modulator," Dr. Johnson replied. "For autoimmunity. When we don't get people better, we blood let, you know that," Dr. Johnson joked. "But really, I would fall off my chair if you don't respond to [this treatment]."

In his lighthearted reassurance, Dr. Johnson captured a prevailing sentiment among mainstream Lyme physicians: in approaching symptoms as a legitimate basis for diagnosis, Lyme-literate physicians practice a "medieval medicine" at odds with contemporary biomedicine. For Dr. Johnson and Eve, however, symptom-based diagnosis is a more comprehensive approach whose contemporary legitimacy is anchored in the validation of the patients whose symptomatic bodies they integratively treat.[10]

The Lyme Revolutionary

Like Dr. Johnson, Dr. Braun is a biomedically trained Lyme-literate physician who approaches symptoms as signs in the diagnosis of Lyme disease. Unlike Dr. Johnson, however, Dr. Braun does not use CAM in his treatment of Lyme. Soft spoken and serious, Dr. Braun has pensive eyes framed by round-rimmed glasses and an affinity for wearing a tiepin that he received when he was inducted into the AOA (Alpha Omega Alpha) medical honor society during his junior year of medical school.[11] He talks and moves with measured pace, but his energy is boundless. Especially when it comes to anything related to Lyme disease. Since he opened his practice in the late 1980s, Dr. Braun has kept meticulous records of almost every Lyme disease document that has found its way to his hands: letters from patients and physicians, newspaper and article clippings, pamphlets and announcements. I observed Dr. Braun's practice on two separate occasions, and each time, he generously allowed me to pore over his archive. For Dr. Braun, the history of Lyme disease is a history of social and medical injustice; for him, speaking out about Lyme disease is a necessary moral corrective. During a conversation we had on my first visit to his office, and to convey the seriousness of Lyme's political landscape, Dr. Braun revealed his omnivorous reading habits when he made references to Thomas Kuhn, Karl Marx, and Philip Agee.

"Thomas Kuhn and *The Structures of Scientific Revolution* showed that it's dangerous to be right when the establishment is wrong," he explained. "This experience has been very radicalizing."[12] For Dr. Braun, the way in which "academicians attack patients" is "analogous to the labor struggles of the thirties and forties," the stuff that "Woody Guthrie wrote songs about." Although he was careful to explain that he is not a Marxist, he observed that "a Marxist analysis shows that this is prototypical Klassenkampf. Corporations have too much power, and as George Soros said, the collusion of corporations and the government equals fascism."[13]

In Dr. Braun's opinion, chronic Lyme patients and Lyme-literate physicians face a range of challenges: academic researchers whose "paradigm has been threatened," insurance industries whose ultimate goal is "social control," corporations that are driven by "ruthless pursuit of profit," and an "intrusive" government. For this reason, he explained, "I've always recognized how dangerous it is for the physician who treats these patients. That's why I document the hell out of what I do." In addition to detailed patient notes, Dr. Braun also makes an audio recording of every patient's initial intake.[14] "Have you discovered the animus that mainstream physicians have against doctors like us?" he asked me.

I would soon learn, however, that Dr. Braun is unique among other Lyme-literate physicians in that he is not reviled by mainstream Lyme physicians.[15] Two mainstream physicians I spoke with talked about him with a certain degree of admiration. Although they did not agree with his approach to treating Lyme disease, they spoke about him in the same way that one might refer to an acquaintance who had started hanging out with the "wrong crowd." It was one of these physicians who described Dr. Braun as a "crusader," someone who was smart and passionate, albeit, in this physician's opinion, misguidedly passionate. Even Dr. Braun described having felt at times like a "revolutionary" and a "pioneer." Referencing Henrik Ibsen's 1882 play, *The Enemy of the People*, in which the "town physician" discovers and makes known that the health bath for which the town is known is contaminated, Dr. Braun explained that "being a good and ethical physician can put you in conflict with the mainstream. Being a good physician sometimes requires courage and is sometimes a revolutionary act, especially in a time in which medicine has become corporatized."

On the morning of my first visit to Dr. Braun's office, I was greeted by his administrative assistant and nurse. Dr. Braun's first appointment of the day typically begins at 6:45 a.m.; by the time I arrived at 7:30 a.m., he had already moved on to the second appointment, which was a phone consultation.

"The first visit has to be in person," the assistant explained. "After that, patients can do follow-ups by phone. Patients come from all over: Austria, Texas, California, Germany. A lot of it has to be done at a distance because they can't get treated where they live." In the waiting room, photographs that Dr. Braun had taken were hung on the wall alongside framed newspaper articles on Lyme disease. Like almost all Lyme-literate physicians, Dr. Braun does not take insurance. As to why, he explained,

> It's important not to take insurance. For example, I've known cases in which physicians have billed insurers and took the money and then the insurers turned it around and made it about fraud because chronic Lyme disease doesn't exist. That is why a lot of LLMDs [Lyme-literate medical doctors] don't take insurance. If you accept money from insurers, they can interfere and sanction you. When you're deselected from a network, you become reportable to the National Practitioner Data Bank. See how it works? It's about social control. Why social control? It's about predictable income, expenses, and profits. Anything that seemingly threatens profit may be targeted for destruction.[16]

And like other Lyme-literate physicians, Dr. Braun did not begin his career as a Lyme-literate physician. A board-certified internist, Dr. Braun described the challenge of trying to find a niche in the early years of his practice. When, by chance, he began to see more patients with Lyme disease, he "read all the literature" and began to "do things to build a practice." For example, he explained, "I deliberately set up a lecture series on Lyme disease at the library. That made my practice explode. After a couple years, I gave up general medical practice." Ultimately, he clarified,

> It's all about the care of my patients. It's all about what I, through observation of my patients and what happened to them when you treated them and what happened to them when you didn't treat them, that informed my care of them based on what was my best judgment as an autonomous physician. That was informed by just general ethics, period. And, more specifically, old-fashioned Hippocratic medical ethics.

Dr. Braun is adamant that his dogged pursuit of a Lyme disease "paradigm shift" is not a matter of belief:

> Once *Borrelia* was discovered to be a spirochete, the early work always talked about spirochetal persistence. It's not a matter of what I believe. There is PCR-demonstrated spirochetal persistence. But more impor-

tantly, there is a wealth of worldwide peer-reviewed scientific literature that overwhelmingly supports persistence. What I respect is honesty in presenting data. Honest science could solve the problem.

Finally, like some Lyme-literate physicians, but unlike Dr. Johnson and other Lyme-literate physicians who practice CAM, Dr. Braun, who describes having had "pretty conservative mainstream training," is wary about it. He explained, "I'm slow to adapt CAM. Some of the stuff out there, for example, I don't know what to think of the Cowden Protocol."

I observed two appointments on my first visit to Dr. Braun's office, both of which were follow-up appointments. The first appointment was with a woman in her early thirties who, nine months prior, had developed pain in both knees and a right knee that had "doubled in size." Upon consulting a primary care physician who ordered a Lyme test and told her that it was positive, she was treated with twenty-one days of antibiotics, but afterward, she developed new symptoms, which she described as fatigue, muscle aches, joint pains, migraines, and memory problems. Since that time, she had been under Dr. Braun's care and was being treated for Lyme disease in addition to babesiosis. She described having improved "80 percent." "There were days when I couldn't get out of bed," she explained. "But the medication is working; there's steady improvement."

The second patient I observed was a middle-aged woman who had been bitten by a tick in the summer of 2004. By the fall of that year, she had developed muscle pain, fatigue, and twitching. Having been healthy and active all of her life, her first instinct was to "hide her pain from her family." "My husband thought I was depressed and avoiding him," she said. She finally consulted her primary care provider, who ordered a Lyme test and recommended that she see a neurologist. Her ELISA and Western blot tests were interpreted to be positive for Lyme disease, so she was prescribed a course of doxycycline. By the second day of antibiotic treatment, all of her symptoms had "stopped," "so it was clearly Lyme," she deduced. Unfortunately, within twenty-four hours of finishing the antibiotics, her "twitching" returned. She sought care from a physician who treats Lyme disease "aggressively" but is considered to be neither Lyme-literate nor mainstream. After one and a half more years of antibiotic therapy, the patient stopped taking antibiotics and reported feeling "fine" for eighteen months before her symptoms again returned. Since that time, she had been under the care of Dr. Braun. She had made enough progress that she had resumed working out six to seven times a week, but, she explained, "I know that I'll never be cured. The idea is to get a longer remission. If I have nerve damage, then that will never go away." After the patient had finished speaking, Dr. Braun carefully examined her mouth. "There's a pocket toward that back that's white-ish," he said as he reached toward the medical supplies stored on the exam room counter. "I'll take a swab to culture to see if it's yeast."

The next time I observed Dr. Braun's practice, almost a year later, he had moved his office to a new building in a different town. He was delighted with the new space and was excited to lead me on a tour that took us through the hallway, into the examination rooms, and back through the large room that held all of Dr. Braun's patient records.[17] That day, I again had the opportunity to observe two of Dr. Braun's appointments. The first was a new patient appointment with a woman in her late forties who grew up in the southern United States and, as an avid hiker and traveler, had a long history of tick exposure. She had traveled from another state to see Dr. Braun and arrived at the appointment with a large and meticulously documented binder of medical records. Her story had begun three years prior to the appointment when she had consulted a functional medical physician for a range of complaints, including joint pain, insomnia, and persistent headaches.[18] Although the physician suggested that she might have Lyme disease, she dismissed this idea because, she explained, "at the time I didn't believe in Lyme disease." The following year she developed Bell's palsy, vertigo, memory problems, and began to have asthma-like reactions in which she described being "starved for air"; she also continued to have painful headaches and became so disoriented that she could no longer drive, which forced her to quit her job.

In 2010, after feeling unwell for two years, her functional medicine physician persuaded her to get tested for Lyme disease. When both the conventional and alternative laboratory tests were interpreted as positive, she began the Cowden Protocol. Dr. Lewis "doesn't believe in antibiotics," she explained. "It's not part of his belief system." Although a month of this protocol provided some relief, she continued to feel unwell, so, under the care of another doctor, she began six weeks of IV Rocephin. "The Rocephin was amazing!" she exclaimed. After six weeks of IV Rocephin, she switched to oral doxycycline, which she did not tolerate well.

Having tried a few other therapies and having consulted with another Lyme-literate physician, she was now in Dr. Braun's office seeking answers. "I'm here to do what you tell me to do," she said. "I'm tired. I need for you to give me direction." After listening to the patient's story and conducting a thorough physical exam, Dr. Braun said, "I do feel OK endorsing a diagnosis of Lyme and other tick-borne diseases." He explained that her physical exam was normal but that that did not exclude the possibility of Lyme disease; he told her that they needed more "data to fill in the blanks," that a SPECT scan might be useful, and that he would need to do a spinal tap before further IV treatment. While they waited for more data, Dr. Braun advised his patient to remain on the treatment that she was on. "It often takes me a while to figure out what to do for a patient. There are multiple ways to skin a cat. There's not a right way; it's a matter of trial and error."

The second patient Dr. Braun saw that day was a middle-aged woman who had been diagnosed with MS twenty years ago. Although she reported that the white lesions on her MRI remained stable and that none of her MS-related symptoms had progressed, she said that she now had new symptoms that she thought might be related to Lyme disease. "I don't feel well," she said. "Something's going on. I've had MS for twenty years; this is something else. I have lack of strength, fatigue, and when I don't feel well, I don't get sleep." In addition to what she thought might be related to Lyme disease, she also described having "strange fibers" growing in her skin, a controversial condition known as Morgellons disease. She had taped one of these fibers to a Post-It note and had brought it to her appointment to show Dr. Braun. The week prior to her appointment, she had developed a scaly rash that "covered her arm." She had also had a "raised plaque-like bump" on her face, "crawling sensations" in her belly, thinning hair, and "random scratches" on her hand. And, she said, "When I'm submerged under water, I get red splotches." She described the frustration of being "passed off" by her doctors, who believed that Morgellons disease is "delusional parasitosis."

After the patient finished her story, Dr. Braun paused briefly before speaking. Based in part on the results of her blood work, Dr. Braun was willing to entertain a diagnosis of tick-borne disease. "At the very least, I would regard it as suspicious. Band 23 is not enough to hang your hat on, but if you see it, it raises questions." As for Morgellons disease, he responded, "It is very controversial. I don't know what to make of it. We have one other patient in the practice that reports fibers, and I am respectful of patients that report them. But I have enough controversy, and my hands are full with Lyme." Dr. Braun suggested that the patient get a spinal tap and ended the appointment with a discussion about testing and treatment options.

Since I last observed his practice, Dr. Braun has continued to check in from time to time. He sends me references that he thinks might be relevant to my research and asks about the well-being of my children. Although he conveyed to me in an email exchange that he believed me to be "a person of integrity" who "will try to honestly evaluate and analyse what has been happening in the 'Lyme world,'" his own experience in the Lyme world over the last four decades has taught him that trust is hard won. In another email, he continued to explain these concerns when he wrote,

> I told you, you're "in the belly of the beast." 'course, I don't really know what your "take" on all of this Lyme "phenomenon" is—but hopefully it'll be honest and with integrity. If so, like I said, don't be surprised if they try to "shut you down" or "water-down" what you'd like to say!!!!!!!! !![19]

CAM and the Medically Explainable

The stories of Dr. Childs, Dr. Smith, Dr. Johnson, and Dr. Braun reveal a striking difference in how Lyme disease is understood across its standard-of-care divide in the United States. While both mainstream and Lyme-literate physicians insist that Lyme disease is a clinical diagnosis, they diverge over the diagnostic validity of interpreting symptoms as signs. For Dr. Johnson and Dr. Braun, the quantity, temporality, and qualitative specificity of symptoms provide a diagnostic road map that differentiates chronic Lyme disease from other illnesses and renders it explainable, irrespective of the presence or absence of signs. For Dr. Childs and Dr. Smith, however, symptoms only become meaningful in the presence of a sign that can be visually verified, measured, and compared across cases. In the absence of these signs, symptoms often become insignificant and, as a result, unexplainable.

These physicians' stories also reveal the complicated manner in which the epistemic frameworks of biomedicine and CAM inform how mainstream and Lyme-literate physicians make diagnoses. Like Dr. Johnson and Dr. Braun, most Lyme-literate physicians are biomedically trained; even though some incorporate CAM therapies into their practices, many do not. However, because Lyme-literate physicians embrace a symptom-based diagnosis at odds with the mainstream paradigm, the practices of Lyme-literate physicians tend to look like those of CAM practitioners in their attention to the diagnostic significance of patients' symptoms. In this vein, the stories told here illuminate a critical epistemic difference between biomedicine and CAM more generally, as well as a difference that tends to characterize the divided bodies of contested illness: the legitimacy of using symptoms as the basis for diagnosis. This difference is also why medically unexplained illness as a diagnostic category is both unique and intrinsic to biomedicine. As one of the above-quoted mainstream Lyme physicians explained, clinical diagnosis in biomedicine "boils down to subjective symptoms and objective signs." This fundamental delineation between signs and symptoms simultaneously generates biomedical explainability *and* unexplainability and "include[s]" unexplainable conditions *within* biomedicine "through [their diagnostic] exclusion" (Agamben 1998, 18).

In contrast, because CAM and Lyme-literate practitioners do not delineate between symptoms and signs as legitimate bases for diagnosis, illness, by way of symptoms, always has the potential to be explained. Although mainstream physicians criticize Lyme-literate physicians (and CAM practitioners in general) for attributing specificity to an ambiguous multitude of symptoms, Lyme-literate physicians and CAM practitioners maintain that, along the lines of the blind men and the elephant, they are merely practicing more comprehensive medicine. For Lyme patients, this is an important difference in therapeutic philosophy. One patient I interviewed explained,

> [Lyme-literate physicians] believe me; that's the biggest thing. The allopathic doctor wouldn't believe my symptoms and would say there's no such thing as Lyme, and [the problem is that I'm a single mother and depressed and morbidly obese]. . . . I can't listen to another doctor telling me there's no such thing as Lyme.

A mainstream Lyme physician I spoke with also recognized this difference. Although he did not "believe in alternative medicine," he thought that patients' attraction to it could be explained by biomedical physicians' "failure to treat the symptoms that they have." In his observation, this physician captured a possible side effect of an epistemology that hierarchizes signs over symptoms: patient dissatisfaction. While biomedicine remains the "dominative medical system" in the United States (Baer 2004, xvii), CAM has continued to gain legitimacy, and its use has grown, despite associated out-of-pocket costs and biomedical physicians' concerns about the efficacy and "potential harm" of CAM therapies (Lantos et al. 2015, 1776). For example, in 2007, estimated out-of-pocket expenditures for CAM office visits and therapies were $33.9 billion (compared with $27 billion in 1997) (Nahin et al. 2009, 1), and in 2012, around 34 percent of US adults reported having used CAM in the previous year (T. Clarke et al. 2015, 6).

As this chapter demonstrates, chronic Lyme patients' attraction to Lyme-literate and CAM practitioners—and the popularity of CAM among individuals in the United States in general—provides a compelling case for the continued importance of "What's the matter with you?," the question that Foucault identified as the outdated antecedent to the question, "Where does it hurt?" ([1973] 1994b, xviii). Despite advances in technologically enhanced ways of "seeing," patients still interpret the experience of disease through symptoms, which, for them, are the transparent effects of what *cannot* be seen (Mol 2002, 126). In contrast to the biomedical model of "patient-centered medicine," which seeks to achieve better health outcomes by taking into account patients' "preferences, needs, and values" and engaging them in medical decision-making, the popularity of Lyme-literate and CAM practitioners among many chronic Lyme patients seems to be achieved not merely in their attention to patient experience but in the explanatory alignment of their medical practice with patients' symptoms.[20]

More critically, by drawing on ethnographic data on two different approaches to diagnosing Lyme disease, I have broadly explored epistemic differences between biomedicine and CAM in the United States to highlight the tensions that often characterize contested illness's divided bodies of thought. On one hand, medically unexplained illness is a diagnosis that is notably absent from CAM and Lyme-literate practitioners' diagnostic tool kits because, as I have suggested, both types of practitioners approach symptoms as *signs* in the process of making a diagnosis. On the other hand, as biomedicine's diagnostic tool kit grows more sophisticated and as it continues to correlate the legitimacy of symptoms with observable pathophysiology, it struggles to address bodily conditions that it categorizes as medically unexplained illnesses. But this is not a coincidence. As I have argued, because biomedical epistemology is grounded in a fundamental delineation between symptoms and signs as legitimate bases for clinical diagnosis, the bodily conditions that biomedicine cannot explain form the constitutive outside of the bodily conditions it can explain. In this way, despite their perceived marginality, medically unexplained illnesses are an intrinsic feature of biomedicine that are included *within* biomedicine through their diagnostic exclusion. If biomedical explainability hinges on the presence of bodily signs, then "medically unexplained illnesses"—or symptoms in the absence of signs—are but the other side of the same coin.

LYME DISEASE, EVIDENCE-BASED MEDICINE,

AND THE BIOPOLITICS OF TRUTHMAKING

On September 28, 2012, in the lead-up to the American presidential election, *Mother Jones* reported that Mitt Romney's campaign had distributed mailers in the battleground state of Virginia that pledged to "fight the spread of Lyme disease" and "provide local physicians with protection from lawsuits to ensure that they can treat the disease with the aggressive antibiotics that are required" (T. Murphy 2012). Within twenty-four hours of this report, Romney's Lyme disease mailers—and Lyme disease itself—had been colorfully debated between and among political bloggers, Lyme patients, and physicians. For example, a *New Yorker* post, "Mitt Romney versus Lyme Disease and Science," argued that Romney's pledge "would be pretty good news if there was something called chronic Lyme disease . . . but, according to the Infectious Diseases Society of America, there is 'no convincing biological evidence' of any such condition" (Specter 2012). In response, seventy-five readers left impassioned comments, ranging from Lyme anecdotes to citations of scientific studies to criticisms about biomedical conflicts of interest.

This exchange highlights the political salience and volatility of contested illnesses. In addition to their uptake by politicians in an attempt to address constituents' concerns, contested illnesses tend to be associated with class action lawsuits, political rallies, congressional hearings, and state and federal investigations. In its controversy over how diagnosis and treatment should be standardized and regulated across time and space, the case of Lyme disease also highlights the biopolitical dimension of the relationship between contested illness and evidence-based medicine. As pillars of evidence-based medicine, standards of care are institutionalized through medical guidelines, which are often drafted by the medical society whose specialty most overlaps with the disease in question. In this chapter, I explore the relationship between evidence-based medicine, the standards it creates, and the controversy over whose truths about Lyme disease get to count. Drawing from interviews and conversations with Lyme physicians and scientists, I argue that, in addition to standardizing medical practice, evidence-based medicine has the unintended consequence of amplifying differences in practice and opinion by providing a platform of legitimacy on which all individuals—from patients and physicians to scientists and politicians—can make claims to medical truth. Finally, I suggest that evidence-based medicine can be more fully understood as a technology of biopower that regulates bodies in the pursuit of more "effective and efficient" medicine, as well as a form of "biolegitimacy" that, in its emphasis on the evidentiary legitimacy of bodily signs, simultaneously produces a categorical division between the "right way to be sick" (medically explainable) and the "wrong way to be sick" (medically unexplainable), which are correspondingly perceived to be *worthy* and *unworthy* of biomedical attention.

This chapter is organized into three sections. In the first section, I examine the historical emergence of the parts that have come to constitute evidence-based medicine's whole: a hierarchy of scientific evidence, clinical guidelines, and evidence-based medicine treatment centers. I then turn to my interlocutors' experiences with and understandings of evidence-based medicine, particularly as they relate to Lyme disease. In doing so, I flesh out how physicians who diagnose and treat Lyme disease understand the role of evidence-based medicine in their own medical practice and in relationship to the Lyme disease controversy. In the second section, I undertake a fine-toothed exploration of the political event that has had the widest-ranging impact on perceptions and experiences related to Lyme disease: the Connecticut attorney general's 2006 investigation into the clinical guideline–writing process of the Infectious Diseases Society of America (IDSA), which hinged on the claim that IDSA guideline panelists had significant financial conflicts of interest and that, in violating antitrust laws, the guidelines "restrain[ed] doctor and patient choices for the treatment of the disease" and "prevent[ed] physicians' clinical judgment" (Asher 2011, 124). The attorney general and the IDSA reached a settlement two years later, with both sides declaring that they had been vindicated. I then examine another significant political event in the Lyme disease controversy: a medical board's review of a prominent Lyme-literate physician's practice. These ethnographic moments provide a springboard into a broader final analysis of the perceived power relations and conflicted interests that undergird Lyme's controversy, as well as the relationship between biopower and biolegitimacy in the everyday experience and practice of evidence-based medicine.

The Emergence of "Evidence" in Medicine

Described as both a "paradigm shift" and a "social movement," evidence-based medicine is an approach to standardizing clinical practice that gained momentum in the late 1980s and is often defined as "the conscientious, explicit, and judicious use of current best evidence in making decisions about the care of individual patients" (Timmermans and Berg 2003, 3). In addition to promoting the "use of clinical practice guidelines to disseminate proven diagnostic and therapeutic knowledge," evidence-based medicine creates a hierarchy of scientific evidence, at the top of which is the randomized controlled trial and at the bottom of which is "expert opinion" (3). Like any locus of power, evidence-based medicine is simultaneously many things. It is a set of practices; a discourse; an assemblage of individuals, technologies, and institutions; and a term that is simply understood to describe the experience of contemporary biomedicine itself. For many individuals, the term "evidence-based medicine" has become so taken for granted that, when asked to define it, patients would often make comments such as, "It's medicine! What other kind of medicine is there?"[1] This highlights the extent to which evidence-based medicine is now embedded in the biomedical imaginary. As Ludwik Fleck observes, "When a conception permeates a thought collective strongly enough, so that it penetrates as far as everyday life and idiom and has become a viewpoint in the literal sense of the word, any contradiction appears unthinkable and unimaginable" ([1935] 1981, 28).

Evidence-based medicine's embeddedness, however, is a rather recent phenomenon. As late as the early 1980s, Timmermans and Berg observe that "the application of scientific knowledge" in the practice of medicine was "an art that only an experienced, true professional could master" (13). Although efforts to standardize medicine began in the early twentieth century—an outgrowth of a broader movement in which "standards emerged as one of the hallmarks of rationalization" and "modernity"—these efforts were directed at standardizing "skills, tools, and facilities" rather than medical decision-making (8, 13). For example, according to Timmermans and Berg, one of the most consequential developments of early twentieth-century medical standardization was the emergence of "paper-based patient records," whereby the medical record was transformed from a "bound casebook in the physician's private office, with handwritten notes gradually and consecutively filling the empty pages with descriptions of the working day" into a "patient-centered case file" in which "all patients now had their own personalized records" (32). The idea that the way in which physicians diagnose and treat conditions of the body could be similarly standardized only began to crystallize in the late 1980s and early 1990s, a development that also coincided with the "emergence of information technology in medicine," particularly the electronic medical record (17).

Three individuals are often credited with having led the charge of biomedicine's shift to evidence-based medicine (2003, 14–15). The first, responsible for the term "evidence-based medicine" and for outlining its defining features, is David Sackett, a clinical epidemiologist whose own research has centered on how to study and assess data derived from randomized controlled trials (15). The second is epidemiologist John Wennberg, who is the founding editor of the *Dartmouth Atlas of Health Care*, a publication that documents the "glaring variations in how medical resources are distributed and used in the United States."[2] For example, a 2010 report found that "amputation rates were 4.7 times greater in blacks than in whites nationally during the study period from 2003 to 2007" (Goodman et al. 2010, 2). Findings such as these and others have highlighted the extent to which differences in the application of medical knowledge affect patient care. The third is Archie Cochrane, a Scottish physician whose experience as a medical officer caring for prisoners of war in World War II led him to believe that "unsubstantiated claims plagu[e] medicine" (Shah and Chung 2009, 985). In his 1972 text, *Effectiveness and Efficiency*, Cochrane argued that randomized controlled trials should be used to determine which medical interventions were actually effective and efficient. Today, an organization called the Cochrane Collaboration, one of the flagship institutions of evidence-based medicine, is devoted to systematically reviewing randomized controlled trials for a range of health-care interventions and publishing its findings.

Although Sackett, Wennberg, and Cochrane, among others, set the stage for the emergence of clinical practice guidelines, Timmermans and Berg suggest that a more significant historical moment brought the widespread institutionalization of evidence-based medicine into being: biomedicine's fear of its own demise. They argue that, in the face of growing patient consumerism and "spiraling health costs," biomedical thought leaders reasserted the dominance and authority of biomedicine through the standardization of clinical practice (2003, 16). Like any tectonic shift, however, evidence-based medicine, in its success, has been met with significant resistance even among conventional practitioners of biomedicine. For all who welcomed the transition to evidence-based medicine, there have been as many practitioners and scholars who have criticized evidence-based medicine for unduly regulating medical decision-making on an individual basis, obscuring "subjectivity," and reinforcing "monopolies of knowledge."[3] Others point to the fact that despite its rhetorical success, evidence-based medicine has had a "marginal effect" on everyday clinical practice (Timmermans 2007, 353). For example, Timmermans notes sociologist Jeanne Daly's observation that there is "a fifty-percent chance that your physician will provide care that conforms to the current best evidence available" (353). This observation was echoed by a mainstream Lyme disease physician-scientist, who explained,

> I don't think evidence-based medicine has actually changed the practice of medicine that much. Even though we study and promulgate evidence-based medicine, I don't think it has changed the average practitioner's management, because they might not be familiar with the evidence. . . . Current trainees are more attuned to the guidelines and the evidence-based theses, but I'm not sure it's infiltrated practice as much.

Through praise, discontent, and indifference, evidence-based medicine, in its entirety, has come to encompass several key components: a hierarchy of scientific evidence, clinical guidelines, and evidence-based practice centers. Within the framework of evidence-based medicine, evidence is most commonly understood to fall within five categories, two categories of which have three subcategories of evidence and one of which has two subcategories of evidence. Table 5.1 shows the "evidence rating scale" created by the Centre for Evidence-Based Medicine at Oxford University, which appears to be one scale that is commonly used.[4] There are other recognized "evidence rating scales," some of which eliminate subcategories and some of which do not include expert opinion, but all scales of evidence are organized according to the probability of bias. That is, systemic reviews of randomized controlled trials are understood to be the strongest evidence because they are understood to contain the least bias, while expert opinion is understood to be the weakest evidence because it is understood to contain the most bias.

American clinical guidelines, which are drafted by representatives from American medical societies and are understood to be based on comprehen-

TABLE 5.1. LEVELS OF EVIDENCE

1a   Systematic reviews (with homogeneity) of randomized controlled trials

1b   Individual randomized controlled trials (with narrow confidence interval)

1c   All or none randomized controlled trials

2a   Systematic reviews (with homogeneity) of cohort studies

2b   Individual cohort study or low quality randomized controlled trials (e.g., <80% follow-up)

2c   "Outcomes" research; ecological studies

3a   Systematic review (with homogeneity) of case-control studies

3b   Individual case-control study

4   Case series (and poor quality cohort and case-control studies)

5   Expert opinion without explicit critical appraisal, or based on physiology, bench research, or "first principles"

Source: Oxford Centre for Evidence-Based Medicine, https://www.cebm
.net/2009/06/oxford-centre-evidence-based-medicine-levels-evidence-march-2009

sive reviews of all available evidence, were, until July 17, 2018, housed within the National Guidelines Clearinghouse (NGC), an online database sponsored by the Agency for Healthcare Research and Quality (AHRQ), which is part of the US Department of Health and Human Services.[5] Prior to its discontinuation, the NGC housed more than two thousand clinical guidelines that were free to the public and were required to be updated every five years. The inclusion criteria for the NGC's guidelines were first developed in 1997, but after the Institute of Medicine updated its definition of clinical practice guidelines in March 2011 in a report titled *Clinical Guidelines We Can Trust*, the NGC adopted the Institute of Medicine's revised criteria. Beginning in June 2014, the Institute of Medicine and the NGC collectively defined clinical practice guidelines as "statements that include recommendations intended to optimize patient care that are informed by a systematic review of evidence and an assessment of the benefits and harms of alternative care options."[6] The primary changes in this definition included documentation of systematic reviews of evidence, as well as documentation of an assessment of benefits and harms, neither of which was part of the original 1997 criteria for inclusion. In addition to the revised definition, the Institute of Medicine's 2011 report also laid out eight standards for "developing trustworthy clinical practice guidelines," which include "establishing transparency," "management of conflicts of interest," "guideline development group composition," "methods for systematic reviews of evidence," "establishing evidence foundations for rating strength of recommendations," "articulation of recommendations," "external review," and "updating" (Institute of Medicine et al. 2011). As a result, each set of guidelines listed in the NGC was graded to demonstrate the extent to which it meets these eight standards.

Finally, evidence-based medicine is structurally manifested through evidence-based practice centers (of which, as of this writing, there are twelve, including Mayo Clinic Evidence-Based Practice Center, in Rochester, Minnesota; the Brown University Center for Evidence-Based Medicine, in Providence, Rhode Island; and the Kaiser Permanente Research Affiliates, in Portland, Oregon). Established in 1997 by the AHRQ, evidence-based practice centers are located at research hospitals, medical centers, and other research institutions, and their purpose is to conduct "evidence reports" for the Effective Health Care Program, which provides funding to individuals and organizations to "hel[p] consumers, health care professionals, and policymakers make informed and evidence-based health care decisions."[7] The three primary "products" that the Effective Health Care Program distributes are "systematic reviews," "research protocols," and "research reports."[8] From 2010 to 2014, the Effective Health Care Program and the evidence-based practice centers that conduct research for the program were part of a larger government initiative called the National Initiative for Promoting Evidence-Based Health Information, one of the primary goals of which was to use "campaigns and marketing activities to promote the use of evidence-based health information to help consumers and health care professionals make informed health care decisions."[9] Perhaps more than any other feature of evidence-based medicine, evidence-based practice centers highlight the extent to which evidence-based medicine has become an important part of the biopolitical management of health in the United States.

"It's Anecdotal; That's Not Evidence"

Among mainstream Lyme physicians, including those who participated in the writing of the IDSA's Lyme disease guidelines, evidence-based medicine is nearly unanimously celebrated. One physician described evidence-based medicine as "very helpful." "It's very objective stuff," he explained.

"It doesn't mean that we'll have the same guidelines in twenty years, but it's very helpful." Another physician reflected, "I think guidelines are helpful because they raise the average level of care. They help physicians understand what leading thought leaders think. Often there are not studies for a specific intervention, but expert opinion is important. Guidelines are only there as recommendations." Echoing this thought, a third physician explained,

> What I like about evidence-based medicine is that it provides some rationale to justify medical interventions and noninterventions. I don't know if every aspect of medicine lends itself to evidence-based medicine. When I was in school, people said, "This is what you do!" There weren't too many times when people said there were four randomized controlled double-blind studies that showed this to be the case. But I think we should all strive to do evidence-based medicine.

Drawing on evidence-based medicine's rich lexicon, mainstream Lyme physicians are quick to emphasize that all evidence is not equal, and that "strength" of evidence matters. One physician-scientist described the problem as an "inability to differentiate between different kinds of evidence." She continued,

> ILADS refers to evidence, but it's anecdotal; that's not evidence. These are the problems you have when you have impressions. That's why we have placebo-controlled studies as the highest level of evidence. Unless you control for all of the bias that you have, you're going to end up with very different levels of evidence. It's about pseudoscience and science, science that looks like science but is not science.

Another physician-scientist echoed these ideas when he exclaimed,

> The lack of a perfect science is exploited by those who uphold things that are totally unscientific. There is such a huge body of evidence for certain things. For example, the earth is smaller than the sun, and the moon is smaller than the earth. Our eyes are imperfect. The body of evidence against chronic Lyme infection is strong; the body of evidence against long-term antibiotic treatment is strong. On the other side, the evidence is very weak. One has to go with the science of it all, as best one can.

Lyme-literate physicians and Lyme patients are acutely aware that mainstream physicians and scientists perceive their evidence to be "weaker" evidence. In response, they tend to emphasize that the case reports and studies on which they make claims for the existence of chronic Lyme disease are "peer reviewed," another feature by which the strength of evidence is judged within an evidence-based medicine framework. Moreover, the clinical trials that mainstream physicians and scientists refer to as the strongest available evidence—evidence which, in their opinion, does not support the Lyme-literate standard of care—is as central to Lyme patients' and Lyme-literate physicians' claims to truth as it is to those of mainstream physicians and scientists. The catch, however, is that each side interprets the evidence from those studies differently. Perhaps not surprisingly, while mainstream physicians argue that the data from those studies show that long-term antibiotics have no benefit, Lyme-literate physicians argue that the data from those studies demonstrate measurable improvement in fatigue. As one Lyme-literate physician explained when discussing one of these studies, "My reading of the study is that there is evidence to support the idea that some patients benefit from re-treatment. I try to be as objective as possible, and I am convinced that the evidence is there." In this way, although intended to resolve disputes, evidence-based medicine provides a means by which each of Lyme's two camps reinforces its respective standard of care through different "styles of scientific practice" and, in so doing, often produces the very "uncertainty" that evidence-based medicine attempts to "settle" (Fujimura and Chou 1994; Epstein 1996, 333).[10]

The phenomenon of differently interpreting data to reinforce a preexisting opinion is not unique to Lyme disease—it is a hallmark feature of evidence-based medicine. Across a wide range of topics and specialties, evidence-based medicine inadvertently produces and legitimizes differences in medical practice and opinion by providing a language of legitimacy through which all individuals can make claims to medical truth. A non-Lyme-related example of this was a much-publicized meta-analysis of the health benefits of saturated fats. Depending on the position of those who read the study, the data derived from the study suggest that saturated fats offer either some health benefits or no benefits at all. Chef and *New York Times* columnist Mark Bittman made waves by publishing a column entitled, "Butter Is Back!," while physicians and public health officials from prestigious universities decried Bittman's lack of scientific knowledge and argued that his interpretation of the data was not only misguided but that the study itself was flawed. In a *Science Insider* article published on March 24, 2014, Walter Willett, the chair of the Department of Nutrition at Harvard University, used the example of the controversy over saturated fats to make a case for the "dangers" of meta-analyses more generally. Quoting Willett, journalist Kai Kupferschmidt writes,

The controversy should serve as a warning about meta-analyses, Willett adds. . . . "[These] days meta-analyses are often done by people who are not familiar with a field, who don't have the primary data or don't make the effort to get it. . . . Often the strengths and weaknesses of individual studies get lost," Willett says. "It's dangerous."[11]

As one of evidence-based medicine's most heavily relied-on tools, meta-analyses aggregate and synthesize all available evidence on a particular topic to arrive at one encompassing truth. Although the goal of performing a meta-analysis is to distill similarity from difference and achieve consensus, the end result is that meta-analyses also reinforce preexisting differences by providing a platform on which anyone with access to evidence-based information can make a claim to truth.[12]

While the trappings of evidence-based medicine are just as important for maintaining the legitimacy of the Lyme-literate standard of care as they are for maintaining the legitimacy of the mainstream standard of care (e.g., medical societies, peer-reviewed articles, and clinical guidelines), I found that Lyme-literate physicians were quicker than their mainstream counterparts to voice concerns about the potential pitfalls of evidence-based medicine. Where mainstream concerns about evidence-based medicine tend to be related to diminished clinical autonomy, concerns among Lyme-literate physicians tend to be related to how evidence-based medicine—primarily in the form of guidelines—is wielded and leveraged as a form of power. One Lyme-literate physician explained,

> The IDSA is very powerful. I mean, they're eight thousand members strong, and they're very influential. And insurance companies will go along with their guidelines. And as a neurologist, I happen to know also that the American Neurological Association [ANA] always follows suit—whatever the IDSA says, the ANA will say, too. So you'll have all the other medical subspecialties going along with it. So you're kind of outnumbered. And they have the credibility on their side.

This physician also expressed concern about what the recently passed Affordable Care Act would mean for the standardization of medicine and how guidelines would be used in the future. She continued,

> The one thing I am concerned about is guidelines. Whose guidelines are they going to follow? How are they going to restrict care and treatment? What's the role of the subspecialist in all of this? . . . It's very, very complicated. I guess from a physician's point of view, you really just

can't have somebody reading from a cookbook over the phone to you and telling you, "Yes, you can do that. No, you can't." . . . It's insane. You can't do it. Medicine is an art; it's not a science.

When I followed up on whether her opinion that "medicine is an art, not a science" meant that she thought evidence-based medicine was at odds with the Lyme-literate standard of care, she was quick to counter,

No, definitely not. That's our goal—to get evidence-based medicine by promoting and funding research that's going to get to the bottom of this and not have people or organizations put up obstacles to that because it's just so much simpler to keep it the status quo. It's just too many things that are unexplained. No, I'm all for evidence-based medicine!

Beyond concerns about how evidence-based medicine could be used to deny Lyme patients care and treatment, Lyme-literate physicians also expressed concerns about the variability with which evidence can be interpreted and how, in these cases, the interpretation held by the more powerful entity is the one that is perceived to be more legitimate. One physician explained, "I'm still 100 percent for evidence-based medicine. I have papers to every statement I make. The problem is that evidence can be presented in a misleading way." Another physician echoed this thought when he reflected,

In the scientific pursuit, when you have one shred of evidence, you go with the evidence. But there is conflicting evidence invariably in most fields; it's never that clear. What I don't like is that the IDSA will say that their guidelines are voluntary, but when it comes to a political setting, they send someone that says that they're standards. It's like freedom of religion or anything else. Evidence-based medicine is like religious doctrine—it can either be a good thing or misused. In pure evidence-based medicine, you have clinical judgment, the best research available, and patient preference. When it is misused, you have absolute evidence quoted out of context, and you ignore clinical judgment and patient preferences. It's really only useful with very well-defined things. With complexity, it falls apart. Here, in this practice, we treat patients; we never treat disease. I don't care about Lyme; I care about patients.

These two physicians take for granted that evidence will be always be interpreted differently or that two studies on the same topic might point to different conclusions. And for this reason, they believe that evidence-based medicine must be used judiciously: always paired with clinical judgment and never used to infringe on *others'* clinical judgment.

The second physician's comparison of evidence-based medicine to religion was one that also surfaced many times in my conversations with physicians and scientists. It is a comparison that not only highlights concerns about the power of ideas and institutions but also points to concerns about the problem of "belief" in science. For individuals entangled in medical controversy, the opinions of the other side always seem to resemble beliefs more than they do facts. One mainstream scientist found it helpful to explain the phenomenon of chronic Lyme disease through what astronomer Carl Sagan described as "the invisible dragon theory." She said,

> They tell you, "You cannot see the dragon, because it's invisible." It becomes an infallible hypothesis. It's impossible to prove that they don't have it. We've set it up in science so that you can never prove a negative. Scientists tend to be cautious—we can never say never. That is so hard to explain to people. People hear that, and they think, "So there's a chance that it might be!" I don't have a belief. I'm a scientist. We know that things change. And that's the problem of representing science to people. It's very hard for people to understand that.

However, another mainstream physician who was critical of what he perceived to be the stridency with which some of his colleagues approached chronic Lyme disease explained, "You would think that a real scientist would always be skeptical. They just seem so arrogant. It gets to the point of religion. Just because it doesn't fit the paradigm doesn't mean that it's not an 'it.' People should be open-minded." And still another mainstream physician became quite reflective when he acknowledged that he, like all physicians, is susceptible to the problem of belief in his own practice. He said, "With that said, there are lots of things that people don't know. Doctors can be too pretentious. I'm one of them. We give the appearance that we know when we certainly do not."

For some Lyme-literate physicians, the perception that belief masquerades as fact among those who practice evidence-based medicine has led them to discount the value of evidence-based medicine altogether. One Lyme-literate physician exclaimed,

> Evidence-based medicine has gone from good to misused. Just look at the strength of evidence behind all the IDSA guidelines. It's hard to de-

velop evidence that's good. That's why we've moved away from evidence-based medicine. There are huge amounts of medicine where there's no evidence. It just goes to show how you can misuse guidelines.

And for other Lyme-literate physicians, the fact that evidence-based medicine does not take into account "what can't be seen" is its greatest weakness. These physicians, who were in the minority of Lyme-literate physicians I spoke with, argued that evidence often obscures medical decisions that should be made with intuition. One such physician exclaimed, "We are confronted with a medical world that must see data. If I can't see it, it must be mental. I can't see air, but should I be sent to a psych ward if I say it?" And a second physician explained,

> This is what I say. On this table are all of your beliefs, everything you know. Let's just say that the thing to help you is off the table of what you accept or think is everything that could be done for you. Some people hesitate, and some take a leap of faith.

Across the board, however, Lyme-literate physicians' most common criticism of evidence-based medicine guidelines is that, despite being promulgated as recommendations supported by the highest level of evidence, the majority of recommendations are supported only by "expert opinion," the lowest-ranking form of evidence in evidence-based medicine. This criticism seemed to be informed by a study published in January 2010 in which the investigators reviewed a representative subset of all guidelines published by the IDSA and concluded that "more than half of the current recommendations of the IDSA are based on level III evidence only" (Lee and Vielemeyer 2011, 18). They continued, "[U]ntil more data from well-designed controlled clinical trials become available, physicians should remain cautious when using current guidelines as the sole source guiding patient care decisions" (18).[13] When I interviewed one of the investigators on this study, he, unlike Lyme-literate physicians, did not believe that the results of his study diminished the value of the IDSA's guidelines on Lyme disease. In fact, he argued that guidelines were sometimes *most* necessary in the absence of good evidence. He explained,

> If there are three beautifully designed trials with clear results to a clinical question that everyone knows, there's no reason for guidelines. What you need guidelines for is when there's little data, because poor data can be confused with good evidence. The problem is that people think that if something is printed, it must be true. . . . The idea of the study was

that if we clarify the issue about levels of evidence, maybe it will trigger thoughts not to blindly follow guidelines. This is important for patient care. Physicians have to be careful when patients are not improving when managing diseases based on guidelines. If the patient is not getting better, you may have to think that in this individual case, you might want to do something different diagnostically and/or therapeutically.

In his reflections about the need for guidelines in the absence of "good data," this physician provided a nuanced understanding of clinical guidelines, one that approaches them as necessary precisely because they function as signposts for what evidence *cannot* determine as much as what it *can*.

Despite mainstream Lyme physicians' nearly unanimous embrace of evidence-based medicine and the IDSA's guidelines for treating and diagnosing Lyme disease, they were unsurprised that the bulk of the guidelines they adhere to are based on expert opinion. In our conversations together, some mainstream Lyme physicians went further by explaining how evidence-based medicine sometimes requires producing evidence when no evidence actually exists. One example of this was given by a scientist who described the process by which the duration for the popular antibiotic azithromycin was determined. He explained that most patients and physicians assume that azithromycin is prescribed for five days because that amount of time is pharmacologically specific, but, according to this scientist, the antibiotic's duration was actually determined by public marketing. He continued to explain,

> When Pfizer brought the med to the United States back in the eighties, they said, "This drug is given in three days." But when it was brought before focus groups, that changed. The perception from the public was that three days wasn't enough time to be effective. Medical decisions are not always based in science. A lot of what we do is empirical, even if we think it's evidence based. Someone just decided it. Or we just picked ten because it was a nice round number, but there was very little work behind it.

In a similar example related to Lyme disease, one physician-scientist described the process by which a recommendation to prescribe antibiotics came to be determined. "We went back and forth over [the duration]. And then one of our colleagues said, 'No, [shorter duration] is more exciting.' That's how we got it published," he explained. He also explained that shorter treatment durations can be more practical and can translate to better patient compliance. Based in part on their decision to test the effectiveness of this antibiotic for these reasons, the investigators performed a study that demonstrated that the selected shorter dose was effective. Nevertheless, these physicians, like the investigator who published the study on the strength of evidence in the IDSA's guidelines, still believed that even "weak" evidence is better than the alternative of not having guidelines to help clinicians make decisions.

Most mainstream Lyme physicians object to the description of the Lyme-literate approach to diagnosing and treating Lyme disease as a "standard of care." For mainstream physicians, Lyme-literate physicians' medical society and their guidelines constitute a well-crafted marketing stunt that has successfully deceived many patients and politicians. For Lyme-literate physicians, however, their approach to diagnosing and treating Lyme disease constitutes a more sophisticated standard of care than that of the IDSA, and, for them, evidence-based medicine provides a path toward vindication and a means to reducing what is perceived to be the disparity of power between themselves and the mainstream. Take, for example, a prominent Lyme advocate and blogger, who in a blog post titled "Who Died and Made You King? Eminence Based Medicine in Lyme Disease Breaks All the Rules" embraces the Cochrane Collaboration as a "leader in true evidence based medicine," an institution at the center of evidence-based medicine's move to "downgrade the ultimate authority of the clinical expert in favour of impersonal scientific research evidence" (L. Johnson 2011; Lambert 2006, 2639). In her embrace of evidence-based medicine, this advocate claims that what mainstream Lyme physicians actually practice is "eminence-based medicine," a term borrowed from the Cochrane Collaboration to describe "guidelines that hinge upon the opinion, bias and arrogance of physicians that hold a particular viewpoint rather than science." She continues, "Eminence is not evidence, it is power. When it is used to shut down treatment options for patients with Lyme, it is an abuse of power that harms patients" (L. Johnson 2011).

On November 10, 2017, six years after this blog's posting, twenty-eight individuals filed a federal antitrust lawsuit that "asserts that key architects of Lyme policy, naming seven physician-researchers, took money from and worked with insurers to develop guidelines that allowed claims to be denied."[14] Three weeks later, the CDC removed the IDSA guidelines from its website, explaining to a reporter, "It has been over a decade since the IDSA guidelines on treatment of Lyme disease, developed in 2006, were published. Since then, additional published research further informs Lyme disease treatment" (Leland 2017).[15] Although the CDC still lists treatment recommendations consistent with the IDSA guidelines on its website, Lyme advocates nevertheless celebrated this development as a small victory. Despite contestations over who has a *legitimate* claim to truth, this section has demonstrated how evidence-based medicine provides a set of tools with which a range of individuals can make a claim to medical truth and expect to have that claim become part of a debate.

An Attorney General, a Set of Guidelines, and the Medical Society That Wrote Them

To fully understand the significance of the IDSA's guidelines being removed from the CDC's website in 2017, a quick historical detour is in order. The IDSA first published its diagnosis and treatment guidelines on Lyme disease in 2000. Six years later, in 2006, the guidelines were reviewed and updated to include new findings. Soon after they were published, Richard Blumenthal, the former Connecticut attorney general and current Connecticut senator, launched an antitrust investigation into the IDSA's guideline-making process by issuing the IDSA a subpoena. It was the first investigation of its kind. Influenced by the appeals of three prominent Lyme advocacy organizations, this investigation was premised on two major claims.[16] The first was that the guideline panelists had significant undisclosed financial conflicts of interest. The second, which followed from the first, was that, in violating antitrust laws, the guidelines "'restrain[ed] doctor and patient choices for the treatment of the disease'" and "prevent[ed] physicians' clinical judgment" (Asher 2011, 124). Attorney General Blumenthal's investigation, which received national media attention and became somewhat of a cautionary tale among mainstream physicians and scientists, never made it to the courtroom. On April 30, 2008, after two years of much anticipation among individuals across the standard-of-care divide, Blumenthal and the IDSA reached a settlement. In a press release posted to his office's website, Blumenthal explained his findings:

> This agreement vindicates my investigation—finding undisclosed financial interests and forcing a reassessment of IDSA guidelines. . . . My office uncovered undisclosed financial interests held by several of the most powerful IDSA panelists. The IDSA's guideline panel improperly ignored or minimized consideration of alternative medical opinion and evidence regarding chronic Lyme disease, potentially raising seri-

ous questions about whether the recommendations reflected all relevant science.[17]

On the same day that the Office of the Attorney General issued its press release, the IDSA also released its own. Not surprisingly, the IDSA provided a much different interpretation of the meaning of its settlement with the attorney general, an interpretation well captured by the press release's heading, "Agreement Ends Lyme Disease Investigation by Connecticut Attorney General: Medical Validity of IDSA Guidelines Not Challenged."[18] In its account, the IDSA emphasized that the guidelines remained in effect and that its members had agreed to a voluntary review of the guidelines process, not because they were concerned that the guidelines were not "the best advice that medicine currently has to offer," but to put to rest the "unfounded" assertion that the IDSA had "ignored divergent opinion." It also denied the validity of the investigation's findings, all of which centered on conflicts of interest and the exclusion of divergent opinion. It countered that none of the panelists had conflicts of interest that would have affected the guidelines' recommendations and that none of the panelists stood to benefit financially from any of the recommendations. As I was told on several occasions by mainstream physicians and scientists, the release further added that, in not recommending long-term antibiotic therapy, IDSA physicians were actually denying themselves an income-generating opportunity. Finally, the release insisted that far from ignoring divergent opinion, the IDSA had welcomed and reviewed all evidence in its guideline-generating process and that the "dissenting" panelist whom Blumenthal had mentioned in his findings had not been removed from the panel but had voluntarily resigned.

On April 22, 2010, two years after Blumenthal and the IDSA reached a settlement, the IDSA announced the findings of its review. In the lead-up to the IDSA's announcement, the Lyme ethersphere was abuzz. Lyme advocates had received word two months prior to the announcement that the guidelines would remain unchanged and that Blumenthal had found errors in the IDSA's voting process. On February 1, 2010, Blumenthal's office sent a four-page letter to the IDSA that documented what it perceived as the panel's procedural mistakes and asked that the review panel revote in compliance with the terms of the settlement agreement. These terms, which the IDSA had agreed to and indicated knowledge of in an internal memo dated July 9, 2009, required a two-step voting procedure, each step of which required a supermajority of six out of eight panel members. All panel members were infectious disease physicians without previous connection to Lyme disease and had been selected by a medical ethicist agreed on by Blumenthal and the IDSA. The first step required that the panel vote on whether the recommendation was "medically/scientifically justified in light of all of the evidence and information provided"; the second step, which followed from the first, was to vote on whether the recommendation required (1) no changes, (2) sectional revisions, or (3) complete rewriting.[19] When, according to Blumenthal's office, some of its members visited the IDSA's office to review minutes of the panel's meetings, it described finding that the panel had only enacted the second part of the voting procedure. Of particular concern to Blumenthal was that a recommendation found in the executive summary of the guidelines had received a vote of 4–4. For chronic Lyme patients, this statement, which recommends that "diagnostic testing performed in laboratories with excellent quality-control procedures [be] required for confirmation of extracutaneous Lyme disease, HGA, and babesiosis," is particularly important because, in the absence of confirmatory laboratory results, they argue that it is the basis on which insurance companies deny them antibiotic therapy coverage (Wormser et al. 2006, 1089–90). Nonetheless, because this statement is located in the executive summary and did not technically qualify as a guideline recommendation, the IDSA argued that this vote did not need to be enforced.

On the heels of Blumenthal's admonishing letter to the IDSA and his request for a second vote, Lyme advocacy organizations sent emails to patients and physicians across the country and informed them of Blumenthal's findings. They also requested that residents of Connecticut contact Blumenthal to thank him and that residents of other states contact their own attorney general to ask that they stand in public support of Blumenthal. Given the possibility that the panel might concede to Blumenthal's request, individuals across the standard-of-care divide waited in suspense. The day before the release of the IDSA's announcement, I received an email from a mainstream Lyme scientist that read, "The IDSA guidelines will remain unchanged—a unanimous decision by the special review board." In a follow-up email two days later, the scientist wrote, "Looks like Blumenthal is on ice with this. Hope he concedes." In the report released by the IDSA on April 22, it announced that the review panel had voted to keep all of the guidelines' recommendations. In a footnote, it revealed that the panel had initially conducted a one-step vote but, after communicating with Blumenthal, had redone the vote according to the two-step procedure. The results of the vote remained the same.

For mainstream physicians and scientists, the IDSA's final report was a moment of great vindication. For them, it unequivocally demonstrated that their approach to diagnosing and treating Lyme disease is the only approach supported by the best available evidence. For Lyme patients and advocates, the report was a discouraging defeat. However, it was a defeat that many did not find entirely surprising. Indeed, most chronic Lyme patients and Lyme-literate physicians have come to perceive the IDSA to be such a powerful and corrupt organization that few had hope that "justice would prevail." For them, the final results of the IDSA's review merely confirmed their long-held suspicions that the IDSA would, in their opinion, brazenly circumvent rules to ensure that their guidelines remained intact.

An Inside Perspective

The beginning of my research in February 2010 coincided with Attorney General Blumenthal's request that the IDSA's special review panel redo their vote. Even in my early conversations with patients and physicians, as I worked to gain footing on Lyme disease's slippery terrain, it was clear that the attorney general's investigation was understood by individuals across the standard-of-care divide to be a significant moment in the history of the Lyme disease controversy. This investigation not only carried with it the possibility that the way in which Lyme disease is diagnosed and treated could be changed but also brought to the fore a question that haunts the Lyme world more generally: What role should politics play in medicine?

To better understand the context in which the attorney general's investigation had been launched, I met with Mr. Smith, one of Connecticut's assistant attorney generals, at his office. Upon my arrival, Mr. Smith and I made our way to a windowless conference room with a long narrow table surrounded by matching office chairs. When we sat down, under the yellow cast of fluorescent lights, Mr. Smith made it clear that he could not speak on behalf of the attorney general and that he could only discuss general background information related to the activities of the Office of the Attorney General.[20]

The involvement of the Office of the Attorney General in issues related to Lyme disease reaches back to 1998, when it began a "health care advocacy effort" for Connecticut residents. One part of this campaign involved working to get insurance coverage for treatments recommended by some patients' physicians, including insurance coverage for antibiotic treatment prescribed for Lyme disease, the duration of which was longer than that recommended by the IDSA's Lyme disease guidelines. In December 1998, six months into this health care advocacy effort, Blumenthal, with the commissioner of the Connecticut Insurance Department as his cochair, decided to organize a state legislative hearing on Lyme disease, which took place on February 24, 1999.

The momentum generated by the legislative hearing translated into the passing of Public Act 99-284. As described on the Connecticut General Assembly website, this bill

> requires health insurers to cover Lyme disease treatment under certain conditions. Specifically, individual and group insurance policies must cover Lyme disease treatment, including at least 30 days of intravenous antibiotic therapy, 60 days of oral antibiotic therapy, or both. Such policies must provide further treatment if recommended by a board-certified rheumatologist, infectious disease specialist, or neurologist licensed in the state.[21]

Although Public Act 99-284, which was amended in 1999 to include specialists who are licensed in another state, was considered to be landmark legislation, patients and Lyme-literate physicians with whom I spoke observed that because most Lyme-literate physicians do not take insurance, many chronic Lyme patients had not felt the anticipated financial impact of the bill.[22] Years later, the Connecticut House of Representatives, through efforts not related to those of the attorney general, passed Connecticut House Bill No. 6200, named by Lyme advocates as the Lyme Doctor Protection Bill. This bill, which went into effect on July 1, 2009, effectively sanctioned the use of long-term antibiotics in the treatment of Lyme disease in Connecticut; it also protected physicians from being "subject to disciplinary action by the Connecticut Medical Examining Board solely on the basis of prescribing, administering, or dispensing long-term antibiotic therapy."[23] Together, Public Act 99-284 and House Bill No. 6200 provide more legal accommodations for the extended treatment of Lyme disease in Connecticut than exist in most states. Nevertheless, a Lyme-literate physician with whom I spoke, who does not practice in Connecticut, observed that despite Connecticut's legal safety net, relatively few physicians actually treat with extended antibiotics because of "peer pressure."

Aside from another hearing in 2004, the next major event in Blumenthal's efforts to help Lyme disease patients was the antitrust investigation that began in 2006. For the Office of the Attorney General, the impetus for the investigation was a complaint that the IDSA, as a respected standard-setting organization, was neglecting its responsibility to follow due and fair process by ignoring divergent medical opinions. In the wake of the investigation, the major criticism leveled at the Office of the Attorney General has been that it took a political stance on a medical issue and that it responded to the concerns of Lyme advocacy groups over and above those of other constituents. In an article titled "Danger Ahead: Politics Intrude in Infectious Diseases Society of America Guidelines for Lyme Disease," the author writes,

> The action of the AG against the IDSA should raise concern for all medical and scientific groups that issue practice recommendations or guidelines. The door is open to any constituency that feels it was not adequately represented in the process of developing the recommendations. If an AG can undermine evidence-based guidelines on the basis of dissenting views of medical and nonmedical advocacy groups, then every guideline for management of a disease or condition presented by any medical organization is at risk of challenge. (Klein 2008, 1198–99)

But the Connecticut Office of the Attorney General has consistently maintained that the investigation was always about accountability and transparency. I left Mr. Smith's office with little more insight into Lyme's political machinations than I had arrived with. But, in this case, failure to gain insight was instructive, as it highlighted the reality that, even at the source of things, the gap between divergent perceptions remains difficult to bridge.

A Standard of Care on Trial

When the IDSA review panel voted to uphold the IDSA's guidelines on Lyme disease, Lyme-literate physicians went on high alert. Despite the Lyme Doctor Protection Bill, Lyme-literate physicians worried that state medical boards would increasingly target them for following the ILADS standard of care. During our discussions about the risks that Lyme-literate physicians face, physicians often mentioned Dr. Albert, a prominent Lyme-literate physician, who at the time of my research had been subject to two investigations by his state medical board. While the medical board argued that its investigation had nothing to do with Lyme disease and was instead related to violations of general medical standards, Lyme-literate physicians, patients, and advocates contended that the investigation was a "witch hunt," a continuation of what they perceived to be a long string of attacks on Lyme-literate physicians for practicing a different standard of care.

On February 16, 2010, I attended the public medical board hearing in which the charges that had been brought against Dr. Albert were voted on. When I arrived, the room's chairs, divided into two sections by a small aisle, had already been filled to reflect Lyme disease's standard-of-care divide. On the right side of the room, Dr. Albert sat quietly in the front row, surrounded by a few family members and friends. Two sets of parents accompanied by their children were seated behind him, and as the start of the hearing approached, more families arrived, hugging Dr. Albert in greeting before taking a seat. Reporters and other members of the community were seated on the left side of the room, and the medical board's panel members were seated around a long U-shaped table at the front of the room. The panel was composed of six physicians, one physician's assistant, three public members, and an assistant attorney general. By the time the hearing began, everyone in the room was seated and still, except for a sheriff who stood and kept watch at the back of the room, lending an even more somber air to an already somber occasion.

In 2010, Dr. Albert was charged by his state medical board with violating medical standards in the cases of four patients. Although the case of the fourth patient was dismissed by the board, the other three cases included one patient in whom Dr. Albert had diagnosed babesiosis and had prescribed treatment prior to examination, and two other patients for whom Dr. Albert had ordered blood tests prior to examination. In 2007, Dr. Albert had also been charged with diagnosing and treating Lyme disease in two patients prior to examining them. He was fined ten thousand dollars and placed on two years' probation. Although Dr. Albert appealed the medical board's decision to both the appellate and supreme courts in his state, both appeals were reviewed and denied. Dr. Albert, his attorney, and Dr. Albert's supporters maintained that he had done nothing wrong. They argued that the claims brought against Dr. Albert were by "disgruntled parents" involved in heated custody disputes and that all the patients under the medical board's consideration had gotten better under Dr. Albert's care. Some of Dr. Albert's supporters conceded that he had taken "short cuts" in his medical practice, but they were concerned that the "punishment" did not fit the "crime." One Lyme blogger explained,

> While no one disputes that [Dr. Albert] took "short cuts," a review of all [state name] Physician Disciplinary Actions 2009 rendered by the [state name] medical board raises questions about fairness of his punishment for these procedural issues.

Last year the medical board punished 43 physicians for serious charges such as substance abuse, sexual misconduct, mental illness, and negligence; not one of these physicians received a fine larger than $5,000. And only one other physician, accused of drug abuse, received a longer supervised probation period than [Dr. Albert]—though this drug-addict doctor did not receive the additional $20,000 in fines levied on [Dr. Albert].[24]

Dr. Albert's hearing proceedings on February 16, 2010, began with a brief update on developments related to his case. Each attorney was then given fifteen minutes for oral arguments. Dr. Albert's attorney spoke last, and his argument was impassioned. "As everyone knows, Lyme disease is a very controversial issue in medicine," he began. Dr. Albert's attorney again reiterated that "no patient had complained, and no patient was harmed" in any of the cases before the board. "Think very carefully as you think about approving the panel's decision. Tests were conducted, but no treatment was pursued. Think about you doctors on the panel. This could set a dangerous precedent," he warned. After Dr. Albert's attorney had finished his argument, one of the panel's physicians responded. He criticized Dr. Albert's attorney for attempting to legitimize the practice of managing care prior to the examination of a patient. "Diagnosing and treating patients you've never seen is third-world medicine," he exclaimed. "This is what this board does, we bring before us doctors who test and treat without seeing their patients, and we punish them." On the heels of this physician's comments, the chair of the panel concluded, "Perhaps because of the size of Dr. Albert's practice, he takes shortcuts and orders tests without examination." With that, the panel members voted and unanimously agreed to discipline Dr. Albert on both counts by fining him ten thousand dollars and placing him on probation for four years.

After the panel voted, the public portion of the hearing came to an end, and those in attendance filed out so that the panel could continue to meet in private. Dr. Albert and his supporters gathered in the hallway to catch up with one another and to stand in solidarity with Dr. Albert, who was clearly shaken. Later that week, during my observation of a mainstream Lyme practice, I mentioned that I had attended the medical board hearing of Dr. Albert. My announcement piqued the attention of the physicians I was observing, and, as they gathered around me in the break room, they asked me to recount what I had seen. I described the counts against Dr. Albert and how the panel had come to a vote. Seemingly disappointed, the physicians looked at one another and shrugged. One physician exclaimed, "Ordering tests before seeing a patient? What's the harm in that?" Later conversations with these physicians revealed that they continued to hold Dr. Albert in low regard; however, in that fleeting moment in the break room, Dr. Albert and his mainstream counterparts were, for perhaps the first and only time, on the same team, a team whose experiences shed light on the disjuncture that can happen between medical practices and the medical standards put in place to regulate them.

Conflicted Interests

In addition to providing a window into how physicians perceive evidence-based medicine to both enable and constrain particular kinds of clinical practice in the United States, Lyme's controversy, in the examples of the IDSA investigation and Dr. Albert's medical board hearings, also helps to shed light on relations of power and the politics of "conflicts of interest" in clinical medicine and medical science. The asymptotic ideal of "disinterested" and "unbiased" judgment is a pillar of clinical guideline-making, the putative aim of which, as one of the primary features of evidence-based medicine, is to supplant "subjective" expert opinion with "objective" scientific evidence. And yet, David J. Hess describes how the "autonomy" of scientific research fields has been increasingly diminished by "changes in the academic and private-sector research-and-development enterprises" and how, through "academic capitalism" (D. Kleinman 2003) and "mode-2 knowledge production" (Gibbons et al. 1994), researchers are, for example, "offered incentives to enhance their level of external funding and to develop research products that can be patented and licensed" (Hess 2004b, 700). Beyond incentives, Frickel et al. also describe instances of "intellectual suppression" and "purposeful policy decisions" as attempts to impede research that "challenge[s] powerful industrial interests (MacKenzie and Spinardi 1995; Zavestoski et al. 2002; [B.] Martin 2007)" (2010, 447).

The role of standardization and evidence-based practices in the reinforcement of these academic and private-sector alliances is especially striking. Because standardization is a reductive and extractive process, sociologists Martha Lampland and Susan Leigh Star observe that "size limits become political limits: whose ideas and whose things matter? . . . Authority arises from classification as well as from ownership" (2009, 23). The politics of whose ideas matter and the authority-generating potential of how these ideas are classified is also powerfully illustrated in Sarah Vogel's (2012) work on bisphenol A (BPA) and the scientific debate over its safety. Vogel describes how, in the wake of a chemical testing scandal in the 1970s, the FDA and EPA, in collaboration with the "chemical industry," created a set of standards for good laboratory practices (GLP), which established rules for how to conduct research on drug and chemical safety (85). Although the intent of GLP was to provide quality assurance and to "enhance the validity of the data and the reliability of the methods," Vogel argues that, instead, GLP provided a means by which the FDA could rely on "industry studies to uphold the safety standard" by dismissing smaller studies that questioned BPA's safety on the grounds that they did not follow GLP standards (85, 208).

In the case of clinical guidelines and similar concerns about how guidelines could be used to reinforce industrial interests, some physicians and scientists have been vocal in calling attention to the risks and realities of conflicted interests in guideline-making and their implications for patient care. For example, in a 2009 *Journal of the American Medical Association* commentary, "Why Guideline-Making Requires Reform," two physicians argue that "by favoring one test over another, or one therapy over another, guidelines often create commercial winners and losers, who cannot be disinterested in the result and who therefore must be separated from the process" (Sniderman and Furberg 2009, 430). In addition to a range of corrective measures, these authors recommend that "all financial relationships with industry should be disclosed in detail, including amounts received, and should be publicly available" (431). They also recommend that significant "benefit" from any particular company should disqualify that individual from being able to participate in guideline-making related to that company's particular product. In a similar *American Family Physician* article, "How Do Clinical Practices Go Awry?," the authors discuss the pervasiveness of conflicts of interest in clinical guidelines *across* specialties, referring to "a review of 17 ACC/AHA [American College of Cardiology/American Heart Association] guidelines involving 498 contributors" that "revealed that 56 percent of the guidelines had an author with a conflict of interest" and a "2002 survey of 100 specialty society guidelines" that "revealed that 87 percent had ties to the pharmaceutical industry" (Dachs, Darby-Stewart, and Graber 2012, 515). And still other physicians have drawn attention to the fact that conflicts of interest not only are financial but also stem from sources such as "long service to government committees or private insurers," "participants' previously established 'stake' in an issue," "the way you make your living," and "inherent influences that come from personal experiences" (Detsky 2006, 1033).

As David J. Hess writes, "Scientists develop strong, sometimes emotionally charged, intellectual commitments to their research programs, and they develop deep social loyalties to their networks of colleagues" (2016, 19). On the other hand, he observes, "they also develop relations of fear, loathing, pity, and disdain for their opponents" (2016, 19). This is especially true for Lyme disease, in which, during my conversations with individuals across the divide, affection for those within one's own camp and animus against those in the opposing camp were often palpable.

In response to this range of concerns about conflicts of interest in guideline-making, the Institute of Medicine (IOM) published *Clinical Practice Guidelines We Can Trust* in 2011, which, as I mentioned earlier in this chapter, outlines eight standards for the creation of "trustworthy guidelines," not least of which is the disclosure of conflicts of interest. But the impact of the IOM's "guidelines for guidelines" remains to be seen. A study conducted the same year that the IOM standards were published reviewed 130 randomly selected guidelines from the NGC and found that they "demonstrated poor compliance with IOM standards," with information on conflicts of interest "given in fewer than half of the guidelines surveyed" (Kung, Miller, and Mackowiak 2012, 1628).

Perceptions of conflicts of interest clearly continue to fuel the Lyme disease controversy. Indeed, perceived conflicts of interest spurred Attorney General Blumenthal's investigation into the IDSA guideline-making process, and, in his eyes, these conflicts were irrefutably confirmed by his investigation. As journalist and patient advocate Pamela Weintraub writes about the investigation's findings, "Of the fourteen authors, nine received money from vaccine manufacturers and four were funded to create test kits, products that would be more likely to reap profit if the definition of Lyme disease remained essentially unchanged" (2008, 350). Beyond these claims, Blumenthal claimed that IDSA authors "received fees as expert witnesses in medical-malpractice, civil, and criminal cases related to Lyme disease; and they were paid by insurance companies to field—and help reject—Lyme-related claims" (350).

The conflicts of interest that were described in Blumenthal's findings were not new to Lyme patients and advocates since, years prior to the IDSA investigation, a prominent Lyme advocacy organization had created and circulated a 182-page document, "Conflicts of Interest in Lyme Disease: Laboratory Testing, Vaccination, and Treatment Guidelines." And after the investigation, two vocal proponents of the Lyme-literate standard of care also published a widely circulated article, "The Infectious Diseases Society of America Lyme Guidelines: A Cautionary Tale about the Development of Clinical Practice Guidelines" (2010). In this article, the authors observe how guidelines have the potential to function as a "sword or shield." As a shield, they write, they can be used "against liability by those who comply with their protocols"; as a sword, however, they can be used "against those who do not comply" (L. Johnson and Stricker 2010, 11). For many Lyme patients, advocates, and Lyme-literate physicians, the IDSA guidelines are perceived to function as a "sword" not only by disciplining Lyme-literate physicians like Dr. Albert who do not follow its standard of care but also by providing the basis on which insurance companies can deny coverage for extended antibiotic treatment and, in doing so, reduce costs. As one patient reflected, "There seems to be a lot of conflicts of interest involved in all of [the guidelines]. You know, again, money. If you're going to pay people, if they have a vested interest, it corrupts the system."

A woman I interviewed named Ellen described the experience of trying to get antibiotic treatment for her daughter that did not conform to the IDSA guidelines. She explained, "The pediatrician felt she needed IV, and when she tried to put her on IV, the insurance company, of course, said, 'No way. You're only a pediatrician,' which she was very offended by." Ellen continued, "This was ten years ago . . . but, um, we actually fought the insurance company. They denied it, and then we fought it. You know, there's three different levels. We went through the whole thing, and it took six months, and eventually, we got her on IV." In total, Ellen estimated that her family's end-of-the-year tax write-offs were close to thirty-five thousand dollars for "unreimbursed medical expenses." Stories like Ellen's make clear why there is so much at stake in how guidelines define Lyme's diagnostic and treatment criteria. For many of the Lyme-literate physicians and patients I spoke with, the IDSA's perceived ties to the insurance industry appeared to be the most compelling explanation for why it refused to recognize chronic Lyme disease. One Lyme-literate physician I interviewed exclaimed, "Understand the insurance and follow the money!" And Dr. Braun, whose opinions about insurance as a form of "social control" are detailed in the previous chapter, explained that he thought "the insurance industry probably has something to do with [Lyme's controversy]," but he also thought "it's more than that."

Of course, accusations of conflicts of interest go both ways in the battle over how to diagnose and treat Lyme disease. As one mainstream physician I interviewed exclaimed, "They claim that we have all these conflicts of interest. They're the ones with conflicts of interest!" For example, in a *Lancet* article written by members of the IDSA, "Antiscience and Ethical Concerns Associated with Advocacy of Lyme Disease," the authors claim that many Lyme-literate physicians benefit financially by prescribing long-term antibiotics, that they receive grants from "activist organizations," and that they have an unethical relationship with "Lyme specialty laboratories" from which many Lyme-literate physicians order their lab tests (Auwaerter et al. 2011, 715–16). Of particular concern, the authors write, is that "an owner of one such diagnostic company is an ILADS director and an adviser to three Lyme organisations," in addition to the fact that "he was one of the authors of the treatment guidelines by ILADS, although his company affiliation is not disclosed in that document" (796).

Shared conflicts of interest aside, when it comes to whose ideas about Lyme disease *matter*, the primary difference between the two standards of care, their guidelines, and their associated medical societies is unequal "capital." Drawing from French sociologist Pierre Bourdieu's work on the "scientific field [as] a social space with some actors in more dominant positions and others in more subordinate positions," David J. Hess categorizes science-related capital into five groups:

> symbolic capital (the esteem of a researcher, indicated by citations, prizes, and other rewards), social capital (the networks of allies and contacts), cultural capital (the scientist's knowledge about the specific research field and the scientific field in general), temporal capital (the organizational positions that a scientist holds), and financial capital (access to resources that can fund research, postdoctoral fellows, and students). (2016, 19)

In the case of Lyme's controversy, the most consequential capital appears to be symbolic, a difference often described as "prestige" or "authority" that "is recognized, accepted as legitimate, [and] provid[es] a profit of distinction" (Bourdieu 2013, 297). Even though both standards of care have their own set of guidelines, which is a critical component of evidence-based legitimacy, the guidelines are not broadly perceived to have the same authority and legitimacy, or to be equally "true." For example, while the IDSA's guidelines were published in a prestigious peer-reviewed journal, the ILADS guidelines were published in a less prestigious peer-reviewed journal. Moreover, whether the 2004 ILADS guidelines were subjected to peer review by this journal appears to be a point of contention. In a letter to the *British Medical Journal,* a member of the IDSA, citing a "personal communication," claims that the 2004 ILADS guidelines "apparently had not undergone the peer review process of the journal in which they appeared as a supplement."[25]

Beyond this difference, and to draw again on Bourdieu, other "signs of distinction" that make possible "forms of profit and power" and transform social relations within medicine into "relations of legitimate domination, authority, or prestige" include the IDSA's composition of primarily academic physicians (many of whom have positions at prestigious academic research institutions) and its endorsement by a range of governmental and nongovernmental institutions, including the CDC, the NIH, and other medical societies, such as the American Neurological Association (298). By contrast, ILADS is largely composed of nonacademic primary care physicians and, aside from Lyme advocacy organizations and private foundations, does not have the endorsements of governmental and nongovernmental institutions. For example, as of this writing, while fifteen of the sixteen members of IDSA's board of directors are academic physicians or physicians affiliated with a major hospital, only four of the ten members of ILADS' board of directors have academic affiliations.

In this book's introduction, I describe the mainstream standard of care as an example of a "dominant epidemiological paradigm," a paradigm created by a range of individuals who draw on institutional knowledge to set the terms of how a disease is understood (P. Brown et al. 2004). In thinking about Lyme's standards of care in the context of symbolic capital, legitimacy, and attendant relations of power, they can also be understood as examples of what Didier Fassin and Robert Aronowitz have both described as "orthodox" versus "heterodox" entities, entities that, in relation to each other, are characterized by unequal relations of epistemic authority (Aronowitz 2012; Fassin 2007). More recently, in Hess's work on movements associated with a range of industries, he has also coined the terms "mobilized publics" (the "incumbent" public) and "mobilized counterpublics" (the "challenger" public) to describe how groups and organizations (composed of various configurations of science professionals *and* citizen activists) use a range of action-oriented strategies to "vie for the legitimacy of public support in the form of public opinion . . . by configuring their views as aligned with public benefit" (2016, 10).

As a mobilized counterpublic, the patients, physicians, and scientists that make up the Lyme-literate "movement" have vied for the legitimacy of public support for almost four decades. Although some patients and Lyme-literate physicians point to what they perceive as important gains, including the creation of private foundations that fund "undone science" on the persistence of Lyme disease, others worry that too little has changed. As one patient advocate, who has been involved in Lyme advocacy for eighteen years, reflected in a phone conversation seven years after I concluded my fieldwork, "Not much has changed. I don't think you'd see a difference. There are the same number of [Lyme-literate doctors], maybe less. Support groups are full. The needle has not moved. People are still asking the same question, 'Why doesn't my doctor believe me?'"

As to why the "needle has not moved," the answer that mainstream physicians provide is that, after all these years, the evidence still does not support Lyme patients' and Lyme-literate practitioners' claims that chronic Lyme disease has a biological basis. Some Lyme-literate proponents, however, point to the resource control and "powerful mobilizing structures" of the physicians and scientists who compose Lyme's mainstream "public" (Hess 2016, 12). One Lyme-literate physician I interviewed gestured to this possibility when he exclaimed, "The IDSA control[s] the field and the publications. . . . The IDSA [has gone] in and prevented publication. These people have gone into institutions and tried to get the people from getting PhDs. In many cases, they're successful. That's the history of medicine: publication bias." For this reason, another mainstream physician who epistemically positions himself between Lyme's two camps, emphasized the importance of using language that is consistent with the IDSA's standard of care to be able to publish data that challenge the dominant paradigm. This physician explained, "We have to use [recognized] words so that we can be published in the literature; if we used 'chronic Lyme disease,' we wouldn't get anything published." And yet another mainstream physician-scientist who inhabits Lyme's middle ground said, "Most of the evidence favors the conventional side of things; on the other hand, that's who's doing the research and creating the evidence. They have a corner on the NIH and funding." In this way, although financial conflicts of interest and industrial ties tend to be the most frequently cited reasons for the persistence and intractability of Lyme's controversy, the competing claims to biological legitimacy and epistemo-legitimacy that characterize Lyme's divided bodies may stem more from differences over *what* kind of evidence matters and *how* that evidence gets produced than from the overt conflicts and conspiratorial collusions that lie at Lyme's surface.

Evidence-Based Medicine as Biopower and Biolegitimacy

As this chapter makes clear, Lyme disease is a dynamic site of political activity. Like all contested illnesses, Lyme disease is political because contestations over how to diagnose and treat it entail politician involvement, medical board hearings, legislative hearings, class action lawsuits, patient advocacy, and, not least of all, claims of bias and conflicts of interest. But because the controversy over Lyme disease is equally about how evidence-based medicine is used to regulate bodies and produce medical truths about those bodies, it also highlights how evidence-based medicine operates as a potent form of biopower and biolegitimacy.

The suggestion that evidence-based medicine is political is not novel. Timmermans and Berg have argued that the standards of evidence-based medicine are "inherently political because their construction and application transform the practices in which they are embedded" (2003, 22). That is, standards "change positions of actors: altering relations of accountability, emphasizing or deemphasizing preexisting hierarchies, changing expectations of patients" (22). Other scholars have gone further to suggest that evidence-based medicine constitutes the defining feature of biomedicine's "dominant *episteme*," and that it is "a political movement, one that suppresses non-conforming ideas, subjugates some clinicians and exalts others and imposes this method of care to the person in need of care" (Holmes and Byrne 2012, 45, 56). These arguments, like my own, highlight the way in which evidence-based medicine is more than just a tool to guide clinical decision-making. As demonstrated by the examples of its institutionalization in agencies and initiatives within the US government, evidence-based medicine is also a means by which state and nonstate authorities can more "efficiently and effectively" manage the health of their population. However, I also suggest that this entails not only an investment in "making live" that legitimizes "life itself" but also an attendant hierarchization of bodily conditions, some of which are deemed to matter more, and some of which are deemed to matter less.

In this way, my argument departs from others in its attention to the biopolitical *and* biolegitimizing features of evidence-based medicine. Following Rabinow and Rose, the way in which evidence-based medicine simultaneously encompasses a "form of truth discourse about living beings," "strategies for intervention upon collective existence in the name of life and health," and "modes of subjectification, in which individuals can be brought to work on themselves . . . by means of practices of the self in the name of individual or collective life or health" exemplifies biopower, or "power over life" (2006, 203–4; Fassin 2018b). As Didier Fassin points out, however, the biopolitical in this sense does not also encompass the tension between the "legitimacy of life" and the "politics of life," or "what politics does with human lives and how it treats them" (2018b, 85). An equally salient feature of evidence-based medicine is the way in which it simultaneously hierarchizes and differentially treats the very biological lives that it holds up and legitimizes as a "supreme good" (16). If evidence-based medicine operates as a form of biopower that centers on "discourses and technologies" and "strategies and tactics," it also operates as a form of biolegitimacy that "sacralizes" life even as it hinges on the "concrete way in which individuals and groups are treated, under which principles and in the name of which morals, implying which inequalities and misrecognitions" (Fassin 2009, 57).

Foregrounding these features is consequential because it more fully captures how evidence-based medicine is discursively and practically produced in everyday life. In the beginning of this chapter, I argued that evidence-based medicine simultaneously produces similarities and differences in medical practice and opinion because it provides a platform of legitimacy on which any individual regardless of their background can make a claim to medical truth. That this is so highlights the extent to which evidence-based medicine is more complex than a "political movement that suppresses nonconforming ideas" (Holmes and Byrne 2012, 56). Indeed, evidence-based medicine's power is located not in unilateral control and dominance but in its broad and democratic appeal, in the perception that it is a "good thing," and, as anthropologist Helen Lambert observes, in its "encompassing character" and "inherent malleability" (2009, 18). It is these features that allow evidence-based medicine to be enacted across the boundary between laboratory and life and to be individually internalized and repurposed as a foundation for competing claims to biological and epistemic legitimacy.

Because of the biopolitical nature of evidence-based medicine and medicine more generally, it is not surprising that ideas about evidence-based medicine's "power over life"—or the management and regulation of individual and population health—are fraught with tension. In my conversations with mainstream Lyme physicians, many were adamant that politicians should have no role in determining how medicine is practiced and that only physicians possess the knowledge and experience necessary to make decisions that affect clinical care. Many Lyme-literate physicians and patients conceded that political involvement in medicine is not ideal, but they also expressed the idea that, as one patient explained, "Politics might be patients' only option." Another patient specified that the goal of political involvement is not to have politicians "play doctor" but to ensure the autonomy of clinical decision-making. He explained,

> Well, if you look at the law we just got passed in Connecticut, the argument was that the legislators were legislating medical care, which is a big jump from what they were actually doing. They were legislating that physicians were allowed to treat is what the law really says. Unfortunately, the dogma that comes out of certain groups manipulates that message and twists it around and says that legislators are playing doctor, and it's just not true.

Still others point to the subtler biopolitical dimensions of evidence-based medicine. For example, on a personal website, one patient advocate posted several letters that he had sent to prominent political figures. One letter, addressed to former President Obama, described evidence-based medicine as "a foundation for health care denials." It continued,

> A core tool for the manipulation of medical standards is the use of "evidence-based medicine." This can involve such tactics as basing recommendations on highly selective and exclusionary references as well as using disease definitions that are so restrictive, few can meet the definition. Evidence-based medicine results in clinical practice guidelines. The authors of these guidelines can have massive conflicts of interest including, for example, arrangements with pharmaceutical companies, interests in test kits and vaccines, and financial relationships with HMO's [sic] and other health insurers.[26]

Although these ideas would likely be characterized as conspiratorial by mainstream Lyme physicians, they nevertheless gesture to more generally held concerns about medical decision-making and its regulation, which is a question that has itself attracted the attention of both medical and legal scholars. In the United States, physicians' insistence that medicine and the law be separate spheres has a long history. Historian James C. Mohr has explored the rise and fall of medical jurisprudence—or the "interaction between those who possess medical knowledge and those who exercise legal authority"—in the United States (1993, xiii). He argues that while American physicians during the first half of the nineteenth century "believed that the future of their profession lay in civic-minded interaction with the nation's courts, legislatures, and lawyers," most physicians by the end of the nineteenth century had "withdrawn from most legal processes" and "relations between doctors and lawyers were, to say the least, strained" (xiv). Mohr observes that an important development in the permanent decline of US medical jurisprudence was the formation of the first medical professional organization, the American Medical Association, in 1847 (225). This development, followed by the formation of state medical boards, effectively placed the responsibility of licensure in the hands of physicians. With the exception of medical malpractice, which falls within the jurisdiction of legal courts, the formation of medical professional societies and state medical boards gave physician leaders the power to regulate physicians and how they practice medicine.

The idea that politico-legal involvement is antithetical to medical decision-making continues to be salient in the contemporary United States, even among those in the political sector. This was made clear during Attorney General Blumenthal's investigation of the IDSA's guideline-writing process. For example, one of the most striking features of Blumenthal's investigation was his insistence that the investigation was not about "the science" but about the "guidelines process." In the press release mentioned above, Blumenthal was quoted as explaining,

> Our investigation was always about the IDSA's guidelines process—not the science. IDSA should be recognized for its cooperation and agreement to address the serious concerns raised by my office. Our agreement with IDSA ensures that a new, conflicts-free panel will collect and review all pertinent information, reassess each recommendation and make necessary changes.[27]

Contrary to what Blumenthal said, however, many of the statements released by the Office of the Attorney General mentioned the existence of "chronic Lyme disease," which, for those in the Lyme world, is an unmistakable position on the "science" of Lyme disease, since Lyme's controversy hinges on whether chronic Lyme disease "exists." Fittingly, mainstream Lyme physicians, Lyme-literate physicians, and Lyme patients all perceived the investigation to be a politician's attempt to expand—and make more accessible—treatment options for chronic Lyme disease patients. The difference, however, was that mainstream Lyme physicians understood the investigation to be an egregious violation of the integrity of medical decision-making, while Lyme-literate physicians and patients understood the investigation to be an attempt to politically rectify medical missteps justified by the urgency of Lyme's "state of exception" (Agamben 2005).[28]

Beyond biopolitics and its regulatory features, however, and within a diagnostic framework that emphasizes the importance of signs over symptoms, an equally consequential concern for the Lyme patients I spent time with was evidence-based medicine's "politics of life," that is, the biological hierarchization of—and categorical distinction between—bodily conditions that biomedically matter and those that do not. Like the "delegitimation" that patients with chronic fatigue syndrome experience (Ware 1992) or the "abjection" of patients with multiple chemical sensitivity (M. Murphy 2006), chronic Lyme patients, in company with all individuals with contested illnesses whose biological basis is in dispute, suffer the misfortune of being sick in the wrong way. As one patient wrote on her blog, "I'm tired of seeing Lyme warrior after warrior dying knowing that they were thought of as crazy and ridiculous. Discarded by society feeling as if they didn't matter!"[29] Another patient I observed at a Lyme-literate practice exclaimed, "We are Lyme untouchables!" The experience of "not mattering" was what one patient described as "the nightmare of this disease." She continued, "If someone says 'I have cancer,' [physicians] say, 'What can I do?' [With Lyme], there's no validation whatsoever." In this way, the lived political implications of evidence-based medicine are as much about how bodies are differently legitimized and treated as they are about the regulation of those bodies.

This chapter has explored the politics of the Lyme disease controversy by attending to one of its most salient features: the disagreement over how to diagnose and treat Lyme disease and the attendant emergence of its competing standards of care. Prior to the 1980s in the United States, medical decision-making was generally understood to be the prerogative of individual physicians. After the institutionalization of evidence-based medicine in the late 1980s and early 1990s, medical decision-making became the object of standardization. As the case of Lyme disease reveals, one of the unintended consequences of evidence-based medicine is that, in addition to achieving medical consensus, it also reinforces differences in medical practice and opinion by providing a platform on which a range of individuals can make claims to medical truth. That evidence-based medicine is enacted, internalized, and repurposed by individuals inside and outside the medical arena underscores its biopolitical and biolegitimizing nature and the key to its power, for it is in its ecumenical appeal and "encompassing character" that evidence-based medicine both regulates and differentially legitimizes biological bodies (Lambert 2009, 18).

THROUGH LYME'S LOOKING GLASS

On July 31, 2016, in what was described as a "historic landslide victory" by Lyme advocates and Lyme-literate physicians, the Massachusetts legislature passed bill H.4491 (An Act Relative to Long-Term Antibiotic Therapy for the Treatment of Lyme Disease).[1] Having been decried by representatives from the Infectious Diseases Society of America, and vetoed by Massachusetts governor, Charlie Baker, four days prior to its passing, the bill requires all insurance companies in Massachusetts to cover long-term antibiotic treatment for Lyme disease that is prescribed by a licensed physician. In response to the bill's passing, one advocate exclaimed, "It's our hope that the bitter polarization will end. That includes not only people talking nice, but really taking a look at the emerging science and trying to have open minds."[2]

The example of the Massachusetts Lyme bill nicely captures how, in the context of contested illnesses over which bodies of thought are divided, individuals inside and outside the biomedical arena mobilize evidence-based medicine as a biopolitical and biolegitimizing technology to adjudicate and make claims about which truths related to those illnesses matter. This example also reveals how claims to biological legitimacy are always bound up with epistemo-legitimacy, since the legitimacy of knowledge that convincingly draws on "emerging science" bolsters the legitimacy of bodily conditions whose biological basis is in dispute and vice versa. As an infectious disease that is often perceived to be an illness, the complex case of Lyme disease holds a revealing mirror up to the experience of living and treating contested illness within the increasingly standardized bounds of the US medical system. And as chapter 1 highlights, what ends up being controversial about contested illnesses is often more than just disputed etiology;

as a result, these illnesses can be fully understood only in their rhizomatic entirety.

More broadly, Lyme disease sheds light on how the experience of living and treating contested illness in the United States is characterized by what I have termed "divided bodies," or the duality of epistemic and embodied division. That is, contested illnesses like Lyme disease are lived realities over which bodies of thought are divided, and they are also states of discomfort that straddle the chasm between being experienced as diseases and being perceived as illnesses. These tensions are ultimately rooted in what I have suggested is biomedicine's unresolvable conundrum: the enduring clinical importance of the symptom within an epistemic framework that, in the context of diagnosis, almost exclusively values the sign. Chapters 3 and 4 ethnographically fleshed out the embodied and epistemic dimensions of contested illness by exploring how Lyme patients *and* physicians "do" and know disease (Mol 2002). For the five patients featured in chapter 3, these experiences ranged from persistent Bell's palsy to disabling pain and fatigue to overwhelming anxiety and rage. And although these patients' experiences were somatically diverse, they were all—with the exception of one patient—characterized by the simultaneity of some degree of physical *and* social suffering, in addition to the challenge of how to live "the most intense life possible" in the face of not feeling well (Fassin 2010, 82). For the Lyme patients I spent time with, I described how the most salient themes that emerged were suffering, survival, and surfeit, and how, in the context of suffering, the "double burden" of being doubted by others is further complicated by the everyday enactment and disruption of the historically constructed binaries of sex/gender and body/mind. I subsequently argued that Lyme patients often perceive CAM to be a means to daily survival because it is perceived to offer the possibility of "being healed" over "being cured," and that, at the same time that inequalities of race and class make some bodies invisible within Lyme's landscape, the widely held perception that Lyme patients have a surfeit of resources often results in a shortfall of compassion.

For the physicians featured in chapter 4, of whom two were mainstream physicians and two were Lyme-literate physicians, their experiences of treating a controversial disease like Lyme, although also wide ranging, were characterized by shared feelings of mistrust, suspicion, and misunderstanding. More broadly, ethnographic attention to physicians who diagnose and treat Lyme disease in the United States revealed how epistemic divergences and convergences between and among biomedicine and

CAM help to explain the differences and similarities in how the Lyme body is understood across its standard-of-care divide. Along these lines, I suggested that the primary difference between mainstream and Lyme-literate approaches is the relative importance they assign to the diagnostic potential of clinical symptoms. For mainstream Lyme physicians—and biomedical physicians more generally—symptoms in the absence of signs are medically unexplainable. However, because Lyme-literate physicians—and CAM practitioners more generally—approach symptoms as signs in the diagnosis of disease, explanations for the symptomatic experience of suffering are nearly limitless, and as a result, "medically unexplained illness" as a diagnostic category is noticeably absent from CAM and Lyme-literate practices. For this reason, I suggested that patients' attraction to Lyme-literate and CAM approaches can, in part, be explained by the validation of having their symptoms recognized as diagnostically explainable and therapeutically responded to in accordance with their symptoms. That Lyme-literate physicians describe themselves as "literate" does not seem coincidental, since a core feature of Lyme's controversy is which approach to *reading* the Lyme body is more legitimate. I ultimately argued that, in contrast to CAM, "medically explained illness" is a foundational feature of biomedicine that makes possible the conditions that biomedicine *can explain*.

As a window into the relationship between contested illness and evidence-based medicine in the United States, Lyme disease highlights two critical ways in which the emergence and institutionalization of evidence-based medicine has made contested illnesses *more contested*. The first is that evidence-based medicine and its requirement that bodily disorders be biomedically legible have further entrenched biomedicine's distinction between "normal pathology" and "abnormal pathology," or, as I have described it, the "wrong way to be sick" (Canguilhem [1966] 2007, 203). The perception that some bodily disorders are less legitimate and more "made up" than others is not new and, as I discussed in chapter 4, appears to be at least as old as biomedicine (Hacking 1999). But because contested illnesses tend to be plagued by clinical ambiguity and disagreement over etiology, what is new is the way in which evidence-based medicine, in relying on objective measurements to produce the "strongest" evidence, has furthered these illnesses' marginality by categorizing them as "medically unexplainable."

The second way in which the rise of evidence-based medicine has informed the experience of contested illnesses is that, at the same time that it has contributed to their perceived delegitimation, it has also provided *a means to legitimacy* by offering patients a platform on which to make claims to medical truth. As I discussed in chapter 5, the power of evidence-based medicine—and the key to its functioning as a technology of biopower and a form of biolegitimacy—is that it is more than just a tool to guide medical decision-making: it is also a set of practices, a discourse, and an assemblage of individuals, technologies, and institutions, the sum of which is widely perceived—inside and outside the medical arena—to be a "good thing." In this way, patients, physicians, and scientists alike draw on evidence-based medicine to participate in conversations about health and have their truth claims heard, even if evidence-based medicine also hierarchizes the very bodily conditions it is invested in improving within a "legitimacy of life" framework (Fassin 2018b, 66).

In bridging the embodied and epistemic dimensions of contested illness by bringing together patients, physicians, and scientists within the same field of analysis, the broader aim of this book has been to provide another kind of map for how social scientists approach contested illness. Previous approaches to contested illnesses have emphasized disputes over environmental causation (P. Brown, Morello-Frosch, and Zavestoski 2012) or the characteristic features and effects of their contestation (Dumit 2000, 2006) and have often focused primarily on patients' experiences to the exclusion of the experiences of the practitioners who treat them and the medical frameworks within which these practitioners work.[3] However, by defining contested illness as "any condition whose biological basis is disputed," I have suggested (1) that contested illness encompasses more bodily conditions than just those whose environmental causation is in dispute, and (2) that these illnesses can be more fully understood through attention to their epistemic conditions of possibility and, in particular, their relationship to evidence-based medicine.

Of course, as chapter 2 illustrated, even if dispute over environmental causation is not the universal feature of contested illnesses, the environment remains an important dimension of these illnesses, particularly in the case of Lyme disease. In a warmer and increasingly contaminated anthropocenic world, and following an "epidemiology of affect," how individuals feel about their microbial and chemical environments in the context of environmental risk *and* privilege has implications for how they understand their health and how they therapeutically act on their health (Park and Pellow 2011). Beyond the salience of the environment, however, contested illness's relationship to evidence-based medicine has been this book's primary focus. Although the social science literature on evidence-based medicine is emergent, it has already asked critical questions about what constitutes evidence, how evidence-based medicine changes social relations, the way in which medical knowledge is produced, and the means by which medical standardization creates "new worlds" (Timmermans and Berg 2003, viii).[4] To better understand these "new worlds," I have suggested that analytical attention be paid to the spectrum of individuals who inhabit them: the scientists who materially generate evidence, the physicians who apply evidence, and the patients whose bodies are evidence's source and end— all of whom draw on evidence-based medicine to make claims to medical truth.

This shift in analytical focus is particularly pertinent to medical anthropology, where explorations of biomedicine have often been distinguished by two types of approaches: (1) "medicine and culture" and (2) "(bio)medicine as culture" (Burri and Dumit 2007, 1). While the "medicine and culture" approach has often attended to the phenomenological experience of illness and considers how aspects of biomedicine are "meaningful for different communities of people" (Dumit 2004, 14), the "biomedicine as culture" approach has often explored how the production of biomedical knowledge shapes and is shaped by cultural context.[5] What has been lost in the gap between these approaches is an attention to the increasingly blurred line between "lay/alternative knowledge" and "scientific knowledge," as well as the relationship between the embodied and the epistemic in the context of "epistemic challenges to medicine" (Hess 2004b, 699). By attending to how individuals experience Lyme disease in the United States *and* to how knowledge about contested illness is produced and practiced inside and outside the medical arena, this book is a call to an engagement with the embodied *and* the epistemic in the creation of a theoretical framework that can more flexibly accommodate the "divided bodies" of contested illness and the "inherent pluralism" that characterizes the contemporary production of biomedical truths (699).

The issue of what counts as evidence and who gets to make claims to truth based on that evidence has never been more salient in the United States. When Stephen Colbert coined the term "truthiness" on October 17, 2005, during a taping of his late-night show, *The Colbert Report*, it was only the beginning of a growing national preoccupation with—and concern about—what counts as the truth. Created to capture "the quality of seeming or being felt to be true, even if not necessarily true," truthiness, Colbert argued, helped to explain the way in which "[America is] a divided nation . . . between those who *think* with their *head* and those who *know* with their *heart*."[6] Named by *Merriam-Webster Dictionary* as the Word of the Year in 2006, "truthiness" was formally included in the *New Oxford American Dictionary* in 2010, and a range of books followed in its wake, including *True Enough: Learning to Live in a Post-Fact Society* (Manjoo 2008) and *Truth or Truthiness: Distinguishing Fact from Fiction by Learning to Think Like a Data Scientist* (Wainer 2015). The lead-up to—and fallout from—the 2016 American presidential election, which saw the addition of terms such as "fake news" and "alternative facts" to the national conversation, only heightened concerns about the country's defection from truth. That year, "post-truth" followed in truthiness's footsteps as the *Oxford Dictionary*'s Word of the Year, and, in a May 30, 2018, *New Yorker* article, journalist Alan Burdick wrote, "If we can agree on anything anymore, it's that we live in a post-truth era. Facts are no longer correct or incorrect; everything is potentially true unless it's disagreeable, in which case it's fake" (2018; see also Sismondo 2017). Not surprisingly, the idea of a "post-truth era" replete with "fake news" found traction on both sides of Lyme's divide when, in a June 16, 2017, blog post, "Who Controls Fake Lyme Disease News," the blogger wrote, "[to] shape good public health policy for the good of patients, in place of fake news, let's have real answers really soon" (Smith 2017); in a July 2017 commentary in the *American Journal of Medicine*, three mainstream proponents also described how recent "interest in the topic of fake news" is not new for "infectious disease physicians" who have grown accustomed to "false and misleading information about the diagnosis and treatment of Lyme disease" (Shapiro, Baker, and Wormser 2017, 771).

The contemporary tension within popular American discourse between truth as something "absolute" and "irrefutable" and truth as something "relative" and "refutable" invites comparison to a long-standing tension within the academy between "classical epistemology" and "constructivist epistemology" (which includes the social studies of science) (Smith 2006). As literary scholar Barbara Herrnstein Smith observes, where classical epistemology is "normative (determining, directing, judging, justifying) in aim," the aims of constructivist epistemology are "descriptive and explanatory, not normative" (3). That is, where classical epistemology embraces the idea that "theories" are "nets" that "catch truth," constructivist epistemology embraces the "net, a web of shifting, intersecting, interacting beliefs and practices, [as] truth" (51).

Another term used to describe this approach, with a reach that includes the work of Thomas Kuhn, Michel Foucault, and Bruno Latour, among others, is "genealogy," that is, an interest in "identifying what counts for true and false in a given world at a given moment" (Fassin 2017, 14). The contextual nature of this approach (both social and historical) is captured by philosopher Ludwig Wittgenstein when he writes, "Knowledge is in the end based on acknowledgement," by which he means that "to call a statement 'true' is not that it corresponds to how things are, but that our criterion for accepting it is met" ([1969] 1975, 49e; Ellenbogen 2003, xiv). Similarly, in Ludwik Fleck's work on the production of scientific knowledge, particularly as it related to the discovery of syphilis (like Lyme disease, a spirochetal infection), he argues that "evidence conforms to conceptions just as often as conceptions conform to evidence," and that "in science, just as in art and in life, only that which is true to culture is true to nature" ([1935] 1981, 28, 35).

In light of these parallel tensions within popular and academic discourses, and the fact that my approach to the controversy over Lyme disease is itself genealogical, what is at stake in this book is not only how people variously understand and make claims to truth but also how, as ethnographers and social scientists, we *represent* those truths. In "The Endurance of Critique," Didier Fassin explores how some social scientists, particularly Bruno Latour, have grown concerned that their work on "the lack of scientific certainty" has been "absorbed, appropriated and recycled" in everyday life and manifests, for example, in the "contesting of climate change" (2017, 6). This concern has led Latour and others to renounce their "former faith" in critique and call for what Fassin describes as the "rejection of the social construction of facts" and a "nostalgic return to positivism" (10). However, Fassin suggests (and I agree) that blaming critique for its perceived "misappropriation" in everyday life is misplaced and that a more productive response is the rearticulation and "reaffirmation" of critique's importance, as well as an insistence, as Donna Haraway argues, that "an account of radical historical contingency for all knowledge claims and knowing subjects" is not mutually exclusive with a "no-nonsense commitment to faithful accounts of the 'real' world" (8; Haraway 1988, 579).

I would also push Fassin's observation further and suggest that the perceived causal relationship between social scientific critique and its application in everyday life might be a problem of *misrecognition*, and that the similarity between these processes is not identical but, rather, "uncanny." It is clear, of course, that there is something "familiar" between genealogical approaches and their application, and the appearance of being *too similar* is perhaps the reason that critique is "under attack" and perceived to be "in crisis" (Fassin 2017, 4). As anthropologist Robert Levy observes, "When an event cannot be thus categorized and identified, we experience terror in the face of the uncanny" (1973, 152). But there is something equally "strange" at work here, and it is in the space between the familiar and the strange that we might locate their difference: where everyday applications are often decontextualized assertions of what *is*, genealogical approaches to understanding how knowledge is produced are often contextualized descriptions of what things are *perceived to be*. It is in this spirit that I have approached Lyme's truths as the net *itself* rather than that which the net *catches*.

The case of Lyme disease, then, provides important methodological and representational insights into the ethnographic and social scientific study of medical controversy. Germane to any fieldwork experience is the impression that things are not as they seem. But this is particularly so when the object of study is controversy. In calling this conclusion "Through Lyme's Looking Glass," I draw fully on its reference to Lewis Carroll's *Through the Looking-Glass and What Alice Found There* ([1871] 2009), in which the main character, Alice, climbs through a mirror to discover a fantastical world where, among other things, books are printed in reverse and people remember the future. Like Alice, when I stepped through Lyme's looking glass, I found an inverted world in which what appeared to be insignificant was quite significant, and where the meaning of things was protean, polarized, and always emotionally charged. In the introduction, I described the methodology I enacted during my fieldwork as quantum ethnography, the conceptual practice of simultaneously inhabiting multiple perspectives within the parameters of my project's field, while also mapping out relations between these perspectives and between myself and these relations.

This conceptual practice, however, is as relevant to representation as it is to methodology. For example, during the writing of this book, I was contacted by a friend from graduate school, who, as a physician with a doctoral degree in sociology, now writes about a range of contemporary health issues as a medical science journalist. When he reached out to me, he was working on a piece directed at journalists to give them tips when reporting on contested illness, and he asked for recommendations to "help them navigate the structural constraints of their writing (word count, audience, pressure to generate clicks) as well as honor and respect patients who are suffering from illnesses that lack definitive diagnostic tests." My first response was to recommend that journalists reach out to a social scientist with expertise on the contested illness at hand and spend more time observing and talking to the people they interview—two strategies that might provide paths to the descriptive "thickness" that ethnographic saturation makes possible. But on further reflection, I realized that of even more importance in the representation of medical controversy is consistent and transparent contextualization.

To illustrate what I mean, I offer the example of an article published on June 27, 2018, in *Slate*, "The Science Isn't Settled on Chronic Lyme: A Close Look at the Evidence Suggests the Controversial Diagnosis Should Be Taken More Seriously, and That Decades of Sexism May Be to Blame for Our Collective Dismissal" (Dusenbery and Rehmeyer). Although this particular article supports the Lyme-literate standard of care, the representational strategies used here are equally found in pieces that support the mainstream. In this article, the authors, in describing Lyme's competing truths, inconsistently contextualize the claims that individuals make and subsequently represent one set of truths as *the way things are* rather than what things are *perceived to be*. For example, when quoting evidence from studies that support the mainstream standard of care, the authors contextualize the evidence by linking it to the positionality of the individuals who produced that evidence, which gives the impression that the evidence is partial and positioned within a particular world view (e.g., "A 2009 article by two prominent mainstream Lyme experts noted that men and women are represented roughly equally among CDC-reported cases of Lyme disease but that patients with a chronic Lyme diagnosis are disproportionately female"). When quoting evidence from studies that support the Lyme-literate standard of care, however, the authors decontextualize the evidence by not linking it to the positionality of the individuals who produced it and, in doing so, strengthen the perceived legitimacy of that evidence by making it seem more impartial and objective (e.g., "Recent research suggests that the current antibody tests may be even less accurate for women"). A quantum ethnographic approach, however, would consistently contextualize all perspectives, taking care to tether each truth claim to the individual or individuals who make it and to describe the individuals as thickly as possible. In this way, the reader can independently assess the type of claims—or, in the context of medical controversy, as one scientist I interviewed described it, "the gradient in the quality of science"—as fully as possible.

Quantum ethnography, in its emphasis on simultaneously occupying and consistently contextualizing multiple perspectives within the parameters of one's field, attempts to contribute to what Didier Fassin more broadly envisions as "critical ethnography," a methodology and a mode of representation in which the ethnographer "stand[s] on the threshold of the cave," inside of which are her interlocutors and outside of which are "texts and theories," and who "alternately [steps] inside and outside, belonging partially to each world but entirely to none" (2017, 21). In this way, through quantum ethnography's simultaneous inhabitation and consistent representation of multiple interlocutors, an ethnographer working on controversial topics like contested illness can engage more fully in an analysis of how, in what context, and with what implications a range of truths is produced (17). Like genealogical approaches before them, both quantum and critical ethnography refrain from making an "ultimate judgment" (17). However, in refraining, their intent is not, as their critics worry, to participate in the distortion of truths but, rather, to better understand them.

Beyond the Looking Glass

In May 2014, as I prepared to leave Connecticut and move to Michigan with my family, I met with the patients, physicians, and scientists who had been most involved with my project to thank them for their help and to say goodbye. Before that, I also attended one final patient support group meeting, a meeting at which a Lyme-literate physician was scheduled to give a much-anticipated presentation. When I arrived at the meeting, the support group leaders were busy setting up the room and shepherding members to their seats. Before the presentation began, and in between conversations with other members who were arriving, I was able to briefly catch up with both leaders. After giving me a big hug, one leader asked, "Is it like coming home? Everything's the same. Nothing's changed," by which I understood her to mean that she and her co-leader were still leading weekly meetings, that patients were still struggling, and that the Lyme patient community was still fighting for better access to diagnosis and treatment.

When I later met with the support group's other leader, she described the discouragement she felt at having put years of work into trying to make things better for Lyme patients only to have nothing change. "People don't understand that it's not getting better," she sighed.

> When we were sick, the people that helped us were the ones that called us and guided us to care that saved my children. When I started this, I said to God, "If you get my children better, I'll give you five years." I thought it'd be better by then, but I'm still getting the same phone calls.

This support group leader was particularly discouraged by the lack of progress that had been made with Lyme disease prevention, which, in addition to patient support, was the issue toward which she now directed most of her energy. Having gone back to school to get a public health–related degree, she was surprised that "more credentials" to "build people's trust" had not enabled her to make more inroads. She explained, "I thought if I became part of the system, I could find a way. But I can't find a way. I thought I could understand the logjam if I got closer to the source, but I have no clue."

Individuals on the other side of the divide also echoed the sentiment that "little had changed," except, for them, the "little that had changed" was what they perceived to be the indefatigable persistence and power of the Lyme advocacy movement. One mainstream Lyme physician described seeing the same chronic Lyme patients with the same complaints that he had seen for the last thirty years. A Lyme scientist also observed that relations between the two camps were as venomous as ever. During my research, this same scientist had on one occasion exclaimed, "We're outnumbered, and we're losing the battle!" And during an email exchange, he reflected,

> I will be retired (soon), and I probably will not want to do much with Lyme disease after that either. I think all of the craziness that has been allowed to go on has been discouraging for many members of the research community. It is not something they will want to pursue during retirement. Who needs it? We do science. If people don't want to believe it, that's their problem. Sorry to be so blunt.

The exception to this shared sense of discouragement among my interlocutors was one Lyme-literate physician and one mainstream physician. In June 2014, the Lyme-literate physician sent me an enthusiastic email to update me on the passing of a bill similar to the Massachusetts Lyme bill described above. In this instance, the New York State Senate would protect Lyme-literate physicians who treat patients with extended courses of antibiotics, a development which he described as "incredible." Prior to this bill being signed by Governor Cuomo in December 2014, Lyme patients and advocates distributed electronic petitions in support of the governor's signing the bill into law, while the Medical Society of the State of New York, the New York State Academy of Family Physicians, the New York chapter of the American College of Physicians, and the American Academy of Pediatrics, District II, fervently opposed the bill and demanded that the governor veto it.[7] The mainstream physician, on the other hand, expressed optimism that Lyme's "madness" was "dying down" because, in contrast to previous years in which he would be referred "three to four" chronic Lyme cases per month, he is now seeing only "three to four" chronic Lyme cases per year.

He reflected, "It's gratifying to see that happening, to know that it's trending in the proper perspective."

In the years that have passed since I left Connecticut, one of the most significant developments has been the establishment of the Tick-Borne Disease Working Group, which, as part of the 21st Century Cures Act, was included within the Department of Health and Human Services on August 10, 2017. As described on its website, the goal of the group is "the development of a report to the Secretary of Health and Human Services and Congress on the findings and any recommendations of the Working Group for the federal response to tick-borne disease prevention, treatment and research, as well as how to address gaps in these areas."[8] Funded and authorized for six years, the Tick-Borne Disease Working Group is expected to submit a report every two years. The most striking feature of the group, however, is its composition of a range of individuals from across the standard-of-care divide, including patient advocates, Lyme-literate physicians, mainstream physicians, scientists, and government officials, who, having locked horns for years over how to understand Lyme disease, now meet semiregularly for in-person and online meetings that are open to the public. Having witnessed firsthand how tense encounters between individuals from Lyme's two camps can be, the fact that these meetings have appeared to proceed with relative cooperation is itself remarkable.

Of course, this is not to say that the process has been without controversy. When the working group's members were first announced, patient advocates objected to the fact that one mainstream physician had been included and, citing financial conflicts of interest, quickly launched a MoveOn.org campaign to protest his inclusion. In its wake, the Department of Health and Human Services announced that this physician had "declined the invitation to serve on the Tick-Borne Disease Working Group."[9] Although one advocate struck a tone of optimism when she wrote in a blog post that she "appreciated the opportunity for the patient voice to be heard, the transparency of the process, and the ability of those who dissented from the group to have their views memorialized in a minority report," another patient advocate I spoke with said, "Everyone's pinning their hope on this, but I don't think it's going to be the game changer" (L. Johnson 2018). She continued to explain how, having been around long enough to know the contours of the controversy, she had come to accept that "everything is a stepping stone, and nothing is one breakthrough." "It's like North Korea," she explained. "You have to be optimistic, but cautious." A physician I spoke with echoed a similar feeling of being "cautiously hopeful," noting that his source of caution was that the working group has "no authority to make decisions or spend money and can only make recommendations."

From where I stand, with one foot in the middle of the Lyme world and one foot on its periphery, it seems that, despite their differences, what both sides have in common is deep discontent that the Lyme controversy persists. In this book's exploration of Lyme disease across the standard-of-care divide and in the context of the relationship between contested illness and evidence-based medicine in the United States, it is one voice in a dissonant chorus of voices that I hope might eventually contribute toward the shared goal of a harmonious resolution. Whether this is wishful thinking is, of course, up for debate. As one mainstream scientist reflected after reviewing a draft of the dissertation on which this book is based, "I doubt there will be a 'harmonious resolution.' The two interpretations of 'Lyme disease' are incommensurate." Either way, as anthropologist Roy Rappaport observes, "An important first step in rectifying disorders in relations between and among discourses is to make all of them intelligible and audible" (1993, 301). At the very least, I hope that this book has made the range of understandings about Lyme disease more "intelligible," more "audible," and, as a result, more "comprehensible"—to those who bear witness from the outside and, more importantly, to those who live and treat it.

Notes

Introduction

1 Many find the term "Lyme literate" offensive because it implies that those who do not recognize chronic Lyme disease and do not treat it with extended antibiotics are not literate in Lyme disease. Because this is the term that most patients and many physicians who treat chronic Lyme disease use, it is the term that best captures this category of identification.

2 Paul Rabinow coined the term "biosociality" to describe "'new groups and individual identities and practices arising out of [the] new truths' of genomic research"; since then, the term has been used more broadly to describe "the ways in which the practices of science, public health, and medicine enable the formation of new subjects and social groups" (Klawiter 2008, 27; see also Rabinow 1999). In Norma C. Ware's exploration of chronic fatigue syndrome, she describes the experience of socially "doubted" or "disconfirmed" illness as "delegitimation" (1992, 34).

3 From "lay expertise" (Epstein 1995, 1996), "patient groups and health movements" (Epstein 2007b), and "health social movements" (including "embodied health movements"; P. Brown, Morello-Frosch, and Zavestoski 2012) to "evidence-based activism" (Rabeharisoa 2013) and the "socialization of biomedicine" (Burri and Dumit 2007), there is a rich social scientific literature on the ways in which patients and individuals outside of the medical arena become knowledge producers by engaging with and, in turn, shaping scientific and medical knowledge, for example, in the form of "citizen-science alliances" (P. Brown, Morello-Frosch, and Zavestoski 2012, 20). My approach to this phenomenon in the context of Lyme disease is a departure in its ethnographic focus on the embodied and epistemologic implications of everyday practical and discursive engagements with evidence-based medicine among patients, practitioners, and scientists—engagements that do not necessarily happen in the context of activism or advocacy.

4 Rosenberg et al. 2018; DVBD (Division of Vector-Borne Diseases), NCEZID (National Center for Emerging and Zoonotic Infectious Diseases), "Lyme Disease:

Recent Surveillance Data," CDC, last reviewed December 21, 2018, https://www
.cdc.gov/lyme/datasurveillance/recent-surveillance-data.html.

5 The blacklegged tick is commonly referred to as the deer tick.

6 When chronic fatigue syndrome (CFS) first emerged in the 1980s, it was described as the "yuppie flu" because it was perceived to be more prevalent among
affluent, highly educated women. Like CFS, chronic Lyme has also been described as "yuppie disease" because of the perception that it disproportionately
affects affluent White women. Maya Dusenbery argues that CFS only *appeared*
to be more prevalent among this demographic because the structural violence
of economic and racial inequalities meant that these individuals "had the resources to pay for repeated doctor's visits" and "enough authority to repeatedly
reject those doctors' conclusions that they were just 'depressed'" (2018, 261).
This issue is further discussed in chapter 3.

7 For incisive analyses of differences in medical thought and practice, see Berg
and Mol 1998; Lock 1993b, 2002.

8 Although the *institutionalization* of two standards of care is exceptional, conflicting guideline recommendations are not. A report by the Institute of Medicine
quoted a finding by the National Guidelines Clearinghouse that there are "at
least 25 different conditions in which conflicting guidelines exist" (Institute of
Medicine et al. 2011, 60).

9 For a comparative sense of these organizations' membership composition, full
ILADS membership is open to "physicians with a doctoral degree in a health-
related field (MD, DO, DDS, DVM), those holding a PhD in life sciences, or
those with an AANMC-accredited Doctor of Naturopathic Medicine degree, (or
equivalent international degree) who have passed the Naturopathic Physicians
Licensing Exam (NPLEX) and completed a naturopathic medicine residency"
("Join ILADS," accessed November 7, 2019, International Lyme and Associated
Diseases Society, https://www.ilads.org/providers-and-members/join-ilads/).
Full IDSA membership is open to "individuals who have completed post-
doctoral or equivalent training in infectious diseases or a related field"
("Membership," IDSA, accessed November 7, 2019, https://www.idsociety.org
/MemberTypes/FullMember.aspx).

10 In related work, Charles Briggs and Mark Nichter describe the shared and often
contested "production, circulation, and reception of knowledge" within biomedicine as "biocommunicability" (2009, 194; see also Briggs and Hallin 2007).

11 For further reading on "embodied health movements," see P. Brown et al. 2004;
P. Brown, Morello-Frosch, and Zavestoski 2012.

12 Sociologist Alissa Cordner explores how "all individuals and institutions interested in contested environmental health issues use science to make competing
and strategic claims in pursuit of institutional and regulatory goals" but notes
that "they do so on an uneven playing field" and in the process "develop different definitions of risk and different interpretations of science" (2016, 4).

13 Phil Brown, "Contested Environmental Illness" syllabus, Northeastern University, accessed December 28, 2019, https://web.northeastern.edu/philbrown/wp-content/uploads/2012/07/syllabus-Cont-Ill.docx. I cite Brown's course syllabus because it provides a succinct definition of how he approaches contested illness. For further reading on Brown's approach, see Kroll-Smith, Brown, and Gunter 2000; P. Brown 2007; P. Brown, Morello-Frosch, and Zavestoski 2012. P. Brown, Morello-Frosch, and Zavestoski describe contested illness as "conditions whose causes are either unexplained by current medical knowledge or whose purported environmental explanations are in dispute" (2012, 18). Here, Brown and his colleagues broaden contested illness's definition beyond the environment but still link contested illness to causation rather than dispute over biological reality. In 2012, Brown left Brown University for Northeastern University, where he is the director of the Social Science Environmental Health Research Institute, which continues the work of the Contested Illness Research Group.

14 P. Brown, "Contested Environmental Illness" syllabus.

15 For further reading on the anthropology and sociology of contested illness, see Barker 2005; P. Brown 2007; P. Brown, Morello-Frosch, and Zavestoski 2012; Crix et al. 2012; Dumit 2000, 2005, 2006; Kilshaw 2010; Klawiter 2008; Krimsky 2000; Kroll-Smith and Floyd 1997; Mitman, Murphy, and Sellers 2004; Moss and Teghtsoonian 2008; M. Murphy 2006; T. Phillips 2010; Schone 2014; Trundle and Scott 2013; Ware 1992.

16 In this book, I approach medically unexplained illness as a biomedical category of practice and contested illness as its corresponding category of analysis.

17 For further reading on anthropological understandings of "disease" versus "illness" and the implications of biomedicine's "tenacious assumptions," see Eisenberg 1977; M.-J. Good et al. 1992; Hahn and Kleinman 1983; A. Kleinman 1988; A. Kleinman, Eisenberg, and Good 1978; Lock and Gordon 1988.

18 Describing contested illness as the "wrong way to be sick" builds on previous social scientific scholarship but also pushes it further. For example, unlike Talcott Parsons's "sick role," which describes sickness as a time-limited phenomenon, the "wrong way to be sick" takes into account illness chronicity *and* the fact that, because "there are normal ways of being ill (ways that our society regards as appropriate) as well as anomalous ways," being ill is also a morally imbued phenomenon (A. Kleinman 1988, 5; see also Parsons 1975). Furthermore, unlike Ian Hacking's "ecological niche," which describes the sociohistorical conditions of possibility that allow disorders to be expressed or "made up" in a particular way at a particular historical moment (Hacking 1998), the "the wrong way to be sick" directs attention to sickness *in practice* and how individuals "enact" and "do" disease (Mol 2002).

19 For thoughtful ruminations on medicalization and biomedicalization, see A. Clarke et al. 2010; Klawiter 2008; Lock and Nguyen 2010; Nichter 1998; Scheper-Hughes and Lock 1987; V. Taylor 1996; S. Williams and Calnan 1996. In Michelle

Murphy's work on multiple chemical sensitivity (MCS), she describes the experience of MCS as "abjection," which, beyond "a form of social exclusion," "ma[kes] and mark[s] a domain of supposed impossibility" (2006, 152).

20 Sociologist Steven Epstein describes the policy shift within biomedical research to include—and measure differences between—"previously underrepresented groups" as a "biopolitical paradigm," which he defines as a "framewor[k] of ideas, standards, formal procedures, and unarticulated understandings that specify how concerns about health, medicine, and the body are made the simultaneous focus of biomedicine and state policy" (2007a, 17, 26). In my analysis of evidence-based medicine, I instead use the term "technology" to draw on Foucault's argument that biopower is a "technology" of power ([1976] 1990, 139), to highlight the work that evidence-based medicine does in *practice*, and to underscore that, in its uptake and internalization by individuals inside and outside the medical arena, evidence-based medicine can *also* be understood as a "technology of the self" (Foucault 1988).

21 Fassin (2018b) notes the convergence between "life as such" and other related work on "bare life" (Agamben 1998) and "life itself" (N. Rose 2007), in addition to concepts such as "biological citizenship" (Petryna 2002; N. Rose and Novas 2005) and "patient citizenship" (Biehl and Eskerod 2007), which attempt to capture how individuals make claims to belonging through biological life. These concepts describe instances in which individuals, whose lives have otherwise been "stripped of their political and social qualities" (Ticktin 2011, 14), gain access to biomedical belonging in the context of contemporary biolegitimacy, in which value is placed on the "supreme good" of life itself (Fassin 2018b, 123). In the case of contested illness, individuals' lives are often politically intact, but because the biological basis of their suffering is not generally recognized, they do not have an established pathway to biological or patient citizenship.

22 The phrase "effective and efficient" is drawn from one of evidence-based medicine's founding texts, *Effectiveness and Efficiency* (Cochrane 1972).

23 For explorations on the deterritorialization and decentralization of power and sovereignty, see Biehl and Eskerod 2007; K. Clarke 2009; Hansen and Stepputat 2005; Ong 2006.

24 For further social scientific perspectives on evidence-based medicine, see Adams 2013, 2016; Bell 2016; Berg 1998; Brody, Miller, and Bogdan-Lovis 2005; Broom and Adams 2012; Cambrosio et al. 2006; Colvin 2015; Daly 2005; Geltzer 2009; Goldenberg 2006; Holmes and O'Byrne 2012; Lambert 2006, 2009; Lowy 2000; Mykhalovskiy 2003; Mykhalovskiy and Weir 2004; Nadav and Dani 2006; Nichter 2013; Pope 2003; Timmermans and Berg 2003; Timmermans and Epstein 2010; Worrall 2002.

25 Here and throughout the book, I use the term "biopolitical" as the adjectival form of "biopower," which encompasses both biopolitics and anatomo-politics.

26 Jonathan M. Metzl makes a similar observation about health by suggesting that it is "a concept, a norm, and a set of bodily practices who[se] ideological work

is often rendered invisible by the assumption that it is a monolithic, universal good" and is "used to make moral judgments, convey prejudice, sell products, or even to exclude who[le] groups of persons from health care" (Metzl and Kirkland 2010, 2, 9). Similarly, anthropologist Kirsten Bell has described health, together with evidence and ethics, as "unassailable values" (2016).

27 Among the Lyme-literate practitioners I formally interviewed, three were mental health practitioners with degrees in either social work or clinical psychology.

28 This term was used by Elizabeth Vann (1995). Vann's application differs in its description of quantum ethnography as a method by which the ethnographer "should represent possibilities, not probabilities, within human realities" (78).

29 For scholarship influenced by the "practical turn," see Bourdieu [1980] 1990; Latour 1987; Pickering 1992; Schatzki, Knorr-Cetina, and von Savigny 2001. For constructivist scholarship, see Fleck [1935] 1981; Foucault [1969] 1972; Golinski 1998; Kuhn [1962] 1996; B. Smith 2006. For an overview of genealogical approaches within the social sciences, see Fassin 2017.

30 In 2017, *Collins Dictionary* defined fake news, a term often used by US president Donald Trump, as "false, often sensational, information disseminated under the guise of news reporting"; "alternative facts" is a neologism created by US presidential counselor Kellyanne Conway during an interview about the crowd size at the 2017 presidential inauguration.

31 Quotations from emails I received from project participants are anonymized and included with participants' permission.

32 This idea was inspired by a Lyme-literate physician I spoke with who emphasized that when it comes to chronic Lyme patients, attention needs to be directed to the question of morbidity and patients' quality of life.

1. Mapping the Lyme Disease Controversy

1 Division of Vector-Borne Diseases (DVBD), National Center for Emerging and Zoonotic Infectious Diseases (NCEZID), "What You Need to Know about *Borrelia mayonii*," CDC, September 12, 2019, https://www.cdc.gov/ticks/mayonii.html.

2 I was told by entomologists that nonendemic areas can have *Borrelia burgdorferi*–infected ticks, but these entomologists argue that the low infectivity rate means that actual disease risk is considered to be very low. Furthermore, the CDC is a primary referent in this book because it is a source of knowledge production to which individuals from both the mainstream and Lyme-literate camps commonly refer.

3 Beyond the United States, Lyme disease is considered by most to be endemic in North America (in particular, the United States and Canada) and Eurasia (including China, Japan, and Korea). Cases of Lyme disease have also been reported in Turkey (Polat et al. 2010), Mexico (Gordillo-Perez et al. 2007), and Brazil (Carranza-Tamayo, Costa, and Bastos 2012), and *Ixodes* ticks infected with

Borrelia burgdorferi sensu lato have been collected in Chile (Ivanova et al. 2014), Egypt (Adham et al. 2010), Mexico (Gordillo-Perez et al. 2009), and Turkey (Güner et al. 2003). Whether this means that these locations are endemic for Lyme disease or whether individuals in these locations are at risk for contracting Lyme disease are points of contention. Of most debate related to this question is whether Lyme disease exists in Australia. Lyme disease case reports from Australia were first published in the late 1980s and continue to be published, but the tick that seeks human hosts in Australia, *Ixodes holocyclus*, has never been found to be infected with *Borrelia burgdorferi* sensu lato (Hudson et al. 1998; Irwin et al. 2017; Mayne 2011, 2012; McCrossin 1986; Piesman and Stone 1991; R. C. Russell 1995; R. C. Russell et al. 1994).

4 The issue of Lyme disease case reporting is plagued by the tension between perceptions of underreporting and perceptions of overdiagnosis. Individuals from both the mainstream and Lyme-literate camps recognize that Lyme disease is underreported. Although 42,743 confirmed cases of Lyme disease were reported in 2017 (DVBD, NCEZID, "Lyme Disease: Recent Surveillance Data," CDC, last reviewed December 21, 2018, https://www.cdc.gov/lyme/datasurveillance/recent-surveillance-data.html), CDC officials estimate actual numbers to be "10 times higher than the yearly reported number" (CDC, "CDC Provides Estimate of Americans Diagnosed with Lyme Disease Each Year," press release, August 19, 2013, http://www.cdc.gov/media/releases/2013/p0819-lyme-disease.html). However, individuals from the mainstream and Lyme-literate camps are divided over diagnosis. Mainstream physicians and scientists argue that an inability to distinguish between real and false positive test results has led to overdiagnosis, particularly in "nonendemic" states; patients and Lyme-literate physicians argue that Lyme disease is underdiagnosed and that many patients suffer from the burden of underrecognition.

5 When Masters first reported cases of STARI, they included EM-like rashes accompanied by ELISA serologies that were positive in 50 percent of patients. However, when some laboratories, including the CDC, switched from a whole-cell sonicate ELISA test to a flagellin-based ELISA test in response to problems with specificity, STARI patients tested positive far less frequently (Masters, Grigery, and Masters 2008). Since then, mainstream physicians and scientists argue that STARI patients have not met the CDC criteria for Western blot positivity, although STARI patients do have Western blot patterns that are dissimilar from case controls (Masters and Donnell 1995, 1996). This fact led Masters and others to suspect an etiological agent that was different from but related to *Borrelia burgdorferi* sensu stricto.

6 Although *Ixodes scapularis* ticks in the southern United States can be infected with *Borrelia burgdorferi* sensu stricto (Oliver, Chandler, et al. 1993; Stromdahl et al. 2015), two entomologists I interviewed argued that the incidence is very low, and one argued that these ticks, unlike their northern counterparts, rarely

attach to humans. One study, which sampled 304 sites between 2004 and 2007, collected nine *Ixodes scapularis* nymphs in twelve states in the southern United States (Diuk-Wasser et al. 2010), and of these nine nymphs, none was positive for *Borrelia burgdorferi* sensu stricto (Diuk-Wasser et al. 2012; personal communication with one of the study's authors). In a similar study, Piesman et al. (1999) collected 284 *Ixodes scapularis* adults from South Carolina, Georgia, Florida, and Mississippi, none of which was infected with spirochetes. In another study done in North Carolina, of 3,746 ticks collected by the dragging method, only 0.5 percent were *Ixodes scapularis*. However, of the fifteen *Ixodes scapularis* nymphs tested, six, or 40 percent, were positive for *Borrelia burgdorferi* sensu lato (M. Smith et al. 2010).

A couple of studies have also examined the frequency with which *Ixodes scapularis* ticks attach to humans (Felz, Durden, and Oliver 1996; Goddard 2002). Related to these, one study described the difficulty of collecting *Ixodes scapularis* nymphs by the dragging method in the southern United States (Goddard and Piesman 2006). For example, of 894 nymphs collected in an area "known to have high populations of the blacklegged tick," only three *Ixodes scapularis* nymphs and twelve *Ixodes scapularis* larvae were collected (2006, 421). The authors of this study argue that the difficulty of collecting *Ixodes scapularis* nymphs in the southern United States and the reported low frequency with which they attach to humans can be explained by "behavioral differences." They postulate that "immatures of this species are feeding on lizards and therefore not questing on higher vegetation. This behavioral difference may explain in part why Lyme disease is not common in the southern United States" (422). Although Herman-Giddens (2012), in a comment on Diuk-Wasser et al. (2012), argues that "by the authors' own description," the collection method of dragging is "not suitable to the south"(1085), several entomologists argue that because the "drag cloth collecting method" is "directly correlated with human contact with host-seeking ticks, it is considered a direct measure of risk for tick bites" (Diuk-Wasser et al. 2012, 325; see also Falco and Fish 1992; Mather et al. 1996).

Although mainstream physicians and scientists argue that *Borrelia burgdorferi* sensu stricto or lato has not been isolated from a STARI rash or a Lone Star tick (Stromdahl et al. 2015), they observed that a different strain of Borrelia, *Borrelia lonestari*, has. One article reports that 1 to 9 percent of Lone Star ticks are infected with *Borrelia lonestari* (Barbour et al. 1996), while a more recent study reports that 6.8 percent are (Schulze et al. 2011). Finally, while there have been many case reports of STARI rashes following the bite of a Lone Star tick (recently described in a young girl from Connecticut who was bitten by a tick on Long Island [Feder et al. 2011]), mainstream physicians and scientists observe that only one of the STARI rashes biopsied in the literature has been PCR positive for *Borrelia lonestari* (A. James et al. 2001).

7　More complicated still is contestation over whether, in areas of the United States not commonly understood to be endemic for Lyme disease like the South, the cause of patients' Lyme-like illnesses is a novel *Borrelia burgdorferi* sensu lato species or a novel strain of *Borrelia burgdorferi* sensu stricto. In a 1996 review article, the investigator wrote, "Although Lyme disease cases have been reported from southern states, some researchers doubt the presence of *B. burgdorferi* or of human Lyme disease in the south. However, new data show that *B. burgdorferi* is widely distributed in the south and that strains are genetically more varied than in the north. Moreover, *B. burgdorferi* enzootic cycles appear to be more complex and more tick species are identified as vectors of the spirochete in the southern states" (Oliver et al. 1996, 926).

Since that publication, the investigator and other colleagues have published a series of articles reporting discoveries of *Borrelia burgdorferi* sensu lato species and strains (and, in a few cases, the detection of *Borrelia burgdorferi* sensu stricto [Oliver et al. 2000, 2003]) in *Ixodes scapularis* ticks and other ticks not known to bite humans throughout the southern United States (Clark et al. 2002; Lin et al. 2001; Lin, Oliver, and Gao 2002; Mathiesen et al. 1997; Oliver et al. 1996, 1998; Rudenko et al. 2009, 2011a, 2011b; Rudenko, Golovchenko, Grubjoffer, et al. 2013; Rudenko, Golovchenko, Hönig, et al. 2013). To the chagrin of patients, advocates, and Lyme-literate physicians, much of this research has not been embraced by the mainstream entomological community. More recently, Clark, Leydet, and Hartman (2013) reported the detection of *Borrelia burgdorferi* sensu lato DNA in blood and skin samples from ten patients with Lyme-like illness in Florida and Georgia. The authors conclude, "We suggest that human Lyme borreliosis occurs in Florida and Georgia, and that some cases of Lyme-like illness referred to as southern tick associated rash illness (STARI) in the southern United States may be attributable to previously undetected *B. burgdorferi* sensu lato infections" (915). However, a follow-up study by Stromdahl et al. (2015), which tried to reproduce Clark's results by using that study's assay, did not detect *Borrelia burgdorferi* in 1,097 Lone Star ticks collected from humans. The authors of this study suggested that Clark's assay produces "indistinct and inconsistent results" and concluded that "human-biting *A. americanum* ticks are not a vector of *B. burgdorferi*" (1703). Felz et al. (1999) did report culturing *Borrelia garinii* from the EM of a patient who had had known tick attachments in Georgia and South Carolina. However, this patient had also vacationed in Holland, Sweden, and Denmark a month before the appearance of his EM, so the study authors concluded that "it is uncertain whether this patient acquired his infection in the United States or Europe" (1322).

8　A study published in 2008 suggests that, unlike previously thought, *Borrelia burgdorferi* originated in what is now Europe and spread to North America (Margos et al. 2008). Although precise dating is not possible, this study estimates that European and North American populations of *Borrelia burgdorferi* have been separated for at least a couple million years. Another study published in 2009 suggests that *Borrelia burgdorferi* expanded west from the northeastern United States, and that "genetically distinct but phylogenetically related" populations in the northeastern and midwestern United States were "present many thousands of years before European settlements" (Hoen et al. 2009, 15013).

9 On November 13, 2010, the *New York Times* reported that, following WWII, US intelligence officials provided a safe haven for Nazi scientists through a secret process known as Operation Paperclip (Eric Lichtblau, "Nazis Were Given 'Safe Haven' in U.S., Report Says," *New York Times*, November 13, 2010, http://www.nytimes.com/2010/11/14/us/14nazis.html?pagewanted=all; see also Jacobsen 2014). The goal of Operation Paperclip was to gain scientific knowledge and to prevent other countries from having access to this knowledge. One of these scientists was Erich Traub, a veterinarian and an "expert on animal infectious diseases," who worked at the Naval Medical Research Institute in Bethesda, Maryland, from his arrival in the United States until 1953 (M. Carroll 2004, 8). Before the Plum Island Animal Disease Center was created in 1954, he was actively recruited to lead the center but never took the job. Whether Traub was involved with tick experiments on Plum Island and whether biological warfare research related to Lyme disease was conducted are points of much debate within the Lyme community.

10 "National Bio and Agro-defense Facility," Kansas State University, updated September 6, 2019, https://www.k-state.edu/nbaf/.

11 One of the primary sources of these ideas within the Lyme community seems to be John Loftus's *Belarus Secret* (later reissued as *America's Nazi Secret*), in which Loftus, a former prosecutor for the US Department of Justice, writing about "the records of Nazi germ warfare scientists who came to America," claimed, "They experimented with poison ticks dropped from planes to spread rare diseases. I have received some information suggesting that the United States tested some of these poison ticks on the Plum Island artillery range off the coast of Connecticut during the early 1950's" (2010, 68).

Another primary source is Michael C. Carroll's *Lab 257*, in which Carroll writes, "A source who worked on Plum Island in the 1950s recalls that animal handlers and a scientist released ticks outdoors on the island. 'They called him the Nazi scientist, when they came in, in 1951—they were inoculating these ticks,' and a picture he once saw 'shows the animal handler pointing to the area on Plum where they released the ticks'" (2004, 15–16). Although a former director of the center, Jerry Callis, and a former center scientist, Richard Endris, confirmed that "Plum Island experimented with ticks," Endris denied any connection between the tick colonies and Lyme disease when he said, "Those kinds of comments . . . indicate a gross ignorance of Lyme disease" (M. Carroll 2004, 23–25). In a series of personal communications, Carroll clarified that he "never stated that Traub was involved in tick experiments," so he cautioned about "connect[ing] Traub to Lyme." But he explained that he believes the Lyme connection is an "inescapable conclusion" hinging on the combination of the timing and proximity of the Lyme outbreak to Plum Island, the disrepair of Plum Island's lab (specifically "quarter inch holes in its roof" [264]), and the fact that "scientists were conducting foreign animal disease studies on animals with hard and soft ticks." More recently, science writer and senior producer of *Under Our Skin*, Kris Newby, postulates that "the most likely scenario" for the origin of "agents discovered in ticks from the Long Island Sound" was "a military experiment gone wrong or an accidental release from Plum Island Animal Disease Center of New York" (2019, 224). In response, a mainstream scientist wrote a *Washington Post* opinion piece on August 11, 2019, that rebutted these claims, arguing that "decades before Lyme was identified—and before military scientists could have altered or weaponized it—the bacterium that causes it was living in the wild" (Sam Telford, "No, Lyme Disease Is Not an Escaped Military Bioweapon, Despite What Conspiracy Theorists Say," *Washington Post*, August 11, 2019, https://www.washingtonpost.com/health/no-lyme-diease-is-not -an-escaped-military-bioweapon-despite-what-conspiracy-theorists-say/2019 /08/09/5bbd85fa-afe4-11e9-8e77-03b30bc29f64_story.html).

12 John Rather, "Plum Island Reports Disease Outbreak," *New York Times*, August 22, 2004, https://www.nytimes.com/2004/08/22/nyregion/plum-island-reports -disease-outbreak.html; "Plumbing the Mysteries of Plum Island," CBS News, June 10, 2012, https://www.cbsnews.com/news/plumbing-the-mysteries-of-plum -island/.

13 Mark Zaretsky, "Tour Reveals Real Purpose of Plum Island Research," *New Haven (CT) Register*, November 17, 2012, https://www.nhregister.com/news/article/Tour -reveals-real-purpose-of-Plum-Island-research-11462955.php.

14 Jackson Parr, "Discovering Plum Island: Historic Island Now Open to Public," *Door County (WI) Pulse*, June 9, 2017, https://doorcountypulse.com/discovering -plum-island-historic-island-now-open-public/; Rachel Siford, "Plum Island Group Tours Halted by Homeland Security," *Suffolk Times* (Suffolk County, New York), June 20, 2018, http://suffolktimes.timesreview.com/2018/06/82582/plum -island-group-tours-halted-by-homeland-security/.

15 "Plum Island Animal Disease Center," DHS, accessed November 9, 2019, https:// www.dhs.gov/science-and-technology/plum-island-animal-disease-center.

16 *United States Animal Health Association Newsletter* 30, no. 4 (2003), http://www .usaha.org/upload/Publication/Newsletters/2003/USAHA_Newsletter_Oct2003 .pdf.

17 Adam Dunn, "The Mysterious Lab off New York's Shore," CNN, April 2, 2004, http://www.cnn.com/2004/SHOWBIZ/books/04/02/lab.257/index.html; Denise Buffa, "Plum Island May Lose Its Dark Secrets," *Hartford Courant*, September 8, 2012, https://www.courant.com/news/connecticut/hc-xpm-2012-09-08-hc-plum -island-20120908-story.html.

18 "Plum Island Animal Disease Center," Wikipedia, last updated September 28, 2019, https://en.wikipedia.org/wiki/Plum_Island_Animal_Disease_Center.

19 Ralph Ginzburg, "Top-Secret Plum I. Beckons Public," *New York Times*, August 28, 1994, https://www.nytimes.com/1994/08/28/nyregion/top-secret-plum-i-beckons-public.html.

20 The tick that transmits Lyme disease was initially thought to be a separate species from *Ixodes scapularis* because of differences in host-seeking behavior during its juvenile stage. It was named *Ixodes dammini*. In 1993, a study using DNA analysis demonstrated that *Ixodes dammini* and *Ixodes scapularis* are the same species (Oliver, Owsley, et al. 1993; see also Wesson et al. 1993). Following this publication, most began to refer to the tick as *Ixodes scapularis*. However, one scientist I interviewed exclaimed that he disagreed with the results of this consequential study, that he still uses the term *Ixodes dammini* in all of his publications, and that the unification of the two tick species was ultimately a ploy by researchers in the South to be eligible for Lyme disease funding.

The life cycle of *Ixodes scapularis* has four stages: egg, larva, nymph, and adult. Both the nymphal and adult stages are understood to transmit *Borrelia burgdorferi* to humans, although the small nymphal tick is understood to pose greater transmission risk because it is more difficult to detect once it is attached to its host (Clover and Lane 1995; Diuk-Wasser et al. 2006; Embers et al. 2013). It has been widely understood that larva do not pose a transmission risk to humans because most agree that *Borrelia burgdorferi* is not transmitted transovarially from adult to larva; however, there have been conflicting reports in the literature (Rollend, Fish, and Childs 2013). Recently, Rollend, Fish, and Childs (2013) discovered that *Borrelia miyamotoi* is transmitted transovarially, and they suggest that this might account for some of the conflicting reports.

21 See chapter 2 for a discussion of Paul Slovic's work on "risks as feelings."

22 There is a slightly larger literature on mosquitoes as possible vectors of *Borrelia burgdorferi* transmission. The first articles appeared in 1986 (Magnarelli, Anderson, and Barbour), 1987 (Magnarelli, Freier, and Anderson), 1988 (Magnarelli and Anderson), and, more recently, in 2002 (Kosik-Bogacka, Bukowska, and Kuźna-Grygiel), 2007 (Kosik-Bogacka, Kuźna-Grygiel, and Jaborowska), and 2010 (Sikutová et al.). Only the 1987 study attempted to demonstrate whether mosquitoes are capable of transmitting *Borrelia burgdorferi* infection. This study, which has not been replicated, suggested that while *Borrelia burgdorferi* can be isolated from the guts of mosquitoes, mosquitoes are not able to transmit *Borrelia burgdorferi* to their host. In a 2002 commentary, "Mosquitoes and Soft Ticks Cannot Transmit Lyme Disease Spirochetes," Matuschka and Richter argue that Ixodid ticks are the only competent vectors for *Borrelia burgdorferi* because "neither mosquitoes nor (soft) ticks are likely: (1) to ingest many Lyme disease spirochetes from an infected host, (2) to permit spirochetes to develop to a stage that is adapted to their hemocoelic environment, (3) to invade their salivary glands

before becoming replete, (4) to successfully implant these pathogens into the skin of a vertebrate host" (284). Nevertheless, knowledge that mosquitoes and biting flies have been found to be infected with Borrelia burgdorferi is knowledge enough for many patients. For example, one photo that has been widely discussed among patients, shown at support group meetings, and circulated on listservs is of an infant girl who appears to have been bitten multiple times by mosquitoes and then developed what patients understand to be several small EM rashes at the bite sites. Knowledge of these case reports has only expanded the perceived field of risk for some patients.

23 MacDonald 1986b; MacDonald et al. 1987; Markowitz et al. 1986; Schlesinger et al. 1985; Shirts et al. 1983; Trevisan et al. 1997; Weber 1988.

24 Among those studies conducted on animal models, three showed no evidence of intrauterine transmission in mice, hamsters, and rats (Mather, Telford, and Adler 1991; Moody and Barthold 1991; Woodrum and Oliver 1999), while one showed evidence of intrauterine transmission in dogs (Gustafson et al. 1993) and another in mice (Burgess, Wachal, and Cleven 1993).

Most retrospective and prospective studies have also not been able to find a correlation between maternal Lyme disease and adverse fetal outcomes (Carlomagno et al. 1988; Figueroa et al. 1996; Gerber and Zalneraitis 1994; Hercogová et al. 1993; Maraspin et al. 1996, 1999, 2011; Nadal et al. 1989; Strobino et al. 1993; Strobino et al. 1999; C. Williams et al. 1995), although Strobino et al. (1993) described a "significant" association between tick bites three years prior to conception and congenital malformations (367). The authors of this study, however, suggest that this association might have been the result of "reporting differences between 'exposed' and 'unexposed' women" (367). Finally, the results of a more recent study demonstrated a possible association between untreated maternal infection and adverse fetal outcome (Lakos and Solymosi 2010). The discrepancies in some findings among and between animal and human studies have done little to resolve debate across the divide and have resulted in articles that still begin with sentences like the following: "There is disagreement whether Lyme disease is associated with adverse pregnancy outcome" (e494).

25 Studies to determine whether Lyme can be transmitted sexually were conducted in a hamster model (Woodrum and Oliver 1999) and a rat model (Moody and Barthold 1991), and both studies reported that venereal transmission did not occur. Another study investigated the viability of Borrelia burgdorferi that had been injected into dog, ram, and bull semen samples after these samples had been either chilled or cryopreserved and reported that "storage had no significant adverse effect on the viability of B. burgdorferi" (Kumi-Diaka and Harris 1995, 223). A more recent study conducted by researchers associated with the Lyme-literate standard of care examined a semen sample from one male patient and vaginal secretions from two female patients, all of whom had

tested positive for Lyme disease. This study reported that *Borrelia burgdorferi* was detected in all three samples (Middelveen et al. 2014). In a follow-up study by some of the same authors (Middelveen et al. 2018), the genital secretions and blood of twelve individuals with persistent Lyme symptoms were "subjected to corroborative microscopic, histopathological and molecular testing for *Borrelia* organisms in four independent laboratories in a blinded manner" (1). The authors reported finding "mobile" Borrelia spirochetes in culture specimens, which were confirmed by PCR, in addition to identifying Borrelia spirochetes that were cultured from blood (7), genital (10), and skin specimens (1). Finally, one study detected *Borrelia burgdorferi* DNA by PCR assay in breast milk (Schmidt et al. 1995). The CDC responded to this study by arguing that "PCR assays detect DNA from dead or living organisms, do not demonstrate the presence of living organisms, and are prone to false positive results" ("Lyme Disease Frequently Asked Questions [FAQ]," CDC, accessed 2014, http://www.cdc.gov /lyme/faq/).

26 A study documenting persistent babesiosis was published in 1998 (P. Krause et al.), followed by studies documenting persistent and/or relapsing babesiosis in immunocompromised patients in 2008 (P. Krause et al. 2008; see also Raffalli and Wormser 2016).

27 Angelakis, Billeter, et al. write, "To date, 13 *Bartonella* species and subspecies have been associated with an increasing spectrum of clinical syndromes in humans" (2010, 385). But, as Telford and Wormser observe, *Bartonella henselae* is "the most common *Bartonella* spp. infection in the United States" (2010, 379).

28 Case reports of bartonellosis after a known tick bite have been reported (Breitschwerdt et al. 2008; Eskow, Rao, and E. Mordechai 2001; Lucey et al. 1992), and small studies and serological surveys have documented *Bartonella* spp. infections in patients presenting with symptoms of neuroborreliosis (Angelakis, Pulcini, et al. 2010; Arnez et al. 2003; Breitschwerdt et al. 2007; Morozova, Chernousova, and Morozov 2005; Podsiadły, Chmielewski, and Tylewska-Wierzbanowska 2003). Although several studies have detected *Bartonella* spp. DNA in ticks using PCR assays, only one was successful in isolating *Bartonella* spp. from a tick (Kruszewska and Tylewska-Wierzbanowska 1996). Finally, one study documented the potential transmission of *Bartonella henselae* by *Ixodes ricinus* ticks through an artificial feeding system (Cotté et al. 2008).

The combined weight of the abovementioned studies led to the publication of two review articles in *Emerging Infectious Diseases*: "Bartonella spp. Transmission by Ticks Not Established" (Telford and Wormser 2010) and "Potential for Tick-Borne Bartellonoses" (Angelakis, Billeter, et al. 2010). Telford and Wormser argue that the presence of *Bartonella* spp. in ticks does not necessarily translate to "epidemiologic significance" nor does it mean that ticks are necessarily "competent vectors" for *Bartonella* spp. (380–81). They also question the relevance of Cotté et al. 2008 and argue that the level of bacteremia in the blood on which the study's ticks fed and the type of *Bartonella* strain that investigators used do not reflect the conditions of natural infection. While Angelakis, Billeter, et al. suggest that ticks "might serve as potential *Bartonella* vectors" (390), the authors of both review articles agree that to prove that ticks are competent vectors for *Bartonella* spp., "definitive" evidence of live transmission of *Bartonella* from a tick to an animal or human is needed. Telford and Wormser also argue that were live transmission to be documented, "epidemiologic relevance" of *Ixodes* ticks as vectors of *Bartonella henselae* would need to be demonstrated (381). A year following the publication of these review articles, Reis et al. (2011) published a study that demonstrated the live transmission of *Bartonella birtlesii* from *Ixodes ricinus* ticks to a mouse model. However, *Bartonella birtlesii* is not known to cause disease in humans. Whether a study on the live transmission of *Bartonella henselae* to a mouse model will also be successful— and whether *Bartonella* spp. can be successfully cultured from ticks (Wormser and Pritt 2015)—remains to be seen.

29 CDC, "Lyme Disease (*Borrelia burgdorferi*): 2017 Case Definition," National Notifiable Diseases Surveillance System (NNDSS), 2017, https://wwwn.cdc.gov/nndss /conditions/lyme-disease/case-definition/2017/.

30 For example, in 1983, a year after the spirochete that causes Lyme disease was first isolated from ticks, a study published in the *New England Journal of Medicine* reported that "the later manifestations of Lyme disease may mimic several immune-mediated disorders, including juvenile rheumatoid arthritis, Reiter's syndrome, rheumatic fever, the Guillain-Barré syndrome, and multiple sclerosis" (Steere, Grodzicki, et al. 1983, 739). A 1989 review article describes Lyme disease as "the new great imitator" and suggests that "third-stage" Lyme "can be confused with conditions such as multiple sclerosis, brain tumor, and psychiatric derangements" (Pachner 1989, S1482). Recently, in a review article on Lyme disease published in 2009, the authors write, "When the characteristic prodrome of erythema migrans, exposure history, or arthritis is lacking, the multifocal clinical findings on neurologic examination and positive oligoclonal bands and white matter patterns on MR imaging may confuse the diagnosis with that of MS" (Hildenbrand et al. 2009, 1083).

31 For references related to multiple sclerosis and Lyme disease, see Agosta et al. 2006; Baranova et al. 2012; Batinac et al. 2007; Bednárová, Stourac, and Adam 2005; Brinar and Habek 2010; Brorson et al. 2001; Chmielewska-Badora, Cisak, and Dutkiewicz 2000; Coyle 1989; Coyle, Krupp, and Doscher 1993; Drozdowski 2006; Dupuis 1988; Forrester et al. 2015; Garcia-Monco et al. 1990; Halperin 2011; Halperin et al. 1989; Hartmann and Pfadenhauer 2003; Heller, Holzer, and Schimrigk 1990a, 1990b; Karussis, Weiner, and Abramsky 1999; Lana-Peixoto 1994; Pohl-Koppe et al. 1999; Schmutzhard 1989, 2002; Spirin et al. 2011; Tardieu and Deiva 2013; Triulzi and Scotti 1998; Wolfson and Talbot 2002.

For references related to ALS and Lyme disease, see Burakgazi 2014; De Cauwer et al. 2009; Deibener et al. 1997; Halperin et al. 1990; Hänsel, Ackerl, and Stanek 1995; Hemmer et al. 1997; Kristoferitsch et al. 2018; Qureshi, Bedlack, and Cudkowicz 2009.

For references related to Parkinson's disease and Lyme disease, see Cassarino et al. 2003; García-Moreno et al. 1997.

For references related to Alzheimer's disease and Lyme disease, see Blanc et al. 2014; Galbussera et al. 2008; Gutacker et al. 1998; MacDonald 1986a, 2006a, 2006b, 2007a, 2007b; Marques, Weir, et al. 2000; Mattsson et al. 2010; Meer-Scherrer et al. 2006; Miklossy 1993, 2008, 2011a, 2011b; Miklossy et al. 2004, 2006; O'Day and Catalano 2014; Pappolla et al. 1989.

32 Despite their differences, Lyme-literate and mainstream physicians agree that most early Lyme disease cases that are *immediately* treated with antibiotics have very few sequelae. This rare agreement between Lyme-literate and mainstream physicians is also a small point of misrecognition, as several mainstream physicians told me that Lyme-literate physicians think that Lyme disease is always chronic.

Since the beginning of Lyme's diagnosis and treatment as a bacterial infection, there have been case reports and studies in which researchers have isolated Borrelia burgdorferi DNA or have cultured Borrelia burgdorferi spirochetes from humans and animals after treatment with antibiotics (Battafarano et al. 1993; Bradley, Johnson, and Goodman 1994; Cimmino et al. 1989; Häupl et al. 1993; Hunfeld et al. 2005; Lawrence et al. 1995; Li et al. 2011; Liegner et al. 1993; Oksi et al. 1995, 1999; S. Phillips et al. 1998; Pícha et al. 2008; Preac-Mursic et al. 1989; Priem et al. 1998; Rudenko et al. 2016; Sapi et al. 2013; Straubinger et al. 1997; Strle et al. 1993, 1996; Yrjänäinen et al. 2010). In the case of two of these studies (S. Phillips et al. 1998; Sapi et al. 2013), which were conducted by researchers affiliated with the Lyme-literate standard of care, follow-up studies conducted by mainstream researchers were not able to reproduce initial findings (B. Johnson, Pilgard, and Russell 2014; Marques, Stock, and Gill 2000; Tilton, Barden, and Sand 2001). There have also been studies in which researchers have not been able to isolate Borrelia burgdorferi after administration of antibiotics (Berger et al. 1992; Malawista, Barthold, and Persing 1994; Nadelman et al. 1993), and one in which the authors concluded that "repeat episodes of erythema migrans in appropriately treated patients were due to reinfection and not relapse" (Nadelman et al. 2012, 1883). Studies and literature reviews also describe treatment failure with antibiotics, which, in some cases, prompted recommendations for longer treatment regimens or the use of different antibiotics, such as intravenous ceftriaxone for late-stage Lyme disease (Dattwyler and Halperin 1987; Luft et al. 1989; Steere, Grodzicki, et al. 1983; Strle et al. 1993, 1996; Weber 1996). Many studies also describe treatment success (Barsic et al. 2000; Dattwyler et al. 1987; Gerber and Zalneraitis 1994; Luger et al. 1995; Nadelman et al. 1992; Nowakowski et al. 2003; R. Smith et al. 2002; Steere, Hutchinson, et al. 1983; Tory, Zurakowski, and Sundel 2010; Wormser et al. 2003).

33 Initially documented in dogs through PCR detection of DNA in tissues (and, with less success, the cultivation of spirochetes) (Straubinger 2000; Straubinger et al. 1997, 2000), later studies performed in mice resulted in two divergent findings. Two described persistence of nondividing infectious *Borrelia burgdorferi* spirochetes after antibiotic therapy (Barthold et al. 2010; Hodzic et al. 2008); another study described persistence of nondividing noninfectious *Borrelia burgdorferi* spirochetes after antibiotic therapy (Bockenstedt et al. 2002). The lead author of this study later reported that "*Borrelia burgdorferi* antigens, but not infectious spirochetes, can remain adjacent to cartilage for extended periods after antibiotic treatment" and proposed that these antigens "could contribute to the development of antibiotic-refractory Lyme arthritis" (Bockenstedt et al. 2012, 2652). A study published by Embers et al. (2012) also reported the detection of *Borrelia burgdorferi* spirochetes in macaques after antibiotic treatment through xenodiagnosis, culture, immunofluorescence, and PCR. In 2014, Hodzic et al. reproduced previous studies by reporting the persistence of nondividing infectious spirochetes in a mouse model after antibiotic treatment, in addition to the "resurgence" of noncultivable spirochetes at up to twelve months after antibiotic treatment. A more recent study by Crossland, Alvarex, and Embers (2018), continuing the work of Embers et al. (2012), reported the "first study in primates to comprehensively examine pathologic findings associated with the persistence of B. *burgdorferi* in the late stage of LD after antibiotic therapy" and concluded that "chronic Lyme disease symptoms can be attributable to residual inflammation in and around tissues that harbor a low burden of persistent host-adapted spirochetes and/or residual antigen" (680, 672). A follow-up to this study has not yet been published.

34 In a comprehensive review of the literature, Lantos, Auwaerter, and Wormser (2014) identified forty-one references in which "morphological variants" of *Borrelia burgdorferi* were reported, of which nine involved human subjects, three involved mice, one involved ticks, and twenty-eight were in vitro experiments. Of the in vitro studies, one demonstrated metabolic changes in starvation-induced *Borrelia burgdorferi* cysts (Alban, Johnson, and Nelson 2000), but this study was not replicated. Criticisms leveled at both in vivo and in vitro studies are the lack of standardization of variant classification, faulty use of the medium in which the spirochetes were grown, inability to reproduce results, and lack of distinction between morphological structure and metabolic change.

35 Over the past twenty years, several in vitro studies have reported the intracellular location of *Borrelia burgdorferi* in skin cells (Chmielewska-Badora, Cisak, and Dutkiewicz 2000; Klempner, Noring, and Rogers 1993; Y. Ma, Sturrock, and Weis 1991; Wu et al. 2011), synovial cells (Girschick et al. 1996), and neuronal

cells (Livengood and Gilmore 2006; Miklossy et al. 2008). Of these studies, the 2006 study by Livengood and Gilmore has enjoyed the most circulation among Lyme patients and Lyme-literate physicians because it was undertaken by scientists at the CDC, an institution commonly understood by Lyme patients and Lyme-literate physicians to promulgate a perspective on Lyme disease that is at odds with theirs but whose resources are also, in the right contexts, operationalized as a source of credibility. The primary criticism of these studies is that in vitro results are limited in their ability to describe what would *actually* happen in vivo. The difficulty of in vivo–in vitro extrapolation is a much-discussed topic, particularly regarding the question of chemical exposure. Many have described the "toxicodynamic and toxicokinetic problems" (the fact that "endpoints of toxic action are less complex in vitro" and that "toxic concentrations determined in vitro are not equivalent to toxic doses or concentrations in vivo") that "hamper the application of in vitro assays for hazard assessment" (Gülden and Seibert 2005, 218; Strikwold et al. 2017). Alternative approaches have been suggested, but assessments of chemical hazards still primarily rely on extrapolations from animal studies (S. Vogel 2008).

Another criticism, made by a scientist I interviewed, is the difference between the rule and the exception. "Intracellularity is the exception," he explained. "Whereas extracellularity is consistent. It's all about where the organism wants to be, and this organism wants to be in the extracellular matrix." In this vein, a publication by members of the ad hoc committee that formulated the IDSA's 2006 Lyme disease guidelines lists as one of several "concepts about Lyme disease that are unsubstantiated or proven to be inaccurate" the idea that *Borrelia burgdorferi* is an intracellular organism (Auwaerter et al. 2011, 714).

36 Aucott et al. 2013; Batheja et al. 2013; Berglund et al. 2002; Bujak, Weinstein, and Dornbush 1996; Cairns and Godwin 2005; Chandra et al. 2010, 2011a, 2011b, 2013; Clarissou et al. 2009; Djukic et al. 2011; J. Fallon et al. 1999; Gaudino, Coyle, and Krupp 1997; Jacek et al. 2013; Kaplan et al. 2003; Klempner 2002; Klempner, Hu, et al. 2001; Kohlhepp, Oschmann, and Mertens 1989; Krupp et al. 2003; Marques, Brown, and Fleisher 2009; Moniuszko et al. 2009; Morgen et al. 2001; Palmieri et al. 2013; Rebman et al. 2014; Schutzer et al. 2011; Shotland et al. 2003; Sjöwall et al. 2011; Stupica et al. 2011; Tager et al. 2001; A. Weinstein and Britchkov 2002.

37 Barsic et al. 2000; Dattwyler and Luft 1991; Luger et al. 1995; Nadelman et al. 1992; Nowakowski et al. 2003; Seltzer et al. 2000; R. Smith et al. 2002; Strle et al. 1993; Wormser et al. 2003.

38 Asch et al. 1994; Aucott et al. 2013; Bujak, Weinstein, and Dornbush 1996; Shadick et al. 1994, 1999. In response to a question about what could have been done differently to avoid the current standoff between the mainstream and the Lyme-literate camps, one mainstream physician scientist I interviewed suggested that the CDC should have recognized post-treatment Lyme disease syndrome sooner.

39 Drouin, Glickstein, and Steere 2004; Drouin et al. 2008a, 2008b; Ghosh et al. 2006; Kalish, Leong, and Steere 1995; Katchar, Drouin, and Steere 2013; Londoño et al. 2014; Steere et al. 2006; Steere, Drouin, and Glickstein 2011; Strle et al. 2012).

40 Aucott et al. 2016; Chandra et al. 2010, 2011a, b; Strle et al. 2014.

41 In an attempt to determine whether symptoms after standard antibiotic treatment are related to ongoing Borrelia burgdorferi infection, Marques et al. conducted the "first study of the use of I. scapularis larvae for xenodiagnosis ['the use of a vector to detect the presence of an organism'] of Borrelia burgdorferi in humans" (2014, 938). In this study, ticks were allowed to feed to repletion on ten patients with post-treatment Lyme disease syndrome (PTLDS), ten patients with high C6 antibody levels, five patients with EM who had completed therapy, one patient with EM on antibiotic therapy, and ten healthy controls. Ticks were then tested for Borrelia burgdorferi by PCR, and "attempts were made to infect immuno-deficient mice by tick bite or inoculation of tick contents" (937). Xenodiagnosis was negative in all but two patients: the patient with EM on antibiotic therapy and one PTLDS patient. The investigators concluded that further studies are necessary to determine whether "positive xenodiagnostic results" for Borrelia burgdorferi "represent viable organisms or remnants of infection, and whether these results can be related to ongoing symptoms in patients after therapy for Lyme disease" (944). In an editorial commentary, Bockenstedt and Radolf express "reservations" about "the use of xenodiagnosis to address the question of Borrelia burgdorferi persistence in humans" (2014, 947). They argue that PCR detection of Borrelia burgdorferi does not necessarily indicate active infection, and that the only definitive evidence of active infection is the "recovery of live spirochetes," which Marques et al. were unable to do (947). They also suggest that recovering live spirochetes from humans might, in fact, be impossible because, unlike mice, "the consensus among entomologists is that humans are not reservoir-competent hosts" for Borrelia burgdorferi (947).

42 For perspectives on early support among patients and advocates of a Lyme disease vaccine, see Aronowitz 2012; McSweegan 2007.

43 Although Smith Kline-Beecham was the pharmaceutical company that ended up getting a Lyme vaccine to market, it was initially joined in the research and development phase by Connaught Pharmaceuticals. Both ended up with similar vaccines that they put through large clinical trials, the data on which they published within months of each other in the New England Journal of Medicine. Why Connaught dropped its bid remains unclear.

For perspectives on the social and political history of the vaccine, including background on the Lyme vaccine's class action lawsuits, see Aronowitz 2012; Hanson and Edelman 2003; Lantos 2013; Nigrovic and Thompson 2007; Plotkin 2011; Poland 2011; Shen, Mead, and Beard 2011; Stricker and Johnson 2014.

44 Robert Ball, "FDA Powerpoint on Lymerix Vaccine," Lyme Disease Association, May 12, 2018, https://lymediseaseassociation.org/government/federal-government/govt-departments-a-policies/hhsfood-a-drug-administration-fda/powerpoint-by-fda-on-lymerix-vaccine-2/.

45 Chen et al. 1999; Drouin et al. 2004; Drouin et al. 2008a, 2008b; Gross et al. 1998a, 1998b; Kalish et al. 1993, 1995; Kamradt et al. 1995, 1996; Kannian et al. 2007; Lengl-Janssen et al. 1994; Steere et al. 2001, 2003, 2006, 2011; Trollmo et al. 2001.

46 Holcomb B. Noble, "Concerns Grow over Reactions to Lyme Shots," *New York Times*, November 21, 2000, https://www.nytimes.com/2000/11/21/science/concerns-grow-over-reactions-to-lyme-shots.html.

47 Lawrence K. Altman, "Lyme Vaccine Is Approved, with Caveat," *New York Times*, December 22, 1998, http://www.nytimes.com/1998/12/22/us/lyme-vaccine-is-approved-with-caveat.html.

48 The logic here hinges on the argument that most diagnoses are made—and are more critical—in early disease, and that by late disease, there would be enough reactivity to a number of *Borrelia burgdorferi* antigens that having one or two bands missing would not affect diagnostic power. Critics argue that patients who *are not* diagnosed in early disease and who do not present with late objective signs, such as arthritis, might be rendered invisible by the band's absence.

49 Many patients and advocates have criticized the integrity of this decision by arguing that those who were involved in formulating diagnostic criteria also had a financial stake in vaccine development. Journalist and Lyme patient advocate Pamela Weintraub argues that three members of the nine-member voting panel had conflicts of interest related to vaccine development (2008, 315).

50 Valneva, "Valneva Reports Positive Phase I Interim Results for Its Lyme Vaccine Candidate VLA15," *Global News Wire*, March 19, 2018, https://globenewswire.com/news-release/2018/03/19/1441705/0/en/VALNEVA-Reports-Positive-Phase-I-Interim-Results-for-Its-Lyme-Vaccine-Candidate-VLA15.html; Brittany Flaherty, "Can a New Lyme Disease Vaccine Overcome a History of Distrust and Failure?," STATnews, August 22, 2019, https://www.statnews.com/2019/08/22/lyme-disease-vaccine-market/.

51 DVBD, NCEZID, "Signs and Symptoms of Untreated Lyme Disease," CDC, last reviewed August 15, 2019, http://www.cdc.gov/lyme/signs_symptoms/.

52 Many mainstream physicians and scientists argue that, following antibiotic treatment, physicians and patients often interpret a positive ELISA or Western blot to mean active infection even though studies have demonstrated that antibody levels remain positive after the infection is cleared and cannot be reliably correlated with cure (Feder et al. 1992; Fleming et al. 2004; Glatz et al. 2006; Kalish et al. 2001; Kannian et al. 2007; Magnarelli and Anderson 1987; Oksi et al. 2007; C. Rose et al. 1996). On the other hand, some studies have demonstrated that antibody level, the *rate* of antibody decline, and, more recently, the C6 antibody *can* be correlated with cure (Lomholt et al. 2000; Panelius et al.

1999; Philipp et al. 2001, 2003, 2005). A more specific disagreement between mainstream and Lyme-literate physicians is how to interpret persistent or recurrent IgM results in late disease. Mainstream physicians and scientists argue that IgM bands are highly cross-reactive and that their presence should not be read as persistent infection; Lyme-literate physicians and patients, citing early studies (Craft et al. 1984, 1986), argue that IgM bands *can* be interpreted as evidence of persistent or new infection and that IgG is more cross-reactive than IgM (Berardi, Weeks, and Steere 1988; Fawcett et al. 1992; Jain et al. 1996; B. Ma et al. 1992; Sivak et al. 1996). Finally, many mainstream physicians and scientists also decry the fact that some physicians disregard the protocolled order of two-tier testing and order a Western blot test even if the ELISA is negative. In these instances, they argue that positive Western blot bands in the absence of a positive ELISA are often false positives (Seriburi et al. 2012). As one scientist explained, "Any test, doesn't matter whether it's Lyme disease or HIV or hepatitis, if you use it as a screening test without any regard for the patient history, they're awful. The positive predictive value is virtually not there."

53 Discrepancies in laboratory results were first published in 1990 in a study that sent blood samples to nine laboratories and demonstrated interlaboratory variability (Luger 1990b). This study was followed by similar ones in 1992 (Bakken et al.), 1997 (Bakken et al.), and 2014 (B. Fallon et al.).

54 The Western blot also has recognized limitations, the most high profile of which is that interpreting antigen bands is a highly subjective process. Antigen bands are printed along a spectrum that runs from faint to dark, and lab technicians must interpret which band is dark enough to be a positive and which band is faint enough to be a negative. Some laboratories have transitioned to computerized readings (despite their own limitations), but many Western blots are still interpreted by technicians.

55 On August 16, 2019, the CDC issued an "updated recommendation for serologic diagnosis in Lyme disease." It announced that, after recent FDA clearance, "serologic assays that utilize EIA rather than western immunoblot assay in a two-test format are acceptable alternatives for the laboratory diagnosis of Lyme disease" (Mead, Petersen, and Hinckley 2019, 703).

56 While surveillance criteria require "true" or "strict" disease cases, diagnostic criteria are often more accommodating.

57 These tests include (1) Western blot tests that report all antigen bands; (2) a test called CD57 that measures a natural killer cell that some Lyme-literate physicians argue is found at lower levels in patients with chronic Lyme disease (Stricker and Winger 2001; Stricker et al. 2002), but which one follow-up study found was not significantly lower than in controls (Marques, Brown, and Fleisher 2009); and (3) a urine PCR test that some mainstream scientists initially found promising (Bayer, Zhang, and Bayer 1996; Dorward, Schwan, and Garon 1991; Hyde et al. 1989; Magnarelli, Anderson, and Stafford 1994) until a study

in 2001 demonstrated high rates of false positive results in controls (Klempner, Schmid, et al. 2001).

58 Part of the confusion stems from the fact that studies and case reports have described seronegativity in late Lyme disease (Dattwyler et al. 1988; Dejmková et al. 2002; Dressler, Yoshinari, and Steere 1991; Lomholt et al. 2000; Oksi et al. 1995; Steere 1993). The most cited of these studies, Dattwyler et al. 1988, has been discredited by many mainstream scientists and physicians—and even by some of the authors themselves—as "understanding of Lyme disease has increased" (Steere 2009, 310). In "Common Misconceptions about Lyme Disease," Halperin, Baker, and Wormser argue that "seronegativity occurs rarely—if ever—in individuals with later manifestations or chronic symptoms of B. burgdorferi infection" (2013, 264.e2). Halperin, Baker, and Wormser continue to argue that the Dattwyler et al. 1988 study "was flawed for multiple reasons," perhaps, most importantly, because the "T-cell proliferative assay used was later shown to be nonspecific" (264.e2).

One of the scientists involved in Dattwyler et al.'s 1988 study continues to maintain that its results are accurate. He argues that the claim that the T-cell proliferative assay is "non-specific" hinges primarily on one study done in 1991 that has not been reproduced (Zoschke, Skemp, and Defosse 1991). On the other hand, several studies report that, despite suboptimal sensitivity (Dressler, Yoshinari, and Steere 1991) and the clinical impracticality of "labor-intensive" "limiting dilution assays" to increase sensitivity (Horowitz et al. 1994, 377), lymphocyte reactivity can be a good indicator of Borrelia burgdorferi infection, especially when used in conjunction with other assays and in individuals who have "nondiagnostic levels of antibodies against Borrelia burgdorferi" (Buechner et al. 1995, 676; see also Bauer et al. 2001; A. Krause et al. 1991, 1992; R. Martin et al. 1988; Neumann et al. 1989; Pachner et al. 1985; Rutkowski, Busch, and Huppertz 1997; Vaz et al. 2001; Weyand and Goronzy 1989; Yoshinari, Reinhardt, and Steere 1991). This scientist also maintains that there is evidence of antibiotics aborting antibody responses in other diseases more generally (Hollander, Turner, and Nell 1952), as well as evidence of seronegative Lyme disease resulting from "inadequate doses of antibiotics" more specifically (Volkman 2011, 100; see also T. Keller, Halperin, and Whitman 1992; Mouritsen et al. 1996; Nadelman et al. 2001; Oksi et al. 1995), the best evidence for which, in his opinion, is that provided by Nadelman et al. 2001. He argues that the authors of this study, which demonstrated the efficacy of a single dose of prophylactic doxycycline to prevent Lyme disease after a tick bite, "showed that their single-dose regimen was 87% effective in blocking both the erythema migrans (EM) and the appearance of anti-Borrelia antibodies expected with borreliosis, but they did not show that it blocked actual infection in the antibiotic recipients" (Volkman 2010, 2271). As a result, he argues, a single oral dose of doxycycline "may actually promote persistent borreliosis that will be seronegative, and therefore difficult to diagnose" (2271). A 2015 study of 104 patients with "physician diagnosed erythema migrans rashes" who underwent three weeks of doxycycline treatment found that 39.4 percent were seronegative before and after treatment (Rebman et al. 2015, 585).

59 Many Lyme-literate physicians would argue that because patients in these studies who did not seroconvert were not followed for symptom sequelae and were not tested for *Borrelia* persistence by PCR or culture, it cannot be assumed that these patients were "cured."

60 The 2006 IDSA guidelines also recommend a single dose of prophylactic doxycycline administered within seventy-two hours of being bitten by a blacklegged tick that was attached for more than thirty-six hours. A study on a mouse model, however, demonstrated that administering doxycycline after twenty-four hours decreased protection by 27 percent, and administering doxycycline after forty-eight hours provided no protection (Piesman and Hojgaard 2012). An earlier study in a mouse model investigating a single oral dose of doxycycline as prophylaxis reported that only 20–43% percent of mice that received oral doxycycline were protected from *Borrelia burgdorferi* infection; however, "100% of mice receiving [a single injection of] sustained-release doxycycline were protected" (Zeidner et al. 2008, 463; see also Zeidner et al. 2004).

61 In 2016, Berende et al. published the results of a randomized controlled trial on the effect of longer-term antibiotics for Lyme patients with persistent symptoms in the Netherlands. The authors concluded that "in patients with persistent symptoms attributed to Lyme disease, longer-term antibiotic treatment did not have additional beneficial effects on health-related quality of life beyond those with shorter-term treatment" (1209). The authors stated that their findings confirmed those of the Klempner studies. In response, Lyme-literate physicians and advocates argued that the Berende et al. study, which compared one group that had received two weeks of IV ceftriaxone with another group that had received two weeks of IV ceftriaxone with an additional twelve weeks of doxycycline, did "not have a true control group because all chronic Lyme disease patients received an additional two weeks of intravenous ceftriaxone therapy," and that it "clearly shows that this additional antibiotic treatment was associated with significant improvement in the SF-36 quality of life scale in all patient groups" (Laura Iyer, March 31, 2016, comment on "Randomized Trial of Longer-Term Therapy for Symptoms Attributed to Lyme Disease," *New England Journal of Medicine* 374 (2016), https://www.nejm.org/doi/full/10.1056/NEJMoa1505425?page=3#article_comments; L. Johnson 2016).

62 The results of the US clinical trials and their implications were revisited in a series of articles (Delong et al. 2012; B. Fallon et al. 2012; Klempner et al. 2013). In a biostatistical review, Delong et al. (2012, 1132) conclude that "retreatment can be beneficial," and B. Fallon et al. (2012, 79) conclude that "future treatment guidelines should clarify that efficacy of IV ceftriaxone for post-treatment Lyme

fatigue was demonstrated in one RCT and supported by a second RCT, but that its use was not recommended primarily due to adverse events stemming from the IV route of treatment." Responding to both articles, Klempner et al. (2013) address many of the criticisms that the Lyme-literate community has of the four clinical trials and how their results have been interpreted. Klempner et al. conclude that "Delong et al. fail to provide credible or convincing evidence that the methodology, findings, and conclusions of the study by Klempner et al. are invalid or that the other National Institutes of Health's sponsored retreatment trials show any evidence that post-treatment symptoms of Lyme disease are due to persistent infection. Neither of the analyses provided by Delong et al. or Fallon et al. justify a conclusion that there is a meaningful clinical benefit to be gained from retreatment with parenteral antibiotic therapy" (7).

63 Concerns about antibiotic use related to chronic Lyme disease seem to be amplified by an increasing public awareness about antibiotic use in livestock, increasing cases of antibiotic-resistant bacteria, and recent discoveries about the critical role of the microbiome in all aspects of human health.

2. Preventing Lyme

1 CDC, "Illnesses from Mosquito, Tick, and Flea Bites Increasing in the US," press release, May 1, 2018, https://www.cdc.gov/media/releases/2018/p0501-vs -vector-borne.html.

2 Ernst 2018; Donald G. McNeil Jr., "Tick and Mosquito Infections Spreading Rapidly, C.D.C. Finds," *New York Times*, May 1, 2018, https://www.nytimes.com /2018/05/01/health/ticks-mosquitoes-diseases.html.

3 David Scales, "As Ticks and Lyme Disease Spread, Prevention Efforts Limited to 'Shoestring,'" *Common Health*, WBUR, July 14, 2017, https://www.wbur.org /commonhealth/2017/07/14/losing-lyme-ticks-spread.

4 For further reading on the anthropology of affect and emotion, see Abu-Lughod and Lutz 1990; Berlant and Greenwald 2012; Leavitt 1996; Lutz and White 1986; Massumi 1995; Silverman 2011; Skoggard and Waterston 2015.

5 For further reading on nature as a "cultural invention" or "cultural construct," see Fine 1997 and Cronon 1995, respectively.

6 One of the defining features of Romanticism was the idea of the "sublime," which came to be understood as qualitatively different from "the beautiful" but still capable of instilling pleasure and delight through feelings that skirted the line between "terror" and "exaltation," "horror" and "awe" (Nash [1967] 2001, 45; Brady 2012). For the Romantics, nature, in its most desolate and unreach-able corners, was sublimity's truest source.

7 Pam Belluck, "Tick-Borne Illnesses Have Nantucket Considering Some Deer-Based Solutions," *New York Times*, September 5, 2009, http://www.nytimes.com /2009/09/06/us/06nantucket.html.

8 Dwight Garner, "Colorless, Tasteless, but Not Dangerous," *New York Times*, November 16, 2010, http://www.nytimes.com/2010/11/16/books/16book.html?_r=0.

9 Lornett Vestal, "The Unbearable Whiteness of Hiking and How to Solve It," Sierra Club, December 7, 2016, https://www.sierraclub.org/outdoors/2016/12/unbearable-whiteness-hiking-and-how-solve-it; Tanya Golash-Boza, Safiya Noble, Vilna Bashi Treitler, and Zulema Valdez, "Why America's National Parks Are So White," *Al Jazeera America*, July 23, 2015, http://america.aljazeera.com/opinions/2015/7/heres-why-americas-national-parks-are-so-white.html; Francie Latour, "Hiking While Black: The Untold Story," *Boston Globe*, June 20, 2014, https://www.bostonglobe.com/ideas/2014/06/20/hiking-while-black-the-untold-story-black-people-great-outdoors/ssRvXFYogkZs2e4RX3z6JP/story.html.

10 Valdez, "Why America's National Parks Are So White."

11 Glenn Nelson, "Why Are Our Parks So White?," *New York Times*, July 10, 2015, https://www.nytimes.com/2015/07/12/opinion/sunday/diversify-our-national-parks.html.

12 Nelson, "Why Are Our Parks So White?"

13 "Quick Facts: United States," US Census Bureau, last updated July 1, 2018, https://www.census.gov/quickfacts/fact/table/US/PST045218; Mireya Navarro, "National Parks Reach Out to Blacks Who Aren't Visiting," *New York Times*, November 2, 2010, https://www.nytimes.com/2010/11/03/science/earth/03parks.html?_r=0.

14 "Our Impact," Outdoor Afro, 2018, http://outdoorafro.com/impact/.

15 "Early Research and the Treatment of Tuberculosis in the 19th Century," accessed January 31, 2020, http://exhibits.hsl.virginia.edu/alav/tuberculosis/.

16 I emphasize the phrase "end up" to underscore the contingency of the relationship between having Lyme disease and loving nature.

17 Alex Gregory, "It's Eden. You don't have to keep checking for ticks," cartoon, *New Yorker*, accessed November 13, 2019, https://www.newyorker.com/cartoon/a151158.

18 Scholars of risk have shown that it (1) has become a ubiquitous idea in the Global North, (2) is understood to be manageable through "human intervention," and (3) is increasingly linked with individual "choice, responsibility and blame" (Lupton 1999, 25; see also Beck 1992; Douglas 1992; Giddens 1991; Harthorn and Oaks 2003; Lash, Wynne, and Szerszynski 1996). In the context of public health and the environment, risk is managed through biopolitical (collective) and anatomo-political (individual) interventions (Foucault [1976] 1990; see also Nadesan 2008; Petersen and Lupton 1996). More critically, depending on the type of risk (from nuclear power plant radiation to infectious disease), individuals are perceived to be either "at risk" (and exempted from blame) or "risky" (and held fully accountable) (Petersen and Lupton 1996, 115). Finally, against earlier work on risk perception that approached it as a "form of deliberative analytic information processing," more recent scholarship in social psychology has demonstrated that risk perception hinges on "emotional and affective processes," that it is

"inherently subjective," and that its "conception and assessment" is a "socially constructed phenomenon" (Slovic 2000, xxxi, xxxvi).

19 CDC, "New CDC Chemical Exposure Report Begins to Fill Critical Information Gaps in Environmental Health for the U.S. Population," press release, March 21, 2001, http://www.cdc.gov/media/pressrel/r010321.htm.

20 In January 2019, the CDC released updated tables, which include data for 352 chemicals. CDC, "Updated Tables, January 2019," *National Report on Human Exposure to Environmental Chemicals*, http://www.cdc.gov/exposurereport/.

21 For further anthropological reading on the placebo effect, see Kirmayer 2011; Ostenfeld-Rosenthal 2012; J. Thompson, Ritenbaugh, and Nichter 2009.

22 Many mainstream physicians perceive subscription to the idea of the Herxheimer—particularly a Herxheimer that is believed to occur at any point during treatment—as further proof that Lyme-literate physicians practice sham medicine. As one physician exclaimed, "If patients believe they are getting cured whether they feel better or worse, then these doctors can do no wrong." Several mainstream physicians I interviewed who actively treat Lyme disease recognize the Herxheimer reaction but only as something that occurs within the first twenty-four hours after antibiotic treatment.

23 This observation is again consistent with the work of Paul Slovic and colleagues, who conclude that "for any given level of benefit, greater risk was tolerated if that risk was *voluntary*, immediate, known precisely, *controllable* and familiar" (94; emphasis added).

24 For some, the opposite is true. Another woman I interviewed said that she would not spray her yard because she did not want to be exposed to any more chemicals. But when I asked her if the same logic applied to her food, she replied, "No. A little funny, huh? Anything but. You know what, if I had all the money in the world, I'd probably eat organic, but, to me, it's too expensive."

25 After my fieldwork ended, a study published in 2016 showed that while a single lawn application did reduce the number of ticks on properties sprayed with pesticides, it did not reduce Lyme disease infection rates (Hinckley, Meek, and Ray 2016); a systematic review of studies on "interventions to prevent Lyme disease in humans" found the quality of the four studies conducted on "personal protection" since 2002 to be "low" and that repellants, protective clothing, and bathing within two hours of coming indoors "may be associated with a lower incidence of LD" (Richardson et al. 2019, 18).

3. Living Lyme

1 In Stephen Kroll-Smith and Hugh Floyd's work on multiple chemical sensitivity, they draw on Clifford Geertz to describe the way in which MCS patients "join science with biography" as a "practical epistemology" (1997, 11). Similarly, in Steven Epstein's work on AIDS activism, he suggests that AIDS activists

achieved new "pathways to credibility" by "imbib[ing] and appropriat[ing] the languages and cultures of the biomedical sciences" (1996, 335). Although there is convergence here with my work, my study also departs from this work in its exploration of how patients *and* physicians enact *and* know disease within the same field of analysis.

2   For a range of anthropological work on "illness experiences," see Ablon 1999; Biehl and Eskerod 2007; Briggs and Mantini-Briggs 2003; Garro 1994; Jackson 2000; A. Kleinman 1986, 1988; Ware 1992; White 2009; Young 1995.

3   I observed and interacted with acute Lyme patients during my visits to mainstream physicians' practices and walk-in clinics. These encounters inform my analysis in the chapter that follows.

4   Light sensitivity was a common complaint among Lyme patients with whom I spoke.

5   Mainstream Lyme physicians typically reserve the use of ceftriaxone for neurological and rheumatological features of late Lyme disease and typically for no longer than six weeks.

6   This interaction and others like it were upsetting to Dr. Childs. Irrespective of whether he believed that his patient had Lyme disease, it was important to Dr. Childs that his patient felt listened to and taken seriously. During conversations with patients, he would allow for as many questions as the patient had and would often exclaim, "Don't let me off the hook too easily!" in an attempt to invite more questions.

7   Dr. Childs later explained, "Most of the time my disagreement with the treatment practices of Lyme-literate doctors is with giving antibiotics to people who don't have Lyme disease in the first place. In such individuals, antibiotics are not indicated for any duration of time. . . . But in the patient who actually has Lyme disease, I am open to a longer duration of therapy in more refractory cases. Also, my experience as a specialist receiving referrals biases me toward these more difficult to treat cases."

8   Only one of the many Lyme-literate physicians I spoke with also echoed this sentiment when he said, "These people are miserable, and there's no solution. The majority of them don't really have Lyme disease. For example, the people in *Under Our Skin*, they didn't have Lyme or chronic Lyme. Eighty percent of the patients that I see think they have Lyme. I end up with 50 percent or more that don't have active Lyme."

9   Lyme-literate physicians and patients adamantly contest this and argue that Lyme disease has claimed many lives. A well-circulated Lyme advocacy newsletter features an "In Memoriam" section that documents lives claimed to be lost to Lyme disease.

10 For further work on the experience of pain in social context, see Aronowitz 1998; M.-J. Good et al. 1992; A. Kleinman 1988, 1995; Mattingly and Garro 2000; Sontag 2001.

11 For further reading on social scientific approaches to the intersection of bio-medicine, gender, and chronic pain/illness, see Bendelow 2000, 2006; Greenhalgh 2001; Lorber and Moore 2002; Manderson and Smith-Morris 2010; Moss and Dyck 2002; Wendell 1996.

12 Lyme-literate physicians would also occasionally provide gendered explanations to delegitimize the biological reality of Lyme disease. For example, during an interview, one physician exclaimed, "You've seen those moms, the 'Greenwich ladies.' There's a lot of overprotection there. A lot of over-amplification of their children's symptoms. Some of their kids are not that sick."

13 For further interdisciplinary reading on women's experiences in biomedical clinical settings, see Fee and Krieger 1994; Pringle 1998; D. Russell 1995; Todd 1989; Vertinsky 1994; Waitzkin 1991.

14 One woman at a support group meeting did muse about whether the overrepresentation of women among chronic Lyme disease patients could be hormonally related.

15 For insightful reflections on whether analytical attention to materiality "produce[es] a politics that does not really matter" and the need for a "contextualized and situated materialism" that engages with postcolonial science studies, see Washick, Wingrove, and Ferguson 2015, 277, and Roy and Subramaniam 2016, 36, respectively.

16 For further "new materialist" readings, see Alaimo and Hekman 2008; Barad 2003; Coole and Frost 2010; Fausto-Sterling 2005; Hekman 2010; Hird 2004; E. Keller 2010; C. Roberts 2007; Wilson 1998, 2011.

17 "Lyme Disease Prevalence: Does Sex Matter?," lymedisease.org, January 6, 2020, https://www.lymedisease.org/lyme-disease-prevalence-gender-bias/.

18 In a later essay, Butler seems to pivot slightly by suggesting that "sexual difference is neither fully given nor fully constructed, but partially both" (2004, 186). Even here, however, she reaffirms a nonentangled division between the biological and the social by concluding that "what is constructed is of necessity prior to construction, even as there appears no access to this prior moment except through construction" (186).

19 *Biology of Sex Differences Journal* home page, accessed November 13, 2019, http://www.bsd-journal.com/. See also Anne Fausto-Sterling's opinion piece in the *New York Times*, "Why Sex Is Not Binary," October 25, 2018, https://www.nytimes.com/2018/10/25/opinion/sex-biology-binary.html.

20 This interview was different from other interviews I conducted because it was a simultaneous exercise in participant observation. My role during this interview was as a participant observer of two practitioners who were conducting a qualitative study on chronic Lyme disease.

21 I was told by several mainstream physicians that the way in which individuals use the word "Lyme" indexes their credibility vis-à-vis Lyme disease. For

example, an individual who says "Lyme's disease" instead of "Lyme disease," as Renee does here, is often perceived by mainstream Lyme physicians to be less credible and less informed.

22 Because I am only interested in individuals' reports of their experiences, it is difficult to decipher what actually happened in this instance. It is possible that the pediatrician made a mistake and did not communicate Dylan's test results; it is also possible that the pediatrician did not interpret Dylan's test as positive and, therefore, saw no need to communicate them to Dylan's family.

23 The use of IVIG was initially intended for immune deficiency syndromes, but in recent years, it has been used experimentally for a range of conditions and has become quite controversial.

24 There have been several studies on Lyme disease and psychiatric comorbidities. One study concluded, "Psychiatric comorbidity and other psychological factors distinguished chronic Lyme disease patients from other patients commonly seen in Lyme disease referral centers, and were related to poor functional outcomes" (Hassett et al. 2008, 1742). In a later study, these same authors observe, "Psychiatric comorbidity and other psychological factors are prominent in the presentation and outcome of some patients who inaccurately ascribe long-standing symptoms to 'chronic Lyme disease'" (Hassett et al. 2009, 843). Despite these conclusions, the results of the 2008 study demonstrate that (1) patients categorized as having post-Lyme disease syndrome and those categorized as having "medically unexplained symptoms thought to be CLD" had almost no history of depression, and (2) the rate of current depression among patients with "medically unexplained symptoms thought to be CLD" was not significantly different from that among the "medical diagnosis comparison group" (1743–46). Another study by a different group published in 2005 also suggests that post–Lyme borreliosis in Europe fits a different pattern than CFS, fibromyalgia, and depression (Cairns and Godwin 2005). The lead author on this study, however, acknowledges in the article that she suffers from "post–Lyme borreliosis," and for this reason, several mainstream physicians discount this study as biased.

25 On a couple occasions during my research, Lyme-literate physicians also made comments to the same effect. While observing a Lyme-literate physician's practice, one staff member said, "The crazies are calling!" Another looked at me and said, "You've probably seen that, shadowing Lyme practices. These patients demand a lot of time and energy." Another Lyme-literate physician I interviewed exclaimed, "Some of the Lyme patients are crazy!" And a Lyme patient who had led a support group for years said that he stopped doing so, in part, because support groups "pull the margins of people."

26 One Lyme-literate practitioner, who is in the minority of Lyme-literate practitioners I spoke with, expressed doubt about some diagnoses of chronic Lyme disease in children.

27 This bolsters mainstream physicians' suspicions that children's chronic Lyme disease diagnoses can, in some cases, be the result of Munchausen syndrome by proxy, a controversial psychological condition in which parents or caregivers fabricate or exaggerate the health of those under their care. Lyme patients argue that this diagnosis is offensive and unfounded, and that family clusters of Lyme disease can more easily be explained by congenital and sexually transmitted Lyme disease or by shared patterns of peridomestic tick exposure.

28 Reference to the internet in the context of the Lyme disease controversy is common. Among the mainstream physicians I spoke with, it was often used to describe how the controversy had been, in the words of one mainstream physician, "hugely accelerated" by patients making self-diagnoses based on symptoms that they had read about on the internet. In contrast, the Lyme-literate physicians I spoke with were more inclined to identify the internet as a tool of empowerment and medical democratization for patients. Despite their differences, ideas about the internet among both types of physicians often conflated the distinction between the internet as *form* and the internet as *content*. That is, reference to the internet included a particular type of knowledge content (i.e., patient forums and blogs but not peer-reviewed articles), even though the internet in *form* is almost ubiquitously the means by which scientists, physicians, and patients alike access and produce knowledge.

29 The perception that Lyme patients are knowledge producers leads some mainstream physicians and scientists to believe that Lyme patients are "self-diagnosers." Several mainstream physicians I spoke with said that patients often come to their office having already made a diagnosis of Lyme disease.

30 Mainstream physicians and scientists I spoke with often described how stories like these about Lyme-literate practitioners who claim to have treated so many chronic Lyme patients made them all the more suspicious of Lyme-literate practitioners.

31 Some mainstream physicians I spoke with and observed also use similar "screening strategies." One physician described how he used an inverse calculus to determine which of his patients might actually be "legitimate" Lyme disease patients. He said, "The farther they drive to see me and the more doctors they have been to see, the less likely it is that they actually have Lyme disease."

32 This, of course, is not universally true. Susan Greenhalgh observes that "when the use of alternative medicine is a major theme in illness autobiographies, the authors often write as converts to the cause"; Greenhalgh offers an autoethnographic case example in which "instead of 'opening the blocks' to healing, some alternative medicines can block healing instead" (2001, 50–51).

33 "Introduction," NIH National Center for Complementary and Integrative Health, last modified September 24, 2017, https://nccih.nih.gov/about/plans /2011/introduction.htm.

34 For further social scientific explorations of CAM, see Badone 2008; Baer 2001, 2004; Barcan 2011; L. Barnes 2003, 2005; Cant and Sharma 1996, 1999; Cant and Watts 2018; Easthope, Tranter, and Gill 2000; Gevitz 1988; Hess 1996, 2004a; Kelner and Wellman 2000; McGuire 1988; Nissen 2011, 2012; Nissen and Manderson 2013; Ross 2012; Ruggie 2004; Scott 1998; Siahpush 2000; Sointu 2006, 2012; J. Thompson and Nichter 2015; Tovey, Easthope, and Adams 2004.

35 CAM practitioners often distinguish themselves from biomedical practitioners through their interest in treating the "root cause" of symptoms and not symptoms themselves, whereas biomedical practitioners are understood to operate within a pharmaceutical-sponsored industry of symptom treatment.

36 The phrase "gentle intervention" is inspired by a support group leader who, at one meeting, explained, "Our bodies are so fragile that they need a gentle intervention."

37 The everyday rituals and regimens of CAM are in no way comforting to every patient. One patient exclaimed, "It scares me a bit because they have these herbal protocols for Lyme. I ordered cat's claw. Herbal medicine is serious stuff. It made me feel horrible. It scared me. I thought of it as a herx. Made me think that I really wanted to treat this pharmaceutically. But if the pharmaceuticals don't work by the end of the summer, I will go to an herbalist."

38 For further reading on the inverse relationship between poverty and health, see Krieger, Williams, and Moss 1997; Leon, Walt, and Gilson 2001; Meer, Miller, and Rosen 2003; Nguyen and Peschard 2003; Pick, Rispel, and Naidoo 2008; Wagstaff 2002.

39 Tom Dart, "Texas Teenager Suffering 'Affluenza' Avoids Jail for Second Time," *Guardian*, February 5, 2014, http://www.theguardian.com/world/2014/feb/06/texas-teenager-affluenza-escapes-jail-second-time.

40 One notable exception is the relationship between affluence, allergies, and other autoimmune disorders, the proposed explanation for which is the "hygiene hypothesis," which posits that "changes of lifestyle in industrialized countries have led to a decrease of the infectious burden and are associated with the rise of allergic and autoimmune diseases" (Okada et al. 2010, 1).

41 For further reading on environmental racism and the environmental justice movement, see Agyeman 2005; Bullard 2000; Cole and Foster 2001; Mohai, Pellow, and Roberts 2009; Park and Pellow 2011; Pellow and Park 2002; Sze 2007; D. Taylor 2009, 2014, 2016.

42 Because I relied on purposive and snowball sampling and not random sampling, it is possible that the demographic picture of the Lyme patients I encountered through support groups, fundraisers, and conferences represents a self-selected sample of chronic Lyme patients. However, because knowledge about chronic Lyme is largely produced within these spaces, this demographic picture is likely an accurate representation of individuals who identify with chronic Lyme disease.

43 "Black People and Lyme," discussion thread, MDJunction, May 2014, https://www.mdjunction.com/forums/lyme-disease-support-forums/general-support/11102097-black-people-and-lyme/limitstart/20.

44 Hoffman et al. found that "disparities in pain management" are correlated with clinician biases about biologically based racial differences, including the belief that "blacks age more slowly than whites," and that their "nerve endings are less sensitive" (2016, 4298), while Singhal et al. found that "there are significant racial-ethnic disparities in opioid prescription and administration for non-definitive conditions" (2016, 11).

45 In addition to physical distance, Fassin, quoting sociologist Everett Hughes, highlights the critical role of "social distance" in the creation of "unequal" and "devalued" lives: "The greater their social distance from us, the more we leave in the hands of others a sort of mandate by default to deal with them on our behalf" (2018b, 120).

4. Diagnosing and Treating Lyme

1 While Colleen Derkatch (2016) explores how the "boundary" between what counts as biomedicine and CAM is made and remade, I am interested in how, in contrast to CAM, biomedicine's delineation between signs and symptoms generates a limit within biomedicine between medical explainability and medical unexplainability.

2 Dr. Childs later explained, "One observation that I think you have not made is why not just give every patient antibiotics if they want to be treated? What is the reluctance? The risk of side effects is not zero, but it is low. The answer is that by treating the patient for a disease that he or she does not have, you are validating a false belief. If you tell the patient on the one hand that they don't have Lyme disease, but you treat them at the same time, the message you are really conveying is that you are making this diagnosis."

3 Dr. Childs explained to me that a "real case" of Lyme disease was a "good case in the teaching sense." He continued to explain that he knew I would "see a lot of patients who didn't have Lyme disease" at his practice and other practices, so it was important to him that I see some "real cases." But he was careful to clarify that he did not believe that a "non-Lyme case is a bad case."

4 Any information that a project participant described as "off the record" was explicitly designated as such within my notes and was not entered into my coding program for analysis.

5 There is also disagreement among biomedical physicians about the usefulness of medically unexplained illness as a diagnostic category. In the UK, in particular, there appears to be an emergent movement within biomedicine to "take symptoms seriously" (Greco 2017, 119). For further reading, see Greco 2012, 2017; Kirmayer et al. 2004; Launer 2009.

6 My work builds on this argument by suggesting that medically unexplained illness is not only a "product" or "iatrogenic product" of biomedicine but also a constitutive feature that makes possible the bodily conditions that biomedicine *can* explain (Greco 2017, 118). For further reading on the historical dimension of biomedical categorization, see Armstrong 2011; Fabrega 1990; Greco 2012; S. Johnson 2008.

7 CDC, "Lyme Disease (*Borrelia burgdorferi*): 2017 Case Definition," National Notifiable Diseases Surveillance System (NNDSS), 2017, https://wwwn.cdc.gov/nndss /conditions/lyme-disease/case-definition/2017/.

8 Many thanks to one of my anonymous reviewers for this insight.

9 International Lyme and Associated Diseases Education Foundation, "Frequently Asked Questions about Lyme Disease," ILADEF, accessed November 13, 2019, https://iladef.org/education/lyme-disease-faq/.

10 Since my observation of Dr. Johnson's practice in 2011, he explains that "a lot has changed." For example, due to availability, he no longer uses SyDetox. He also does not use chelation on a regular basis. He explains, "The key to getting people better turned out to be the persister and biofilm forms of [*Borrelia burgdorferi*]. . . . I have developed new treatments that are short-term antibiotics, addressing the biofilms and persister forms, and these are working better than many other strategies we tried years before. Many resistant patients now have their lives back."

11 Dr. Braun explained that he likes to wear this pin when he gives talks and presentations because it "lends 'cred.'"

12 Dr. Braun later shared that his experiences had been "radicalizing" in large part because he had undergone two investigations by his state's Office of Professional Medical Conduct (OPMC). "A lot of the passion comes from that," he explained. "And a lot of the radicalization comes from that. That happened in 2000 and 2010, and it was extremely stressful and also costly. Each took about two years to resolve. But I was able to, as they say in the trade, defend on the merits."

13 Klassenkampf is a German word that means "class struggle." Dr. Braun explained that "from a certain point of view," the idea of Klassenkampf "fits." "The patients are the proletariat, the physicians are the radicals trying to man the ramparts, so to speak, and the academicians who consult for the insurance industry and produce guidelines that personally I believe are fraudulent and who then serve as expert witnesses for boards of medical practice in actions being taken against physicians who treat persons with Lyme disease, and whom I regard as the goons, they're the thugs for the insurance company bosses."

14 Dr. Braun explained that recording patient interviews has been "invaluable." "As you know, these patients have a career as a patient. That documentation, not only does it help to defend myself but it also serves the patients very well as they pursue their career in different venues they may go to. It has also been very expensive but well worth it."

15 Dr. Braun was careful to clarify that he does not use the term "Lyme literate in relation to himself." He continued, "Maybe people apply it to me, but I don't particularly use it."

16 With regard to being reported to the National Practitioner Data Bank, Dr. Braun explained, "That's a really black mark on you. If you get reported to the National Practitioner Data Bank, what that means is that potentially you will be prohibited from getting any reimbursement from any insurers and from Medicare and Medicaid. That's why it's so dangerous to do what we do. . . . All of these insurers have internal so-called quality control committees, and if you digress from what's recommended, you become targeted. Especially if you're costing the plan more than they want you to cost, you're going to be destroyed."

17 Dr. Braun was adamant about not using electronic medical records. He explained that he was philosophically opposed to them because of their "inability to assure patient privacy"; he also explained that they are a "key 'element' in 'social control' and assuring 'uniformity' of approach," "violate the 'sanctity' of the physician–patient relationship," and "undermine physician autonomy and individualization of patient care."

18 Functional medicine is a type of integrative medicine that focuses on the "root cause" of disease and often uses CAM therapies and diagnostics.

19 Dr. Braun explained that these concerns were based on the story of a mainstream scientist who, according to Dr. Braun, contacted the academic department of a graduate student working on a Lyme disease–related book in the hopes of getting her "sanctioned."

20 AHRQ, "Six Domains of Health Care Quality," accessed January 26, 2020, https://www.ahrq.gov/talkingquality/measures/six-domains.html.

5. Lyme Disease, Evidence-Based Medicine, and the Biopolitics of Truthmaking

1 Patients' use of the term "evidence-based medicine" could alternatively be interpreted as a "commonsense" understanding of contemporary biomedicine that does not also encompass an understanding of evidence-based medicine's operational specificities. Although this could be the case among a broader patient population in the United States, I suspect that, in contrast to previous generations of patients, even these patients likely associate biomedicine and its pharmaceutical and procedural accessories with something highly "scientific." Because the controversy over Lyme disease is so overtly linked to clinical guidelines, I found that many patients had a working understanding of "evidence-based medicine" as something that differentiates between "strong" and "weak" forms of evidence (an understanding that impressed on them the

importance of having randomized controlled trials validate their experience)
and is linked to the creation of clinical guidelines.

2   "Understanding Geographic Variations in Health Care," *Dartmouth Atlas Projec-
tion*, November 15, 2019, https://www.dartmouthatlas.org/.

3   For further reading, see Daly 2005; Davidovitch and Filc 2006; Goldenberg 2006;
Worrall 2002.

4   Centre for Evidence-Based Medicine, "OCEBM Levels of Evidence," CEBM,
May 1, 2016, http://www.cebm.net/ocebm-levels-of-evidence/.

5   On July 17, 2018, the NGC database "went dark" due to federal "budget cuts"
(AAFP, "AHRQ: National Guideline Clearinghouse to Shut Down July 16,"
press release, June 27, 2018, https://www.aafp.org/news/government
-medicine/20180627guidelineclearinghouse.html); that day, the ECRI Institute, a nonprofit organization based at the University of Pennsylvania, announced it would continue the NGC's work by creating a "centralized reposi-
tory of current, properly vetted evidence-based clinical practice guideline
summaries and other information" later in 2018 (ECRI, "ECRI Institute to
Continue Clinical Guideline Work Shuttered by Federal Government," press
release, July 17, 2018, https://www.ecri.org/press/Pages/ECRI_Guideline
_Website.aspx).

6   AHRQ, "Guidelines and Measures," accessed November 14, 2019, http://www
.guideline.gov/about/inclusion-criteria.aspx.

7   AHRQ, "Evidence-Based Practice Centers," Effective Health Care Program, accessed November 14, 2019, https://effectivehealthcare.ahrq.gov/about/epc.

8   AHRQ, Product Search, Effective Health Care Program, accessed November 14,
2019, https://effectivehealthcare.ahrq.gov/products.

9   AHRQ, "Former Projects," Effective Health Care Program, accessed November 14, 2019, https://effectivehealthcare.ahrq.gov/about/former.

10 In a related example about "autism litigation" and the vaccine court, in which,
after losing in court, "families and their advocates transformed their scientific
arguments into an indictment of procedural injustice," Anna Kirkland describes
how, oftentimes, "design meant to produce legitimacy ends up being used to
upend legitimacy" (2012, 237, 256).

11 Kai Kupferschmidt, "Scientists Fix Errors in Controversial Paper about Saturated Fats," *Science Insider*, March 24, 2014, http://news.sciencemag.org/health
/2014/03/scientists-fix-errors-controversial-paper-about-saturated-fats?utm
_content=buffer24ca2&utm_medium=social&utm_source=facebook.com&utm
_campaign=buffer; https://www.nytimes.com/2014/03/26/opinion/bittman
-butter-is-back.html.

12 John Ioannidis has written extensively about the problems of bias in random-
ized controlled trials and meta-analyses. For representative readings, see "Why
Most Published Research Findings Are False" (2005) and "Evidence-Based
Medicine Has Been Hijacked: A Report to David Sackett" (2016).

13 This study used a three-level hierarchy of evidence. In this hierarchy, Level III is expert opinion.

14 Mary Beth Pfeiffer, "10 Points about Suing the Architects of Lyme Policy—As a Task Force Meets to Review It," *Huffington Post*, December 7, 2017, https://www .huffingtonpost.com/entry/10-points-about-suing-the-architects-of-lyme -policy_us_5a2764bbe4b0650db4d40bb5.

15 Pfeiffer, "10 Points about Suing the Architects of Lyme Policy—As a Task Force Meets to Review It."

16 Lyme Disease Association, "Historic Move by CT Attorney General to Investigate IDSA Guidelines Process," press release, November 16, 2006, http://www .lymediseaseassociation.org/index.php/lda-press-releases/319-historic-move-by -ct-attorney-general-to-investigate-idsa-guidelines-process.

17 Lyme Disease Association, written testimony to Connecticut Public Health Committee, February 6, 2009, https://www.cga.ct.gov/2009/PHdata/Tmy /2009HB-06200-R000206-Lyme%20Disease%20Association-TMY.PDF.

18 IDSA, "Agreement Ends Lyme Disease Investigation by Connecticut Attorney General," press release, May 1, 2008, http://www.idsociety.org/Agreement _Ends_Lyme_Disease_Investigation_by_Connecticut_Attorney_General/.

19 PRWeb, "Connecticut Attorney General Charges IDSA with Violating Lyme Antitrust Settlement Agreement," February 1, 2010, http://www.prweb.com /releases/2010/02/prweb3566094.htm.

20 Richard Blumenthal's tenure as attorney general of Connecticut began in 1991 and ended in 2011 when he was elected to the US Senate. When I refer to the Office of the Attorney General, I am referring to the administration prior to 2011.

21 John Kasprak, "Lyme Disease," OLR Research Report, June 16, 2000, http:// www.cga.ct.gov/2000/rpt/2000-R-0638.htm.

22 As per Public Act 99-284, specialists do not need to be in a patient's insurance network to recommend treatment. While the office visit fee might not be covered by insurance, the antibiotic treatment is required to be.

23 Connecticut House of Representatives, An Act Concerning the Use of Long-Term Antibiotics for the Treatment of Lyme Disease, May 4, 2009, http://www .cga.ct.gov/2009/FC/2009HB-06200-R000903-FC.htm.

24 I do not cite this blog entry to protect the identity of the physician whom the blogger mentions.

25 Susan O'Connell, "Re: 'Lyme Wars,'" response, *British Medical Journal* 335 (2007): 910, https://www.bmj.com/rapid-response/2011/11/01/re-lyme-wars.

26 Miguel A. Perez-Lizano to President Barack Obama, March 7, 2009, https://lyme .kaiserpapers.org/pdfs/Obama-Evidence-based-medicine-and-CDC-Corruption .pdf.

27 Kasprak, "Lyme Disease."

28 Despite its general unpopularity, the idea that political action is sometimes needed to guide medical decision-making was voiced by two politicians I interviewed.

29 "Lyme Lives Matter!," *Lyme Aware* (blog), June 8, 2016, http://lyme-aware.org /lyme-lives-matter/.

Conclusion

1 Felice J. Freyer, "Legislature Overrides Baker Veto on Lyme Treatment Coverage," *Boston Globe*, August 1, 2016, https://www.bostonglobe.com/metro/2016 /08/01/legislature-orders-insurers-cover-long-term-lyme-treatment-overriding -baker-veto/YBZ3DGaUy8bHRWMYaOyQdM/story.html.

2 Freyer, "Legislature Overrides Baker Veto."

3 For scholarship on contested illnesses that explores patients' experiences and their role as knowledge producers, see Barker 2005; Dumit 2000, 2006; Kilshaw 2010; Kroll-Smith and Floyd 1997; Moss and Teghtsoonian 2008; M. Murphy 2006; Nettleton 2006; Nettleton et al. 2004; Ware 1992.

4 For reading about "what constitutes evidence," see Goldenberg 2006; Worrall 2002. For reading about "how evidence-based medicine changes social relations," see Geltzer 2009; Nadav and Dani 2006. For reading about "the way in which medical knowledge is produced," see Adams 2013; Broom and Adams 2012; Cambrosio et al. 2006; Lambert 2006, 2009. For reading about "the means by which medical standardization creates 'new worlds'" (Timmermans and Berg 2003, viii), see Berg 1998; Daly 2005; Timmermans and Berg 2003.

5 For further "medicine and culture" reading, see Ablon 1999; Gaines and Hahn 1985; B. Good 1994; A. Kleinman 1988; Lock 1986; Lupton 1994. For further "biomedicine as culture" reading, see Franklin and Lock 2003; Inhorn 2003; Lock and Gordon 1988; E. Martin 1990; Rajan 2006; Rapp 1999; C. Thompson 2013.

6 Oxford Dictionaries Lexico, s.v., "truthiness," accessed November 14, 2019, https://en.oxforddictionaries.com/definition/truthiness; "The Word Truthiness," clip, *Colbert Report*, October 17, 2005, http://www.cc.com/video-clips /63ite2/the-colbert-report-the-word-truthiness.

7 Medical Society of the State of New York, Memorandum of Concern, accessed November 14, 2019, http://www.mssny.org/MSSNY/Governmental_Affairs/Lyme _Disease.aspx.

8 "Tick-Borne Disease Working Group," Office of the Assistant Secretary for Health, February 21, 2018, https://www.hhs.gov/ash/advisory-committees /tickbornedisease/index.html.

9 David Michael Conner, "Federal Tick-Borne Disease Working Group Meets Today and Tomorrow," *Huffington Post*, December 11, 2017, https://www .huffingtonpost.com/entry/statement-to-the-federal-tick-borne-disease -working_us_5a2e8c90e4b0d7c3f26224af.

Glossary

ANTIBODY: A protein produced by the immune system in response and counteraction to an antigen.

ANTIGEN: A foreign substance in the body that induces an immune response.

BORRELIA BURGDORFERI: The bacterium that causes Lyme disease.

CAM: Complementary and alternative medicine

CDC: Centers for Disease Control and Prevention

CFS: Chronic fatigue syndrome

DOXYCYCLINE: An oral antibiotic commonly used in the treatment of Lyme disease.

ELISA: Enzyme-linked immunosorbent assay; a laboratory procedure that measures antibodies to an infectious agent's antigens and, with the Western blot (see below), is one of two laboratory procedures in the standard two-tiered test for Lyme disease.

EM: *Erythema migrans*, the characteristic bull's-eye rash often seen in the early stages of Lyme disease.

IDSA: Infectious Diseases Society of America

IGG: Immunoglobulin G, an antibody produced in the later stages of an infection.

IGM: Immunoglobulin M, an antibody produced in the early stages of an infection.

ILADS: International Lyme and Associated Diseases Society

IXODES SCAPULARIS (BLACKLEGGED TICK): The tick most commonly understood to transmit the bacterium that causes Lyme disease in the United States.

LYME-LITERATE PHYSICIAN: A physician who claims that Lyme disease can persist beyond standard antibiotic treatment in the form of chronic Lyme disease and that, when it does, it should be treated with extended courses of antibiotics.

MAINSTREAM LYME PHYSICIAN: A physician who claims that Lyme disease does not persist beyond standard antibiotic treatment in the form of chronic Lyme disease and should not be treated with extended courses of antibiotics.

MCS: Multiple chemical sensitivity

NGC: National Guidelines Clearinghouse, the organization that formerly housed all US clinical practice guidelines.

OSP: Outer surface protein, or a protein on the surface of a cell; in the case of Lyme disease, the outer surface proteins of *Borrelia burgdorferi* (and the antibodies produced in response to them) have been important in establishing laboratory diagnostic criteria and in the development of the now discontinued Lyme vaccine, LYMErix, which was formulated with an outer surface protein referred to as Osp A.

PCR: Polymerase chain reaction; a laboratory procedure used to make copies of segments of DNA and, in the case of Lyme disease, employed to detect evidence of *Borrelia burgdorferi* in skin, blood, and spinal fluid samples.

STARI: Southern tick-associated rash illness

WESTERN BLOT: A laboratory procedure that measures antibodies to an infectious agent's antigens by separating the antigens by molecular weight; with the ELISA, the Western blot comprises one of two laboratory procedures used in the standard two-tiered test for Lyme disease.

References

Ablon, Joan. 1999. *Living with Genetic Disorder: The Impact of Neurofibromatosis 1*. West-port, CT: Auburn House.

Abu-Lughod, Lila, and Catherine Lutz. 1990. "Introduction: Emotion, Discourse and the Politics of Everyday Life." In *Language and the Politics of Emotion*, edited by Catherine Lutz and Lila Abu-Lughod, 1–23. Cambridge: Cambridge University Press.

Adams, Vincanne. 2013. "Evidence-Based Global Public Health: Subjects, Profits, Erasures." In *When People Come First: Critical Studies in Global Health*, edited by João Guilherme Biehl and Adriana Petryna, 54–90. Princeton, NJ: Princeton University Press.

Adams, Vincanne. 2016. *Metrics*. Durham, NC: Duke University Press.

Adekoya, N. 2005. "Racial Disparities in Nationally Notifiable Diseases—United States, 2002." MMWR 54 (1): 9–11.

Adham, F. K., E. M. El-Samie-Abd, R. M. Gabre, et al. 2010. "Detection of Tick Blood Parasites in Egypt Using PCR Assay II—*Borrelia burgdorferi* Sensu Lato." *Journal of the Egyptian Society of Parasitology* 40 (3): 553–64.

Afzelius, A. 1910. "Verhandlungen der Dermatologischen Gesellschaft zu Stockholm." *Archives Dermatologia Syphilagia* 101:405–6.

Agamben, Giorgio. 1998. *Homo Sacer: Sovereign Power and Bare Life*. Stanford, CA: Stanford University Press.

Agamben, Giorgio. 2004. *The Open: Man and Animal*. Stanford, CA: Stanford University Press.

Agamben, Giorgio. 2005. *State of Exception*. Chicago: University of Chicago Press.

Agosta, F., M. A. Rocca, B. Benedetti, et al. 2006. "MR Imaging Assessment of Brain and Cervical Cord Damage in Patients with Neuroborreliosis." *American Journal of Neuroradiology* 27 (4): 892–94.

Aguero-Rosenfeld, M. E, J. Nowakowski, S. Bittker, et al. 1996. "Evolution of the Serologic Response to *Borrelia burgdorferi* in Treated Patients with Culture-Confirmed Erythema Migrans." *Journal of Clinical Microbiology* 34 (1): 1–9.

Aguero-Rosenfeld, M. E., J. Nowakowski, D. F. McKenna, et al. 1993. "Serodiagnosis in Early Lyme Disease." *Journal of Clinical Microbiology* 31 (12): 3090–95.

Aguero-Rosenfeld, M. E., G. Wang, I. Schwartz, et al. 2005. "Diagnosis of Lyme Borreliosis." *Clinical Microbiology Reviews* 18 (3): 484–509.

Agyeman, Julian. 2005. *Sustainable Communities and the Challenge of Environmental Justice.* New York: New York University Press.

Alaimo, Stacy, and Susan Hekman, eds. 2008. *Material Feminisms.* Bloomington: Indiana University Press.

Alban, P. S., P. W. Johnson, and D. R. Nelson. 2000. "Serum-Starvation-Induced Changes in Protein Synthesis and Morphology of *Borrelia burgdorferi.*" *Microbiology* 146 (part 1): 119–27.

Anderson, Elijah. 2015. "The White Space." *Sociology of Race and Ethnicity* 1 (1): 10–21.

Angelakis, E., S. A. Billeter, E. B. Breitschwerdt, et al. 2010. "Potential for Tick-Borne Bartonelloses." *Emerging Infectious Diseases Journal* 16 (3): 385–91.

Angelakis, E., C. Pulcini, J. Waton, et al. 2010. "Scalp Eschar and Neck Lymphadenopathy Caused by *Bartonella henselae* after Tick Bite." *Clinical Infectious Diseases* 50 (4): 549–51.

Arendt, Hannah. (1963) 2006. *On Revolution.* New York: Penguin.

Armstrong, David. 1983. *Political Anatomy of the Body: Medical Knowledge in Britain in the Twentieth Century.* Cambridge: Cambridge University Press.

Armstrong, David. 2011. "Diagnosis and Nosology in Primary Care." *Social Science and Medicine* 73 (2011): 801–7.

Arnez, M., T. Luznik-Bufon, T. Avsic-Zupanc, et al. 2003. "Causes of Febrile Illness after a Tick Bite in Slovenian Children." *Pediatric Infectious Disease Journal* 22 (12): 1078–83.

Aronowitz, Robert A. 1991. "Lyme Disease: The Social Construction of a New Disease and Its Social Consequences." *Milbank Quarterly* 69 (1): 79–112.

Aronowitz, Robert A. 1998. *Making Sense of Illness: Science, Society, and Disease.* Cambridge: Cambridge University Press.

Aronowitz, Robert A. 2012. "The Rise and Fall of the Lyme Disease Vaccines: A Cautionary Tale for Risk Interventions in American Medicine and Public Health." *Milbank Quarterly* 90 (2): 250–77.

Asch, E. S., D. I. Bujak, M. Weiss, et al. 1994. "Lyme Disease: An Infectious and Postinfectious Syndrome." *Journal of Rheumatology* 21 (3): 454–61.

Asher, Tammy. 2011. "Unprecedented Anti-Trust Investigation into the Lyme Disease Treatment Guidelines Development Process." *Gonzaga Law Review* 46 (1): 117–45.

Assous, M. V., D. Postic, G. Paul, et al. 1993. "Western Blot Analysis of Sera from Lyme Borreliosis Patients According to the Genomic Species of the Borrelia Strains Used as Antigens." *European Journal of Clinical Microbiology and Infectious Disease* 12 (4): 261–68.

Aucott, J. N., A. W. Rebman, L. A. Crowder, et al. 2013. "Post-Treatment Lyme Disease Syndrome Symptomatology and the Impact on Life Functioning: Is There Something Here?" *Quality of Life Research Journal* 22 (1): 75–84.

Aucott, J. N., M. J. Soloski, A. W. Rebman, et al. 2016. "CCL19 as a Chemokine Risk Factor for Posttreatment Lyme Disease Syndrome: A Prospective Clinical Cohort Study." *Clinical and Vaccine Immunology* 23 (9): 757–66.

Auwaerter, P. G., J. S. Bakken, R. J. Dattwyler, et al. 2011. "Antiscience and Ethical Concerns Associated with Advocacy of Lyme Disease." *Lancet Infectious Diseases* 11 (9): 713–19.

Bacon, R. M., B. J. Biggerstaff, M. E. Schriefer, et al. 2003. "Serodiagnosis of Lyme Disease by Kinetic Enzyme-Linked Immunosorbent Assay Using Recombinant VlsE1 of Peptide Antigens of *Borrelia burgdorferi* Compared with 2-Tiered Testing Using Whole-Cell Lysates." *Journal of Infectious Disease* 187 (8): 1187–99.

Badone, E. 2008. "Illness, Biomedicine, and Alternative Healing in Brittany, France." *Medical Anthropology* 27 (2): 190–218.

Baer, Hans. 2001. *Biomedicine and Alternative Healing Systems in America: Issues of Class, Race, Ethnicity, and Gender.* Madison: University of Wisconsin Press.

Baer, Hans. 2004. *Toward an Integrative Medicine: Merging Alternative Therapies with Biomedicine.* Walnut Creek, CA: AltaMira Press.

Bakken, L. L., S. M. Callister, P. J. Wand, et al. 1997. "Interlaboratory Comparison of Test Results for Detection of Lyme Disease by 516 Participants in the Wisconsin State Laboratory of Hygiene/College of American Pathologists Proficiency Testing Program." *Journal of Clinical Microbiology* 35 (3): 537–43.

Bakken, L. L., K. L. Case, S. M. Callister, et al. 1992. "Performance of 45 Laboratories Participating in a Proficiency Testing Program for Lyme Disease Serology." *Journal of the American Medical Association* 268 (7): 891–95.

Ball, R., S. V. Shadomy, A. Meyer, et al. 2009. "HLA Type and Immune Response to *Borrelia burgdorferi* Outer Surface Protein A in People in Whom Arthritis Developed after Lyme Disease Vaccination." *Arthritis and Rheumatism* 60 (4): 1179–86.

Barad, K. 2003. "Posthuman Performativity: Toward an Understanding of How Matter Comes to Matter." *Signs* 28 (3): 801–31.

Baranova, N. S., N. N. Spirin, O. A. Fadeeva, et al. 2012. "Lyme Disease in Patients with Multiple Sclerosis: Clinical, Diagnostic, and Therapeutic Features." *Zhurnal nevrologii i psikhiatrii imeni S. S. Korsakova* 112 (2, part 2): 64–68.

Barbour, A. G., G. O. Maupin, G. J. Teltow, et al. 1996. "Identification of an Uncultivable *Borrelia* Species in the Hard Tick *Amblyomma americanum*: Possible Agent of a Lyme Disease-Like Illness." *Journal of Infectious Diseases* 173 (2): 403–9.

Barcan, Ruth. 2011. *Complementary and Alternative Medicine: Bodies, Therapies, Senses.* New York: Berg.

Barker, Kristin K. 2005. *The Fibromyalgia Story: Medical Authority and Women's Worlds of Pain.* Philadelphia: Temple University Press.

Barnes, Linda L. 2003. "The Acupuncture Wars: The Professionalizing of American Acupuncture—A View from Massachusetts." *Medical Anthropology* 22:261–301.

Barnes, Linda L. 2005. "American Acupuncture and Efficacy: Meanings and Their Points of Insertion." *Medical Anthropology Quarterly* 19:239–66.

Barnes, Patricia, Barbara Bloom, and Richard L. Nahin. 2008. "Complementary and Alternative Medicine Use among Adults and Children: United States, 2007." *National Health Statistics Reports* 12:1–23. http://nccam.nih.gov/sites/nccam.nih.gov/files/news/nhsr12.pdf.

Barsic, B., T. Maretic, L. Majerus, et al. 2000. "Comparison of Azithromycin and Doxycycline in the Treatment of Erythema Migrans." *Infection* 28 (3): 153–56.

Barthold, S. W., E. Hodzic, D. M. Imai, et al. 2010. "Ineffectiveness of Tigecycline against Persistent *Borrelia burgdorferi*." *Antimicrobial Agents Chemotherapy* 54 (2): 643–51.

Batheja, S., J. A. Nields, A. Landa, et al. 2013. "Post-Treatment Lyme Syndrome and Central Sensitization." *Journal of Neuropsychiatry and Clinical Neuroscience* 25 (3): 176–86.

Batinac, T., D. Petranovic, G. Zamolo, et al. 2007. "Lyme Borreliosis and Multiple Sclerosis Are Associated with Primary Effusion Lymphoma." *Medical Hypotheses* 69 (1): 117–19.

Battafarano, D. F., J. A. Combs, R. J. Enzenauer, et al. 1993. "Chronic Septic Arthritis Caused by *Borrelia burgdorferi*." *Clinical Orthopaedics and Related Research* (297): 238–41.

Bauer, Y., H. Hofmann, O. Jahraus, et al. 2001. "Prominent T Cell Response to a Selectively in Vivo Expressed *Borrelia burgdorferi* Outer Surface Protein (pG) in Patients with Lyme Disease." *European Journal of Immunology* 31 (3): 767–76.

Bayer, M. E., L. Zhang, and M. H. Bayer. 1996. "*Borrelia burgdorferi* DNA in the Urine of Treated Patients with Chronic Lyme Disease Symptoms: A PCR Study of 97 Cases." *Infection* 24 (5): 347–53.

Beck, Ulrich. 1992. *Risk Society: Towards a New Modernity*. Newbury Park, CA: Sage.

Bednárová, J., P. Stourac, and P. Adam. 2005. "Relevance of Immunological Variables in Neuroborreliosis and Multiple Sclerosis." *Acta Neurologica Scandinavica* 112 (2): 97–102.

Bell, Kirsten. 2016. *Health and Other Unassailable Values: Reconfigurations of Health, Evidence, and Ethics*. New York: Routledge.

Bendelow, Gillian A. 2000. *Pain and Gender*. Essex: Pearson Education.

Bendelow, Gillian A. 2006. "Pain, Suffering, and Risk." *Health, Risk, and Society* 8 (1): 59–70.

Bennett, Jane. 2002. *Thoreau's Nature: Ethics, Politics, and the Wild*. New ed. Lanham, MD: Rowman and Littlefield.

Berardi, V. P., K. E. Weeks, and A. C. Steere. 1988. "Serodiagnosis of Early Lyme Disease: Analysis of IgM and IgG Antibody Responses by Using an Antibody-Capture Enzyme Immunoassay." *Journal of Infectious Diseases* 158 (4): 754–60.

Berende, A., H. J. M. ter Hofstede, F. J. Vos, et al. 2016. "Randomized Trial of Longer-Term Therapy for Symptoms Attributed to Lyme Disease." *New England Journal of Medicine* 374 (13): 1209–20.

Berg, Marc. 1998. "Order(s) and Disorder(s): Of Protocols and Medical Practices." In *Differences in Medicine: Unraveling Practices, Techniques, and Bodies*, edited by Marc Berg and Annemarie Mol, 226–46. Durham, NC: Duke University Press.

Berg, Marc, and Annemarie Mol, eds. 1998. *Differences in Medicine: Unraveling Practices, Techniques, and Bodies*. Durham, NC: Duke University Press.

Berger, B. W., R. C. Johnson, C. Kodner, et al. 1992. "Failure of *Borrelia burgdorferi* to Survive in the Skin of Patients with Antibiotic-Treated Lyme Disease." *Journal of the American Academy of Dermatology* 27 (1): 34–37.

Berglund, J., L. Stjernberg, K. Ornstein, et al. 2002. "5-Y Follow-Up Study of Patients with Neuroborreliosis." *Scandinavian Journal of Infectious Diseases* 34 (6): 421–25.

Berlant, Lauren, and Jordan Greenwald. 2012. "Affect in the End Times: A Conversation with Lauren Berlant." *Qui Parle: Critical Humanities and Social Sciences* 20 (2): 71–89.

Biehl, João Guilherme, and Torben Eskerod. 2007. *Will to Live: AIDS Therapies and the Politics of Survival*. Princeton, NJ: Princeton University Press.

Blanc, F., N. Philippi, B. Cretin, et al. 2014. "Lyme Neuroborreliosis and Dementia." *Journal of Alzheimer's Disease* 41 (4): 1087–93.

Bockenstedt, L. K., D. G. Gonzalez, et al. 2012. "Spirochete Antigens Persist Near Cartilage after Murine Lyme Borreliosis Therapy." *Journal of Clinical Investigation* 122 (7): 2652–60.

Bockenstedt, L. K., J. Mao, E. Hodzic, et al. 2002. "Detection of Attenuated, Noninfectious Spirochetes in *Borrelia burgdorferi*-Infected Mice after Antibiotic Treatment." *Journal of Infectious Diseases* 186 (10): 1430–37.

Bockenstedt, L. K., and J. D. Radolf. 2014. "Xenodiagnosis for Posttreatment Lyme Disease Syndrome: Resolving the Conundrum or Adding to It?" *Clinical Infectious Diseases* 58 (7): 946–48.

Boltanski, Luc. 1999. *Distant Suffering: Morality, Media, and Politics*. Translated from the French by Graham Burchell. Cambridge: Cambridge University Press.

Bourdieu, Pierre. (1980) 1990. *The Logic of Practice*. Cambridge: Polity.

Bourdieu, Pierre. 2013. "Symbolic Capital and Social Classes." *Journal of Classical Sociology* 13 (2): 292–302.

Bradley, J. F., R. C. Johnson, and J. L. Goodman. 1994. "The Persistence of Spirochetal Nucleic Acids in Active Lyme Arthritis." *Annals of Internal Medicine* 120 (6): 487–89.

Brady, Emily. 2012. "The Environmental Sublime." In *The Sublime: From Antiquity to Present*, edited by Timothy M. Costelloe, 171–82. Cambridge: Cambridge University Press.

Branda, J. A., K. Linskey, Y. A. Kim, et al. 2011. "Two-Tiered Antibody Testing for Lyme Disease with Use of 2 Enzyme Immunoassays, a Whole-Cell Sonicate Enzyme Immunoassay Followed by a VlsE c6 Peptide Enzyme Immunoassay." *Clinical Infectious Diseases* 53 (6): 541–47.

Branda, J. A., K. Strle, L. E. Nigrovic, et al. 2017. "Evaluation of Modified 2-Tiered Serodiagnostic Testing Algorithms for Early Lyme Disease." *Clinical Infectious Disease* 64 (8): 1074–80.

Breitschwerdt, E. B., R. G. Maggi, A. W. Duncan, et al. 2007. "*Bartonella* Species in Blood of Immunocompetent Persons with Animal and Arthropod Contact." *Emerging Infectious Diseases* 13 (6): 938–41.

Breitschwerdt, E. B., R. G. Maggi, W. L. Nicholson, et al. 2008. "*Bartonella* sp. Bacteremia in Patients with Neurological and Neurocognitive Dysfunction." *Journal of Clinical Microbiology* 46 (9): 2856–61.

Bridges, Khiara M. 2011. *Reproducing Race: An Ethnography of Pregnancy as a Site of Racialization.* Berkeley: University of California Press.

Briggs, Charles L., and Daniel C. Hallin. 2007. "Biocommunicability: The Neoliberal Subject and Its Contradictions in News Coverage of Health Issues." *Social Text,* no. 25, 43–66.

Briggs, Charles L., and Clara Mantini-Briggs. 2003. *Stories in the Time of Cholera: Racial Profiling During a Medical Nightmare.* Berkeley: University of California Press.

Briggs, Charles L., and Mark Nichter. 2009. "Biocommunicability and the Biopolitics of Pandemic Threats." *Medical Anthropology* 28 (3): 189–98.

Brinar, V. V., and M. Habek. 2010. "Rare Infections Mimicking MS." *Clinical Neurology and Neurosurgery* 112 (7): 625–28.

Brody, Howard, Franklin G. Miller, and Elizabeth Bogdan-Lovis. 2005. "Evidence-Based Medicine: Watching Out for Its Friends." *Perspectives in Biology and Medicine* 48 (4): 570–84.

Broom, Alex, and Jon Adams, eds. 2012. *Evidence-Based Healthcare in Context: Critical Social Science Perspectives.* Burlington, VT: Ashgate.

Brorson, O., S. H. Brorson, T. H. Henriksen, et al. 2001. "Association between Multiple Sclerosis and Cystic Structures in Cerebrospinal Fluid." *Infection* 29 (6): 315–19.

Brotherton, Sean. 2012. *Revolutionary Medicine: Health and the Body in Post-Soviet Cuba.* Durham, NC: Duke University Press.

Brown, M. J., T. Willis, B. Omalu, et al. 2006. "Deaths Resulting from Hypocalcemia after Administration of Edetate Disodium: 2003–2005." *Pediatrics* 118 (2): e534–36.

Brown, Phil. 2007. *Toxic Exposures: Contested Illness and the Environmental Health Movement.* New York: Columbia University Press.

Brown, Phil, Rachel Morello-Frosch, and Stephen Zavestoski. 2012. *Contested Illness: Citizens, Science, and Health Social Movements.* Berkeley: University of California Press.

Brown, Phil, S. Zavestoski, S. McCormick, et al. 2004. "Embodied Health Movements: New Approaches to Social Movements in Health." *Sociology of Health and Illness* 26 (1): 50–80.

Brulle, Robert J. 2009. "The U.S. Environmental Movement." In *Twenty Lessons in Environmental Sociology,* edited by K. Gould and T. Lewis, 211–27. New York: Oxford University Press.

Buchanan, Brett. 2008. *Onto-Ethologies: The Animal Environments of Uexküll, Heidegger, Merleau-Ponty, and Deleuze.* SUNY Series in Environmental Philosophy and Ethics. Albany: SUNY Press.

Buechner, S. A., S. Lautenschlager, P. Itin, et al. 1995. "Lymphoproliferative Responses to *Borrelia burgdorferi* in Patients with Erythema Migrans, Acrodermatitis Chronica Atrophicans, Lymphadenosis Benigna Cutis, and Morphea." *Archives of Dermatology* 131 (6): 673–77.

Bujak, D. I., A. Weinstein, and R. L. Dornbush. 1996. "Clinical and Neurocognitive Features of the Post Lyme Syndrome." *Journal of Rheumatology* 23 (8): 1392–97.

Bullard, Robert. 2000. *Dumping in Dixie: Race, Class, and Environmental Quality.* 3rd ed. Boulder, CO: Westview.

Bunikis, J., B. Olsén, G. Westman, et al. 1995. "Variable Serum Immunoglobulin Responses against Different *Borrelia burgdorferi* Sensu Lato Species in a Population at Risk for and Patients with Lyme Disease." *Journal of Clinical Microbiology* 33 (6): 1473–78.

Burakgazi, A. Z. 2014. "Lyme Disease-Induced Polyradiculopathy Mimicking Amyotrophic Lateral Sclerosis." *International Journal of Neuroscience* 124 (11): 859–62.

Burdick, Alan. 2018. "Looking for Life on a Flat Earth." *New Yorker*, May 30, 2018. https://www.newyorker.com/science/elements/looking-for-life-on-a-flat-earth.

Burgdorfer, W. 1986. "Discovery of the Lyme Disease Spirochete: A Historical Review." *Zentralbl Bakteriol Mikrobiol Hyg A* 263 (1–2): 7–10.

Burgdorfer, W., A. G. Barbour, S. F. Hayes, et al. 1982. "Lyme Disease—A Tick-Borne Spirochetosis?" *Science* 216 (4552): 1317–19.

Burgess, E. C., M. D. Wachal, and T. D. Cleven. 1993. "*Borrelia burgdorferi* Infection in Dairy Cows, Rodents, and Birds from Four Wisconsin Dairy Farms." *Veterinary Microbiology* 35 (1–2): 61–77.

Burri, Regula Valérie, and Joseph Dumit, eds. 2007. *Biomedicine as Culture: Instrumental Practices, Technoscientific Knowledge, and New Modes of Life.* New York: Routledge.

Burton, C. 2003. "Beyond Somatisation: A Review of the Understanding and Treatment of Medically Unexplained Physical Symptoms (MUPS)." *British Journal of General Practice* 53 (488): 231–39.

Butler, Judith. 1993. *Bodies That Matter: On the Discursive Limits of "Sex."* New York: Routledge.

Butler, Judith. 2004. *Undoing Gender.* New York: Routledge.

Cairns, V., and J. Godwin. 2005. "Post-Lyme Borreliosis Syndrome: A Meta-Analysis of Reported Symptoms." *International Journal of Epidemiology* 34 (6): 1340–45.

Cambrosio, A., P. Keating, T. Schlich, et al. 2006. "Regulatory Objectivity and the Generation and Management of Evidence in Medicine." *Social Science and Medicine* 63 (1): 189–99.

Cameron, D., L. B. Johnson, and E. L. Maloney. 2014. "Evidence Assessments and Guideline Recommendations in Lyme Disease: The Clinical Management of

Known Tick Bites, Erythema Migrans Rashes and Persistent Disease." *Expert Review of Anti-infectious Therapy* 12 (9): 1103–35.

Canguilhem, Georges. (1965) 2008. *Knowledge of Life.* New York: Fordham University Press.

Canguilhem, Georges. (1966) 2007. *The Normal and the Pathological.* Brooklyn, NY: Zone Books.

Cant, Sarah, and Ursula Sharma, eds. 1996. *Complementary and Alternative Medicines: Knowledge in Practice.* London: Free Association Books.

Cant, Sarah, and Ursula Sharma. 1999. *A New Medical Pluralism.* London: Routledge.

Cant, Sarah, and Peter Watts. 2018. "Hidden in Plain Sight: Exploring Men's Use of Complementary and Alternative Medicine." *Journal of Men's Studies* 27 (1): 45–65.

Carlomagno, G., V. Luksa, G. Candussi, et al. 1988. "Lyme *Borrelia* Positive Serology Associated with Spontaneous Abortion in an Endemic Italian Area." *Acta Europaea Fertilitatis* 19 (5): 279–81.

Carranza-Tamayo, C. O., J. N. Costa, and W. M. Bastos. 2012. "Lyme Disease in the State of Tocantins, Brazil: Report of the First Cases." *Brazilian Journal of Infectious Disease* 16 (6): 586–89.

Carroll, Lewis. (1871) 2009. *Through the Looking-Glass and What Alice Found There.* Cnoc Sceichin, Ireland: Evertype.

Carroll, Michael C. 2004. *Lab 257: The Disturbing Story of the Government's Secret Germ Laboratory.* New York: William Morrow.

Caskey, J. R., and M. E. Embers. 2015. "Persister Development by *Borrelia burgdorferi* Populations In Vitro." *Antimicrobial Agents and Chemotherapy* 59: 6288–95.

Cassarino, D. S., M. M. Quezado, N. R. Ghatak, et al. 2003. "Lyme-Associated Parkinsonism: A Neuropathologic Case Study and Review of the Literature." *Archives of Pathology and Laboratory Medicine* 127 (9): 1204–6.

Cerar, D., T. Cerar, E. Ruzić-Sabljić, et al. 2010. "Subjective Symptoms after Treatment of Early Lyme Disease." *American Journal of Medicine* 123 (1): 79–86.

Chandra, A., N. Latov, G. P. Wormser, et al. 2011a. "Anti-*Borrelia burgdorferi* Antibody Profile in Post-Lyme Disease Syndrome." *Clinical Vaccine Immunology* 18 (5): 767–71.

Chandra, A., N. Latov, G. P. Wormser, et al. 2011b. "Epitope Mapping of Antibodies to VlsE Protein of *Borrelia burgdorferi* in Post-Lyme Disease Syndrome." *Clinical Immunology* 141 (1): 103–10.

Chandra, A., G. P. Wormser, M. S. Klempner, et al. 2010. "Anti-Neural Antibody Reactivity in Patients with a History of Lyme Borreliosis and Persistent Symptoms." *Brain, Behavior, and Immunity* 24 (6): 1018–24.

Chandra, A. M., J. G. Keilp, and B. A. Fallon. 2013. "Correlates of Perceived Health-Related Quality of Life in Post-Treatment Lyme Encephalopathy." *Psychosomatics* 54 (6): 552–59.

Chen, J., J. A. Field, L. Glickstein, et al. 1999. "Association of Antibiotic Treatment-Resistant Lyme Arthritis with T Cell Responses to Dominant Epitopes of Outer Surface Protein A of *Borrelia burgdorferi*." *Arthritis and Rheumatism* 42 (9): 1813–22.

Chmielewska-Badora, J., E. Cisak, and J. Dutkiewicz. 2000. "Lyme Borreliosis and Multiple Sclerosis: Any Connection? A Seroepidemic Study." *Annals of Agricultural and Environmental Medicine* 7 (2): 141–43.

Cimmino, M. A., A. Azzolini, F. Tobia, et al. 1989. "Spirochetes in the Spleen of a Patient with Chronic Lyme Disease." *American Journal of Clinical Pathology* 91 (1): 95–97.

Clarissou, J., A. Song, C. Bernede, et al. 2009. "Efficacy of a Long-Term Antibiotic Treatment in Patients with a Chronic Tick Associated Poly-Organic Syndrome (TAPOS)." *Médecine et Maladies Infectieuses* 39 (2): 108–15.

Clark, K. L., B. Leydet, and S. Hartman. 2013. "Lyme Borreliosis in Human Patients in Florida and Georgia, USA." *International Journal of Medical Science* 10 (7): 915–31.

Clark, K. L., J. H. Oliver Jr., A. M. James, et al. 2002. "Prevalence of *Borrelia burgdorferi* Sensu Lato Infection among Rodents and Host-Seeking Ticks in South Carolina." *Journal of Medical Entomology* 39 (1): 198–206.

Clarke, Adele, Laura Mamo, Jennifer R. Fosket, et al. 2010. *Biomedicalization: Technoscience, Health, and Illness in the U.S.* Durham, NC: Duke University Press.

Clarke, Kamari Maxine. 2009. *Fictions of Justice: The International Criminal Court and the Challenges of Legal Pluralism in Sub-Saharan Africa.* New York: Cambridge University Press.

Clarke, T. C., L. I. Black, B. J. Stussman, et al. 2015. "Trends in the Use of Complementary Health Approaches among Adults: United States, 2002–2012." *National Health Statistics Reports* 79:1–16.

Clover, J. R., and R. S. Lane. 1995. "Evidence Implicating Nymphal *Ixodes pacificus* (Acari: Ixodidae) in the Epidemiology of Lyme Disease in California." *American Journal of Tropical Medicine and Hygiene* 53 (3): 237–40.

Cochrane, Archie L. 1972. *Effectiveness and Efficiency: Random Reflections on Health Services.* London: Nuffield Provincial Hospitals Trust.

Coggon, D., Geoffrey Rose, and D. J. P. Barker. 1997. "What Is Epidemiology?" In *Epidemiology for the Uninitiated.* London: British Medical Association. https://www.bmj.com/about-bmj/resources-readers/publications/epidemiology-uninitiated/1-what-epidemiology.

Cole, Luke, and Sheila Foster. 2001. *From the Ground Up: Environmental Racism and the Rise of the Environmental Justice Movement.* New York: New York University Press.

Colvin, Christopher J. 2015. "Anthropologies in and of Evidence Making in Global Health Research and Policy." *Medical Anthropology* 34 (2): 99–105.

Cook, Michael J. 2014. "Lyme Borreliosis: A Review of Data on Transmission Time after Tick Attachment." *International Journal of General Medicine* 8: 1–8.

Coole, Diana, and Samantha Frost, eds. 2010. *New Materialisms: Ontology, Agency, and Politics.* Durham, NC: Duke University Press.

Cordner, Alissa. 2016. *Toxic Safety: Flame Retardants, Chemical Controversies, and Environmental Health.* New York: Columbia University Press.

Côté, S. D., T. P. Rooney, J.-P. Tremblay, C. Dussault, and D. M. Waller. 2004. "Ecological Impacts of Deer Overabundance." *Annual Review of Ecology, Evolution, and Systematics* 35:113–47.

Cotté, V., S. Bonnet, M. Cote, et al. 2010. "Prevalence of Five Pathogenic Agents in Questing *Ixodes ricinus* Ticks from Western France." *Vector-Borne and Zoonotic Diseases* 10 (8): 723–30.

Cotté, V., S. Bonnet, D. Le Rhun, et al. 2008. "Transmission of *Bartonella henselae* by *Ixodes ricinus*." *Emerging Infectious Diseases Journal* 14 (7): 1074–80.

Coulter, Ian. 2004. "Integration and Paradigm Clash: The Practical Difficulties of Integrative Medicine." In *The Mainstreaming of Complementary and Alternative Medicine: Studies in Social Context*, edited by Philip Tovey, Gary Easthope, and Jon Adams, 103–22. New York: Routledge.

Coulter, P., C. Lema, D. Flayhart, et al. 2005. "Two-Year Evaluation of *Borrelia burgdorferi* Culture and Supplemental Tests for Definitive Diagnosis of Lyme Disease." *Journal of Clinical Microbiology* 43:5080–84.

Coyle, P. K. 1989. "*Borrelia burgdorferi* Antibodies in Multiple Sclerosis Patients." *Neurology* 39 (6): 760–61.

Coyle, P. K., L. B. Krupp, and C. Doscher. 1993. "Significance of Reactive Lyme Serology in Multiple Sclerosis." *Annals of Neurology* 34 (5): 745–47.

Craft, J. E., D. K. Fischer, G. T. Shimamoto, et al. 1986. "Antigens of *Borrelia burgdorferi* Recognized during Lyme Disease: Appearance of a New Immunoglobulin M Response and Expansion of the Immunoglobulin G Response Late in the Illness." *Journal of Clinical Investigation* 78 (4): 934–39.

Craft, J. E., R. L. Grodzicki, M. Shrestha, et al. 1984. "The Antibody Response in Lyme Disease." *Yale Journal of Biological Medicine* 57 (4): 561–65.

Creary, Melissa. 2018. "Biocultural Citizenship and Embodying Exceptionalism: Biopolitics for Sickle Cell Disease in Brazil." *Social Science and Medicine* 199:123–31.

Crix, D., J. Stedmon, C. Smart, and R. Dallos. 2012. "Knowing 'ME' Knowing You: The Discursive Negotiation of Contested Illness within a Family." *Journal of Depression and Anxiety* 1:119.

Cromley, R. G., and E. K. Cromley. 2009. "Choropleth Map Legend Design for Visualizing Community Health Disparities." *Journal of Health Geographics* 8:52.

Cronon, William. 1995. "The Trouble with Wilderness; or, Getting Back to the Wrong Nature." In *Uncommon Ground: Toward Reinventing Nature*, edited by William Cronon, 69–90. New York: Norton.

Crossland, N. A., X. Alvarex, and M. E. Embers. 2018. "Late Disseminated Lyme Disease: Associated Pathology and Spirochete Persistence Posttreatment in Rhesus Macaques." *American Journal of Pathology* 188 (3): 672–82.

Dachs, Robert, Andrew Darby-Stewart, and Mark A. Graber. 2012. "How Do Clinical Practice Guidelines Go Awry?" *American Family Physician* 86 (6): 514–16.

Daly, Jeanne. 2005. *Evidence-Based Medicine and the Search for a Science of Clinical Care.* Berkeley: University of California Press.

Dattwyler, R. J., and P. M. Arnaboldi. 2014. "Comparison of Lyme Disease Serologic Assays and Lyme Specialty Laboratories." *Clinical Infectious Disease* 59 (12): 1711–13.

Dattwyler, R. J., and J. J. Halperin. 1987. "Failure of Tetracycline Therapy in Early Lyme Disease." *Arthritis and Rheumatism* 30 (4): 448–50.

Dattwyler, R. J., J. J. Halperin, H. Pass, et al. 1987. "Ceftriaxone as Effective Therapy in Refractory Lyme Disease." *Journal of Infectious Diseases* 155 (6): 1322–25.

Dattwyler, R. J., and B. J. Luft. 1991. "Overview of the Clinical Manifestations of *Borrelia burgdorferi* Infection." *Canadian Journal of Infectious Diseases* 2 (2): 61–63.

Dattwyler, R. J., D. J. Volkman, B. J. Luft, et al. 1988. "Seronegative Lyme Disease: Dissociation of Specific T- and B-Lymphocyte Responses to Borrelia burgdorferi." *New England Journal of Medicine* 319 (22): 1441–46.

Davidovitch, N., and D. Filc. 2006. "Reconstructing Data: Evidence-Based Medicine and Evidence-Based Public Health in Context." *Dynamis* 26:287–306.

Davis, Dána-Ain. 2019. *Reproductive Injustice: Racism, Pregnancy, and Premature Birth*. Durham, NC: Duke University Press.

Davis, Georgia, and Mark Nichter. 2015. "The Lyme Wars: The Effects of Biocommunicability, Gender, and Epistemic Politics on Health Activation and Lyme Science." In *Diagnostic Controversy: Cultural Perspectives on Competing Knowledge in Healthcare*, edited by C. Smith-Morris, 215–46. New York: Routledge.

Davis, Noela. 2009. "New Materialism and Feminism's Anti-Biologism." *European Journal of Women's Studies* 16 (1): 67–80.

Davis, T. N., M. O'Reilly, S. Kang, et al. 2013. "Chelation Treatment for Autism Spectrum Disorders: A Systematic Review." *Research in Autism Spectrum Disorders* 7:49–55.

De Cauwer, H., S. Declerck, J. De Smet, et al. 2009. "Motor Neuron Disease Features in a Patient with Neuroborreliosis and a Cervical Anterior Horn Lesion." *Acta Clinica Belgica* 64 (3): 225–27.

Deibener, J., P. Kaminsky, M. Debouverie, et al. 1997. "Motor Neuron Syndrome and Lyme Disease: Relation of Causality or Fortuitous Association?" *Presse Médicale* 26 (24): 1144.

Dejmková, H., D. Hulinska, D. Tegzová, et al. 2002. "Seronegative Lyme Arthritis Caused by *Borrelia garinii*." *Clinical Rheumatology* 21 (4): 330–34.

Deleuze, Gilles, and Félix Guattari. (1980) 1987. *A Thousand Plateaus: Capitalism and Schizophrenia*. Minneapolis: University of Minnesota Press.

Delong, A. K., B. Blossom, E. L. Maloney, et al. 2012. "Antibiotic Retreatment of Lyme Disease in Patients with Persistent Symptoms: A Biostatistical Review of Randomized, Placebo-Controlled, Clinical Trials." *Contemporary Clinical Trials* 33 (6): 1132–42.

Derkatch, Colleen. 2016. *Bounding Biomedicine: Evidence and Rhetoric in the New Science of Alternative Medicine*. Chicago: University of Chicago Press.

Detsky, Allan S. 2006. "Sources of Bias for Authors of Clinical Practice Guidelines." *Canadian Medical Association Journal* 175 (9): 1033.

Diuk-Wasser, M. A., A. G. Gatewood, M. R. Cortinas, et al. 2006. "Spatiotemporal Patterns of Host-Seeking Ixodes scapularis Nymphs (Acari: Ixodidae) in the United States." *Journal of Medical Entomology* 43 (2): 166–76.

Diuk-Wasser, M. A., A. G. Hoen, P. Cislo, et al. 2012. "Human Risk of Infection with *Borrelia burgdorferi*, the Lyme Disease Agent, in Eastern United States." *American Journal of Tropical Medicine and Hygiene* 86 (2): 320–27.

Diuk-Wasser, M. A., G. Vourc'h, P. Cislo, et al. 2010. "Field and Climate-Based Model for Predicting the Density of Host-Seeking Nymphal *Ixodes scapularis*, an Important Vector of Tick-Borne Disease Agents in the Eastern United States." *Global Ecology and Biogeography* 19:504–14.

Djukic, M., C. Schmidt-Samoa, R. Nau, et al. 2011. "The Diagnostic Spectrum in Patients with Suspected Chronic Lyme Neuroborreliosis—The Experience from One Year of a University Hospital's Lyme Neuroborreliosis Outpatients Clinic." *European Journal of Neurology* 18 (4): 547–55.

Dorward, D. W., T. G. Schwan, and C. F. Garon. 1991. "Immune Capture and Detection of *Borrelia burgdorferi* Antigens in Urine, Blood, or Tissues from Infected Ticks, Mice, Dogs, and Humans." *Journal of Clinical Microbiology* 29 (6): 1162–70.

Douglas, Mary. 1992. *Risk and Blame: Essays in Cultural Theory*. New York: Routledge.

Dressler, F., R. Ackermann, and A. C. Steere. 1994. "Antibody Responses to the Three Genomic Groups of *Borrelia burgdorferi* in European Lyme Borreliosis." *Journal of Infectious Diseases* 169 (2): 313–18.

Dressler, F., J. A. Whalen, B. N. Reinhardt, et al. 1993. "Western Blotting in the Serodiagnosis of Lyme Disease." *Journal of Infectious Diseases* 167 (2): 392–400.

Dressler, F., N. H. Yoshinari, and A. C. Steere. 1991. "The T-Cell Proliferative Assay in the Diagnosis of Lyme Disease." *Annals of Internal Medicine* 115 (7): 533–39.

Drouin, E. E., L. Glickstein, W. W. Kwok, et al. 2008a. "Human Homologues of *Borrelia* T Cell Epitope Associated with Antibiotic-Refractory Lyme Arthritis." *Molecular Immunology* 45 (1): 180–89.

Drouin, E. E., L. Glickstein, W. W. Kwok, et al. 2008b. "Searching for Borrelial T Cell Epitopes Associated with Antibiotic-Refractory Lyme Arthritis." *Molecular Immunology* 45 (8): 2323–32.

Drouin, E. E., L. J. Glickstein, and A. C. Steere. 2004. "Molecular Characterization of the OspA (161–175) T Cell Epitope Associated with Treatment-Resistant Lyme Arthritis: Differences among the Three Pathogenic Species of *Borrelia burgdorferi* Sensu Lato." *Journal of Autoimmunity* 23 (3): 281–92.

Drozdowski, W. 2006. "Multifocal Central Nervous Systems Lesions—Multiple Sclerosis or Neuroborreliosis." *Przeglad epidemiologiczny* 60 (S1): 39–45.

Duden, Barbara. 1991. *The Woman beneath the Skin: A Doctor's Patients in Eighteenth-Century Germany*. Cambridge, MA: Harvard University Press.

Dumit, Joseph. 2000. "When Explanations Rest: 'Good-Enough' Brain Science and the New Socio-Medical Disorders." In *Working and Living the New Medical Technologies: Intersections of Inquiry*, edited by Margaret M. Lock, Allan Young, and Alberto Cambrosio, 209–32. Cambridge: Cambridge University Press.

Dumit, Joseph. 2004. *Picturing Personhood: Brain Scans and Biomedical Identity*. In-Formation Series. Princeton, NJ: Princeton University Press.

Dumit, Joseph. 2005. "'Come on, People . . . We "Are" the Aliens. We Seem to be Suffering from Host-Planet Rejection Syndrome.' Liminal Illnesses, Structural Damnation, and Social Creativity." In *E.T. Culture: Anthropology in Outerspaces*, edited by Debbora Battaglia, 218–34. Durham, NC: Duke University Press.

Dumit, Joseph. 2006. "Illnesses You Have to Fight to Get: Facts as Forces in Uncertain, Emergent Illnesses." *Social Science and Medicine* 63:577–90.

Dupuis, M. J. 1988. "Multiple Neurologic Manifestations of *Borrelia burgdorferi* Infection." *Revue Neurologique* 144 (12): 765–75.

Dusenbery, Maya. 2018. *Doing Harm: The Truth about How Bad Medicine and Lazy Science Leave Women Dismissed, Misdiagnosed, and Sick*. New York: HarperOne.

Dusenbery, Maya, and Julie Rehmeyer. 2018. "The Science Isn't Settled on Chronic Lyme: A Close Look at the Evidence Suggests the Controversial Diagnosis Should Be Taken More Seriously, and That Decades of Sexism May Be to Blame for Our Collective Dismissal." *Slate*, June 27, 2018. https://slate.com/technology/2018/06/the-science-isnt-settled-on-chronic-lyme.html.

DVBD (Division of Vector-Borne Diseases), NCEZID (National Center for Emerging and Zoonotic Infectious Diseases). 2019. "Post-Treatment Lyme Disease Syndrome." CDC, last reviewed November 8, 2019. https://www.cdc.gov/lyme/postlds/index.html.

Easthope, G., B. Tranter, and G. Gill. 2000. "General Practitioners' Attitudes toward Complementary Therapies." *Social Science and Medicine* 51: 1555–61.

Ecks, Stefan. 2008. "Three Propositions for Evidence-Based Anthropology." *Journal of the Royal Anthropological Institute* 14: S77–92.

Eddens, T., D. J. Kaplan, A. J. M. Anderson, A. J. Norwalk, and B. T. Campfield. 2019. "Insights from the Geographic Spread of the Lyme Disease Epidemic." *Clinical Infectious Diseases* 68 (3): 426–34.

Edlow, Jonathan A. 2003. *Bull's-Eye: Unraveling the Medical Mystery of Lyme Disease*. New Haven, CT: Yale University Press.

Ehrenreich, Barbara, and Deirdre English. 1973. *Complaints and Disorders: The Sexual Politics of Sickness*. New York: Feminist Press.

Eisen, Lars. 2018. "Pathogen Transmission in Relation to Duration of Attachment by *Ixodes scapularis* Ticks." *Ticks and Tick-Borne Diseases* 9:535–42.

Eisenberg, Leon. 1977. "Disease and Illness: Distinctions between Professional and Popular Ideas of Sickness." *Culture, Medicine and Psychiatry* 1 (1): 9–23.

Ellenbogen, Sara. 2003. *Wittgenstein's Account of the Truth*. Albany: State University of New York Press.

Embers, M. E., S. W. Barthold, J. T. Borda, et al. 2012. "Persistence of *Borrelia burgdorferi* in Rhesus Macaques Following Antibiotic Treatment of Disseminated Infection." *PLOS One* 7 (1): e29914.

Embers, M. E., B. J. Grasperge, M. B. Jacobs, et al. 2013. "Feeding of Ticks on Animals for Transmission and Xenodiagnosis in Lyme Disease Research." *Journal of Visual Experiments*, no. 78, e50617.

Epstein, Steven. 1995. "The Construction of Lay Expertise: AIDS Activism and the Forging of Credibility in the Reform of Clinical Trials." *Science, Technology, and Human Values* 20 (4): 408–37.

Epstein, Steven. 1996. *Impure Science: AIDS, Activism, and the Politics of Knowledge.* Medicine and Society. Berkeley: University of California Press.

Epstein, Steven. 2007a. *Inclusion: The Politics of Difference in Medical Research.* Chicago: University of Chicago Press.

Epstein, Steven. 2007b. "Patient Groups and Health Movements." In *New Handbook of Science and Technology Studies*, edited by J. Hackett, O. Amsterdamska, M. Lynch, and J. Wajcman, 499–539. Cambridge, MA: MIT Press.

Ernst, Kacey C. 2018. "Tick- and Mosquito-Borne Diseases Are Increasing Dramatically." *Scientific American* (blog), August 10, 2018. https://blogs.scientificamerican .com/observations/tick-and-mosquito-borne-diseases-are-increasing -dramatically/.

Eskow, E., R. V. Rao, and E. Mordechai. 2001. "Concurrent Infection of the Central Nervous System by *Borrelia burgdorferi* and *Bartonella henselae*: Evidence for a Novel Tick-Borne Disease Complex." *Archives of Neurology* 58 (9): 1357–63.

Fàbrega, H. 1990. "The Concept of Somatization as a Cultural and Historical Product of Western Medicine." *Psychosomatic Medicine* 52:653–72.

Falco, R. C., and D. Fish. 1992. "A Comparison of Methods for Sampling the Deer Tick, *Ixodes dammini*, in a Lyme Disease Endemic Area." *Experimental and Applied Acarology* 14 (2): 165–73.

Fallon, B. A., J. G. Keilp, K. M. Corbera, et al. 2008. "A Randomized, Placebo-Controlled Trial of Repeated IV Antibiotic Therapy for Lyme Encephalopathy." *Neurology* 70 (13): 992–1003.

Fallon, B. A., M. Pavlicova, S. W. Coffino, et al. 2014. "A Comparison of Lyme Disease Serologic Test Results from 4 Laboratories in Patients with Persistent Symptoms after Antibiotic Treatment." *Clinical Infectious Diseases* 59 (12): 1705–10.

Fallon, B. A., E. Petkova, J. G. Keilp, et al. 2012. "A Reappraisal of the U.S. Clinical Trials of Post-Treatment Lyme Disease Syndrome." *Open Neurology Journal* 6:79–87.

Fallon, J., D. I. Bujak, S. Guardino, et al. 1999. "The Fibromyalgia Impact Questionnaire: A Useful Tool in Evaluating Patients with Post-Lyme Disease Syndrome." *Arthritis Care and Research* 12 (1): 42–47.

Farmer, Paul. 2004. "An Anthropology of Structural Violence." *Current Anthropology* 45 (3): 305–25.

Farquhar, Judith. 1994. "Eating Chinese Medicine." *Cultural Anthropology* 9 (4): 471–97.

Fassin, Didier. 2007. *When Bodies Remember: Experiences and Politics of AIDS in South Africa.* Berkeley: University of California Press.

Fassin, Didier. 2009. "Another Politics of Life Is Possible." *Theory, Culture, Society* 26 (5): 44–60.

Fassin, Didier. 2010. "Ethics of Survival: A Democratic Approach to the Politics of Life." *Humanity: An International Journal of Human Rights* 1 (Fall 2010): 81–95.

Fassin, Didier. 2011. "Coming Back to Life: An Anthropological Reassessment of Biopolitics and Governmentality." In *Governmentality: Current Issues and Future Challenges*, edited by U. Bröckling, S. Krasmann, and T. Lemke, 185–200. New York: Routledge.

Fassin, Didier. 2017. "The Endurance of Critique." *Anthropological Theory* 17 (1): 4–29.

Fassin, Didier. 2018a. "Legitimizing a Less Exceptional Life in Global Public Health." Discussion comments for a panel at the American Ethnological Association's meeting in Philadelphia, March 23, 2018.

Fassin, Didier. 2018b. *Life: A Critical User's Manual*. Cambridge: Polity Press.

Fausto-Sterling, Anne. 2005. "The Bare Bones of Sex: Part 1—Sex and Gender." *Signs: Journal of Women in Culture and Society* 30 (2): 1491–527.

Fawcett, P. T., K. M. Gibney, C. D. Rose, et al. 1992. "Frequency and Specificity of Antibodies That Crossreact with *Borrelia burgdorferi* Antigens." *Journal of Rheumatology* 19 (4): 582–87.

Feder, H. M., Jr., M. A. Gerber, S. W. Luger, et al. 1992. "Persistence of Serum Antibodies to *Borrelia burgdorferi* in Patients Treated for Lyme Disease." *Clinical Infectious Diseases* 15 (5): 788–93.

Feder, H. M., Jr., D. M. Hoss, L. Zemel, et al. 2011. "Southern Tick-Associated Rash Illness (STARI) in the North: STARI Following a Tick Bite in Long Island, New York." *Clinical Infectious Diseases* 53 (10): e142–46.

Fee, Elizabeth, and Nancy Krieger, eds. 1994. *Women's Health, Politics, and Power: Essays on Sex/Gender, Medicine, and Public Health*. Amityville, NY: Baywood.

Felz, M. W., F. W. Chandler Jr., J. H. Oliver Jr., et al. 1999. "Solitary Erythema Migrans in Georgia and South Carolina." *Archives of Dermatology* 135 (11): 1317–26.

Felz, M. W., L. A. Durden, and J. H. Oliver Jr. 1996. "Ticks Parasitizing Humans in Georgia and South Carolina." *Journal of Parasitology* 82 (3): 505–8.

Feng, J., P. G. Auwaerter, and Y. Zhang. 2015. "Drug Combinations Against *Borrelia burgdorferi* Persisters In Vitro: Eradication Achieved by Using Daptomycin, Cefoperazone, and Doxycycline." *PLOS One* 10:e0117207.

Feng, J., W. Shi, S. Zhang, and Y. Zhang. 2015a. "Identification of New Compounds with High Activity against Stationary Phase *Borrelia burgdorferi* from the NCI Compound Collection." *Emerging Microbes and Infections* 4:e31.

Feng, J., W. Shi, S. Zhang, and Y. Zhang. 2015b. "Persister Mechanisms in *Borrelia burgdorferi*: Implications for Improved Intervention." *Emerging Microbes and Infections* 4:e51.

Feng, J., T. Wang, W. Shi, et al. 2014. "Identification of Novel Activity against *Borrelia burgdorferi* Persisters Using an FDA Approved Drug Library." *Emerging Microbes and Infections* 3:e49.

Feng, J., M. Weitner, W. Shi, et al. 2015. "Identification of Additional Anti-Persister Activity against *Borrelia burgdorferi* from an FDA Drug Library." *Antibiotics* 4:397–410.

Feng, J., S. Zhang, W. Shi, and Y. Zhang. 2016. "Ceftriaxone Pulse Dosing Fails to Eradicate Biofilm-Like Microcolony B. burgdorferi Persisters Which Are Sterilized by Daptomycin/Doxycycline/Cefuroxime without Pulse Dosing." *Frontiers in Microbiology* 4 (7): 1744.

Figueroa, R., L. A. Bracero, M. Aguero-Rosenfeld, et al. 1996. "Confirmation of *Borrelia burgdorferi* Spirochetes by Polymerase Chain Reaction in Placentas of Women with Reactive Serology for Lyme Antibodies." *Gynecologic and Obstetric Investigation* 41 (4): 240–43.

Fine, Gary. 1997. "Naturework and the Taming of the Wild: The Problem of 'Overpick' in the Culture of Mushroomers." *Social Problems* 44 (1): 68–88.

Fix, Alan D., César A. Peña, and G. Thomas Strickland. 2000. "Racial Differences in Reported Lyme Disease Incidence." *American Journal of Epidemiology* 152 (8): 756–59.

Fleck, Ludwik. (1935) 1981. *Genesis and Development of a Scientific Fact*. Edited by Thaddeus J. Trenn and Robert K. Norton. Chicago: University of Chicago Press.

Fleming, R. V., A. R. Marques, M. S. Klempner, et al. 2004. "Pre-Treatment and Post-Treatment Assessment of the C (6) Test in Patients with Persistent Symptoms and a History of Lyme Borreliosis." *European Journal of Clinical Microbiology and Infectious Disease* 23 (8): 615–18.

Forrester, J. D., K. J. Kugeler, A. E. Perea, et al. 2015. "No Geographic Correlation between Lyme Disease and Death Due to 4 Neurodegenerative Disorders, United States, 2001–2010." *Emerging Infectious Diseases* 21 (11): 2036–39.

Foucault, Michel. (1969) 1972. *The Archaeology of Knowledge*. New York: Pantheon.

Foucault, Michel. (1966) 1994a. *The Order of Things: An Archaeology of the Human Sciences*. New York: Vintage Press.

Foucault, Michel. (1973) 1994b. *The Birth of the Clinic: An Archaeology of Medical Perception*. New York: Pantheon Books.

Foucault, Michel. (1976) 1990. *The History of Sexuality*. Vol. 1, *An Introduction*. New York: Vintage Books.

Foucault, Michel. 1988. "Technologies of the Self." In *Technologies of the Self: A Seminar with Michel Foucault*, edited by L. H. Martin, H. Gutman, and P. H. Hutton, 16–49. Amherst: University of Massachusetts Press.

Foucault, Michel. (1997) 2003. *Society Must Be Defended: Lectures at the Collège de France, 1975–76*. New York: Picador.

Franklin, Sarah, and Margaret Lock. 2003. *Remaking Life and Death: Toward an Anthropology of the Biosciences*. Santa Fe, NM: School of American Research Press.

Frey, William H. 2018. *Diversity Explosion: How New Racial Demographics Are Remaking America*. Rev. ed. Washington, DC: Brookings Institution.

Frickel, Scott, S. Gibbon, J. Howard, et al. 2010. "Undone Science: Charting Social Movement and Civil Society Challenges to Research Agenda Setting." *Science, Technology, and Human Values* 35 (4): 444–73.

Frost, Samantha. 2014. "Re-Considering the Turn to Biology in Feminist Theory." *Feminist Theory* 15 (3): 307–26.

Fujimura, J. H., and D. Y. Chou. 1994. "Dissent in Science: Styles of Scientific Practice and the Controversy over the Cause of AIDS." *Social Science and Medicine* 38 (8): 1017–36.

Fullwiley, Duana. 2014. "The 'Contemporary Synthesis': When Politically Inclusive Genomic Science Relies on Biological Notions of Race." *Isis* 105:803–14.

Fung, B. P., G. L. McHugh, J. M. Leong, et al. 1994. "Humoral Immune Response to Outer Surface Protein C of *Borrelia burgdorferi* in Lyme Disease: Role of the Immunoglobulin M Response in the Serodiagnosis of Early Infection." *Infection and Immunity* 62 (8): 3213–21.

Gaines, Atwood D., and Robert A. Hahn. 1985. "Among the Physicians: Encounter, Exchange, and Transformation." In *Physicians of Western Medicine*, edited by Atwood Gaines and Robert Hahn, 3–22. Boston: D. Reidel.

Galbussera, A., et al. 2008. "Lack of Evidence for *Borrelia burgdorferi* Seropositivity in Alzheimer's Disease." *Alzheimer's Disease and Associated Disorders* 22 (3): 308.

Galtung, John. 1969. "Violence, Peace, and Peace Research." *Journal of Peace Research* 6 (3): 167–91.

Garcia-Monco, J. C., J. Miró Jornet, B. Fernández Villar, et al. 1990. "Multiple Sclerosis or Lyme Disease? A Diagnosis Problem of Exclusion." *Medicina Clínica* 94 (18): 685–88.

García-Moreno, J. M., G. Izquierdo, J. Chacón, et al. 1997. "Neuroborreliosis in a Patient with Progressive Supranuclear Paralysis: An Association or the Cause?" *Revista de Neurologia* 25 (148): 1919–21.

Garro, Linda C. 1994. "Narrative Representations of Chronic Illness Experience: Cultural Models of Illness, Mind, and Body in Stories Concerning the Temporomandibular Joint (TMJ)." *Social Science and Medicine* 28 (6): 775–88.

Gaudino, E. A., P. K. Coyle, and L. B. Krupp. 1997. "Post-Lyme Syndrome and Chronic Fatigue Syndrome: Neuropsychiatric Similarities and Differences." *Archives of Neurology* 54 (11): 1372–76.

Geltzer, Anna. 2009. "When the Standards Aren't Standard: Evidence-Based Medicine in the Russian Context." *Social Science and Medicine* 68 (3): 526–32.

Gerber, M. A., and E. L. Zalneraitis. 1994. "Childhood Neurological Disorders and Lyme Disease during Pregnancy." *Pediatric Neurology* 11 (1): 41–43.

Gevitz, Norman, ed. 1988. *Other Healers: Unorthodox Medicine in America.* Baltimore, MD: Johns Hopkins University Press.

Ghosh, S., R. Seward, C. E. Costello, et al. 2006. "Autoantibodies from Synovial Lesions in Chronic, Antibiotic Treatment-Resistant Lyme Arthritis Bind Cytokeratin-10." *Journal of Immunology* 177 (4): 2486–94.

Gibbons, M., C. Limoges, H. Nowotny, et al. 1994. *The New Production of Knowledge.* London: Sage.

Giddens, Anthony. 1991. *Modernity and Self-Identity: Self and Society in the Late Modern Age.* Cambridge: Polity Press.

Gieryn, Thomas. 1983. "Boundary-Work and the Demarcation of Science from Non-Science: Strains and Interests in Professional Ideologies of Scientists." *American Sociological Review* 48 (6): 781–95.

Girard, Y. A., N. Fedorova, and R. S. Lane. 2011. "Genetic Diversity of *Borrelia burgdorferi* and Detection of B. *bissettii*-Like DNA in Serum of North-Coastal California Residents." *Journal of Clinical Microbiology* 49 (3): 945–54.

Girschick, H. J., H. I. Huppertz, H. Rüssmann, et al. 1996. "Intracellular Persistence of *Borrelia burgdorferi* in Human Synovial Cells." *Rheumatology International* 16 (3): 125–32.

Glatz, M., M. Golestani, H. Kerl, and R. R. Müllegger. 2006. "Clinical Relevance of Different IgG and IgM Serum Antibody Responses to *Borrelia burgdorferi* after Antibiotic Therapy for Erythema Migrans: Long-Term Follow-Up Study of 113 Patients." *Archives of Dermatology* 142 (7): 862–68.

Goddard, J. 2002. "A Ten-Year Study of Tick Biting in Mississippi: Implications for Human Disease Transmission." *Journal of Agromedicine* 8 (2): 25–32.

Goddard, J., and J. Piesman. 2006. "New Records of Immature *Ixodes scapularis* from Mississippi." *Journal of Vector Ecology* 31 (2): 421–22.

Goldenberg, Maya J. 2006. "On Evidence and Evidence-Based Medicine: Lessons from the Philosophy of Science." *Social Science and Medicine* 62 (11): 2621–32.

Golinski, Jan. 1998. *Making Natural Knowledge: Constructivism and the History of Science.* Cambridge: Cambridge University Press.

Golovchenko, Maryna, M. Vancová, K. Clark, et al. 2016. "A Divergent Spirochete Strain Isolated from a Resident of the Southeastern United States Was Identified by Multilocus Sequence Typing as *Borrelia bissettii*." *Parasites and Vectors* 9:68.

Good, Byron. 1994. *Medicine, Rationality, and Experience: An Anthropological Perspective.* Cambridge: Cambridge University Press.

Good, Mary-Jo DelVecchio, P. Brodwin, B. J. Good, et al., eds. 1992. *Pain as Human Experience: An Anthropological Perspective.* Berkeley: University of California Press.

Goodman, D. C., S. Brownlee, C.-H. Chang, et al. 2010. "Regional and Racial Variation in Primary Care and the Quality of Care among Medicare Beneficiaries." Edited by K. K. Bronner. *A Report of the Dartmouth Atlas Project*, September 9, 2010, 1–36. http://www.dartmouthatlas.org/downloads/reports/Primary_care_report_090910.pdf.

Gordillo-Pérez, G., J. Torres, F. Solórzano-Santos, et al. 2007. "*Borrelia burgdorferi* Infection and Cutaneous Lyme Disease, Mexico." *Emerging Infectious Disease Journal* 13 (10): 1556–58.

Gordillo-Pérez, G., M. Vargas, F. Solórzano-Santos, et al. 2009. "Demonstration of *Borrelia burgdorferi* Sensu Stricto Infection in Ticks from the Northeast of Mexico." *Clinical Microbiology and Infection* 15 (5): 496–98.

Gorski, David. 2011. "Spin City: Using Placebos to Evaluate Objective and Subjective Responses in Asthma." *Science-Based Medicine*, July 18, 2011. https://sciencebasedmedicine.org/spin-city-placebos-and-asthma/.

Greco, Monica. 2012. "The Classification and Nomenclature of 'Medically Unexplained Symptoms': Conflict, Performativity, and Critique." *Social Science and Medicine* 75 (12): 2362–69.

Greco, Monica. 2017. "Pragmatics of Explanation: Creative Accountability in the Care of 'Medically Unexplained Symptoms.'" *Sociological Review Monographs* 65 (2): 110–29.

Greenhalgh, Susan. 2001. *Under the Medical Gaze: Facts and Fictions of Chronic Pain.* Berkeley: University of California Press.

Grey, Timothy, and Breanne Russell, dirs. 2009. *Under the Eightball.* 120 min. Traverse City, MI: Andalusian Dogs.

Gross, D. M., T. Forsthuber, M. Tary-Lehmann, et al. 1998. "Identification of LFA-1 as a Candidate Autoantigen in Treatment-Resistant Lyme Arthritis." *Science* 281 (5377): 703–6.

Gross, D. M., A. C. Steere, and B. T. Huber. 1998. "T Helper 1 Response Is Dominant and Localized to the Synovial Fluid in Patients with Lyme Arthritis." *Journal of Immunology* 160 (2): 1022–28.

Gülden, M., and H. Seibert. 2005. "In Vitro–In Vivo Extrapolation of Toxic Potencies for Hazard and Risk Assessment—Problems and New Developments." *Altex* 22 (2): 218–25.

Güner, E. S., N. Hashimoto, N. Takada, et al. 2003. "First Isolation and Characterization of *Borrelia burgdorferi* Sensu Lato Strains from *Ixodes ricinus* Ticks in Turkey." *Journal of Medical Microbiology* 52 (part 9): 807–13.

Gustafson, J. M., E. C. Burgess, M. D. Wachal, et al. 1993. "Intrauterine Transmission of *Borrelia burgdorferi* in Dogs." *American Journal of Veterinary Research* 54 (6): 882–90.

Gutacker, M., C. Valsangiacomo, T. Balmelli, et al. 1998. "Arguments against the Involvement of *Borrelia burgdorferi* Sensu Lato in Alzheimer's Disease." *Research in Microbiology* 149 (1): 31–37.

Haas, Lidija. 2018. "Memoirs of Disease and Disbelief." *New Yorker*, May 28, 2018. https://www.newyorker.com/magazine/2018/06/04/memoirs-of-disease-and-disbelief.

Hacking, Ian. 1998. *Mad Travelers: Reflections on the Reality of Transient Mental Illness.* Charlottesville: University of Virginia Press.

Hacking, Ian. 1999. "Making Up People." In *The Science Studies Reader*, edited by M. Biagioli, 161–71. New York: Routledge.

Hahn, Robert A., and Arthur Kleinman. 1983. "Biomedical Practice and Anthropological Theory: Frameworks and Directions." *Annual Review of Anthropology* 12 (1): 305–33.

Halperin, J. J. 2011. "Nervous System Lyme Disease: Is There a Controversy?" *Seminars in Neurology* 31 (3): 317–24.

Halperin, J. J., P. Baker, and G. P. Wormser. 2013. "Common Misconceptions about Lyme Disease." *American Journal of Medicine* 126 (3): 264.e1–7.

Halperin, J. J., G. P. Kaplan, S. Brazinsky, et al. 1990. "Immunologic Reactivity against *Borrelia burgdorferi* in Patients with Motor Neuron Disease." *Archives of Neurology* 47 (5): 586–94.

Halperin, J. J., B. J. Luft, A. K. Anand, et al. 1989. "Lyme Neuroborreliosis: Central Nervous System Manifestations." *Neurology* 39 (6): 753–59.

Hänsel, Y., M. Ackerl, and G. Stanek. 1995. "ALS-Like Sequelae in Chronic Neuroborreliosis." *Wiener Medizinische Wochenschrift* 145 (7–8): 186–88.

Hansen, Thomas Blom, and Finn Stepputat, eds. 2005. *Sovereign Bodies: Citizens, Migrants, and States in the Postcolonial World*. Princeton, NJ: Princeton University Press.

Hanson, M. S., and R. Edelman. 2003. "Progress and Controversy Surrounding Vaccines against Lyme Disease." *Expert Review of Vaccines* 2 (5): 683–703.

Haraway, Donna Jeanne. 1988. "Situated Knowledges: The Science Question in Feminism and the Privilege of Partial Perspectives." *Feminist Studies* 14 (3): 575–99.

Haraway, Donna Jeanne. 1989. *Primate Visions: Gender, Race, and Nature in the World of Modern Science*. New York: Routledge.

Haraway, Donna Jeanne. 1991. *Simians, Cyborgs, and Women: The Reinvention of Nature*. London: Free Association Books.

Harding, Sandra G. 1986. *The Science Question in Feminism*. Ithaca, NY: Cornell University Press.

Harthorn, Barbara H., and Laury Oaks, eds. 2003. *Risk, Culture, and Health Inequality: Shifting Perceptions of Danger and Blame*. Santa Barbara, CA: Praeger.

Hartmann, M., and K. Pfadenhauer. 2003. "Intrathecal Antibody Production against *Borrelia burgdorferi* in a Patient with Relapsing-Remitting Multiple Sclerosis." *European Journal of Neurology* 10 (6): 747–48.

Hassett, A. L., D. C. Radvanski, S. Buyske, et al. 2008. "Role of Psychiatric Comorbidity in Chronic Lyme Disease." *Arthritis and Rheumatism* 59 (12): 1742–49.

Hassett, A. L., D. Radvanski, S. Buyske, et al. 2009. "Psychiatric Comorbidity and Other Psychological Factors in Patients with 'Chronic Lyme Disease.'" *American Journal of Medicine* 122 (9): 843–50.

Hatcher, S., and B. Arroll. 2008. "Assessment and Management of Medically Unexplained Symptoms." *British Medical Journal* 336 (7653): 1124–28.

Häupl, T., G. Hahn, M. Rittig, et al. 1993. "Persistence of *Borrelia burgdorferi* in Ligamentous Tissue from a Patient with Chronic Lyme Borreliosis." *Arthritis and Rheumatism* 36 (11): 1621–26.

Hauser, U., H. Krahl, H. Peters, et al. 1998. "Impact of Strain Heterogeneity on Lyme Disease Serology in Europe: Comparison of Enzyme-Linked Immunosorbent Assays Using Different Species of *Borrelia burgdorferi* Sensu Lato." *Journal of Clinical Microbiology* 36 (2): 427–36.

Heiser, Christina. 2016. "How Lyme Disease Stole the Sanity of This Former 'Rich Girl.'" *Women's Health*, May 11, 2016. https://www.womenshealthmag.com/health/a19995841/ally-hilfiger-lyme-disease/.

Hekman, Susan. 2010. *The Material of Knowledge: Feminist Disclosures*. Bloomington: Indiana University Press.

Heller, J., G. Holzer, and K. Schimrigk. 1990a. "ELISA for Specifying Oligoclonal Bands of Isoelectric Focusing of Cerebrospinal Fluid in Patients with Neuroborreliosis and Multiple Sclerosis." *Nervenarzt* 61 (4): 248–49.

Heller, J., G. Holzer, and K. Schimrigk. 1990b. "Immunological Differentiation between Neuroborreliosis and Multiple Sclerosis." *Journal of Neurology* 237 (8): 465–70.

Heller, J. E., E. Benito-Garcia, N. E. Maher, et al. 2010. "Behavioral and Attitude Survey about Lyme Disease among a Brazilian Population in the Endemic Area of Martha's Vineyard, Massachusetts." *Journal of Immigrant and Minority Health* 12 (3): 377–83.

Hemmer, B., F. X. Glocker, R. Kaiser, et al. 1997. "Generalised Motor Neuron Disease as an Unusual Manifestation of *Borrelia burgdorferi* Infection." *Journal of Neurology, Neurosurgery, and Psychiatry* 63 (2): 257–58.

Hercogová, J., M. Tománková, D. Frösslová, et al. 1993. "Early-Stage Lyme Borreliosis during Pregnancy: Treatment in 15 Women with Erythema Migrans." *Ceskoslovenská Gynekologie* 58 (5): 229–32.

Herman, Daniel Justin. 2001. *Hunting and the American Imagination*. Washington, DC: Smithsonian Institution Press.

Herman-Giddens, M. E. 2012. "Yale Lyme Disease Risk Maps Are Not Accurate for the South in 2012." *American Journal of Tropical Medicine and Hygiene* 86 (6): 1085; author reply, 1086.

Herrmann, Anne C., and Abigail J. Stewart, eds. 1994. *Theorizing Feminism: Parallel Trends in the Humanities and Social Sciences*. Boulder, CO: Westview.

Hess, David J. 1996. "Technology and Alternative Cancer Therapies: An Analysis of Heterodoxy and Constructivism." *Medical Anthropology Quarterly* 10 (4): 657–74.

Hess, David J. 2004a. "CAM Cancer Therapies in Twentieth-Century North America: The Emergence and Growth of a Social Movement." In *The Politics of Healing*, edited by Robert Johnston, 231–43. New York: Routledge.

Hess, David J. 2004b. "Medical Modernisation, Scientific Research Fields and the Epistemic Politics of Health Social Movements." *Sociology of Health and Illness* 26 (6): 695–709.

Hess, David J. 2016. *Undone Science: Social Movements, Mobilized Publics, and Industrial Transitions*. Cambridge, MA: MIT Press.

Hildenbrand, P., D. E. Craven, R. Jones, and P. Nemeskal. 2009. "Lyme Neuroborreliosis: Manifestations of a Rapidly Emerging Zoonosis." *American Journal of Neuroradiology* 30 (6): 1079–87.

Hinckley, A. F., J. I. Meek, and J. A. E. Ray. 2016. "Effectiveness of Residential Acaricides to Prevent Lyme and Other Tick-Borne Diseases in Humans." *Journal of Infectious Diseases* 214 (2): 182–88.

Hird, Myra J. 2004. "Feminist Matters: New Materialist Considerations of Sexual Difference." *Feminist Theory* 5 (2): 223–32.

Hodzic, E., S. Feng, K. Holden, K. J. Freet, et al. 2008. "Persistence of *Borrelia burgdorferi* Following Antibiotic Treatment in Mice." *Antimicrobial Agents and Chemotherapy* 52 (5): 1728–36.

Hodzic, E., D. Imai, S. Feng, and S. W. Barthold. 2014. "Resurgence of Persisting Non-Cultivable *Borrelia burgdorferi* Following Antibiotic Treatment in Mice." PLOS *One* 9 (1): e86907.

Hoen, A. G., G. Margos, S. J. Bent, et al. 2009. "Phylogeography of *Borrelia burgdorferi* in the Eastern United States Reflects Multiple Independent Lyme Disease Emergence Events." *Proceedings of the National Academy of Sciences of the United States of America* 106 (35): 15013–18.

Hoffman, K. M., S. Trawalter, J. R. Axt, et al. 2016. "Racial Bias in Pain Assessment and Treatment Recommendations, and False Beliefs about Biological Differences between Blacks and Whites." *Proceedings of the National Academy of Science* 113 (16): 4296–4301.

Hollander, D. H., T. B. Turner, and E. E. Nell. 1952. "The Effect of Long Continued Subcurative Doses of Penicillin during the Incubation Period of Experimental Syphilis." *Bulletin of the Johns Hopkins Hospital* 90 (2): 105–20.

Hollstrom, E. 1951. "Successful Treatment of Erythema Migrans Afzelius." *Acta Dermato-Venereologica* 31 (2): 235–43.

Holmes, Dave, and Patrick O'Byrne. 2012. "Resisting Stratification: Imperialism, War Machines and Evidence-Based Practice." In *Evidence-Based Healthcare in Context: Critical Social Science Perspectives*, edited by Alex Broom and Jon Adams, 43–58. Burlington, VT: Ashgate.

Horowitz, H. W., C. S. Pavia, S. Bittker, et al. 1994. "Sustained Cellular Immune Responses to *Borrelia burgdorferi*: Lack of Correlation with Clinical Presentation and Serology." *Clinical and Diagnostic Laboratory Immunology* 1 (4): 373–78.

Hoy, Suellen M. 1995. *Chasing Dirt: The American Pursuit of Cleanliness*. New York: Oxford University Press.

Hudson, B. J., M. Stewart, V. A. Lennox, et al. 1998. "Culture-Positive Lyme Borreliosis." *Medical Journal of Australia* 168 (10): 500–502.

Hunfeld, K. P., E. Ruzic-Sabljic, D. E. Norris, et al. 2005. "In Vitro Susceptibility Testing of *Borrelia burgdorferi* Sensu Lato Isolates Cultured from Patients with Erythema Migrans before and after Antimicrobial Chemotherapy." *Antimicrobial Agents and Chemotherapy* 49 (4): 1294–301.

Hyde, F. W., R. C. Johnson, T. J. White, et al. 1989. "Detection of Antigens in Urine of Mice and Humans Infected with *Borrelia burgdorferi*, Etiologic Agent of Lyme Disease." *Journal of Clinical Microbiology* 27 (1): 58–61.

ILADS Working Group. 2004. "Evidence-Based Guidelines for the Management of Lyme Disease." *Expert Review in Anti-Infective Therapy* 2 (S1): S1–13.

Iliopoulou, B. P., J. Alroy, and B. T. Huber. 2008. "Persistent Arthritis in *Borrelia burgdorferi*-Infected HLA-DR4-Positive CD28-Negative Mice Post-Antibiotic Treatment." *Arthritis and Rheumatism* 58 (12): 3892–3901.

Iliopoulou, B. P., M. Guerau-de-Arellano, and B. T. Huber. 2009. "HLA-DR Alleles Determine Responsiveness to *Borrelia burgdorferi* Antigens in a Mouse Model of Self-Perpetuating Arthritis." *Arthritis and Rheumatism* 60 (12): 3831–40.

Imbuluzqueta, E., C. Gamazo, J. Ariza, et al. 2010. "Drug Delivery Systems for Potential Treatment of Intracellular Bacterial Infections." *Frontiers in Bioscience* 15:397–417.

Inhorn, Marcia C. 2003. *Local Babies, Global Science: Gender, Religion, and In Vitro Fertilization in Egypt.* New York: Routledge.

Institute of Medicine, Robin Graham, Michelle Mancher, Dianne Miller Wolman, Sheldon Greenfield, and Earl Steinberg, eds. 2011. *Clinical Practice Guidelines We Can Trust.* Washington, DC: National Academies Press. http://www.nationalacademies.org/hmd/Reports/2011/Clinical-Practice-Guidelines-We-Can-Trust.aspx.

Ioannidis, J. 2005. "Why Most Published Research Findings Are False." *PLOS Medicine* 2 (8): e124.

Ioannidis, J. 2016. "Evidence-Based Medicine Has Been Hijacked: A Report to David Sackett." *Journal of Clinical Epidemiology* 73:82–86.

Irwin, P. J., I. D. Robertson, M. E. Westman, et al. 2017. "Searching for Lyme Borreliosis in Australia: Results of a Canine Sentinel Study." *Parasites and Vectors* 10 (1): 114.

Ivanova, L. B., A. Tomova, D. González-Acuña, et al. 2014. "*Borrelia chilensis*, a New Member of the *Borrelia burgdorferi* Sensu Lato Complex That Extends the Range of This Genospecies in the Southern Hemisphere." *Environmental Microbiology* 16 (4): 1069–80.

Iyer, R., P. Mukherjee, K. Wang, J. Simons, et al. 2013. "Detection of *Borrelia burgdorferi* Nucleic Acids after Antibiotic Treatment Does Not Confirm Viability." *Journal of Clinical Microbiology* 51 (3): 857–62.

Jacek, E., B. A. Fallon, A. Chandra, et al. 2013. "Increased IFNα Activity and Differential Antibody Response in Patients with a History of Lyme Disease and Persistent Cognitive Deficits." *Journal of Neuroimmunology* 255 (1–2): 85–91.

Jackson, Jean E. 2000. *"Camp Pain": Talking with Chronic Pain Patients.* Philadelphia: University of Pennsylvania Press.

Jacobsen, Annie. 2014. *Operation Paperclip: The Secret Intelligence Program That Brought Nazi Scientists to America.* New York: Little, Brown.

Jain, V. K., E. Hilton, J. Maytal, et al. 1996. "Immunoglobulin M Immunoblot for Diagnosis of *Borrelia burgdorferi* Infection in Patients with Acute Facial Palsy." *Journal of Clinical Microbiology* 34 (8): 2033–35.

James, A. M., D. Liveris, G. P. Wormser, et al. 2001. "*Borrelia lonestari* Infection after a Bite by an *Amblyomma americanum* Tick." *Journal of Infectious Disease* 183 (12): 1810–14.

James, S., S. W. Stevenson, N. Silove, et al. 2015. "Chelation for Autism Spectrum Disorder (ASD)." *Cochrane Database of Systematic Reviews* 11 (5): CD010766.

Jenks, N. P., and J. Trapasso. 2005. "Lyme Risk for Immigrants to the United States: The Role of an Educational Tool." *Journal of Travel Medicine* 12 (3): 157–60.

Johnson, B. J., M. A. Pilgard, and T. M. Russell. 2014. "Assessment of New Culture Method for Detection of Borrelia Species from Serum of Lyme Disease Patients." *Journal of Clinical Microbiology* 52 (3): 721–24.

Johnson, L. 2011. "Who Died and Made You King? Eminence Based Medicine in Lyme Disease Breaks All the Rules." *Lyme Policy Wonk*, LymeDisease.org, March 17, 2011. https://www.lymedisease.org/664/.

Johnson, L. 2016. "Chronic Lyme European PLEASE Trial—You Know It's Spin When Treatment 'Success' Is Called 'Failure'?" *Lyme Policy Wonk*, LymeDisease .org, March 30, 2016. https://www.lymedisease.org/lymepolicywonk-lyme -european-please-trial-you-know-its-spin-when-treatment-success-is-called -failure/.

Johnson, L. 2018. "Update on TBD Working Group: How Did We Do?" *Lyme Policy Wonk*, LymeDisease.org, June 1, 2018. https://www.lymedisease.org /lymepolicywonk-update-on-tbd-working-group-how-did-we-do/.

Johnson, L., and R. B. Stricker. 2010. "The Infectious Diseases Society of America Lyme Guidelines: A Cautionary Tale about the Development of Clinical Practice Guidelines." *Philosophy, Ethics, and Humanities in Medicine* 5:1–17.

Johnson, Susan. 2008. *Medically Unexplained Illness: Gender and Biopsychosocial Implications*. Washington, DC: American Psychological Association.

Jutel, Annemarie. 2010. "Medically Unexplained Symptoms and the Disease Label." *Social Theory and Health* 8 (3): 229–45.

Kalish, R. A., J. M. Leong, and A. C. Steere. 1993. "Association of Treatment-Resistant Chronic Lyme Arthritis with HLA-DR4 and Antibody Reactivity to OspA and OspB of *Borrelia burgdorferi*." *Infection and Immunity* 61 (7): 2774–79.

Kalish, R. A., J. M. Leong, and A. C. Steere. 1995. "Early and Late Antibody Responses to Full-Length and Truncated Constructs of Outer Surface Protein A of *Borrelia burgdorferi* in Lyme Disease." *Infection and Immunity* 63 (6): 2228–35.

Kalish, R. A., G. McHugh, J. Granquist, et al. 2001. "Persistence of Immunoglobulin M or Immunoglobulin G Antibody Responses to *Borrelia burgdorferi* 10–20 Years after Active Lyme Disease." *Clinical Infectious Diseases* 33 (6): 780–85.

Kamradt, T., A. Krause, and G. R. Burmester. 1995. "A Role for T Cells in the Pathogenesis of Treatment-Resistant Lyme Arthritis." *Molecular Medicine* 1 (5): 486–90.

Kamradt, T., B. Lengl-Janssen, A. F. Strauss, et al. 1996. "Dominant Recognition of a *Borrelia burgdorferi* Outer Surface Protein A Peptide by T Helper Cells in Patients with Treatment-Resistant Lyme Arthritis." *Infection and Immunity* 64 (4): 1284–89.

Kannian, P., E. E. Drouin, L. Glickstein, et al. 2007. "Decline in the Frequencies of *Borrelia burgdorferi* OspA161 175-Specific T Cells after Antibiotic Therapy in

HLA-DRB10401-Positive Patients with Antibiotic-Responsive or Antibiotic-Refractory Lyme Arthritis." *Journal of Immunology* 179 (9): 6336–42.

Kaplan, R. F., R. P. Trevino, G. M. Johnson, et al. 2003. "Cognitive Function in Post-Treatment Lyme Disease: Do Additional Antibiotics Help?" *Neurology* 60 (12): 1916–22.

Karussis, D., H. L. Weiner, and O. Abramsky. 1999. "Multiple Sclerosis vs Lyme Disease: A Case Presentation to a Discussant and a Review of the Literature." *Multiple Sclerosis* 5 (6): 395–402.

Katchar, K., E. E. Drouin, and A. C. Steere. 2013. "Natural Killer Cells and Natural Killer T Cells in Lyme Arthritis." *Arthritis Research and Therapy* 15 (6): R183.

Keller, Evelyn Fox. 2010. *The Mirage of a Space between Nature and Nurture.* Durham, NC: Duke University Press.

Keller, T. L., J. J. Halperin, and M. Whitman. 1992. "PCR Detection of *Borrelia burgdorferi* DNA in Cerebrospinal Fluid of Lyme Neuroborreliosis Patients." *Neurology* 42 (1): 32–42.

Kelner, Merrijoy, and Beverly Wellman, eds. 2000. *Complementary and Alternative Medicine: Challenge and Change.* London: Routledge.

Kent, Jennifer A., Vinisha Patel, and Natalie A. Varela. 2012. "Gender Disparities in Health Care." *Mt. Sinai Journal of Medicine* 79:555–59.

Kilshaw, Susie. 2010. *Impotent Warriors: Perspectives on Gulf War Syndrome, Vulnerability and Masculinity.* New York: Berghahn.

Kirkland, Anna. 2012. "Credibility Battles in the Autism Litigation." *Social Studies of Science* 42 (2): 237–61.

Kirmayer, L. J. 1988. "Mind and Body as Metaphors: Hidden Values in Biomedicine." In *Biomedicine Examined*, edited by Margaret Lock and Deborah Gordon, 57–93. Boston: Kluwer Academic.

Kirmayer, L. J. 2011. "Unpacking the Placebo Response: Insights from Ethnographic Studies of Healing." *Journal of Mind-Body Regulation* 1 (3): 112–24.

Kirmayer, L. J., D. Groleau, K. J. Looper, et al. 2004. "Explaining Medically Unexplained Symptoms." *Canadian Journal of Psychiatry* 49 (10): 663–72.

Klawiter, Maren. 2008. *The Biopolitics of Breast Cancer: Changing Cultures of Disease and Activism.* Minneapolis: University of Minnesota Press.

Klein, J. O. 2008. "Danger Ahead: Politics Intrude in Infectious Diseases Society of America Guideline for Lyme Disease." *Clinical Infectious Diseases* 47 (9): 1197–99.

Kleinman, Arthur. 1986. *Social Origins of Distress and Disease: Depression, Neurasthenia, and Pain in Modern China.* New Haven, CT: Yale University Press.

Kleinman, Arthur. 1988. *The Illness Narratives: Suffering, Healing, and the Human Condition.* New York: Basic Books.

Kleinman, Arthur. 1995. "Pain and Resistance: The Delegitimation and Relegitimation of Local Worlds." In *Writing at the Margin: Discourse between Anthropology and Medicine*, 120–46. Berkeley: University of California Press.

Kleinman, Arthur, Veena Das, and Margaret M. Lock. 1997. *Social Suffering*. Berkeley: University of California Press.

Kleinman, Arthur, Leon Eisenberg, and Byron Good. 1978. "Culture, Illness, and Care: Critical Lessons from Anthropologic and Cross-Cultural Research." *Annals of Internal Medicine* 88 (2): 251–58.

Kleinman, Daniel. 2003. *Impure Cultures: University Biology and the World of Commerce*. Madison: University of Wisconsin Press.

Klempner, M. S. 2002. "Controlled Trials of Antibiotic Treatment in Patients with Post-Treatment Chronic Lyme Disease." *Vector-Borne and Zoonotic Diseases* 2 (4): 255–63.

Klempner, M. S., P. J. Baker, E. D. Shapiro, et al. 2013. "Treatment Trials for Post-Lyme Disease Symptoms Revisited." *American Journal of Medicine* 126 (8): 665–69.

Klempner, M. S., L. T. Hu, J. Evans, et al. 2001. "Two Controlled Trials of Antibiotic Treatment in Patients with Persistent Symptoms and a History of Lyme Disease." *New England Journal of Medicine* 345 (2): 85–92.

Klempner, M. S., R. Noring, and R. A. Rogers. 1993. "Invasion of Human Skin Fibroblasts by the Lyme Disease Spirochete, *Borrelia burgdorferi*." *Journal of Infectious Diseases* 167 (5): 1074–81.

Klempner, M. S., C. H. Schmid, L. Hu, et al. 2001. "Intralaboratory Reliability of Serologic and Urine Testing for Lyme Disease." *American Journal of Medicine* 110 (3): 217–19.

Kohlhepp, W., P. Oschmann, and H. G. Mertens. 1989. "Treatment of Lyme Borreliosis: Randomized Comparison of Doxycycline and Penicillin G." *Journal of Neurology* 236 (8): 464–69.

Kosik-Bogacka, D., K. Bukowska, and W. Kuźna-Grygiel. 2002. "Detection of *Borrelia burgdorferi* Sensu Lato in Mosquitoes (*Culicidae*) in Recreational Areas of the City of Szczecin." *Annals of Agricultural and Environmental Medicine* 9 (1): 55–57.

Kosik-Bogacka, D., W. Kuźna-Grygiel, and M. Jaborowska. 2007. "Ticks and Mosquitoes as Vectors of *Borrelia burgdorferi* S.L. in the Forested Areas of Szczecin." *Folia Biologica* 55 (3–4): 143–46.

Kosnett, M. J. 2010. "Chelation for Heavy Metals (Arsenic, Lead, and Mercury): Protective or Perilous?" *Clinical Pharmacology and Therapeutics* 88 (3): 412–15.

Krause, A., V. Brade, C. Schoerner, et al. 1991. "T Cell Proliferation Induced by *Borrelia burgdorferi* in Patients with Lyme Borreliosis: Autologous Serum Required for Optimum Stimulation." *Arthritis and Rheumatism* 34 (4): 393–402.

Krause, A., G. R. Burmester, A. Rensing, et al. 1992. "Cellular Immune Reactivity to Recombinant OspA and Flagellin from *Borrelia burgdorferi* in Patients with Lyme Borreliosis: Complexity of Humoral and Cellular Immune Responses." *Journal of Clinical Investigation* 90 (3): 1077–84.

Krause, P. J., B. E. Gewurz, D. Hill, et al. 2008. "Persistent and Relapsing Babesiosis in Immunocompromised Patients." *Clinical Infectious Disease* 46 (3): 370–76.

Krause, P. J., S. Narasimhan, G. P. Wormser, et al. 2013. "Human *Borrelia miyamotoi* Infection in the United States." *New England Journal of Medicine* 368 (3): 291–93.

Krause, P. J., A. Spielman, S. R. Telford, et al. 1998. "Persistent Parasitemia after Acute Babesiosis." *New England Journal of Medicine* 339 (3): 160–65.

Krause, P. J., S. R. Telford 3rd, A. Spielman, et al. 1996. "Concurrent Lyme Disease and Babesiosis: Evidence for Increased Severity and Duration of Illness." *Journal of the American Medical Association* 275 (21): 1657–60.

Krieger, N., D. R. Williams, and N. E. Moss. 1997. "Measuring Social Class in U.S. Public Health Research: Concepts, Methodologies, and Guidelines." *Annual Review of Public Health* 18:341–78.

Krimsky, Sheldon. 2000. *Hormonal Chaos: The Scientific and Social Origins of the Environmental Endocrine Hypothesis.* Baltimore, MD: Johns Hopkins University Press.

Kristoferitsch, W., F. Aboulenein-Djamshidian, J. Jecel, et al. 2018. "Secondary Dementia Due to Lyme Neuroborreliosis." *Wiener Klinische Wochenschrift* 130 (15–16): 468–78.

Kroll-Smith, Steve, Phil Brown, and Valerie J. Gunter, eds. 2000. *Illness and the Environment: A Reader in Contested Medicine.* New York: New York University Press.

Kroll-Smith, Steve, and H. Hugh Floyd. 1997. *Bodies in Protest: Environmental Illness and the Struggle over Medical Knowledge.* New York: New York University Press.

Krupp, L. B., L. G. Hyman, R. Grimson, et al. 2003. "Study and Treatment of Post Lyme Disease (STOP-LD): A Randomized Double Masked Clinical Trial." *Neurology* 60 (12): 1923–30.

Kruszewska, D., and S. Tylewska-Wierzbanowska. 1996. "Unknown Species of Rickettsiae Isolated from Ixodes ricinus Tick in Wałcz." *Roczniki Akademii Medycznej w Białymstoku* 41 (1): 129–35.

Kuhn, Thomas. (1962) 1996. *The Structure of Scientific Revolutions.* Chicago: University of Chicago Press.

Kumi-Diaka, J., and O. Harris. 1995. "Viability of *Borrelia burgdorferi* in Stored Semen." *British Veterinary Journal* 151 (2): 221–24.

Kung, Justin, Ram Miller, and Philip A. Mackowiak. 2012. "Failure of Clinical Practice Guidelines to Meet Institute of Medicine Standards: Two More Decades of Little, If Any, Progress." *Archives of Internal Medicine* 172 (21): 1628–33.

Kuriyama, Shigehisa. 1999. *The Expressiveness of the Body and the Divergence of Greek and Chinese Medicine.* New York: Zone Books.

Lakos, A., and N. Solymosi. 2010. "Maternal Lyme Borreliosis and Pregnancy Outcome." *International Journal of Infectious Diseases* 14 (6): e494–98.

Lamas, Gervasio A., C. Goertz, R. Boineau, et al. 2013. "Effect of Disodium EDTA Chelation Regimen on Cardiovascular Events in Patients with Previous Myocardial Infarction: The TACT Randomized Trial." *Journal of the American Medical Association* 309 (12): 1241–50.

Lambert, Helen. 2006. "Accounting for EBM: Notions of Evidence in Medicine." *Social Science and Medicine* 62 (11): 2633–45.

Lambert, Helen. 2009. "Evidentiary Truths? The Evidence of Anthropology through the Anthropology of Medical Evidence." *Anthropology Today* 25 (1): 16–20.

Lampland, Martha, and Sarah Leigh Star, eds. 2009. *Standards and Their Stories: How Quantifying, Classifying, and Formalizing Practices Shape Everyday Life.* Ithaca, NY: Cornell University Press.

Lana-Peixoto, M. A. 1994. "Multiple Sclerosis and Positive Lyme Serology." *Arquivos de Neuro-Psiquiatria* 52 (4): 566–71.

Lander, Christian. 2008a. "#9 Making You Feel Bad about Not Going Outside." *Stuff White People Like* (blog), January 20, 2008. http://stuffwhitepeoplelike.com/2008 /01/20/9-making-you-feel-bad-about-not-going-outside/.

Lander, Christian. 2008b. *Stuff White People Like: A Definitive Guide to the Unique Taste of Millions.* New York: Random House.

Lander, Christian. 2010. *Whiter Shades of Pale: The Stuff White People Like, Coast to Coast, from Seattle's Sweaters to Maine's Microbrews.* New York: Random House.

Lantos, P. M. 2013. "Lyme Disease Vaccination: Are We Ready to Try Again?" *Lancet Infectious Diseases* 13 (8): 643–44.

Lantos, P. M., P. G. Auwaerter, and G. P. Wormser. 2014. "A Systematic Review of *Borrelia burgdorferi* Morphologic Variants Does Not Support a Role in Chronic Lyme Disease." *Clinical Infectious Diseases* 58 (5): 663–71.

Lantos, P. M., E. D. Shapiro, P. G. Auwaerter, et al. 2015. "Unorthodox Alternative Therapies Marketed to Treat Lyme Disease." *Clinical Infectious Disease* 60 (12): 1776–82.

Lash, Scott, Brian Wynne, and Bronislaw Szerszynski, eds. 1996. *Risk, Environment and Modernity: Towards a New Ecology.* London: Sage.

Latour, Bruno. 1987. *Science in Action: How to Follow Scientists and Engineers through Society.* Cambridge, MA: Harvard University Press.

Launer, J. 2009. "Medically Unexplored Stories." *Postgraduate Medical Journal* (85): 503–4.

Lawrence, C., R. B. Lipton, F. D. Lowy, et al. 1995. "Seronegative Chronic Relapsing Neuroborreliosis." *European Neurology* 35 (2): 113–17.

Leavitt, John. 1996. "Meaning and Feeling in the Anthropology of Emotions." *American Ethnologist* 23 (3): 514–39.

Lee, D. H., and O. Vielemeyer. 2011. "Analysis of Overall Level of Evidence behind Infectious Diseases Society of America Practice Guidelines." *Archives of Internal Medicine* 171 (1): 18–22.

Leland, Dorothy Kupcha. 2017. "CDC Website Removes Link to IDSA Guidelines: Just Lipstick on a Pig?" *Touched by Lyme*, LymeDisease.org, December 2, 2017. https://www.lymedisease.org/touchedbylyme-cdc-lipstick-on-pig/.

Lengl-Janssen, B., A. F. Strauss, A. C. Steere, et al. 1994. "The T Helper Cell Response in Lyme Arthritis: Differential Recognition of *Borrelia burgdorferi* Outer Surface Protein A in Patients with Treatment-Resistant or Treatment-Responsive Lyme Arthritis." *Journal of Experimental Medicine* 180 (6): 2069–78.

Leon, D. A., G. Walt, and L. Gilson. 2001. "Recent Advances: International Perspectives on Health Inequalities and Policy." *British Medical Journal* 322 (7286): 591–94.

Lettau, Ludwig A. 1991. "From the Centers for Fatigue Control (CFC) Weekly Report: Epidemiologic Notes and Reports." *Annals of Internal Medicine* 114 (7): 602.

Levy, Robert. 1973. *Tahitians: Mind and Experience in the Society Islands*. Chicago: University of Chicago Press.

Li, X., G. A. McHugh, N. Damle, et al. 2011. "Burden and Viability of *Borrelia burgdorferi* in Skin and Joints of Patients with Erythema Migrans or Lyme Arthritis." *Arthritis and Rheumatism* 63 (8): 2238–47.

Liegner, K. B., J. R. Shapiro, D. Ramsay, et al. 1993. "Recurrent Erythema Migrans despite Extended Antibiotic Treatment with Minocycline in a Patient with Persisting *Borrelia burgdorferi* Infection." *Journal of the American Academy of Dermatology* 28 (part 2): 312–14.

Lin, T., J. H. Oliver Jr., and L. Gao. 2002. "Genetic Diversity of the Outer Surface Protein C Gene of Southern *Borrelia* Isolates and Its Possible Epidemiological, Clinical, and Pathogenetic Implications." *Journal of Clinical Microbiology* 40 (7): 2572–83.

Lin, T., J. H. Oliver Jr., L. Gao, et al. 2001. "Genetic Heterogeneity of *Borrelia burgdorferi* Sensu Lato in the Southern United States Based on Restriction Fragment Length Polymorphism and Sequence Analysis." *Journal of Clinical Microbiology* 39 (7): 2500–2507.

Lipshutz, B. 1913. "Über Eine Seltene Erythemform (Erythema Chronicum Migrans) [Concerning a Rare Form of Erythema (Erythema Chronicum Migrans)]." *Archives Dermatologica Syphilogia* 118:349–56.

Livengood, J. A., and R. D. Gilmore Jr. 2006. "Invasion of Human Neuronal and Glial Cells by an Infectious Strain of *Borrelia burgdorferi*." *Microbes and Infection* 8 (14–15): 2832–40.

Lock, Margaret M. 1986. "Plea for Acceptance: School Refusal Syndrome in Japan." *Social Science and Medicine* 23:99–112.

Lock, Margaret M. 1993a. "Cultivating the Body: Anthropology and Epistemologies of Bodily Practice and Knowledge." *Annual Review of Anthropology* 22:133–55.

Lock, Margaret M. 1993b. *Encounters with Aging: Mythologies of Menopause in Japan and North America*. Berkeley: University of California Press.

Lock, Margaret M. 2002. *Twice Dead: Organ Transplants and the Reinvention of Death*. Berkeley: University of California Press.

Lock, Margaret M., and Judith Farquhar, eds. 2007. *Beyond the Body Proper: Reading the Anthropology of Material Life*. Durham, NC: Duke University Press.

Lock, Margaret M., and Deborah Gordon, eds. 1988. *Biomedicine Examined*. Dordrecht: Kluwer Academic.

Lock, Margaret M., and Vinh-Kim Nguyen. 2010. *An Anthropology of Biomedicine*. Chichester, West Sussex: Wiley-Blackwell.

Loftus, John. 1982. *The Belarus Secret*. New York: Knopf.

Loftus, John. 2010. *America's Nazi Secret*. Walterville, OR: TrineDay.

Lomholt, H., A. M. Lebech, K. Hansen, et al. 2000. "Long-Term Serological Follow-Up of Patients Treated for Chronic Cutaneous Borreliosis or Culture-Positive Erythema Migrans." *Acta-Dermato Venereologica* 80 (5): 362–66.

Londoño, D., D. Cadavid, E. E. Drouin, et al. 2014. "Antibodies to Endothelial Cell Growth Factor and Obliterative Microvascular Lesions in the Synovium of Patients with Antibiotic-Refractory Lyme Arthritis." *Arthritis and Rheumatology* 66 (8): 2124–33.

Lorber, Judith, and Lisa Jean Moore. 2002. *Gender and the Social Construction of Illness.* Lanham, MD: AltaMira Press.

Louv, Richard. 2005. *Last Child in the Woods: Saving Our Children from Nature-Deficit Disorder.* Chapel Hill, NC: Algonquin Books of Chapel Hill.

Lowy, Ilana. 2000. "Trustworthy Knowledge and Desperate Patients: Clinical Tests for New Drugs from Cancer to AIDS." In *Living and Working with the New Medical Technologies: Intersections of Inquiry,* edited by Margaret M. Lock, Allan Young, and Alberto Cambrosio, 49–81. Cambridge: Cambridge University Press.

Lucey, D., M. J. Dolan, C. Moss, et al. 1992. "Relapsing Illness Due to *Rochalimaea henselae* in Immunocompetent Hosts: Implication for Therapy and New Epidemiological Associations." *Clinical Infectious Diseases* 14 (3): 683–88.

Luft, B. J., J. J. Halperin, D. J. Volkman, et al. 1989. "Ceftriaxone—An Effective Treatment of Late Lyme Borreliosis." *Journal of Chemotherapy* 1 (S4): 917–19.

Luger, S. W. 1990a. "Lyme Disease Transmitted by a Biting Fly." *New England Journal of Medicine* 322 (24): 1752.

Luger, S. W. 1990b. "Serologic Findings in Lyme Disease." *Annals of Emergency Medicine* 19 (11): 1353–54.

Luger, S. W., P. Paparone, G. P. Wormser, et al. 1995. "Comparison of Cefuroxime Axetil and Doxycycline in Treatment of Patients with Early Lyme Disease Associated with Erythema Migrans." *Antimicrobial Agents and Chemotherapy* 39 (3): 661–67.

Lupton, Deborah. 1994. *Medicine as Culture: Illness, Disease and the Body in Western Societies.* London: Sage.

Lupton, Deborah. 1999. *Risk.* London: Routledge.

Lutz, Catherine, and Geoffrey M. White. 1986. "The Anthropology of Emotions." *Annual Review of Anthropology* 15:405–36.

Ma, B., B. Christen, D. Leung, et al. 1992. "Serodiagnosis of Lyme Borreliosis by Western Immunoblot: Reactivity of Various Significant Antibodies against *Borrelia burgdorferi.*" *Journal of Clinical Microbiology* 30 (2): 370–76.

Ma, Y., A. Sturrock, and J. J. Weis. 1991. "Intracellular Localization of *Borrelia burgdorferi* within Human Endothelial Cells." *Infection and Immunity* 59 (2): 671–78.

MacDonald, A. B. 1986a. "Borrelia in the Brains of Patients Dying with Dementia." *Journal of the American Medical Association* 256 (16): 2195–96.

MacDonald, A. B. 1986b. "Human Fetal Borreliosis, Toxemia of Pregnancy, and Fetal Death." *Zentralblatt für Bakteriologie, Mikrobiologie, und Hygiene* 263 (1–2): 189–200.

MacDonald, A. B. 2006a. "Plaques of Alzheimer's Disease Originate from Cysts of Borrelia burgdorferi, the Lyme Disease Spirochete." *Medical Hypotheses* 67 (3): 592–600.

MacDonald, A. B. 2006b. "Transfection 'Junk' DNA—A Link to the Pathogenesis of Alzheimer's Disease?" *Medical Hypotheses* 66 (6): 1140–41.

MacDonald, A. B. 2007a. "Alzheimer's Disease Braak Stage Progressions: Reexamined and Redefined as *Borrelia* Infection Transmission through Neural Circuits." *Medical Hypotheses* 68 (5): 1059–64.

MacDonald, A. B. 2007b. "Alzheimer's Neuroborreliosis with Trans-Synaptic Spread of Infection and Neurofibrillary Tangles Derived from Intraneuronal Spirochetes." *Medical Hypotheses* 68 (4): 822–25.

MacDonald, A. B., J. L. Benach, and W. Burgdorfer. 1987. "Stillbirth Following Maternal Lyme Disease." *New York State Journal of Medicine* 87 (11): 615–16.

MacKendrick, Nora. 2010. "Media Framing of Body Burdens: Precautionary Consumption and the Individualization of Risk." *Sociological Inquiry* 80 (1): 126–49.

MacKenzie, D., and G. Spinardi. 1995. "Tacit Knowledge, Weapons Design, and the Uninvention of Nuclear Weapons." *American Journal of Sociology* 101:44–99.

Magnarelli, L. A., and J. F. Anderson. 1987. "Early Detection and Persistence of Antibodies to *Borrelia burgdorferi* in Persons with Lyme Disease." *Zentralblatt für Bakteriologie, Mikrobiologie, und Hygiene* 263 (3): 392–99.

Magnarelli, L. A., and J. F. Anderson. 1988. "Ticks and Biting Insects Infected with the Etiologic Agent of Lyme Disease, *Borrelia burgdorferi*." *Journal of Clinical Microbiology* 26 (8): 1482–86.

Magnarelli, L. A., J. F. Anderson, and A. G. Barbour. 1986. "The Etiologic Agent of Lyme Disease in Deer Flies, Horse Flies, and Mosquitoes." *Journal of Infectious Diseases* 154 (2): 355–58.

Magnarelli, L. A., J. F. Anderson, and K. C. Stafford 3rd. 1994. "Detection of *Borrelia burgdorferi* in Urine of *Peromyscus leucopus* by Inhibition Enzyme-Linked Immunosorbent Assay." *Journal of Clinical Microbiology* 32 (3): 777–82.

Magnarelli, L. A., J. E. Freier, and J. F. Anderson. 1987. "Experimental Infections of Mosquitoes with *Borrelia burgdorferi*, the Etiologic Agent of Lyme Disease." *Journal of Infectious Diseases* 156 (4): 694–5.

Mahmood, Saba. 2005. *Politics of Piety: The Islamic Revival and the Feminist Subject.* Princeton, NJ: Princeton University Press.

Makhani, N., S. K. Morris, A. V. Page, et al. 2010. "A Twist on Lyme: The Challenge of Diagnosing European Lyme Neuroborreliosis." *Journal of Clinical Microbiology* 49 (1): 455–57.

Malawista, S. E., S. W. Barthold, and D. H. Persing. 1994. "Fate of *Borrelia burgdorferi* DNA in Tissues of Infected Mice after Antibiotic Treatment." *Journal of Infectious Diseases* 170 (5): 1312–16.

Manderson, Lenore, and Carolyn Smith-Morris. 2010. *Chronic Conditions, Fluid States: Chronicity and the Anthropology of Illness.* New Brunswick, NJ: Rutgers University Press.

Mani, A., S. Mullainathan, E. Shafir, et al. 2013. "Poverty Impedes Cognitive Function." *Science* 341 (6149): 976–80.

Manjoo, Farhad. 2008. *True Enough: Learning to Live in a Post-Fact Society*. Hoboken, NJ: John Wiley and Sons.

Maraspin, V., J. Cimperman, S. Lotric-Furlan, et al. 1996. "Treatment of Erythema Migrans in Pregnancy." *Clinical Infectious Diseases* 22 (5): 788–93.

Maraspin, V., J. Cimperman, S. Lotric-Furlan, et al. 1999. "Erythema Migrans in Pregnancy." *Wiener Klinische Wochenschrift* 111 (22–23): 933–40.

Maraspin, V., E. Ružić-Sabljić, D. Pleterski-Rigler, et al. 2011. "Pregnant Women with Erythema Migrans and Isolation of *Borreliae* from Blood: Course and Outcome after Treatment with Ceftriaxone." *Diagnostic Microbiology and Infectious Disease* 71 (4): 446–48.

Margos, G., A. G. Gatewood, D. M. Aanensen, et al. 2008. "MLST of Housekeeping Genes Captures Geographic Population Structure and Suggests a European Origin of *Borrelia burgdorferi*." *Proceedings of the National Academy of Sciences of the United States of America* 105 (25): 8730–35.

Margos, G., S. A. Vollmer, N. H. Ogden, et al. 2011. "Population Genetics, Taxonomy, Phylogeny and Evolution of *Borrelia burgdorferi* Sensu Lato." *Infection, Genetics, and Evolution* 11 (7): 1545–63.

Markowitz, L. E., A. C. Steere, J. L. Benach, et al. 1986. "Lyme Disease during Pregnancy." *Journal of the American Medical Association* 255 (24): 3394–96.

Marques, A. 2018. "Revisiting the Lyme Disease Serodiagnostic Algorithm: The Momentum Gathers." *Journal of Clinical Microbiology* 56 (8): e00749-18.

Marques, A., M. R. Brown, and T. A. Fleisher. 2009. "Natural Killer Cell Counts Are Not Different between Patients with Post-Lyme Disease Syndrome and Controls." *Clinical and Vaccine Immunology* 16 (8): 1249–50.

Marques, A., F. Stock, and V. Gill. 2000. "Evaluation of a New Culture Medium for *Borrelia burgdorferi*." *Journal of Clinical Microbiology* 38 (11): 4239–41.

Marques, A., S. R. Telford 3rd, S. P. Turk, et al. 2014. "Xenodiagnosis to Detect *Borrelia burgdorferi* Infection: A First-in-Human Study." *Clinical Infectious Diseases* 58 (7): 937–45.

Marques, A., S. C. Weir, G. A. Fahle, et al. 2000. "Lack of Evidence of *Borrelia* Involvement in Alzheimer's Disease." *Journal of Infectious Disease* 182 (3): 1006–7.

Martin, Brian. 2007. *Justice Ignited: The Dynamics of Backfire*. Lanham, MD: Rowman and Littlefield.

Martin, Emily. 1990. "Toward an Anthropology of Immunology: The Body as Nation State." *Medical Anthropology Quarterly* 4 (4): 410–26.

Martin, Emily. 1994. *Flexible Bodies: Tracking Immunity in American Culture from the Days of Polio to the Age of AIDS*. Boston: Beacon.

Martin, R., J. Ortlauf, V. Sticht-Groh, et al. 1988. "*Borrelia burgdorferi*—Specific and Autoreactive T-Cell Lines from Cerebrospinal Fluid in Lyme Radiculomyelitis." *Annals of Neurology* 24 (4): 509–16.

Massumi, Brian. 1995. "The Autonomy of Affect." *Cultural Critique* 31:83–109.

Mast, W. E., and W. M. Burrows Jr. 1976. "Erythema Chronicum Migrans in the United States." *Journal of the American Medical Association* 236 (7): 859–60.

Masters, E. J., and H. D. Donnell. 1995. "Lyme and/or Lyme-like Disease in Missouri." *Missouri Medicine Journal* 92 (7): 346–53.

Masters, E. J., and H. D. Donnell. 1996. "Epidemiologic and Diagnostic Studies of Patients with Suspected Early Lyme Disease, Missouri, 1990–1993." *Journal of Infectious Disease* 173 (6): 1527–28.

Masters, E. J., C. N. Grigery, and R. W. Masters. 2008. "STARI, or Masters Disease: Lone Star Tick–Vectored Lyme-Like Illness." *Infectious Disease Clinics of North America* 22 (2): 361–76.

Mather, T. N., M. C. Nicholson, E. F. Donnelly, et al. 1996. "Entomologic Index for Human Risk of Lyme Disease." *American Journal of Epidemiology* 144 (11): 1066–69.

Mather, T. N., S. R. Telford 3rd, and G. H. Adler. 1991. "Absence of Transplacental Transmission of Lyme Disease Spirochetes from Reservoir Mice (*Peromyscus leucopus*) to Their Offspring." *Journal of Infectious Disease* 164 (3): 564–67.

Mathiesen, D. A., J. H. Oliver Jr., C. P. Kolbert, et al. 1997. "Genetic Heterogeneity of *Borrelia burgdorferi* in the United States." *Journal of Infectious Disease* 175 (1): 98–107.

Mattingly, Cheryl, and Linda C. Garro, eds. 2000. *Narrative and the Cultural Construction of Illness and Healing*. Berkeley: University of California Press.

Mattsson, N., D. Bremell, R. Anckarsäter, et al. 2010. "Neuroinflammation in Lyme Neuroborreliosis Affects Amyloid Metabolism." *BioMedCentral Neurology* 10:51.

Matuschka, F. R., and D. Richter. 2002. "Mosquitoes and Soft Ticks Cannot Transmit Lyme Disease Spirochetes." *Parasitology Research* 88 (4): 283–84.

Mayne, P. J. 2011. "Emerging Incidence of Lyme Borreliosis, Babesiosis, Bartonellosis, and Granulocytic Ehrlichiosis in Australia." *International Journal of General Medicine* 4:845–52.

Mayne, P. J. 2012. "Investigations of *Borrelia burgdorferi* Genotypes Obtained from Erythema Migrans Tissues." *Clinical, Cosmetic, and Investigative Dermatology* 5:69–78.

McCrossin, I. 1986. "Lyme Disease on the NSW South Coast." *Medical Journal of Australia* 144 (13): 724–25.

McGuire, Meredith B. 1988. *Ritual Healing in Suburban America*. New Brunswick, NJ: Rutgers University Press.

McSweegan, E. 2007. "The Lyme Vaccine: A Cautionary Tale." *Epidemiology and Infection* 135 (1): 9–10.

Mead, Paul, Jeannine Petersen, and Alison Hinckley. 2019. "Updated CDC Recommendation for Serologic Diagnosis of Lyme Disease." *MMWR* 68 (32): 703. https:// www.cdc.gov/mmwr/volumes/68/wr/mm6832a4.htm?s_cid=mm6832a4_w.

Meer, J., D. L. Miller, and H. S. Rosen. 2003. "Exploring the Health-Wealth Nexus." *Journal of Health Economics* 22 (5): 713–30.

Meer-Scherrer, L., C. Chang Loa, M. E. Adelson, et al. 2006. "Lyme Disease Associated with Alzheimer's Disease." *Current Microbiology* 52 (4): 330–32.

Merchant, Carolyn. 2004. *Reinventing Eden: The Fate of Nature in Western Culture*. New York: Routledge.

Meriläinen, L., H. Brander, A. Herranen, et al. 2016. "Pleomorphic Forms of *Borrelia burgdorferi* Induce Distinct Immune Responses." *Microbes and Infection* 18 (7–8): 484–95.

Metzl, Jonathan M., and Anna Kirkland, eds. 2010. *Against Health: How Health Became the New Morality*. New York: New York University Press.

Micozzi, Marc. 2001. *Fundamentals of Complementary and Alternative Medicine*. New York: Churchill Livingstone.

Middelveen, M. J., C. Bandoski, J. Burke, et al. 2014. "Isolation and Detection of *Borrelia burgdorferi* from Human Vaginal and Seminal Secretions." *Journal of Investigative Medicine* 62 (1): 280–81.

Middelveen, M. J., E. Sapi, J. Burke, et al. 2018. "Persistent *Borrelia* Infection in Patients with Ongoing Symptoms of Lyme Disease." *Healthcare* 6 (2): 33.

Miklossy, J. 1993. "Alzheimer's Disease—A Spirochetosis?" *Neuroreport* 4 (7): 841–48.

Miklossy, J. 2008. "Chronic Inflammation and Amyloidogenesis in Alzheimer's Disease—Role of Spirochetes." *Journal of Alzheimer's Disease* 13 (4): 381–91.

Miklossy, J. 2011a. "Alzheimer's Disease—A Neurospirochetosis: Analysis of the Evidence Following Koch's and Hill's Criteria." *Journal of Neuroinflammation* 8:90.

Miklossy, J. 2011b. "Emerging Roles of Pathogens in Alzheimer Disease." *Expert Reviews in Molecular Medicine* 13:e30.

Miklossy, J., S. Kasas, A. D. Zurn, et al. 2008. "Persisting Atypical and Cystic Forms of *Borrelia burgdorferi* and Local Inflammation in Lyme Neuroborreliosis." *Journal of Neuroinflammation* 5 (40): 1–18.

Miklossy, J., K. Khalili, L. Gern, et al. 2004. "*Borrelia burgdorferi* Persists in the Brain in Chronic Lyme Neuroborreliosis and May Be Associated with Alzheimer Disease." *Journal of Alzheimer's Disease* 6 (6): 639–49; discussion, 673–81.

Miklossy, J., A. Kis, A. Radenovic, et al. 2006. "Beta-Amyloid Deposition and Alzheimer's Type Changes Induced by *Borrelia* Spirochetes." *Neurobiology of Aging* 27 (2): 228–36.

Mitman, Gregg, Michelle Murphy, and Christopher C. Sellers, eds. 2004. *Landscapes of Exposure: Knowledge and Illness in Modern Environments*. Washington, DC: Georgetown University Press.

Mohai, P., D. Pellow, and J. T. Roberts. 2009. "Environmental Justice." *Annual Review of Environment and Resources* 34:405–30.

Mohr, James C. 1993. *Doctors and the Law: Medical Jurisprudence in Nineteenth-Century America*. Baltimore, MD: Johns Hopkins University Press.

Mol, Annemarie. 2002. *The Body Multiple: Ontology in Medical Practice*. Durham, NC: Duke University Press.

Molins, C. R., M. J. Delorey, A. Replogle, et al. 2017. "Evaluation of BioMérieux's Dissociated Vidas Lyme IgM II and IgG II as a First-Tier Diagnostic Assay for Lyme Disease." *Journal of Clinical Microbiology* 55 (6): 1698–1706.

Moniuszko, A., P. Czupryna, J. Zajkowska, et al. 2009. "Post Lyme Syndrome as a Clinical Problem." *Polski Merkuriusz Lekarski* 26 (153): 227–30.

Moody, K. D., and S. W. Barthold. 1991. "Relative Infectivity of *Borrelia burgdorferi* in Lewis Rats by Various Routes of Inoculation." *American Journal of Tropical Medicine and Hygiene* 44 (2): 135–39.

Moore, A., C. Nelson, C. Mollins, P. Mead, and M. Schriefer. 2016. "Current Guidelines, Common Clinical Pitfalls, and Future Directions for Laboratory Diagnosis of Lyme Disease, United States." *Emerging Infectious Diseases* 22 (7): 1169–77.

Morgan, B. W., S. Kori, and J. D. Thomas. 2002. "Adverse Effects in 5 Patients Receiving EDTA at an Outpatient Chelation Clinic." *Veterinary and Human Toxicology* 44 (5): 274–76.

Morgen, K., R. Martin, R. D. Stone, et al. 2001. "FLAIR and Magnetization Transfer Imaging of Patients with Post-Treatment Lyme Disease Syndrome." *Neurology* 57 (11): 1980–85.

Morozova, O. V., N. A. Chernousova, and I. V. Morozov. 2005. "Detection of the *Bartonella* DNA by the Method of Nested PCR in Patients after Tick Bites in Novosibirsk Region." *Molekuliarnaia Genetika, Mikrobiologiia I Virusologiia*, no. 4, 14–17.

Moss, Pamela, and Isabel Dyck. 2002. *Women, Body, Illness: Space and Identity in the Everyday Lives of Women with Chronic Illness.* Lanham, MD: Rowman and Littlefield.

Moss, Pamela, and Katherine Teghtsoonian, eds. 2008. *Contesting Illness: Processes and Practices.* Toronto: University of Toronto Press.

Mouritsen, C. L., C. T. Wittwer, C. M. Litwin, et al. 1996. "Polymerase Chain Reaction Detection of Lyme Disease: Correlation with Clinical Manifestations and Serologic Responses." *American Journal of Clinical Pathology* 105 (5): 647–54.

Moyce, Sally C., and Marc Schenker. 2018. "Migrant Workers and Their Occupational Health and Safety." *Annual Review of Public Health* 39:351–65.

Murphy, Michelle. 2006. *Sick Building Syndrome and the Problem of Uncertainty: Environmental Politics, Technoscience, and Women Workers.* Durham, NC: Duke University Press.

Murphy, Tim. 2012. "Romney's Plan to Win Virginia: Lyme Disease." *Mother Jones*, September 28, 2012. https://www.motherjones.com/politics/2012/09/romneys-plan-win-virginia-lyme-disease/.

Murray, Polly. 1996. *The Widening Circle: A Lyme Disease Pioneer Tells Her Story.* New York: St. Martin's.

Myers, Natasha. 2015. *Rendering Life Molecular: Models, Modelers, and Excitable Matter.* Durham, NC: Duke University Press.

Mykhalovskiy, Eric. 2003. "Evidence-Based Medicine: Ambivalent Reading and the Clinical Recontextualization of Science." *Health: An International Journal for the Social Study of Health, Illness, and Medicine* 7 (3): 331–52.

Mykhalovskiy, Eric, and Lorna Weir. 2004. "The Problem of Evidence-Based Medicine: Directions for Social Science." *Social Science and Medicine* 59 (5): 1059–69.

Nadal, D., U. A. Hunziker, H. U. Bucher, et al. 1989. "Infants Born to Mothers with Antibodies against *Borrelia burgdorferi* at Delivery." *European Journal of Pediatrics* 148 (5): 426–27.

Nadav, D., and F. Dani. 2006. "Reconstructing Data: Evidence-Based Medicine and Evidence-Based Public Health in Context." *Dynamis* 26:287–306.

Nadelman, R. B., K. Hanincová, P. Mukherjee, et al. 2012. "Differentiation of Reinfection from Relapse in Recurrent Lyme Disease." *New England Journal of Medicine* 367 (20): 1883–90.

Nadelman, R. B., S. W. Luger, E. Frank, et al. 1992. "Comparison of Cefuroxime Axetil and Doxycycline in the Treatment of Early Lyme Disease." *Annals of Internal Medicine* 117 (4): 273–80.

Nadelman, R. B., J. Nowakowski, D. Fish, et al. 2001. "Prophylaxis with Single-Dose Doxycycline for the Prevention of Lyme Disease after an *Ixodes scapularis* Tick Bite." *New England Journal of Medicine* 345 (2): 79–84.

Nadelman, R. B., J. Nowakowski, G. Forseter, et al. 1993. "Failure to Isolate *Borrelia burgdorferi* after Antimicrobial Therapy in Culture-Documented Lyme Borreliosis Associated with Erythema Migrans: Report of a Prospective Study." *American Journal of Medicine* 94 (6): 583–88.

Nadesan, Majia Holmer. 2008. *Governmentality, Biopower, and Everyday Life*. New York: Routledge.

Nahin, R. L., P. M. Barnes, B. J. Stussman, et al. 2009. "Costs of Complementary and Alternative Medicine (CAM) and Frequency of Visits to CAM Practitioners: United States, 2007." *National Health Statistics Reports* 18:1–14.

Nash, Roderick. (1967) 2001. *Wilderness and the American Mind*. New Haven, CT: Yale University Press.

Nester, Eugene W., Denise G. Anderson, C. Evans Roberts, and Martha T. Nester. 2012. *Microbiology: A Human Perspective*. New York: McGraw-Hill.

Nettleton, S. 2006. "'I Just Want Permission to Be Ill': Towards a Sociology of Medically Unexplained Symptoms." *Social Science and Medicine* 62 (5): 1167–78.

Nettleton, S., L. O'Malley, I. Watt, and P. Duffey. 2004. "Enigmatic Illness: Narratives of Patients Who Live with Medically Unexplained Symptoms." *Social Theory and Health* 2 (1): 47–66.

Neumann, A., M. Schlesier, H. Schneider, et al. 1989. "Frequencies of *Borrelia burgdorferi*–Reactive T Lymphocytes in Lyme Arthritis." *Rheumatology International* 9 (3–5): 237–41.

Newby, Kris. 2019. *Bitten: The Secret History of Lyme Disease and Biological Weapons*. New York: Harper Collins.

Nguyen, Vinh-Kim, and Karine Peschard. 2003. "Anthropology, Inequality, and Disease: A Review." *Annual Review of Anthropology* 32:447–74.

Nichter, Mark. 1998. "The Mission within the Madness: Self-Initiated Medicalization as Expression of Agency." In *Pragmatic Women and Body Politics*, edited by Margaret Lock and Patricia A. Kaufert, 327–53. Cambridge: Cambridge University Press.

Nichter, Mark. 2013. "The Rise and Transformation of Evidence-Based Medicine." *American Anthropologist* 115 (4): 647–49.

Nigrovic, L. E., and K. M. Thompson. 2007. "The Lyme Vaccine: A Cautionary Tale." *Epidemiology and Infection* 135 (1): 1–8.

Nimnuan, C., M. Hotopf, and S. Wessely. 2001. "Medically Unexplained Symptoms: An Epidemiological Study in Seven Specialties." *Journal of Psychosomatic Research* 51 (1): 361–67.

Nissen, Nina. 2011. "Challenging Perspectives: Women, Complementary and Alternative Medicine, and Social Change." *Interface: A Journal for and about Social Movements* 3:187–212.

Nissen, Nina. 2012. "Women's Bodies and Women's Lives in Western Herbal Medicine in the UK." *Medical Anthropology* 32 (1): 75–91.

Nissen, Nina, and Lenore Manderson. 2013. "Researching Alternative and Complementary Therapies: Mapping the Field." *Medical Anthropology* 32 (1): 1–7.

Norman, G. L., J. M. Antig, G. Bigaignon, and W. R. Hogrefe. 1996. "Serodiagnosis of Lyme Borreliosis by *Borrelia burgdorferi* Sensu Stricto, *B. garinii*, and *B. afzelii* Western Blots (Immunoblots)." *Journal of Clinical Microbiology* 34 (7): 1732–38.

Nowakowski, J., R. B. Nadelman, R. Sell, et al. 2003. "Long-Term Follow-Up of Patients with Culture-Confirmed Lyme Disease." *American Journal of Medicine* 115 (2): 91–96.

Nowakowski, J., I. Schwartz, D. Liveris, et al. 2001. "Laboratory Diagnostic Techniques for Patients with Early Lyme Disease Associated with Erythema Migrans: A Comparison of Different Techniques." *Clinical Infectious Disease* 33 (12): 2023–27.

O'Day, D. H., and A. Catalano. 2014. "A Lack of Correlation between the Incidence of Lyme Disease and Deaths Due to Alzheimer's Disease." *Journal of Alzheimer's Disease* 42:115–18.

Okada, H., C. Kuhn, H. Feillet, and J. F. Bach. 2010. "The 'Hygiene Hypothesis' for Autoimmune and Allergic Diseases: An Update." *Clinical and Experimental Immunology* 160 (1): 1–9.

Oksi, J., J. Nikoskelainen, H. Hiekkanen, et al. 2007. "Duration of Antibiotic Treatment in Disseminated Lyme Borreliosis: A Double-Blind, Randomized, Placebo-Controlled, Multicenter Clinical Study." *European Journal of Clinical Microbiology and Infectious Disease* 26 (8): 571–81.

Oksi, J., J. Uksila, M. Marjamäki, et al. 1995. "Antibodies against Whole Sonicated *Borrelia burgdorferi* Spirochetes, 41-Kilodalton Flagellin, and P39 Protein in Patients with PCR- or Culture-Proven Late Lyme Borreliosis." *Journal of Clinical Microbiology* 33 (9): 2260–64.

Oksi, J., J. Uksila, M. Marjamäki, et al. 1999. "*Borrelia burgdorferi* Detected by Culture and PCR in Clinical Relapse of Disseminated Lyme Borreliosis." *Annals of Medicine* 31 (3): 225–32.

Oliver, J. H., Jr. 1996. "Lyme Borreliosis in the Southern United States: A Review." *Journal of Parasitology* 82 (6): 926–35.

Oliver, J. H., Jr., F. W. Chandler Jr., A. M. James, et al. 1996. "Unusual Strain of *Borrelia burgdorferi* Isolated from *Ixodes dentatus* in Central Georgia." *Journal of Parasitology* 82 (6): 936–40.

Oliver, J. H., Jr., F. W. Chandler Jr., M. P. Luttrell, et al. 1993. "Isolation and Transmission of the Lyme Disease Spirochete from the Southeastern United States." *Proceedings of National Academy of Sciences of the United States of America* 90 (15): 7371–75.

Oliver, J. H., Jr., K. L. Clark, F. W. Chandler Jr., et al. 2000. "Isolation, Cultivation, and Characterization of *Borrelia burgdorferi* from Rodents and Ticks in the Charleston Area of South Carolina." *Journal of Clinical Microbiology* 38 (1): 120–24.

Oliver, J. H., Jr., T. M. Kollars Jr., F. W. Chandler Jr., et al. 1998. "First Isolation and Cultivation of *Borrelia burgdorferi* Sensu Lato from Missouri." *Journal of Clinical Microbiology* 36 (1): 1–5.

Oliver, J. H., Jr., T. Lin, L. Gao, et al. 2003. "An Enzootic Transmission Cycle of Lyme Borreliosis Spirochetes in the Southeastern United States." *Proceedings of the National Academy of Sciences of the United States of America* 100 (20): 11642–45.

Oliver, J. H., Jr., M. R. Owsley, H. J. Hutcheson, et al. 1993. "Conspecificity of the Ticks Ixodes scapularis and I. dammini (Acari: Ixodidae)." *Journal Medical Entomology* 30 (1): 54–63.

Ong, Aihwa. 2006. *Neoliberalism as Exception: Mutations in Citizenship and Sovereignty*. Durham, NC: Duke University Press.

Orsini, Michael. 2008. "Hepatitis C and the Dawn of Biological Citizenship: Unravelling the Policy Implications." In *Contesting Illness: Processes and Practices*, edited by Pamela Moss and Katherine Teghtsoonian, 107–22. Toronto: University of Toronto Press.

Ostenfeld-Rosenthal, Ann M. 2012. "Energy Healing and the Placebo Effect: An Anthropological Perspective on the Placebo Effect." *Anthropology and Medicine* 19 (3): 327–38.

Pachner, A. R. 1989. "Neurologic Manifestations of Lyme Disease, the New 'Great Imitator.'" *Review of Infectious Diseases* 11 (suppl 6): S1482–86.

Pachner, A. R., A. C. Steere, L. H. Sigal, et al. 1985. "Antigen-Specific Proliferation of CSF Lymphocytes in Lyme Disease." *Neurology* 35 (11): 1642–44.

Palmieri, J. R., S. King, M. Case, and A. Santo. 2013. "Lyme Disease: Case Report of Persistent Lyme Disease from Pulaski County, Virginia." *International Medical Case Reports Journal* 6:99–105.

Panelius, J., I. Seppälä, H. Granlund, et al. 1999. "Evaluation of Treatment Responses in Late Lyme Borreliosis on the Basis of Antibody Decrease during the Follow-Up Period." *European Journal of Clinical Microbiology and Infectious Diseases* 18 (9): 621–29.

Pappolla, M. A., R. Omar, B. Saran, et al. 1989. "Concurrent Neuroborreliosis and Alzheimer's Disease: Analysis of the Evidence." *Human Pathology* 20 (8): 753–57.

Park, Lisa Sun-Hee, and David Naguib Pellow. 2011. *The Slums of Aspen: Immigrants vs. the Environment in America's Eden.* New York: New York University Press.

Parsons, Talcott. 1975. "The Sick Role and the Role of the Physician Reconsidered." *Milbank Memorial Fund Quarterly* 53 (3): 257–78.

Pegalaiar-Jurado, A., M. E. Schriefer, R. J. Welch, et al. 2018. "Evaluation of Modified Two-Tiered Testing Algorithms for Lyme Disease Laboratory Diagnosis Using Well-Characterized Serum Samples." *Journal of Clinical* 56 (8): e01943-17.

Pellow, David Naguib, and Robert J. Brulle, eds. 2005. *Power, Justice, and the Environment: A Critical Appraisal of the Environmental Justice Movement.* Cambridge, MA: MIT Press.

Pellow, David Naguib, and Lisa Sun-Hee Park. 2002. *The Silicon Valley of Dreams: Environmental Justice, Immigrant Workers, and the High-Tech Global Economy.* New York: New York University Press.

Perry, Wynne. 2012. "Iceman Mummy May Hold Earliest Evidence of Lyme Disease." *Live Science,* February 12, 2012. https://www.livescience.com/18704-oldest-case -lyme-disease-spotted-iceman-mummy.html.

Petersen, Alan R., and Deborah Lupton. 1996. *The New Public Health: Health and Self in the Age of Risk.* St. Leonards, NSW: Allen and Unwin.

Petryna, Adriana. 2002. *Life Exposed: Biological Citizens after Chernobyl.* Princeton, NJ: Princeton University Press.

Philipp, M. T., L. C. Bowers, P. T. Fawcett, et al. 2001. "Antibody Response to IR6, a Conserved Immunodominant Region of the VlsE Lipoprotein, Wanes Rapidly after Antibiotic Treatment of *Borrelia burgdorferi* Infection in Experimental Animals and in Humans." *Journal of Infectious Diseases* 184 (7): 870–78.

Philipp, M. T., A. R. Marques, P. T. Fawcett, et al. 2003. "C6 Test as an Indicator of Therapy Outcome for Patients with Localized or Disseminated Lyme Borreliosis." *Journal of Clinical Microbiology* 41 (11): 4955–60.

Philipp, M. T., G. P. Wormser, A. R. Marques, et al. 2005. "A Decline in C6 Antibody Titer Occurs in Successfully Treated Patients with Culture-Confirmed Early Localized or Early Disseminated Lyme Borreliosis." *Clinical and Diagnostic Laboratory Immunology* 12 (9): 1069–74.

Philippon, Daniel J. 2005. *Conserving Words: How American Nature Writers Shaped the Environmental Movement.* Athens: University of Georgia Press.

Phillips, S. E., L. H. Mattman, D. Hulinska, et al. 1998. "A Proposal for the Reliable Culture of *Borrelia burgdorferi* from Patients with Chronic Lyme Disease, Even from Those Previously Aggressively Treated." *Infection* 26 (6): 364–67.

Phillips, Tarryn. 2010. "Debating the Legitimacy of a Contested Environmental Illness: A Case Study of Multiple Chemical Sensitivities (MCS)." *Sociology of Health and Illness* 32 (7): 1026–40.

Piacentino, J., and B. Schwartz. 2002. "Occupational Risk of Lyme Disease: An Epidemiological Review." *Occupational and Environmental Medicine* 59 (20): 75–84.

Pícha, D., L. Moravcová, D. Holecková, et al. 2008. "Examination of Specific DNA by PCR in Patients with Different Forms of Lyme Borreliosis." *International Journal of Dermatology* 47 (10): 1004–10.

Pick, W., L. Rispel, and S. Naidoo. 2008. "Poverty, Health and Policy: A Historical Look at the South African Experience." *Journal of Public Health Policy* 29 (2): 165–78.

Pickering, Andrew. 1992. *Science as Practice and Culture*. Chicago: University of Chicago Press.

Pickett, K. E., and R. G. Wilkinson. 2015. "Income Inequality and Health: A Causal Review." *Social Science and Medicine* 128:316–26.

Piesman, J., K. L. Clark, M. C. Dolan, et al. 1999. "Geographic Survey of Vector Ticks (*Ixodes scapularis* and *Ixodes pacificus*) for Infection with the Lyme Disease Spirochete, *Borrelia burgdorferi*." *Journal of Vector Ecology* 24 (1): 91–98.

Piesman, J., and A. Hojgaard. 2012. "Protective Value of Prophylactic Antibiotic Treatment of Tick Bite for Lyme Disease Prevention: An Animal Model." *Ticks and Tick Borne Diseases* 3 (3): 193–96.

Piesman, J., T. N. Mather, R. J. Sinsky, et al. 1987. "Duration of Tick Attachment and *Borrelia burgdorferi* Transmission." *Journal of Clinical Microbiology* 25 (3): 557–58.

Piesman, J., and B. F. Stone. 1991. "Vector Competence of the Australian Paralysis Tick, *Ixodes holocyclus*, for the Lyme Disease Spirochete *Borrelia burgdorferi*." *International Journal of Parasitology* 21 (1): 109–11.

Pizzorno, Joseph E., Jr. 2008. "CAM Differentiated." *Medical Anthropology Quarterly* 16 (4): 405–7.

Plotkin, S. A. 2011. "Correcting a Public Health Fiasco: The Need for a New Vaccine against Lyme Disease." *Clinical Infectious Diseases* 52 (S3): S271–75.

Plotkin, S. A. 2016. "Need for a New Lyme Disease Vaccine." *New England Journal of Medicine* 375 (10): 911–13.

Plotkin, S. A., and G. P. Wormer, eds. 2016. "The Need for a New Lyme Disease Vaccine." *Clinical Infectious Diseases* 52 (3): 247–75.

Podsiadły, E., T. Chmielewski, and S. Tylewska-Wierzbanowska. 2003. "*Bartonella henselae* and *Borrelia burgdorferi* Infections of the Central Nervous System." *Annals of New York Academy of Science* 990:404–6.

Pohl-Koppe, A., E. L. Logigian, A. C. Steere, et al. 1999. "Cross-Reactivity of *Borrelia burgdorferi* and Myelin Basic Protein-Specific T Cells Is Not Observed in Borrelial Encephalomyelitis." *Cell Immunology* 194 (1): 118–23.

Poland, G. A. 2011. "Vaccines against Lyme Disease: What Happened and What Lessons Can We Learn?" *Clinical Infectious Diseases* 52 (S3): S253–58.

Polat, E., V. Turhan, M. Aslan, B. Müsellim, et al. 2010. "First Report of Three Culture Confirmed Human Lyme Cases in Turkey." *Mikrobiyoloji bülteni* 44 (1): 133–39.

Pope, Catherine. 2003. "Resisting Evidence: The Study of Evidence-Based Medicine as a Contemporary Social Movement." *Health: An Interdisciplinary Journal for the Social Study of Health, Illness and Medicine* 7 (3): 267–82.

Pothineni, V. R., D. Wagh, M. M. Babar, et al. 2016. "Identification of New Drug Candidates against Borrelia burgdorferi Using High-Throughput Screening." *Drug Design, Development, and Therapy* 10:1307–22.

Preac-Mursic, V., K. Weber, H. W. Pfister, et al. 1989. "Survival of Borrelia burgdorferi in Antibiotically Treated Patients with Lyme Borreliosis." *Infection* 17 (6): 355–59.

Priem, S., G. R. Burmester, T. Kamradt, et al. 1998. "Detection of Borrelia burgdorferi by Polymerase Chain Reaction in Synovial Membrane, but Not in Synovial Fluid from Patients with Persisting Lyme Arthritis after Antibiotic Therapy." *Annals of Rheumatic Diseases* 57 (2): 118–21.

Pringle, Rosemary. 1998. *Sex and Medicine: Gender, Power and Authority in the Medical Profession*. Cambridge: Cambridge University Press.

Pritt, B. S., P. S. Mead, D. K. H. Johnson, et al. 2016. "Identification of a Novel Pathogenic Borrelia Species Causing Lyme Borreliosis with Unusually High Spirochaetaemia: A Descriptive Study." *Lancet Infectious Diseases* 16 (5): 556–64.

Pulido, Laura. 2000. "Rethinking Environmental Racism: White Privilege and Urban Development in Southern California." *Annals of the Association of American Geographers* 90 (1): 12–40.

Qureshi, M., R. S. Bedlack, and M. E. Cudkowicz. 2009. "Lyme Disease Serology in Amyotrophic Lateral Sclerosis." *Muscle Nerve* 40 (4): 626–28.

Rabeharisoa, Vololona. 2013. "Evidence-Based Activism: Patients' Organisations, Users' and Activist's Groups in Knowledge Society." CSI Working Papers Series 033, Centre de Sociologie de l'Innovation (CSI), Mines ParisTech.

Rabinow, Paul. 1999. "Artificiality and Enlightenment: From Sociobiology to Biosociality." In *The Science Studies Reader*, edited by M. Biagioli, 407–16. New York: Routledge.

Rabinow, Paul, and Nikolas S. Rose. 2006. "Biopower Today." *Biosocieties* 1:195–217.

Raffalli, J., and G. P. Wormser. 2016. "Persistence of Babesiosis for >2 Years in a Patient on Rituximab for Rhematoid Arthritis." *Diagnostic Microbial and Infectious Diseases* 85 (2): 231–32.

Rajan, Kaushik Sunder. 2006. *Biocapital: The Constitution of Postgenomic Life*. Durham, NC: Duke University Press.

Rapp, Rayna. 1999. *Testing Women, Testing the Fetus: The Social Impact of Amniocentesis in America*. New York: Routledge.

Rappaport, Roy A. 1993. "Distinguished Lecture in General Anthropology: The Anthropology of Trouble." *American Anthropologist* 95 (2): 295–303.

Rebman, A. W., K. T. Bechtold, T. Yang, et al. 2017. "The Clinical, Symptom, and Quality-of-Life Characterization of a Well-Defined Group of Patients with Post-Treatment Lyme Disease Syndrome." *Frontiers in Medicine* 4:224.

Rebman, A. W., L. A. Crowder, A. Kirkpatrick, et al. 2015. "Characteristics of Seroconversion and Implications for Diagnosis of Post-Treatment Lyme Disease Syndrome: Acute and Convalescent Serology among a Cohort of Early Lyme Disease Patients." *Clinical Rheumatology* 34 (3): 585–89.

Rebman, A. W., K. Kortte, W. Robinson, et al. 2014. "Sex-Based Differences in the Immune Response in Lyme Disease over Time." *Open Forum Infectious Diseases* 1 (1): S12–13.

Reis, C., M. Cote, D. Le Rhun, et al. 2011. "Vector Competence of the Tick *Ixodes ricinus* for Transmission of *Bartonella birtlesii*." *PLOS Neglected Tropical Diseases* 5 (5): e1186.

Richardson, M., C. Khouia, and K. Sutcliffe. 2019. "Intervention to Prevent Lyme Disease in Humans: A Systematic Review." *Preventive Medicine Reports* 13:16–22.

Roberts, Celia. 2007. *Messengers of Sex: Hormones, Biomedicine, and Feminism.* Cambridge: Cambridge University Press.

Roberts, Elizabeth F. S. 2016. "When Nature/Culture Implodes: Feminist Anthropology and Biotechnology." In *Mapping Feminist Anthropology in the Twenty-First Century*, edited by Ellen Lewin and Leni M. Silverstein, 105–25. New Brunswick, NJ: Rutgers University Press.

Rollend, L., D. Fish, and J. E. Childs. 2013. "Transovarial Transmission of *Borrelia* Spirochetes by *Ixodes scapularis*: A Summary of the Literature and Recent Observations." *Ticks and Tick-Borne Diseases* 4 (1–2): 46–51.

Rose, C. D., P. T. Fawcett, K. M. Gibney, et al. 1996. "Residual Serologic Reactivity in Children with Resolved Lyme Arthritis." *Journal of Rheumatology* 23 (2): 367–69.

Rose, Nikolas S. 2007. *The Politics of Life Itself: Biomedicine, Power, and Subjectivity in the Twenty-First Century*. Princeton, NJ: Princeton University Press.

Rose, Nikolas, and Carlos Novas. 2005. "Biological Citizenship." In *Global Assemblages: Technology, Politics, and Ethics as Anthropological Problems*, edited by Aihwa Ong and Stephen J. Collier, 439–63. Malden, MA: Blackwell.

Rosenberg, R., N. P. Lindsey, M. Fischer, et al. 2018. "Vital Signs: Trends in Reported Vectorborne Disease Cases—United States and Territories, 2004–2016." *MMWR* 67:496–501. http://dx.doi.org/10.15585/mmwr.mm6717e1.

Ross, Anamaria Iosif. 2012. *The Anthropology of Alternative Medicine*. New York: Berg.

Rouse, Carolyn. 2009. *Uncertain Suffering: Racial Health Care Disparities and Sickle Cell Disease.* Berkeley: University of California Press.

Roy, Deboleena, and Banu Subramaniam. 2016. "Matter in the Shadows." In *Mattering: Feminism, Science, Materialism*, edited by Victoria Pitts-Taylor, 23–42. New York: New York University Press.

Rubin, Gayle. 1975. "The Traffic in Women: Notes on the 'Political Economy' of Sex." In *Toward an Anthropology of Women*, edited by Rayna Rapp, 157–210. New York: Monthly Review Press.

Rudenko, N., M. Golovchenko, L. Grubhoffer, et al. 2009. "*Borrelia carolinensis* sp. nov., a New (14th) Member of the *Borrelia burgdorferi* Sensu Lato Complex from the Southeastern Region of the United States." *Journal of Clinical Microbiology* 47 (1): 134–41.

Rudenko, N., M. Golovchenko, L. Grubhoffer, et al. 2011a. "*Borrelia carolinensis* sp. nov., a Novel Species of the *Borrelia burgdorferi* Sensu Lato Complex Isolated from

Rodents and a Tick from the South-Eastern USA." *International Journal of Systematic and Evolutionary Microbiology* 61 (part 2): 381–83.

Rudenko, N., M. Golovchenko, L. Grubhoffer, et al. 2011b. "Updates on *Borrelia burgdorferi* Sensu Lato Complex with Respect to Public Health." *Ticks and Tick-Borne Diseases* 2 (3): 123–28.

Rudenko, N., M. Golovchenko, L. Grubhoffer, et al. 2013. "The Rare OspC Allele L of *Borrelia burgdorferi* Sensu Stricto, Commonly Found among Samples Collected in a Coastal Plain Area of the Southeastern United States, Is Associated with *Ixodes affinis* Ticks and Local Rodent Hosts *Peromyscus gossypinus* and *Sigmodon hispidus*." *Applied and Environmental Microbiology* 79 (4): 1403–6.

Rudenko, N., M. Golovchenko, V. Hönig, et al. 2013. "Detection of *Borrelia burgdorferi* Sensu Stricto OspC Alleles Associated with Human Lyme Borreliosis Worldwide in Non-Human-Biting Tick *Ixodes affinis* and Rodent Hosts in Southeastern United States." *Applied and Environmental Microbiology* 79 (5): 1444–53.

Rudenko, N., M. Golovchenko, M. Vancova, et al. 2016. "Isolation of Live *Borrelia burgdorferi* Sensu Lato Spirochaetes from Patients with Disorders and Symptoms Not Typical for Lyme Borreliosis." *Clinical Microbiology and Infection* 22 (3): 267.

Ruggie, Mary. 2004. *Marginal to Mainstream: Alternative Medicine in America.* Cambridge: Cambridge University Press.

Russell, Denise. 1995. *Women, Madness, and Medicine.* Cambridge: Polity Press.

Russell, R. C. 1995. "Lyme Disease in Australia—Still to Be Proven!" *Emerging Infectious Diseases* 1 (1): 29–31.

Russell, R. C., S. L. Doggett, R. Munro, et al. 1994. "Lyme Disease: A Search for a Causative Agent in Ticks in South-Eastern Australia." *Epidemiology and Infection* 112 (2): 375–84.

Rutkowski, S., D. H. Busch, and H. I. Huppertz. 1997. "Lymphocyte Proliferation Assay in Response to *Borrelia burgdorferi* in Patients with Lyme Arthritis: Analysis of Lymphocyte Subsets." *Rheumatology International* 17 (4): 151–58.

Salkeld, D. J., and R. S. Lane. 2010. "Community Ecology and Disease Risk: Lizards, Squirrels, and the Lyme Disease Spirochete in California, USA." *Ecology* 91 (1): 293–8.

Sapi, E., S. L. Bastian, C. M. Mpoy, et al. 2012. "Characterization of Biofilm Formation by *Borrelia burgdorferi* in Vitro." *PLOS One* 7 (10): e48277.

Sapi, E., N. Pabbati, A. Datar, et al. 2013. "Improved Culture Conditions for the Growth and Detection of *Borrelia* from Human Serum." *International Journal of Medical Sciences* 10 (4): 362–76.

Sayre, Ryan. 2010. "Tokyo, Almost-Encounters, and 'Passing By.'" *3 Quarks Daily,* November 29, 2010. http://www.3quarksdaily.com/3quarksdaily/2010/11/tokyo-almost-encounters-and-passing-by.html.

Scarry, Elaine. 1985. *The Body in Pain: The Making and Unmaking of the World.* New York: Oxford University Press.

Schatzki, Theodore, Karin Knorr-Cetina, and Eike von Savigny, eds. 2001. *The Practice Turn in Contemporary Theory*. London: Routledge.

Scheper-Hughes, Nancy, and Margaret M. Lock. 1987. "The Mindful Body: A Prolegomenon to Future Work in Medical Anthropology." *Medical Anthropology Quarterly* 1:6–41.

Schlesinger, P. A., P. H. Duray, B. A. Burke, et al. 1985. "Maternal-Fetal Transmission of the Lyme Disease Spirochete, *Borrelia burgdorferi*." *Annals of Internal Medicine* 103 (1): 67–68.

Schmidt, B. L., E. Aberer, C. Stockenhuber, et al. 1995. "Detection of *Borrelia burgdorferi* DNA by Polymerase Chain Reaction in the Urine and Breast Milk of Patients with Lyme Borreliosis." *Diagnostic Microbiology and Infectious Disease* 21 (3): 121–28.

Schmutzhard, E. 1989. "Lyme Borreliosis and Multiple Sclerosis." *Biomedicine and Pharmacotherapy* 43 (6): 415–19.

Schmutzhard, E. 2002. "Multiple Sclerosis and Lyme Borreliosis." *Wiener Klinische Wochenschrift* 114 (13–14): 539–43.

Schone, Harry Quinn. 2014. "Learning from Morgellons." Master's thesis, University College London.

Schotthoefer, Anna M., and Holly M. Frost. 2015. "Ecology and Epidemiology of Lyme Borreliosis." *Clinics in Laboratory Medicine* 35:723–43.

Schulze, T. L., R. A. Jordan, J. C. White, et al. 2011. "Geographical Distribution and Prevalence of Selected *Borrelia*, *Ehrlichia*, and *Rickettsia* Infections in *Amblyomma americanum* (Acari: Ixodidae) in New Jersey." *Journal of the American Mosquito Control Association* 27 (3): 236–44.

Schutzer, S. E., T. E. Angel, T. Liu, et al. 2011. "Distinct Cerebrospinal Fluid Proteomes Differentiate Post-Treatment Lyme Disease from Chronic Fatigue Syndrome." *PLOS One* 6 (2): e17287.

Schutzer, S. E., C. M. Fraser-Liggett, W. G. Qiu, et al. 2012. "Whole-Genome Sequences of *Borrelia bissettii*, *Borrelia valaisiana*, and *Borrelia spielmanii*." *Journal of Bacteriology* 194 (2): 545–46.

Schutzer, S. E., C. K. Janniger, and R. A. Schwartz. 1991. "Lyme Disease During Pregnancy." *Cutis* 47 (4): 267–68.

Schutzer, S. E., and J. Luan. 2003. "Early OspA Immune Complex Formation in Animal Models of Lyme Disease." *Journal of Molecular Microbiology and Biotechnology* 5 (3): 167–71.

Schwartz, A. M., A. F. Hinckley, P. S. Mead, S. A. Hook, and K. J. Kugeler. 2017. "Surveillance for Lyme Disease—United States, 2008–2015." *MMWR Surveillance Summaries* 66:1–12.

Schwarzwalder, A., M. F. Schneider, A. Lydecker, et al. 2010. "Sex Differences in the Clinical and Serologic Presentation of Early Lyme Disease: Results from a Retrospective Review." *Gender and Medicine* 7 (4): 320–29.

Scott, Anne. 1998. "The Symbolizing Body and the Metaphysics of Alternative Medicine." *Body and Society* 4 (3): 21–37.

Scrimenti, R. J. 1970. "Erythema Chronicum Migrans." *Archives of Dermatology* 102 (1): 104–5.

Seltzer, E. G., M. A. Gerber, M. L. Cartter, et al. 2000. "Long-Term Outcomes of Persons with Lyme Disease." *Journal of the American Medical Association* 283 (5): 609–16.

Seriburi, V., N. Ndukwe, Z. Chang, et al. 2012. "High Frequency of False Positive IgM Immunoblots for *Borrelia burgdorferi* in Clinical Practice." *Clinical Microbiology and Infection* 18 (12): 1236–40.

Shadick, N. A., C. B. Phillips, E. L. Logigian, et al. 1994. "The Long-Term Clinical Outcomes of Lyme Disease: A Population-Based Retrospective Cohort Study." *Annals of Internal Medicine* 121 (8): 560–67.

Shadick, N. A., C. B. Phillips, O. Sangha, et al. 1999. "Musculoskeletal and Neurologic Outcomes in Patients with Previously Treated Lyme Disease." *Annals of Internal Medicine* 131 (12): 919–26.

Shah, Hriday M., and Kevin C. Chung. 2009. "Archie Cochrane and His Vision for Evidence-Based Medicine." *Journal of Plastic, Reconstructive and Aesthetic Surgery* 124 (3): 982–88.

Shapiro, Eugene, Philip J. Baker, and Gary P. Wormser. 2017. "False and Misleading Information about Lyme Disease." *American Journal of Medicine* 130 (7): 771–72.

Sharma, B., A. V. Brown, N. E. Matluck, et al. 2015. "*Borrelia burgdorferi*, the Causative Agent of Lyme Disease, Forms Drug-Tolerant Persister Cells." *Antimicrobial Agents and Chemotherapy* 59 (8): 4616–24.

Shen, A. K., P. S. Mead, and C. B. Beard. 2011. "The Lyme Disease Vaccine—A Public Health Perspective." *Clinical Infectious Diseases* 52 (S3): S247–52.

Shih, C. M., and A. Spielman. 1993. "Accelerated Transmission of Lyme Disease Spirochetes by Partially Fed Vector Ticks." *Journal of Clinical Microbiology* 31 (11): 2878–81.

Shirts, S. R., M. S. Brown, and J. R. Bobitt. 1983. "Listeriosis and Borreliosis as Causes of Antepartum Fever." *Obstetrics and Gynecology* 62 (2): 256–61.

Shorter, Edward. 1992. *From Paralysis to Fatigue: A History of Psychosomatic Illness in the Modern Era.* New York: Free Press.

Shotland, L. I., M. A. Mastrioanni, D. L. Choo, et al. 2003. "Audiologic Manifestations of Patients with Post-Treatment Lyme Disease Syndrome." *Ear and Hearing* 24 (6): 508–17.

Showalter, Elaine. 1997. *Hystories: Hysterical Epidemics and Modern Culture.* New York: Columbia University Press.

Siahpush, Mohammad. 2000. "A Critical Review of the Sociology of Alternative Medicine: Research on Users, Practitioners, and the Orthodoxy." *Health* 4:159–78.

Sigal, L. H., and A. L. Hassett. 2005. "Commentary: 'What's in a Name? That Which We Call a Rose by Any Other Name Would Smell as Sweet.' Shakespeare W. Romeo and Juliet, II, ii (47–48)." *International Journal of Epidemiology* 34 (6): 1345–47.

Sikutová, S., J. Halouzka, J. Mendel, J. Knoz, et al. 2010. "Novel Spirochetes Isolated from Mosquitoes and Black Flies in the Czech Republic." *Journal of Vector Ecology* 35 (1): 50–55.

Silverman, Chloe. 2011. *Understanding Autism: Parents, Doctors, and the History of a Disorder.* Princeton, NJ: Princeton University Press.

Singhal, Astha, Yu-Yu Tien, and Renee Y. Hsia. 2016. "Racial-Ethnic Disparities in Opioid Prescriptions at Emergency Department Visits for Conditions Commonly Associated with Prescription Drug Abuse." *PLOS One* 11 (8): e0159224.

Sismondo, Sergio. 2017. "Post-Truth?" *Social Studies of Science* 47 (1): 3–6.

Sivak, S. L., M. E. Aguero-Rosenfeld, J. Nowakowski, et al. 1996. "Accuracy of IgM Immunoblotting to Confirm the Clinical Diagnosis of Early Lyme Disease." *Archives of Internal Medicine* 156 (18): 2105–9.

Sjöwall, J., L. Fryland, M. Nordberg, et al. 2011. "Decreased Th1-Type Inflammatory Cytokine Expression in the Skin Is Associated with Persisting Symptoms after Treatment of Erythema Migrans." *PLOS One* 6 (3): e18220.

Skoggard, Ian, and Alisse Waterston. 2015. "Introduction: Toward an Anthropology of Affect and Evocative Ethnography." *Anthropology of Consciousness* 26 (2): 109–20.

Slovic, Paul. 2000. *The Perception of Risk.* London: Earthscan.

Slovic, Paul. 2010. *The Feeling of Risk: New Perspectives of Risk Perception.* London: Earthscan.

Smith, Barbara H. 2006. *Scandalous Knowledge: Science, Truth, and the Human.* Durham, NC: Duke University Press.

Smith, M. P., L. Ponnusamy, J. Jiang, et al. 2010. "Bacterial Pathogens in Ixodid Ticks from a Piedmont County in North Carolina: Prevalence of Rickettsial Organisms." *Vector-Borne and Zoonotic Diseases* 10 (10): 939–52.

Smith, Patricia. 2017. "Who Controls Fake Lyme Disease News?" LymeDisease.org, June 14, 2017. https://www.lymedisease.org/pat-smith-op-ed/.

Smith, R. P., R. T. Schoen, D. W. Rahn, et al. 2002. "Clinical Characteristics and Treatment Outcome of Early Lyme Disease in Patients with Microbiologically Confirmed Erythema Migrans." *Annals of Internal Medicine* 136 (6): 421–28.

Smith-Morris, Carolyn. 2016. *Diagnostic Controversy: Cultural Perspectives on Competing Knowledge in Healthcare.* New York: Routledge.

Sniderman, A. D., and C. D. Furberg. 2009. "Why Guideline-Making Requires Reform." *Journal of the American Medical Association* 301 (4): 429–31.

Sointu, Eeva. 2006. "Healing Bodies, Feeling Bodies: Embodiment and Alternative and Complementary Health Practices." *Social Theory and Health* 4:203–20.

Sointu, Eeva. 2012. *Theorizing Complementary and Alternative Medicine: Wellbeing, Self, Gender, Class.* New York: Palgrave Macmillan.

Sonenshine, D. E. 2018. "Range Expansion of Tick Disease Vectors in North America: Implications for Spread of Tick-Borne Disease." *International Journal of Environmental Research and Public Health* 15 (3): E478.

Sontag, Susan. 2011. *Illness as Metaphor and AIDS and Its Metaphors*. New York: Picador USA.

Soper, Kate. 1995. *What Is Nature?: Culture, Politics and the Non-Human*. Oxford: Blackwell.

Specter, Michael. 2011. "The Power of Nothing: Could Studying the Placebo Effect Change the Way We Think about Medicine?" *New Yorker*, December 4, 2011. http://www.newyorker.com/reporting/2011/12/12/111212fa_fact_specter.

Specter, Michael. 2012. "Mitt Romney versus Lyme Disease and Science." *New Yorker*, October 1, 2012. https://www.newyorker.com/news/news-desk/mitt-romney -versus-lyme-disease-and-science.

Spirin, N. N., N. S. Baranova, O. A. Fadeeva, et al. 2011. "Differential Aspects of Multiple Sclerosis and Chronic Borrelial Encephalomyelitis." *Zhurnal Nevrologii Psikhiatrii Imeni S. S. Korsakova* 111 (7): 8–12.

Stafford, Kirby C., 3rd. 2007. *Tick Management Handbook: An Integrated Guide for Homeowners, Pest Control Operators, and Public Health Officials for the Prevention of Tick-Associated Disease*. New Haven: Connecticut Agricultural Experiment Station.

Stanek, Gerold, G. P. Wormser, J. Gray, and F. Strle. 2012. "Lyme Borreliosis." *Lancet* 379:461–73.

Star, S. L., and J. R. Greisemer. 1989. "Institutional Ecology, 'Translations,' and Boundary Objects: Amateurs and Professionals in Berkeley's Museum of Vertebrate Zoology, 1907–39." *Social Studies of Science* 19:387–420.

Steere, A. C. 1993. "Seronegative Lyme Disease." *Journal of the American Medical Association* 270 (11): 1369.

Steere, A. C. 2009. "Reply to Letter by Volkman Commenting on the Possible Onset of Seronegative Disease in Lyme Arthritis." *Arthritis and Rheumatism* 60 (1): 310.

Steere, A. C., E. E. Drouin, and L. J. Glickstein. 2011. "Relationship between Immunity to *Borrelia burgdorferi* Outer-Surface Protein A (OspA) and Lyme Arthritis." *Clinical Infectious Diseases* 52 (S3): S259–65.

Steere, A. C., B. Falk, E. E. Drouin, et al. 2003. "Binding of Outer Surface Protein A and Human Lymphocyte Function-Associated Antigen 1 Peptides to HLA-DR Molecules Associated with Antibiotic Treatment–Resistant Lyme Arthritis." *Arthritis and Rheumatism* 48 (2): 534–40.

Steere, A. C., R. L. Grodzicki, A. N. Kornblatt, et al. 1983. "The Spirochetal Etiology of Lyme Disease." *New England Journal of Medicine* 308 (13): 733–40.

Steere, A. C., D. Gross, A. L. Meyer, et al. 2001. "Autoimmune Mechanisms in Antibiotic Treatment-Resistant Lyme Arthritis." *Journal of Autoimmunity* 16 (3): 263–68.

Steere, A. C., G. J. Hutchinson, D. W. Rahn, et al. 1983. "Treatment of the Early Manifestations of Lyme Disease." *Annals of Internal Medicine* 99 (1): 22–26.

Steere, A. C., W. Klitz, E. E. Drouin, et al. 2006. "Antibiotic-Refractory Lyme Arthritis Is Associated with HLA-DR Molecules That Bind a *Borrelia burgdorferi* Peptide." *Journal of Experimental Medicine* 203 (4): 961–71.

Steere, A. C., G. McHugh, N. Damle, et al. 2008. "Prospective Study of Serologic Tests for Lyme Disease." *Clinical Infectious Diseases* 47 (2): 188–95.

Steere, A. C., A. R. Pachner, and S. E. Malawista. 1983. "Neurologic Abnormalities of Lyme Disease: Successful Treatment with High-Dose Intravenous Penicillin." *Annals of Internal Medicine* 99 (6): 767–72.

Strasheim, Connie. 2009. *Insights into Lyme Disease Treatment: 13 Lyme-Literate Health Care Practitioners Share Their Healing Strategies.* South Lake Tahoe, NV: BioMed.

Straubinger, R. K. 2000. "PCR-Based Quantification of *Borrelia burgdorferi* Organisms in Canine Tissues over a 500-Day Postinfection Period." *Journal of Clinical Microbiology* 38 (6): 2191–99.

Straubinger, R. K., A. F. Straubinger, B. A. Summers, et al. 2000. "Status of *Borrelia burgdorferi* Infection after Antibiotic Treatment and the Effects of Corticosteroids: An Experimental Study." *Journal of Infectious Diseases* 181 (3): 1069–81.

Straubinger, R. K., B. A. Summers, Y. F. Chang, et al. 1997. "Persistence of *Borrelia burgdorferi* in Experimentally Infected Dogs after Antibiotic Treatment." *Journal of Clinical Microbiology* 35 (1): 111–16.

Stricker, R. B., J. Burrascano, and E. Winger. 2002. "Longterm Decrease in the CD57 Lymphocyte Subset in a Patient with Chronic Lyme Disease." *Annals of Agricultural and Environmental Medicine* 9 (1): 111–13.

Stricker, R. B., and L. Johnson. 2014. "Lyme Disease Vaccination: Safety First." *Lancet Infectious Diseases* 14 (1): 12.

Stricker, R. B., and E. E. Winger. 2001. "Decreased CD57 Lymphocyte Subset in Patients with Chronic Lyme Disease." *Immunology Letters* 76 (1): 43–48.

Strikwold, Marije, B. Spenkelink, L. H. J. de Haan, et al. 2017. "Integrating In Vitro Data and Physiologically Based Kinetic (PBK) Modelling to Assess the In Vivo Potential Developmental Toxicity of a Series of Phenols." *Archives of Toxicology* 91 (5): 2119–33.

Strle, F., V. Maraspin, S. Lotric-Furlan, et al. 1996. "Azithromycin and Doxycycline for Treatment of *Borrelia* Culture-Positive Erythema Migrans." *Infection* 24 (1): 64–68.

Strle, F., R. N. Picken, Y. Cheng, et al. 1997. "Clinical Findings for Patients with Lyme Borreliosis Caused by *Borrelia burgdorferi* Sensu Lato with Genotypic and Phenotypic Similarities to Strain 25015." *Clinical Infectious Diseases* 25 (2): 273–80.

Strle, F., V. Preac-Mursic, J. Cimperman, et al. 1993. "Azithromycin versus Doxycycline for Treatment of Erythema Migrans: Clinical and Microbiological Findings." *Infection* 21 (2): 83–88.

Strle, K., J. J. Shin, L. J. Glickstein, et al. 2012. "Association of a Toll-Like Receptor 1 Polymorphism with Heightened Th1 Inflammatory Responses and Antibiotic-Refractory Lyme Arthritis." *Arthritis and Rheumatism* 64 (5): 1497–507.

Strle, K., D. Stupica, E. E. Drouin, et al. 2014. "Elevated Levels of IL-23 in a Subset of Patients with Post-Lyme Disease Symptoms Following Erythema Migrans." *Clinical Infectious Diseases* 58 (3): 372–80.

Strobino, B., S. Abid, and M. Gewitz. 1999. "Maternal Lyme Disease and Congenital Heart Disease: A Case-Control Study in an Endemic Area." *American Journal of Obstetrics and Gynecology* 180 (3, part 1): 711–16.

Strobino, B., C. L. Williams, S. Abid, et al. 1993. "Lyme Disease and Pregnancy Outcome: A Prospective Study of Two Thousand Prenatal Patients." *American Journal of Obstetrics and Gynecology* 169 (2, part 1): 367–74.

Stromdahl, E. Y., R. M. Nadolny, J. A. Gibbons, et al. 2015. "*Borrelia burgdorferi* Not Confirmed in Human-Biting *Amblyomma americanum* Ticks from the Southeastern United States." *Journal of Clinical Microbiology* 53 (5): 1697–1704.

Stupica, D., L. Lusa, T. Cerar, et al. 2011. "Comparison of Post-Lyme Borreliosis Symptoms in Erythema Migrans Patients with Positive and Negative *Borrelia burgdorferi* Sensu Lato Skin Culture." *Vector-Borne Zoonotic Diseases* 11 (7): 883–89.

Swei, A., R. S. Ostfeld, R. S. Lane, et al. 2011. "Impact of the Experimental Removal of Lizards on Lyme Disease Risk." *Proceedings of the Royal Society: Biological Sciences* 278 (1720): 2970–78.

Szasz, Andrew. 2007. *Shopping Our Way to Safety: How We Changed from Protecting the Environment to Protecting Ourselves*. Minneapolis: University of Minnesota Press.

Szczepanski, A., and J. L. Benach. 1991. "Lyme Borreliosis: Host Responses to *Borrelia burgdorferi*." *Microbiology Review* 55 (1): 21–34.

Sze, Julie. 2007. *Noxious New York: The Racial Politics of Urban Health and Environmental Justice*. Cambridge, MA: MIT Press.

Tager, F. A., B. A. Fallon, J. Keilp, et al. 2001. "A Controlled Study of Cognitive Deficits in Children with Chronic Lyme Disease." *Journal of Neuropsychiatry and Clinical Neuroscience* 13 (4): 500–507.

Tardieu, M., and K. Deiva. 2013. "Rare Inflammatory Diseases of the White Matter and Mimics of Multiple Sclerosis and Related Disorders." *Neuropediatrics* 44 (6): 302–8.

Taylor, Dorceta. 1989. "Blacks and the Environment: Toward an Explanation of the Concern and Action Gaps between Blacks and Whites." *Environment and Behavior* 21 (2): 175–205.

Taylor, Dorceta. 2009. *The Environment and the People in American Cities, 1600s–1990s: Disorder, Inequality, and Social Change*. Durham, NC: Duke University Press.

Taylor, Dorceta. 2014. *Toxic Communities: Environmental Racism, Industrial Pollution, and Residential Mobility*. New York: New York University Press.

Taylor, Dorceta. 2016. *The Rise of the American Conservation Movement: Power, Privilege, and Environmental Protection*. Durham, NC: Duke University Press.

Taylor, E., D. J. Kaplan, A. J. M. Anderson, A. J. Nowalk, and B. T. Campfield. 2019. "Insights from the Geographic Spread of the Lyme Disease Epidemic." *Clinical Infectious Diseases* 68 (3): 426–34.

Taylor, Verta. 1996. *Rock-a-Bye Baby: Feminism, Self-Help, and Postpartum Depression.* New York: Routledge.

Telford, S. R., 3rd, and G. P. Wormser. 2010. "Bartonella spp. Transmission by Ticks Not Established." *Emerging Infectious Diseases* 16 (3): 379–84.

Thompson, Charis. 2013. *Good Science: The Ethical Choreography of Stem Cell Research.* Cambridge, MA: MIT Press.

Thompson, Jennifer Jo, and Mark Nichter. 2016. "Is There a Role for Complementary and Alternative Medicine in Preventive and Promotive Health? An Anthropological Assessment in the Context of U.S. Health Reform." *Medical Anthropology Quarterly* 30 (1): 80–99.

Thompson, Jennifer Jo, Cheryl Ritenbaugh, and Mark Nichter. 2009. "Reconsidering the Placebo Response from a Broad Anthropological Perspective." *Culture, Medicine, Psychiatry* 33 (1): 112–52.

Ticktin, Miriam. 2011. *Casualties of Care: Immigration and the Politics of Immigration in France.* Berkeley: University of California Press.

Tilton, R. C., D. Barden, and M. Sand. 2001. "Culture *Borrelia burgdorferi.*" *Journal of Clinical Microbiology* 39 (7): 2747.

Timmermans, Stefan. 2007. "Evidence-Based Medicine and the Search for a Science of Clinical Care (Jeanne Daly)." *Health Sociology Review* 16 (3–4): 352–54.

Timmermans, Stefan, and Marc Berg. 2003. *The Gold Standard: The Challenge of Evidence-Based Medicine and Standardization in Health Care.* Philadelphia: Temple University Press.

Timmermans, Stefan, and Steven Epstein. 2010. "A World of Standards but Not a Standard World: Toward a Sociology of Standards and Standardization." *Annual Review of Sociology* 36:69–89.

Todd, Alexandra Dundas. 1989. *Intimate Adversaries: Cultural Conflict between Doctors and Women Patients.* Philadelphia: University of Pennsylvania Press.

Tomes, Nancy. 1998. *The Gospel of Germs: Men, Women, and the Microbe in American Life.* Cambridge, MA: Harvard University Press.

Tory, H. O., D. Zurakowski, and R. P. Sundel. 2010. "Outcomes of Children Treated for Lyme Arthritis: Results of a Large Pediatric Cohort." *Journal of Rheumatology* 37 (5): 1049–55.

Touradji, P., J. N. Aucott, T. Yang, et al. 2019. "Cognitive Decline in Post-Treatment Lyme Disease Syndrome." *Archives in Clinical Neuropsychology* 34 (4): 455–65.

Tovey, Philip, Gary Easthope, and John Adams, eds. 2004. *Mainstreaming Complementary and Alternative Medicine: Studies in Social Context.* New York: Routledge.

Trevisan, G., G. Stinco, and M. Cinco. 1997. "Neonatal Skin Lesions Due to a Spirochetal Infection: A Case of Congenital Lyme Borreliosis?" *International Journal of Dermatology* 36 (9): 677–80.

Triulzi, F., and G. Scotti. 1998. "Differential Diagnosis of Multiple Sclerosis: Contribution of Magnetic Resonance Techniques." *Journal of Neurology, Neurosurgery, and Psychiatry* 64 (S1): S6–14.

Trollmo, C., A. L. Meyer, A. C. Steere, et al. 2001. "Molecular Mimicry in Lyme Arthritis Demonstrated at the Single Cell Level: LFA-1 Alpha L Is a Partial Agonist for Outer Surface Protein A–Reactive T Cells." *Journal of Immunology* 166 (8): 5286–91.

Trundle, Catherine, and Brydie Isobel Scott. 2013. "Elusive Genes: Nuclear Test Veterans' Experiences of Genetic Citizenship and Biomedical Refusal." *Medical Anthropology* 32 (6): 501–17.

Vann, Elizabeth. 1995. "Quantum Ethnography: Anthropology in a Post-Einsteinian Era." SOAR, Wichita State Research Publications. http://soar.wichita.edu /bitstream/handle/10057/1217/LAJv.25-26_p75_88.pdf?sequence=1.

Vaz, A., L. Glickstein, J. A. Field, et al. 2001. "Cellular and Humoral Immune Responses to *Borrelia burgdorferi* Antigens in Patients with Culture-Positive Early Lyme Disease." *Infection and Immunity* 69 (12): 7437–44.

Vertinsky, Patricia. 1994. *The Eternally Wounded Woman: Women, Doctors, and Exercise in the Late Nineteenth Century.* Manchester: Manchester University Press.

Vogel, Lise. 1995. *Woman Questions: Essays for a Materialist Feminism.* New York: Routledge.

Vogel, Sarah A. 2008. "From 'the Dose Makes the Poison' to 'the Timing Makes the Poison': Conceptualizing Risk in the Synthetic Age." *Environmental History* 13 (4): 667–73.

Vogel, Sarah A. 2012. *Is It Safe? BPA and the Struggle to Define the Safety of Chemicals.* Berkeley: University of California Press.

Volkman, D. J. 2010. "Comment on: Efficacy of Antibiotic Prophylaxis for the Prevention of Lyme Disease: An Updated Systematic Review and Meta-Analysis." *Journal of Antimicrobial Chemotherapy* 65 (10): 2271; author reply, 2271–73.

Volkman, D. J. 2011. "Recommendation for Management of *I. scapularis* Bites Draws Mixed Reactions." *WMJ* 110 (3): 100.

Wagstaff, A. 2002. "Poverty and Health Sector Inequalities." *Bulletin of the World Health Organization* 80 (2): 97–105.

Wainer, Howard. 2015. *Truth or Truthiness: Distinguishing Fact from Fiction by Learning to Think Like a Data Scientist.* New York: Cambridge University Press.

Waitzkin, Howard. 1991. *The Politics of Medical Encounters: How Patients and Doctors Deal with Social Problems.* New Haven, CT: Yale University Press.

Wang, T. J., M. H. Liang, O. Sangha, et al. 2000. "Coexposure to *Borrelia burgdorferi* and *Babesia microti* Does Not Worsen the Long-Term Outcome of Lyme Disease." *Clinical Infectious Disease* 31 (5): 1149–54.

Ware, Norma C. 1992. "Suffering and the Social Construction of Illness: The Delegitimation of Illness Experience in Chronic Fatigue Syndrome." *Medical Anthropology Quarterly* 6 (4): 347–61.

Washick, B., E. Wingrove, K. E. Ferguson, et al. 2015. "Politics That Matter: Thinking about Power and Justice with the New Materialists." *Contemporary Political Theory* 14 (1): 63–89.

Watson, Stephanie. 2013. "Chelation Therapy Offers Small, If Any, Benefit for Heart Disease." *Harvard Health Blog*, March 26, 2013. https://www.health.harvard .edu/blog/chelation-therapy-offers-small-if-any-benefit-for-heart-disease -201303266030.

Weber, K. 1973. "Tick-Borne Diseases and Their Treatment." *Therapie der Gegenwart* 112 (9): 1402–9.

Weber, K. 1996. "Treatment Failure in Erythema Migrans—A Review." *Infection* 24 (1): 73–75.

Weber, K., H. J. Bratzke, U. Neubert, et al. 1988. "*Borrelia burgdorferi* in a Newborn despite Oral Penicillin for Lyme Borreliosis during Pregnancy." *Pediatric Infectious Diseases* Journal 7 (4): 286–89.

Wechsler, M. E., J. M. Kelley, et al. 2011. "Active Albuterol or Placebo, Sham Acupuncture, or No Intervention in Asthma." *New England Journal of Medicine* 365 (2): 119–26.

Weinstein, A., and M. Britchkov. 2002. "Lyme Arthritis and Post-Lyme Disease Syndrome." *Current Opinion in Rheumatology* 14 (4): 383–87.

Weinstein, E. R., A. W. Rebman, J. N. Aucott, et al. 2018. "Sleep Quality in Well-Defined Lyme Disease: A Clinical Cohort Study in Maryland." *Sleep* 41 (5): 1–8.

Weintraub, Karen. 2016. "For Daring to Study a Discredited Therapy, This Doctor Earned Scorn—And a $37 Million Grant." STAT, December 27, 2016.

Weintraub, Pamela. 2001. "The Bitter Feud over LYMErix: Big Pharma Takes on the Wrong Little Osp." HMS *Beagle*, no. 106. http://www.whale.to/m/lymerix8 .html.

Weintraub, Pamela. 2008. *Cure Unknown: Inside the Lyme Epidemic*. New York: St. Martin's.

Weitzner, E., P. Visintainer, and G. P. Wormser. 2016. "Comparison of Males versus Females with Culture-Confirmed Early Lyme Disease at Presentation and at 11–20 Years after Diagnosis." *Diagnostic Microbiology and Infectious Disease* 85 (4): 493–95.

Wendell, Susan. 1996. *The Rejected Body: Feminist Philosophical Reflections on Disability*. New York: Routledge.

Wesson, D. M., D. K. McLain, J. H. Oliver, et al. 1993. "Investigation of the Validity of Species Status of Ixodes dammini (Acari: Ixodidae) Using rDNA." *Proceedings of the National Academy of Sciences of the United States of America* 90 (21): 10221–25.

Weyand, C. M., and J. J. Goronzy. 1989. "Immune Responses to *Borrelia burgdorferi* in Patients with Reactive Arthritis." *Arthritis and Rheumatism* 32 (9): 1057–64.

White, Cassandra. 2009. *An Uncertain Cure: Living with Leprosy in Brazil*. New Brunswick, NJ: Rutgers University Press.

Williams, C. L., B. Strobino, A. Weinstein, et al. 1995. "Maternal Lyme Disease and Congenital Malformations: A Cord Blood Serosurvey in Endemic and Control Areas." *Paediatric Perinatal Epidemiology* 9 (3): 320–30.

Williams, Simon, and Michael Calnan. 1996. "The 'Limits' of Medicalization?: Modern Medicine and the Lay Populace in 'Late' Modernity." *Social Science and Medicine* 42:1609–20.

Willyard, Cassandra. 2014. "Resurrecting the 'Yuppie Vaccine.'" *Nature Medicine* 20 (7): 698–701.

Wilson, Elizabeth. 1998. *Neural Geographies: Feminism and the Microstructures of Cognition.* New York: Routledge.

Wilson, Elizabeth. 2011. "Neurological Entanglements: The Case of Paediatric Depressions, SSRIs, and Suicidal Ideation." *Subjectivity* 4 (3): 277–97.

Wittgenstein, Ludwig. (1969) 1975. *On Certainty.* Malden, MA: Blackwell.

Wolfson, C., and P. Talbot. 2002. "Bacterial Infection as a Cause of Multiple Sclerosis." *Lancet* 360 (9330): 352–53.

Woodrum, J. E., and J. H. Oliver Jr. 1999. "Investigation of Venereal, Transplacental, and Contact Transmission of the Lyme Disease Spirochete, *Borrelia burgdorferi*, in Syrian Hamsters." *Journal of Parasitology* 85 (3): 426–30.

Wormser, G. P., P. J. Baker, S. O'Connell, et al. 2012. "Critical Analysis of Treatment Trials of Rhesus Macaques Infected with *Borrelia burgdorferi* Reveals Important Flaws in Experimental Design." *Vector-Borne and Zoonotic Diseases* 12 (7): 535–38.

Wormser, G. P., R. J. Dattwyler, E. D. Shapiro, et al. 2006. "The Clinical Assessment, Treatment, and Prevention of Lyme Disease, Human Granulocytic Anaplasmosis, and Babesiosis: Clinical Practice Guidelines by the Infectious Diseases Society of America." *Clinical Infectious Diseases* 43 (9): 1089–134.

Wormser, G. P., and B. Pritt. 2015. "Update and Commentary on Four Emerging Tick-Borne Infections: *Ehrlichia muris*-like Agent, *Borrelia miyamotoi*, Deer Tick Virus, Heartland Virus, and Whether Ticks Play a Role in Transmission of *Bartonella henselae.*" *Infectious Disease Clinics of North America* 29 (2): 371–81.

Wormser, G. P., R. Ramanathan, J. Nowakowski, et al. 2003. "Duration of Antibiotic Therapy for Early Lyme Disease: A Randomized, Double-Blind, Placebo-Controlled Trial." *Annals of Internal Medicine* 138 (9): 697–704.

Wormser, G. P., and I. Schwartz. 2009. "Antibiotic Treatment of Animals Infected with *Borrelia burgdorferi.*" *Clinical Microbiology Review* 22 (3): 387–95.

Wormser, G. P., and E. D. Shapiro. 2009. "Implications of Gender in Chronic Lyme Disease." *Journal of Women's Health* 18 (6): 831–34.

Worrall, John. 2002. "What Evidence in Evidence-Based Medicine?" *Philosophy of Science* 69 (3): S316–30.

Wressnigg, N., E. Pöllabauer, G. Aichinger, et al. 2013. "Safety and Immunogenicity of a Novel Multivalent OspA Vaccine against Lyme Borreliosis in Healthy Adults: A Double-Blind, Randomised, Dose-Escalation Phase 1/2 Trial." *Lancet Infectious Diseases* 13 (8): 680–89.

Wu, J., E. H. Weening, J. B. Faske, et al. 2011. "Invasion of Eukaryotic Cells by *Borrelia burgdorferi* Requires β (1) Integrins and Src Kinase Activity." *Infectious Immunology* 79 (3): 1338–48.

Yakutchik, Maryalice. 2011. "Science of the Sexes: Why Hasn't Infectious Disease Research Reflected Fundamental Differences in Women and Men?" *Magazine of Johns Hopkins Bloomberg School of Public Health*, Spring, 25–31. https://magazine.jhsph.edu/2011/spring/features/science_of_the_sexes/page_1/.

Yoshinari, N. H., B. N. Reinhardt, and A. C. Steere. 1991. "T Cell Responses to Polypeptide Fractions of *Borrelia burgdorferi* in Patients with Lyme Arthritis." *Arthritis and Rheumatism* 34 (6): 707–13.

Young, Allan. 1995. *The Harmony of Illusions: Inventing Post-Traumatic Stress Disorder*. Princeton, NJ: Princeton University Press.

Yrjänäinen, H., J. Hytönen, P. Hartiala, et al. 2010. "Persistence of Borrelial DNA in the Joints of *Borrelia burgdorferi*–Infected Mice after Ceftriaxone Treatment." APMIS 118 (9): 665–73.

Zavestoski, S., P. Brown, M. Linder, et al. 2002. "Science, Policy, Activism, and War: Defining the Health of Gulf War Veterans." *Science, Technology, and Human Values* 27 (2): 171–205.

Zeidner, N. S., K. S. Brandt, E. Dadey, et al. 2004. "Sustained-Release Formulation of Doxycycline Hyclate for Prophylaxis of Tick Bite Infection in a Murine Model of Lyme Borreliosis." *Antimicrobial Agents and Chemotherapy* 48 (7): 2697–99.

Zeidner, N. S., R. F. Massung, M. C. Dolan, et al. 2008. "A Sustained-Release Formulation of Doxycycline Hyclate (Atridox) Prevents Simultaneous Infection of *Anaplasma phagocytophilum* and *Borrelia burgdorferi* Transmitted by Tick Bite." *Journal of Medical Microbiology* 57 (part 4): 463–68.

Zoschke, D. C., A. A. Skemp, and D. L. Defosse. 1991. "Lymphoproliferative Responses to *Borrelia burgdorferi* in Lyme Disease." *Annals of Internal Medicine* 114 (4): 285–89.

Index

activated health citizens, 5–6

active infection, 49; antibody testing and, 253n52; PCR detection and, 252n41

acute Lyme disease, 19, 168, 260n3; as biomedically explainable, 159; gender distribution of, 116; identifying with, 117; symptoms of, 101, 160; treatment of, 16, 152

aesthetic of nature, 66; health and, 74–75; historical construction of, 68–70; in Lyme-endemic areas, 88; political sensibilities and, 71–72; racial dimension of, 72–74

affect: anthropology of, 257n4; nature's relationship to, 66, 75; risk and, 76, 259n18. See also epidemiology of affect

affluence: hygiene hypothesis and, 264n40; perceived somatization and, 163; relationship to suffering and survival, 111, 236n6; suburban context of, 156

Affordable Care Act, 196

Agamben, Giorgio, 67, 97, 221, 238n21

Agency for Healthcare Research and Quality (AHRQ), 192, 193

AHRQ. See Agency for Healthcare Research and Quality

Amblyomma americanum, 32, 38. See also Lone Star tick

American Neurological Association, 196, 215

Anaplasma phagocytophilum, 41

anatomo-politics, 10, 238n25; in context of public health, 258n18

Anderson, Elijah, 73

anecdote, 187; as form of evidence, 28, 40, 46, 50; mainstream criticisms of, 194; as weak evidence, 45, 64, 193

antibiotics, 2, 5, 99, 160, 181, 227; ALS patients and, 45, 46; ambivalence about, 146; Bell's palsy and, 107; CAM and, 142; conflicts of interest and, 214; costs of, 106, 152; debate about, 16, 32, 63, 81, 163, 256n62; dosage of, 201, 203; duration of, 200, 266n10; Herxheimer reaction and, 84, 126, 137, 168–69, 175, 259n22; insurance coverage of, 133, 152, 165, 204, 205–6, 213, 222, 269n22; intravenous, 127, 133; legislation of, 206, 232; maternal-fetal transmission and, 40; persistence and, 46–47, 249n32, 250n33; randomized controlled trials on, 6, 62, 256n61; relapse after, 47, 105, 133; reports of feeling better, 107, 109, 128, 141; Rife machine and, 85–86, 145; risks of, 133, 164–65; seronegativity and, 60, 255n58; test interpretation and, 253n52; treatment antibiotics (cont.)

recommendations of, 61–62; xenodiagnosis and, 252n41

antibody/antibodies, 5, 51; c6, 252n41; correlation with cure and, 253n52; Osp A, 51; seronegativity and, 60, 255n58; test, 57, 58, 161, 230; vaccine development and, 55

Arendt, Hannah, 154–55

autism, 45; chelation and, 81; diagnosed as Lyme disease, 44; litigation and, 268n10; vaccines and, 53

autoimmune reaction: persistent symptoms and, 49–50; Lyme vaccine and, 54

Auwaerter, P. G., 48, 250n34; "Unorthodox Alternative Therapies Marketed to Treat Lyme Disease," 81

Azotobacter, 48

Babesia microti, 41, 42

babesiosis, 41, 133, 163, 168, 181, 208; impact of co-infection with, 42; laboratory confirmation of, 204; persistent, 247n26

Baer, Hans, 170

Baker, P.: "Common Misconceptions about Lyme Disease," 255n58

Bambi, 70–71

"bare life," 111, 238n21

Bartonella, 42, 132, 145; as controversial, 43; debate over transmission by ticks, 247nn27–28

belief, 128, 180; in biologically based racial differences, 265n44; facts and, 18, 199; false, 265n2; Fleck, Ludwik and, 227; masquerading as fact, 198; in science, 198; social disbelief and suffering, 23; system, 5, 114, 182

Bell, Kirsten, 239n26

Bell's palsy, 173, 182; persistent, 107, 223; "self-controlled," 134; as sign, 43

Berg, Marc, 189–90, 217

bias, 194, 260n7; clinicians and racial, 152, 265n44; conflicts of interest and, 217; of diagnosis, 152; eminence-based medicine and, 201; evidence-based medicine and, 8, 191, 268n11; gender, 118, 119; within health care, 154; probability of, 191; publication, 216, 262n24; recall, 169

biocommunicability, 236n10

biocultural citizenship, 121

biolegitimacy: biopower and, 189, 217; in contrast to biological legitimacy, 11; definition of, 10; evidence-based medicine and 24, 188, 218, 225; life itself and, 238n21

biological citizenship, 238n21

biological determinism, 120

biological legitimacy, 99, 216; in contrast to biolegitimacy, 11; epistemo-legitimacy and, 7, 222; evidence-based medicine and, 3; Lyme's psychiatric symptoms and, 136; in relation to wealth and health, 148; sex differences and, 121

biological warfare: Borrelia burgdorferi as weapon of, 33–37, 243n9

Biology of Sex Differences Journal, 123

biomedicine, 4, 11; binaries of, 8–9; biocommunicability and, 236n10; CAM and, 24, 159, 184–85, 186, 265n1; evidence-based medicine and, 2, 189–91, 217, 267n1; gender, chronic pain/illness and, 261n11; historical development of, 170–71; medical anthropology approaches to, 226, 270n5; medically unexplainable illnesses and, 160, 171–72, 186, 224, 265n1, 265nn5–6; mind/body and, 136; moral and political dimensions of, 9; sign vs. symptom as foundational feature of, 8, 43, 223–24; the

Centers for Disease Control (cont.)
cases and, 240nn4; IDSA guidelines and, 201–2, 215; increased risk
of vector-borne diseases and, 65;
laboratory test standardization and,
54, 57, 254n55; Lyme vaccine and,
51; PCR assays and, 247n25; post-
treatment Lyme disease syndrome
and, 16, 251n38; racial statistics and,
151; sexual transmission and, 40; as
source of knowledge production,
239n2, 250n35; study on Lyme disease
mortality and, 110; vectors of transmission and, 37

CFS. See chronic fatigue syndrome

chelation, 105, 177; as detoxification
therapy, 81, 83; TACT study and, 82;
use in Lyme-literate practice, 266n10.
See also Trial to Assess Chelation
Therapy

chronic fatigue syndrome (CFS), 1; as
contested illness, 6, 175, 262n24;
delegitimation and, 112, 221, 235n2;
Lyme disease misdiagnosed as, 44,
45, 175; perceived historical context
of, 117, 173; women and, 100, 236n6;
"yuppie flu" and, 149, 236n6

chronic Lyme disease, 23; affluence
and, 147–48, 163; antibiotics and,
61, 64, 133, 256n61, 257n63; barriers
to research on, 179, 216; belief in,
113, 126; biological basis of, 1, 116,
118, 122, 221, 149; biomedicine and,
136; as boundary movement, 6; CAM
and, 138, 143, 202; children and,
262nn26–27; as constitutive outside,
159; contested illnesses and, 3, 100,
111, 136; debate over existence of, 14,
18, 47; demographics of, 163, 264n42;
depression and, 163; detoxification
therapy and, 83; diagnosis of, 54, 62,
204; distinction between acute Lyme

disease and, 19; divided experience
of, 136, 156; doubt and, 112, 113; as
embodied health movement, 6; financial cost of, 106; gender and, 116–17,
118; Herxheimer reaction and, 84; as
hysteria, 172; IDSA investigation and,
202–5; ILADS guidelines and, 62;
insurance and, 180, 206, 213; lack of
compassion for, 154–55; mainstream
understanding of, 108–109, 110,
119, 149, 166–67, 263n30; medically
unexplained illnesses and, 5, 9, 173,
184–87; medical racism and, 152; migrant workers and, 153; nonspecific
symptoms and, 172–73; pesticide use
and, 87; post-treatment Lyme disease
and, 16; psychiatric symptoms and,
130, 134, 262n24; Rife machine and,
85; sex differences and, 116, 120, 121;
symptomatic specificity and, 175, 184;
tests and, 58, 204, 254n57; toxins and,
79–80, 83–84; women and, 4, 100,
115, 139, 230, 261n14; as "yuppie flu,"
236n6

citizen experts, 4. See also activated
health citizens; lay experts

class: -action lawsuits, 1, 50, 187, 217,
252n43; chronic Lyme disease and
upper middle-, 72, 163; emergent
industrial capitalist, 170; environmental health and, 148; "female
invalidism" and, 117; inequalities
and health, 154, 157, 223; nature and
upper middle-, 72; perceptions of
intelligence and, 150; struggle,
266n13

climate change, 22, 65, 228

clinical guidelines, 200; conflicts of
interest and, 210–11; Lyme disease
controversy and, 267n1; evidence-
based medicine and, 2, 3, 188, 191–92;
IDSA, 5; ILADS, 5; legitimacy and,

diagnosis: bias and, 152; gender disparities and, 119; Lyme disease as a clinical, 165, 184; over-, 240n4; relationship between symptoms and signs
in, 8, 24, 170, 174, 178, 185–86; and
treatment guidelines, 60–62, 202
discourse: "disordered relations
between and among," 234; evidence-
based medicine as, 189, 218, 225;
"form of truth," 10, 217; of nature,
78; scientific discourse and biological
determinism, 120
divided bodies, 99, 226; competing claims and, 216, 223; defining
features of, 7, 184, 223; epistemic
tensions and, 159, 186
dominant epidemiological paradigm,
5, 215
doubt: as double burden, 223; pain and,
112; self-, 113–14; socially doubted,
235n2
doxycycline, 107, 126; acne and, 64;
effects of, 132, 162, 181, 182; IDSA
guidelines and, 61; prophylactic,
255n58, 256n60
Duden, Barbara, 140
Dumit, Joseph, 6,
Dusenbery, Maya, 118–19, 236n6; "The
Science Isn't Settled on Chronic
Lyme," 230

Ecks, Stefan, 8
Edlow, Jonathan, 51
"effective and efficient," 10, 24, 188, 190,
238n22
Ehrenreich, Barbara: "The 'Sick'
Women of the Upper Class," 117
Ehrlichia chaffeensis, 41
electromagnetic sensitivity, 86–87
ELISA. See enzyme-linked immunosor-
bent assay
Embers, M. E., 250n33

embodied health movements, 6, 235n3,
236n11
environmental: health, 6, 89, 148,
236n12; justice, 6, 148, 264n41; movements, 72; privilege, 23, 67, 78, 97;
risk, 22, 67, 78–90, 225
"environment-world," 67, 97
enzyme-linked immunosorbent assay
(ELISA), 57, 58, 123, 162, 181, 240,
253n52
epidemiology of affect, 23, 66, 75, 98, 225
epistemo-legitimacy, 7, 11, 216, 222
epistemology, 185; biomedical, 186;
classical vs. constructivist, 227;
"epistemic challenges to medicine,"
226; epistemic differences between
biomedicine and CAM, 7, 184, 186;
feminist, 13; practical, 259n1
Epstein, Steven, 62, 63, 121, 238n20, 259n1
ethnography, 155; critical, 230, 231; multisited, 13; of ontology, 123; quantum,
13–14, 229, 230, 231, 239n28
evidence, 1; "conforms to conceptions," 228; as differently interpreted,
197–98; objective vs. subjective, 2, 7;
"production of different kinds of," 19,
47, 28; strength of, 191, 194–95, 201
evidence-based medicine, 187–221; anecdote and, 193–202; as biopower and
biolegitimacy, 9–14, 217–21; clinical
guidelines and, 2, 3, 188, 191–192; conflicts of interest and, 59, 189, 210–16;
as technology, 10, 24, 225, 238n20
expert opinion, 28, 194; evidence
scale and, 189, 192; IDSA guidelines
and, 199, 200; as Level III evidence,
269n13; as weak or subjective evidence, 2, 191, 210
extracellular organism, 49, 251n35

Fàbrega, Horacio, 172, 266n6
Facebook, 16, 150

light sensitivity, 99, 155, 260n4

Lock, Margaret, 120

Loftus, John: *America's Nazi Secret*, 33, 243n11; *Belarus Secret*, 33, 243n11

Lone Star tick, 32, 38, 241n6, 242n7. See also *Amblyomma americanum*

Louv, Richard, 75

Lyme brain, 130, 142

Lyme Doctor Protection Bill, 206, 207

Lyme-literate: as a mobilized counterpublic, 215–16; observations of Lyme-literate physicians, 174–184; physicians and antibiotics, 133, 260n7; standard of care, 5, 62; term use, 19, 235n1

Lyme pre-exposure prophylaxis (Lyme PrEP), 55

Lyme rage, 129–30, 135

LYMErix, 50–55

Mahmood, Saba, 67

mainstream: observations of mainstream physicians, 160–70; perceptions of chronic Lyme disease, 19, 31, 37, 43, 45, 50, 59, 81, 110, 116–17, 134, 148–49, 261n21; physicians and cysts, 47; physicians and post-treatment Lyme disease, 16, 251n38; standard of care, 5, 39, 61

Manjoo, Farhad: *True Enough*, 227

Marx, Karl, 178

Masters, Ed, 32, 240n5

materiality, 123, 124, 261n15

Matuschka, F. R.: "Mosquitoes and Soft Ticks Cannot Transmit Lyme Disease Spirochetes," 245n22

MCS. See multiple chemical sensitivity

medical jurisprudence, 219–20

medical racism, 152

medicalization, 9, 237n19

medically unexplained illness, 160, 266n6; chronic Lyme

disease as, 5, 117, 173, 262n24; definition of, 171; as diagnostic category, 24, 159, 185–86, 224, 265n5; historical emergence of, 172; as practice category, 237n16

Merchant, Carolyn, 69

Metzl, Jonathan M., 238n26

migraines, 130, 131, 181

migrant workers, 152–54

mobilized counterpublic/mobilized public, 215–16

morbidity/mortality, 23, 111, 147, 239n32; psychiatric comorbidity, 262n24

Mol, Annemarie, 8, 123, 171

multiple chemical sensitivity (MCS), 1, 172, 221; as abjection, 238n19; chronic Lyme disease and, 80; as contested illness, 6; practical epistemology and, 259n1; social suffering and, 112

Murphy, Michelle, 238n19

Murray, Polly, 43, 115

Mycoplasma bacteria, 42

Myxobacteria, 48

Nash, Roderick, 67–68, 69

National Center on Complementary and Alternative Medicine, 142

National Guidelines Clearinghouse (NGC), 1, 192, 193, 212, 236n8, 268n5

National Institutes of Health (NIH), 10, 82, 215, 216, 257n62; National Center on Complementary and Alternative Medicine, 142

National Park Service, 74

nature, 22; American nationalism and, 69; as beautiful *and* frightening, 66, 68; changed feelings toward, 65; discourse, 78; lovers of, 72–73; racial exclusion and, 73; Romanticism and, 257n6; scholarship on construction of, 257n5. See also aesthetic of nature

Nelson, Glenn: "Why Are Our Parks So White?," 74

New England Journal of Medicine, 83, 248n30, 252n43

new materialism, 122–23, 261n16

New Yorker, 78, 114, 187, 227; "The Power of Nothing," 83

New York Times, 36–37, 73, 74, 167, 195, 243n9

Newby, Kris: *Bitten: The Secret History of Lyme Disease and Biological Weapons*, 33; *Under Our Skin*, 244

NGC. *See* National Guidelines Clearinghouse

Nichter, Mark, 236n10

night sweats, 176, 177

NIH. *See* National Institutes of Health

Notifiable Diseases Surveillance System, 151

Organization for the Study of Sex Differences, 122

Osler, William, 136

OSP. *See* outer surface protein

outer surface protein (OSP): Osp A, 51–55; Osp B, 53, 54

outside/inside: of the body, 79, 96; critical ethnography and, 230; health and, 93; knowledge production and, 14, 48, 221, 222, 226; toxins and, 80, 85; what constitutes the environment, 67, 90, 97

Oxford University: Centre for Evidence-Based Medicine, 191

pain: "aches and pains of daily living," 163, 173; mindfully living with, 140; pain management and racial disparities, 152, 265n44; Scarry, Elaine and, 101, 111–12; scholarship on, 260n10; social expectations and, 111, 156

Paisley, Brad: "Ticks," 95, 96

Park, Lisa Sun-Hee, 78

Parsons, Talcott, 237n18

pathophysiology, 46–50

patient citizenship, 238n21

PCR. *See polymerase chain reaction*

Pellow, David Naguib, 78, 148

persistent symptoms, 42, 49, 63, 101, 109, 256n61

pesticides, 2, 79, 93; environmental health and, 89; Lyme disease patients and, 87–88; studies on efficacy and, 97, 259n25

Philippon, Daniel J., 69

Piesman, J., 241n6

Plaquenil, 47, 132, 133

Pliny the Elder, 90

Plum Island, 33–37, 243n9, 243n11,

political sensibilities: nature and, 72

politics of life, 10, 156, 218, 221

politics of pity, 154, 155

polymerase chain reaction (PCR), 58, 180–81, 241–42, 247n25, 247n28, 250n33, 252n41, 254n57, 256n59

post–Lyme disease syndrome, 16, 116, 118, 262n24

post-treatment Lyme disease syndrome, 16, 63, 251n38, 252n41

poverty, 4, 147–48, 264n38

pregnancy, 40, 246n24

psychosomatic, 112, 117, 134. *See also* somatization and somatoform disorder

Public Act No. 99–284, 206, 269n22

Pulido, Laura, 154

quantum ethnography, 13–14, 229; critical ethnography and, 230–31; term use, 239n28

Rabinow, Paul, 217, 235n2

race: environmental health and, 148; health inequalities and, 154, 157, 190, 223, 236n6, 265n44; Lyme disease and, 150–51; nature and, 72–74. *See also* medical racism

randomized controlled trial, 2, 28, 192; clinical care and, 8; evidence-based medicine and, 10, 189–91, 268n12; Lyme disease and, 6, 256n61, 267n1

Rebman, A. W., 123

Rehmeyer, Julie: "The Science Isn't Settled on Chronic Lyme," 230

relapsing fever, 30

rhizome, 22, 27–28, 43

Rife, Royal, 85

Rife machine, 85–86, 87, 105, 142, 145

right way to be sick, 9, 11, 188

risk: antibiotic use and, 64, 133; benefit and, 10, 76; environmental privilege and, 67, 78, 225; epidemiology of affect and, 23, 75; as feelings, 76, 245n21; pesticides and perceived, 88; residential area and Lyme disease, 151–52; scholarship on, 258n18, 259n23; toxic environment and, 79; worth taking, 76

Rocephin, 105, 132, 182

Romanticism, 67–68, 257n6

Romney, Mitt, 67, 187

Sackett, David, 190

sanitary citizenship, 93

Scarry, Elaine, 101, 111–12

Schutzer, S. E., 40

scientific medicine, 8, 9, 170–71

seronegativity, 60, 255n58

sex differences, 116, 120–24. *See also* gender; sex/gender binary.

sex/gender binary, 120–21, 125. *See also* gender; sex differences.

Shapiro, E. D., 227

sick role, 118, 237n18

Slovic, Paul, 76, 245n21, 259n23

Smith, Patricia: "Who Controls Fake Lyme Disease News?," 227

Sniderman, A. D.: "Why Guideline-Making Requires Reform," 211

social constructionism, 121–22

social suffering, 112, 139, 223. *See also* suffering

somatization, 134, 172, 266n6

somatoform disorder, 3

southern tick-associated rash illness (STARI), 32, 56, 240n5, 241n6, 242n7

SPECT scan, 15, 105, 132, 183

Specter, Michael, 84, 187; "The Power of Nothing," 83

spirochete: description of, 33; syphilis as, 228

Stafford, Kirby, 90

standardization: diagnostic laboratory tests and, 5–758; evidence-based medicine and, 2, 10, 11, 210, 226, 270n4

Star, Susan Leigh, 210

STARI. *See* southern tick-associated rash illness

Strasheim, Connie: *Insights into Lyme Disease Treatment*, 143–44

Stricker, R. B., 213, 254n57

structural violence, 152, 156, 236n6

sublime, 68, 257n6

suburbs, 75; deer and, 4, 90; demographics of, 152; as form of white privilege, 154; Lyme disease and, 31, 91, 148–50, 156; nature and, 69–70, 73; pesticides and, 89

suffering, 2, 110–14; affluence and, 154, 156; delegitimation and, 3; doubt and, 100; spectacle of, 54. *See also* social suffering

support groups, 2; discussions at, 81, 86, 113–14, 141, 144; mainstream perceptions of, 17, 31, 135; as site of observation, 12, 76; as survival, 139–40

surfeit, 145–57